GENDER AND CHRISTIANITY

AF412270

Beyond the Feminization Thesis

Gender and Christianity in Modern Europe

PATRICK PASTURE, JAN ART & THOMAS BUERMAN

JAN DE MAEYER, LEEN VAN MOLLE, TINE VAN OSSELAER, VINCENT VIAENE EDS

Leuven University Press

EDITORIAL BOARD

Urs Altermatt, *Université de Fribourg*
Jan Art, *Universiteit Gent*
Jaak Billiet, *Katholieke Universiteit Leuven*
Jan De Maeyer, *Katholieke Universiteit Leuven - KADOC*
Jean-Dominique Durand, *Université Lyon 3*
Emmanuel Gerard, *Katholieke Universiteit Leuven - KADOC*
James C. Kennedy, *Universiteit van Amsterdam*
Mathijs Lamberigts, *Katholieke Universiteit Leuven*
Emiel Lamberts, *Katholieke Universiteit Leuven*
Jean-Michel Leniaud, *École pratique des hautes études, Sorbonne, Paris*
Patrick Pasture, *Katholieke Universiteit Leuven*
Andrew Saint, *University of Cambridge*
Liliane Voyé, *Université Catholique de Louvain*

Cover: cf. ill. p. 106

© 2012
Leuven University Press/Presses Universitaires de Louvain/Universitaire Pers Leuven
Minderbroedersstraat 4 bus 5602, B-3000 Leuven (Belgium)

All rights reserved. Except in those cases expressly determined by law, no part of this publication may be multiplied, saved in an automated data file or made public in any way whatsoever without the express prior written consent of the publishers.

ISBN 978 90 5867 912 3
D/2012/1869/40
NUR: 704

CONTENTS

Christianity became associated with femininity in different ways: not only did the religion appeal to women more than men, religiosity became a women's affair and femininity sacred. Women dominated in this devotional procession.
[F. Van Leemputten, Candle procession, Montaigu (Belgium), 1903; Antwerp, Koninklijk Museum voor Schone Kunsten]

BEYOND THE FEMINIZATION THESIS:

GENDERING THE HISTORY OF CHRISTIANITY IN THE NINETEENTH AND TWENTIETH CENTURIES

PATRICK PASTURE

The origin of this book lies in a collective research project aimed at developing a gender perspective on socio-religious history. The project focused on Belgium, a country that was relatively understudied - although an extensive literature exists on the social and political aspects of Christendom in Belgium, gender was (and arguably still is) hardly used as a research perspective[1] - but particularly interesting because of the dominant position of Catholicism and the country's geographical position between Germany and France. At the time, the project was conceived in the perspective of the 'feminization thesis' that seemed to be becoming an alternative master narrative replacing secularization - a concept that was increasingly abandoned by historians and sociologists of religion alike (it has returned to some degree since).[2] However, it raised some critical issues, in particular with regard to men and masculinity, the importance of the denominational context, and chronology. It appeared that the concept as we knew it from studies on American Protestantism could not that easily be applied to Europe, and particularly not in Belgium, and that a

* This text bears influence of discussions with the participants in the project *In search of the good Catholic m/f. Feminization and masculinity in Belgian Catholicism (c 1750-1950)*, a research project funded by the FWO (Research Foundation Flanders) with additional funding from KADOC and the Arts faculties of the universities of Ghent and Leuven. The project was supervised by a scientific committee consisting of the editors of this volume. I am particularly grateful to Claude Langlois, Tine Van Osselaer and the anonymous reviewers (who reviewed the whole volume) for their comments on an earlier version of this chapter.

[1] Longman, "De marginalisering van 'religie' binnen genderstudies". Compare Van Osselaer and Buerman, "Feminization Thesis".

[2] The latest state of the art in Brown and Snape eds, *Secularisation in the Christian World*.

more sophisticated approach might be needed. This volume revisits the feminization thesis in the light of the results of the project and other recent research on Europe.[3]

It will discuss the validity of the feminization thesis through a series of case studies mainly relating to Western Europe in the nineteenth and especially twentieth century, and will conclude that while the concept has no doubt made an important contribution to contemporary research on the functioning of religion in society and has fundamentally altered our ways of looking at this past, it is time to move beyond it. Not only is the concept used with different meanings, more specifically it entails a huge risk of failing to properly historicize gender stereotypes and, by doing so, of actually confirming them. Still, it is useful to remember the context in which the concept was developed and to point out some results it has generated, without losing sight of the criticisms that were expressed in earlier studies. This will be done in the first paragraph of this introductionary chapter. Afterwards it will become easier to develop a more sophisticated historical approach that historicizes and problemizes gendered identities and practices, with more attention for ambiguities than for clear-cut differences. This will be also the logic of the order followed to subdivide this book, along with the more obvious chronological order of the subsequent chapters.

THE ORIGINAL FORMULATIONS OF THE FEMINIZATION THESIS

In 1974 Barbara Welter published a seminal article on religion in North America, in which she not only argued that "the *Christianization* [my emphasis] of the West, indeed the domesticating of the West, was probably the most important religious, cultural, and political event of the nineteenth century", but also that Christianity profoundly changed, in its theology, institutions, and membership: it had become, in her words, "more domesticated, more soft and accommodating - in a word, more 'feminine'".[4] A few years later Ann Douglas in her equally seminal *The Feminization of American Culture* confirmed and generalized Welter's conclusions, describing Victorian America as a "perpetual Mother's Day".[5] Indeed, while American public life secularized and industrial capitalism triumphed, a romantic and anti-intellectual counterculture developed which cherished domesticity and sentimentalism while

---

[3] This project also resulted in two PhD dissertations (Buerman, *Katholieke mannelijkheden* and Van Osselaer, *The Pious Sex*, publication in this series forthcoming), and another collective volume Van Osselaer and Pasture et al., eds, *Households of Faith*, which will be published in this series in 2012. The chapters published in both collective volumes were discussed at workshops held at the University of Ghent (*'Dieu changea de sexe?' Christian Feminization and masculinization in Europe*, 3-4 Jan. 2008) and the University of Leuven (*'Households of faith': Domesticity and religion*, 4-6 Sept. 2008). Papers were reviewed by the editors as well as two external reviewers appointed by the editorial board of the series KADOC Studies on Religion, Culture and Society, and subsequently rewritten. For various reasons not all papers were finally included in the present volumes.

[4] Welter, "The Feminization of American Religion: 1800-1860". Some ideas she already developed in "The Cult of True Womanhood: 1820-1860".

[5] Douglas, *The Feminization*, 6.

abandoning serious theological reflection. In many ways, Douglas asserts, this was exactly the opposite of the dominant culture:

> [Sentimentalism] asserts that the values a society's activity denies are precisely the ones it cherishes; it attempts to deal with the phenomenon of cultural bifurcation by the manipulation of nostalgia. Sentimentalism provides a way to protest a power to which one has already in part capitulated. [...] Many nineteenth-century Americans in the Northeast acted every day as if they believed that economic expansion, urbanization, and industrialization represented the greatest good. It is to their credit that they indirectly acknowledged that the pursuit of these 'masculine' goals meant damaging, perhaps losing, another good, one increasingly included under the 'feminine' ideal (p. 12).

Although for Douglas this 'caramel' Christian culture distinguished the young republic from the old European continent, including Britain - which possessed "sufficiently rich and diversified secular traditions to serve as carriers for its ongoing intellectual life" (12) -, the concept of the feminization of Christianity was also applied to the European continent from the 1980s onwards and became particularly popular.[6] However, while Ann Douglas and Barbara Welter used the term feminization to refer to sentimentalism, French historians actually were already using it in another meaning, pointing especially at the high and increasing numbers of women engaging in religious orders in the nineteenth century. They too were exploring 'uncharted territory', referring to quantitative sources to validate their claims.[7] The following different meanings or dimensions of the concept could be identified in the nineteenth and twentieth centuries:[8]

1) The feminization of the faithful, of church membership and participation, referring to the high and arguably increasing numbers of women participating in religious rites - at least compared to men -, from churchgoing to participation in pilgrimages and other forms of popular devotion.

2) The growth of female religious orders - the nineteenth century therefore is labelled the 'century of the nun' (Hugh McLeod)[9] - as well as (one should be attentive to such distinctions) the disproportional involvement of women in lay fraternities and associations.[10] Many of these associations engaged in charity, social work and

---

[6] See Anderson, "Piety and Politics"; Blackbourn, "The Catholic Church" and Ford, "Religion" for overviews. How lasting its success was (and still is) is illustrated by the fact that the *Schwerter Arbeitskreises Katholizismusforschung* organized its 2007 annual meeting, uniting the finest of Germany's historians of Catholicism, entirely to the feminization thesis (*Feminisierung der Religion im 19. und 20. Jahrhundert*).

[7] See esp. the pioneering work of Langlois, *Le catholicisme au féminin*.

[8] Elaborating on distinctions formulated earlier by Schneider, "Feminisierung der Religion" and Van Osselaer and Buerman, "Feminization Thesis".

[9] McLeod, "New Perspectives", 137, 141.

[10] Meiwes, *'Arbeiterinnen des Herrn'*; Tihon, "Les religieuses"; Langlois, *Le catholicisme au féminin*; Gibson, "Le catholicisme"; Gross, *The War Against Catholicism*, 210-216; Abrams, *The Making of the Modern Woman*, 35.

education. As a result, these activities, and Christian charity in general, feminized too: *Die kirchliche Caritas trug ein weibliches Gesicht*.[11] That observation can also be interpreted in a different way, not only referring to the predominance of women in charitable associations and activities, but also in a figurative or metaphorical sense. That meaning, however, should certainly be distinguished from the more 'quantitative' aspect.

3) The 'feminization thesis' also denotes how Christianity became characterized by a change in piety, which became typified by emotion and sentimentality, and in popular theology, which represented God less as a god of fear and wrath and more as loving and caring, more 'cosy', but also a god of humility and sacrifice - associated with women and contrasted to men - and the subject of pious adoration.[12] Mary, especially embodying the 'feminine' values of modern times, became the centre of devotion after her metamorphosis from 'Heavenly Mother' to the pious Virgin-Mother, perfect wife and mother and an example for all women.

4) Lastly, the term feminization is referred to with regard to the shift in Christian culture, or the discursive feminization. In this context one could refer to the development of a sentimentalized and anti-intellectual counterculture in which Christian belief became increasingly associated with womanliness, domesticity and also sentimentalism as anti-intellectualism, as was Ann Douglas' original argument.[13] Discursive feminization, however, should also be understood in a slightly different way.[14] The concept figures prominently in Callum Brown's ground-breaking *The Death of Christian Britain* (2001), in which the author offers a complex gendered reading of Christian practices and discourses. According to Brown, Evangelicalism in Britain feminized piety, which came to the fore not only in higher participation rates but especially in a narrative about femininity. Hence Evangelicalism not only "feminized piety" but also "pietized femininity": "Femininity became sacred *and nothing but sacred*" (emphasis in the original).[15] Brown argues that in contrast to previous centuries when masculinity lay at the core of representations of piety and women were seen as heirs of Eve, this polarity reversed after 1800. His sources not only showed less participation of men in religious activities, but also demonstrated how the religiosity of men increasingly became perceived as worrisome: men, not women, were presented as heathens and likely to succumb to the sirens of Satan: gambling, drinking, sexual debauchery, et cetera.

While the feminization thesis originally was designed in an American Protestant context, it has also often been used as a source of inspiration with regard to Catholicism. From a Protestant point of view, Catholicism, with its 'sensual environment' of

---

[11] Schneider, "Feminisierung der Religion", 137, 141.

[12] See e.g. Busch, "Die Feminisierung der Frömmigkeit".

[13] See also McLeod, "Weibliche Frömmigkeit".

[14] See Borutta, "Antikatholizismus".

[15] Brown, *The Death of Christian Britain*, 59. See also Borutta, "Antikatholizismus". The term Evangelicalism is used here in the common English usage, referring to a particular strand in Anglicanism which emphasises biblicism, redemption, conversion and activism (to be distinguished from the common German meaning of *Evangelisch* as Lutheran and also from the American usage which refers to the heirs of the evangelical revivals of the eighteenth and nineteenth century, known as the First and the Second Great Awakening).

candles and images of saints and Madonnas, often appeared more 'feminine' than the austere and 'rational' forms of Protestant theology and worship - Protestantism hence has more than once been depicted as 'manly'.[16] That representation corroborates remarkably with the imaginaries developed during the European Culture Wars of the nineteenth and twentieth centuries, e.g. when both German Protestant nationalists and Belgian anti-clericals represented the Catholic Church as unmanly and effeminate, inter al. because of its 'irrationality', 'debilitating' anti-intellectualism, and docile submission to the Pope, the 'master-eunuch'.[17] Such representations incidentally have a long life and continue to influence contemporary perceptions as well.

The feminization thesis has had a profound impact on the historical study of French Catholicism, which emphasized the transition during the nineteenth century from a (post-) Tridentine Catholicism and its obsession with sexual morality and *pastorale de la peur* to a more compassionate ultramontane (?) piety, "from a god of fear to a god of love" (Ralph Gibson).[18] As we will see further in this text, his depiction of a loving and compassionate ultramontane clergy, however, certainly does not convince everyone and it must be admitted that Catholic revivalism, just as was the case with Protestant movements, offered opportunities for men to express their piety as well. Moreover, neither lay associations, social Catholicism nor politics fit the feminization narrative.[19] That observation underpins critical attitudes towards the application of the feminization theory in Germany, though the theory has also inspired much research there as well.[20] The main issue in Germany - one that should be extended to much of Europe - regards the different spheres in which Christians are active, including the social and political realm. As Bernhard Schneider emphasizes, developing even a model of concentric circles with regard to the Catholic Church in chapter I, the role of men and women was conceived quite different depending on sphere of activities and symbolic distance to the core of the circle.

Though contemporary historians are more than hesitant to apply broad concepts to their subjects, which usually are well framed within narrow time schemes and firm national boundaries, and limited to 'comparable' (i.e. largely *similar*) phenomena, adopting a feminization perspective in Europe and across denominations has revealed some striking parallels: the Marian century in the Catholic world, for example, coincided in many ways with the Protestant cult of true womanhood. Such generalizations are not without problems though, especially if they include a transatlantic comparison. Neither North America, even if we leave Canada out of the equation, nor

---

[16] Braude, "Women's History *is* American Religious History", 105; Blaschke, "The Unrecognized Piety of Men"; Alderson, *Mansex Fine*.

[17] Hastings, "Fears of a Feminized Church"; Art and Buerman, "Anticléricalisme et genre"; Borutta, "Antikatholizismus".

[18] Gibson, *A Social History of French Catholicism*; Id., "Le catholicisme"; Langlois, *Le catholicisme au féminin*; Hufton, "The Reconstruction"; Cholvy and Hilaire, *Histoire religieuse*; Desan, *Reclaiming the Sacred*; di Giorgio, "La bonne catholique"; Ford, "Religion"; Smith, *Ladies*.

[19] Gibson did focus on Catholic nationalism, however. For an early attempt to complicate the feminization-of-religion thesis by analysing the religious commitments of bourgeois Catholic men, see Seeley, "O Sainte Mère".

[20] Schneider, "Feminisierung der Religion"; Van Osselaer and Buerman, "Feminization Thesis", 498.

Europe can be considered homogenous. Denominations, patterns of religious practice as well as church-state relations differ considerably among European countries.[21] The present volume concentrates on Northwestern Europe, where Roman Catholicism remained either dominant or at least a significant factor in society. Moreover European historiography is fundamentally marked by dechristianization and secularization.[22]

A CRITICAL DISCUSSION

The feminization thesis, indeed, raises a number of problems, both theoretical and empirical, some of which became recognized early on. Harvard historian Ann Braude, in a critical overview (1997) of the way the feminization thesis has been developed relating to North-American Anglo-Protestantism, speaks of a *narrative fiction*.

FICTION 1: WHAT FEMINIZATION?

For Braude, feminization even 'never happened'. Her main argument as regards feminization from a quantitative perspective is that women always formed the majority in the church and that there was at most some relative increase in women's participation as the participation of men possibly declined somewhat. This reveals some major problems indeed, regarding (non)existence and interpretation of statistics of religious participation and regarding the chronology and the beginnings of the alleged feminization. Hence, according to Braude, secularization, declension[23] and feminization

> can be said to have happened only if they are understood as referring not to demographic shifts but *rather to anxieties caused by the belief that such shifts were occurring or the fear that they might occur* [my emphasis]. In each case, the term expresses nostalgia for a world that never existed, a world in which men went to church and were as moved as women by what they heard there, a world in which the clergy felt they had precisely as much public influence as they should. Perhaps it is not women who have sentimentalised American Protestantism, but rather the male clergy who have cherished a romantic notion of a patriarchal past.[24]

Does that comment also apply to European scholarship on the subject? Looking at the data presented by Olaf Blaschke on the basis of Lucian Hölscher's impressive data-atlas of religious practice in Protestant Germany, one may wonder. This data

---

[21] See e.g. Schnabel-Schüle, "Vierzig Jahre". Some interesting observations in this respect in Martin, "Integration" and Baldwin, *The Narcissism*.

[22] Cox, "Master narratives".

[23] Declension: process by which churches and denominations 'soften' their ideological and theological positions, making them more 'this-worldly'. The term has been used in particular for American Protestant denominations falling back from the difficult Calvinist doctrines of their Puritan origins.

[24] Braude, "Women's History *is* American Religious History", 96. Schneider, "Feminisierung der Religion" offers an insightful discussion from a Catholic perspective.

do show that more women than men took Sunday communion, but demonstrate no change over time in the percentage of women doing so.[25] It is, however, also important to note that the demands and significance of religious practices change. Within Catholicism, for example, the Church attached much more importance to attending Sunday Mass, taking communion and annual confession in the early nineteenth century than ever before. Research on Belgium indicates that far more women than men observed these new practices.[26] Moreover, there can be no doubt that female congregations experienced a tremendous growth that far exceeded the increase of the population.[27] Still, Braude is right in pointing out a lack of long-term perspective in much contemporary historical research, and in making us aware that quite a few of the sources we use to analyse feminization are effectively produced by men - especially those containing complaints about men failing to live to the expectations, reflecting 'masculine' concerns and anxieties.

There are other indications that this feminization could never have happened. Blaschke recently observed that in Germanic countries - no doubt the observation holds elsewhere as well - women participated in religious rites for other reasons than piety, for example to attract men, and that for that reason their piety should be qualified.[28] That comment is a very dubious one though, as it suggests the historian can somehow 'measure' the quality of piety and faith. What standard should one then use? Moreover, Blaschke ignores the power of discursive feminization, which made participation socially desirable for women but not for men. Far more valid is the observation that definitions and interpretations of what is feminine and what is masculine should be historicized and contextualized. Which definitions and interpretations do we follow, our own or those of contemporaries? Susan Juster commented that the sentimentalized language with its images of a loving and merciful Christ, which historians consider characteristic of nineteenth-century feminization, "would hardly have been considered 'feminine' by earlier generations of American Protestants".[29] The same holds for Europe in the nineteenth century. This volume will indeed show that many quite different ideals of masculinity and femininity existed.[30] Therefore a careful reconstruction of the way gender ideals are constructed should be a prime concern in any discussion on religion and gender.

FICTION 2: FEMINIZATION AND SECULARIZATION

One of the reasons for the success of the feminization thesis was that it offers an alternative and even an explanation for secularization narratives, which have dominated social scientific discourse since Kant's and Voltaire's 'rational' criticisms of particularly the organized and revealed Christian religion. Many social thinkers since the pioneers of social sciences have analysed the processes that drove religion - and in

---

[25] Blaschke, "The Unrecognized Piety of Men"; Hölscher, *Datenatlas*.
[26] Van Osselaer and Buerman, "Feminization Thesis", 502-503.
[27] See supra, note 10 and 11.
[28] Blaschke, "The Unrecognized Piety of Men".
[29] Juster, "The Spirit and the Flesh", 345. See also Scott, "On Gender".
[30] Likewise in Werner, *Christian Manliness*.

the modern West this meant Christianity - out of the centre of society into the margins of private life, and explained why religion actually was irreconcilable with modernity.[31] In the 1960s the death knell indeed seemed to be ringing for god. However, in the following decades, scholars who doubted the decline of (organized) religion in modern societies seemed to get the wind back in their sails. While Islam became a powerful force in the modernizing Islamic world, in the US church participation remained high and, moreover, a militant conservative Christianity went increasingly public and even political. Europe suddenly seemed to be a secular exception in a world full of religious fervour.[32] Historians started to realize that nineteenth-century revivals and culture wars on the continent were hard to reconcile with secularization, however defined. A gender perspective offered a simple, even crude explanation for the apparent paradox: secularization was the result of gender blindness. By bringing the perspective of women in, religion too returned into the picture.

Before discussing the connections between feminization and secularization we need to clarify the concept of secularization, as the term can be used to mean several different things. There are three clear major distinctions, between (1) a decline in religious participation, (2) the separation of church and state and the privatization of religion as a consequence of functional differentiation; and (3) the evolution by which religious doctrines adapt by becoming more this-worldly and de-emphasizing other-worldliness and transcendence (essentially what Perry Miller calls declension).[33] Callum Brown added a fourth meaning, a loss of discursive religiosity, the interpenetration of religious narrative forms in everyday language.[34] Obviously *secularism*, an ideological movement promoting secular ideas or values in either public or private settings and arguing for the separation of church and state or *laïcité*, should be clearly distinguished from secularization, but in practice there are connections, as secularists consider secularization desirable and 'natural', a result of modernization processes, especially functional differentiation, individualization, rationalization, and urbanization. In any case, secularization in the nineteenth and twentieth centuries is predominantly understood from a Christian and from an institutional perspective, i.e. a perspective which focuses on the Christian churches, with their rituals, doctrines, and apparatus, but one should obviously bear in mind that the concept theoretically could apply to all religious expressions. However, because the secularization theories were formulated from within a Christian tradition and bear witness to Christian and particularly nineteenth-century ('modern') conceptions of the distinctions between the sacred and the profane, and hence are far less culture-free than their advocates admit, they turn out to be very difficult to apply outside

---

[31] E.g. Bruce, *God is Dead*; Id., *Religion in the Modern World*; Lehmann, *Säkularisierung*; Dawson, *Christianity and European Culture*; McLeod, *Secularization*. Historiographical assessments in Tschannen, *Les théories*; Borutta, "Genealogie".

[32] See Pasture, "Religion in Contemporary Europe"; Id., "De-Christianization".

[33] A more sociological approach would start from the process of functional differentiation and differentiate between macro-, meso- and individual levels. See Dobbelaere, "Assessing Secularization Theory"; Id., *Secularization: an analysis at three levels*. See also Gorski, "Historizing the Secularization Debate". On declension see note 23.

[34] Brown, *The Death of Christian Britain*.

of an explicit Christian institutional context.[35] Although this volume only deals with Christian cases, some of these problems are relevant for our purpose as well.

Feminization is associated in different ways with secularization. Sometimes it is considered a particular expression or consequence of it, but more often - certainly in Europe - it is presented as a correction to it or blatantly as an alternative, e.g. by Callum Brown. In the former interpretation the rationale is first of all that men abandoned the churches first, and that in the end women will follow as well - when they finally became 'emancipated', 'educated', thus when they became 'modern' - and secondly that the ensuing feminization (since women remained faithful) is an expression of the 'privatization' of religion: religion in 'modern' *secularized* societies is relegated to the private sphere, which indeed became women's domain - an issue that raises its own set of problems.[36] From that perspective, the public sphere became essentially masculine. The feminization is then seen as a confirmation of the secularization of society.[37] In the eyes of contemporaries the involvement of women with religion actually helps to qualify it as 'only' a women's affair, not worthy of any serious consideration. Present-day historians to be sure will not subscribe to such reasoning, at least not explicitly,[38] but it is no doubt one of the reasons why religion received so little attention in modern history.

FICTION 3: FEMINIZATION EMPOWERING?

According to Welter, the feminization of Christendom empowered Christian women, giving them opportunities to assert themselves and develop personally, among other things through their involvement in female religious orders and laic associations, and by exercising moral authority over men.[39] As Michael O'Sullivan observes in chapter 10 with regard to German Catholicism, few historians of Europe would endorse this view. Generally present day European intellectuals, and historians do not really constitute an exception, consider Christianity, and particularly the Catholic Church, mainly as a reactionary force, confirming social and especially gender inequalities (essentially as women oppressing), in which women could only be considered as subordinate. Hence for many scholars, feminization of Catholicism cannot be dissociated from the development of a conservative, reactionary Church, dominated by the clerical hierarchy with the pope as supreme leader, which firmly imposed a gender-

---

[35] Dubuisson, *The Western Construction of Religion*; Peterson and Walhof, *The Invention of Religion*; Id., "Rethinking Religion"; Dussel, "World Religions"; Fitzgerald, *The Ideology*; McCutcheon, *Manufacturing Religion*; Smith, "Religion, Religions, Religious"; Asad, "The Construction of Religion". A particularly insightful discussion of secularization in Ruff, "The Postmodern Challenge".

[36] Which will be explored in Van Osselaer, Pasture et al., *Households of Faith*. See also note 109.

[37] de Vries, "Rediscovering Christianity"; Brown, *The Death of Christian Britain*; Busch, *Katholische Frömmigkeit und Moderne*; Jonas, *France and the Cult of the Sacred Heart*; McLeod, *Secularization*; Id., "Weibliche Frömmigkeit", 141; Id., "New perspectives", 137-138; Ruff, "The Postmodern Challenge"; Ford, *Divided Houses*, 3; Marks, "'A fragment of heaven on earth'?", 262; Mergel, "Die subtile Macht der Liebe", 46.

[38] That men abandoned church while women 'remained' faithful is still seen as proof of secularization though, e.g. in Chélini-Pont, "French Catholics", 81.

[39] See also Cott, *The Bonds of Womanhood* and the brief discussion in Haynes, "Women and Protestantism".

determined world with women either confined to the household or virtually locked up in nunneries and cloisters, where they were also controlled by men, either directly or indirectly through the confession - a situation that incidentally, in response, paved the way for the rise of a militant 'masculine' *laïcité*, particularly in France.[40] However, the discussion of the feminization thesis and the introduction of more sophisticated gender perspectives have led to other findings and interpretations. It has been noted for example that the French Revolution saw women standing up in resistance against impious men to defend the churches, though once the Revolution was over they went back to their homes.[41] Michael O'Sullivan argues in chapter 10 that women considered attacks on the church as treats to their own position, also within the household.

Relinde Meiwes, among others, has forcefully argued that the massive involvement of women in religious institutions in the nineteenth century, offering opportunities to engage in missions, charity, education and health care in a relatively egalitarian context, was one way women could escape from the narrow boundaries of family life, even if it brought about other constraints.[42] To some extent it created a separate women's world where women held the authority, though this was not always and everywhere the case. There also existed ways through which men and women could act side by side, sometimes in actions with clear social and political perspectives such as the temperance movement, anti-prostitution activities and even women's leagues, friendly societies and trade unions. Michael Gross went one step further and saw in the famous German *Kulturkampf* a gender war of the liberal bourgeoisie against Catholicism, considered 'feminine', and particularly against Catholic women, which to him included the social work of nuns, who trespassed the boundaries of the 'Liberal' bourgeois gender dichotomy.

> The Catholic Church, personified as a woman, and Catholics, as they participated in the missions and practiced their faith in public, undermined the separate spheres of public and private, one reserved, according to liberal social and sexual ideology, for women in the life of the family, and the other reserved for men in the world of social and political citizenship.[43]

By doing so, Gross actually inverts a generally held belief that identifies the Church with the household ideology and secular liberalism with women's liberation. Gross continues by situating some origins of the women's movement in Germany with dissenting churches such as the *Deutschkatholiken*, who incidentally vehemently opposed the ultramontane Catholic renewal as expressed in popular pilgrimages and intellectual anti-liberalism.

Nevertheless, as Ann Braude commented with regard to the US, the alleged increased moral authority came at a cost, and a high one, as their moral elevation

---

[40] Michelet, *Du prêtre*. See the discussion in Ford, *Divided Houses*, 14 ff.; Götz von Olenhausen, "Die Feminisierung von Religion und Kirche".
[41] McLeod, *Religion and the People of Western Europe*, 11.
[42] Meiwes, 'Arbeiterinnen des Herrn'. See also Curtis, *Educating the Faithful*.
[43] Gross, *The War Against Catholicism*, 186.

required their sexual disempowerment.[44] Not only nuns but also lay women militants remained celibate: for mothers there was no alternative but to take care of the children at home - at least as far as that was financially feasible (which was only the case in bourgeois families). Neither did the augmented emphasis on their morality mark the demise of negative views of women: even if men's souls could be more easily corrupted than women's, women could still be held responsible for it. And it should obviously not obliterate the very unequal power relations between men and women: female presence and masculine power formed a strange association, but one characteristic of nineteenth- and twentieth-century Christendom. According to Braude the discrepancy was even greater in American Protestant churches than in the Catholic Church.[45] In this respect one should emphasize that the space allotted to women in all terms remained limited and that the opportunities for charitable and social (including educational) engagement actually prevented further radical involvement with feminism. Pat Starkey suggests that women had "interiorized old and familiar Gospel injunctions to love and service so successfully that they could not easily be dislodged by a new dogma, whatever its potential for personal liberation". Some argue that especially at the end of the nineteenth century women "spoke with forked tongues", paying lip service to Pauline conceptions of the role of women but at the same time pleading for the right of women to paid work outside the home and to speak out on matters of general moral interest, which included politics.[46] Belgian Catholic women in this respect would develop in the twentieth century what they saw as a 'Catholic feminism', a personalist interpretation of feminism as a way of personal liberation and self-development which subscribed to fundamentally different roles for men and women.[47] Starkey therefore considers social Catholicism as part of the political right, a concept that is arguable for more than one reason, but her point is well taken.

MASCULINITY, MANLINESS AND MASCULINIZATION

FEMALE PRESENCE, MASCULINE POWER?

This brings me to men. Obviously the feminization thesis raises a lot of questions relating to the position of men and manliness. The feminization thesis suggests that men became alienated from the churches and that women gained importance within them. Does this mean that power relations within the churches altered as women became 'empowered'? There are indeed indications that by the end of the nineteenth century in some Protestant denominations in the US women were effectively threatening the male positions of power, were about to be ordained and to gain access to leadership positions. Though it was by no means the case in the mainstream denominations, this was perceived as a real threat, provoking a reaction to which we will return. Was that also the case in Europe? Surely not in the mainstream churches,

[44] Braude, "Women's History *is* American Religious History", 99-100.
[45] Ibid., 104.
[46] Starkey, "Women religious and religious women", 196 ff.
[47] Van Molle, "De nieuwe vrouwenbeweging".

but neither was it so in the main dissident sects. There was no question about the ordination of women in the Anglican Church, the Reformed and the Lutheran state Churches nor, least of all, in the Catholic Church. Men continued to occupy the main positions of power within the ecclesiastical structures as they did in the wider society.[48] But, as comes to the fore in the explosive growth of the numbers of women religious, religious 'personnel' did become more feminized.

However, Ann Braude argues that rather than feminization, it was the discrepancy between female presence and masculine power that characterized nineteenth-century American Protestantism. That argument could easily be confirmed in other contexts, including in the Anglican Church on the British isles as well as the Reformed and the Lutheran state Churches on the continent and even the dissident movements, including Quakers and Methodists. Within Catholicism, the hierarchy and in particular the papacy strongly increased its power, leading to a 'clericalization', centralization and ultramontane hierarchization. This started right after the French Revolution, culminated in the First Vatican Council and the promulgation of papal infallibility, and continues even up the present day. After all Peter's Pence (also illustrative of the 'economic' - masculine? - dimension of the church) marked the nineteenth century as much as the devotion to the Virgin Mary.[49] Ralph Gibson, speaking of the "clerical recuperation of popular piety", incidentally saw a cause of the feminization in the greater impact of the clergy, as it drove men away from popular religion.[50] His argument follows the same reasoning as Patricia Bonomi with regard to congregationalism in late colonial North America. Bonomi suggested that the professionalization of the clergy alienated men from the churches, as the clergy took over tasks traditionally taken on by laymen.[51] This is less obvious in Europe, though, especially in Catholic and, perhaps to a lesser extent, Reformed churches. Indeed, while at first sight men abandoned the church, the fact is easily overlooked that there were ways for laymen (actually for laywomen too) to engage as Christians outside the church as narrowly defined.[52] There they engaged in worldly affairs, but did so motivated by their faith and often also manifesting themselves as Christians. Hence there was, as Olaf Blaschke concluded with regard to Germany, a clear "specific male transfer of religion from the ecclesiastical into the professional, public and political sphere".[53] This was the case elsewhere in (continental) Western Europe too, as Catholics and Calvinists reacted against secularization, interpreting it as a largely political onslaught, and subsequently developing a socio-political counteroffensive.[54] It is not difficult to show that men dominated the socio-political action and the representation of the Catholic and Reformed worlds, even if, as mentioned, women sometimes did have a

---

[48] Starkey, "Women religious and religious women".
[49] The concept of *Verkirchlichung* has been introduced in Germany by Kaufmann, *Kirche begreifen* and Hürten, "Zukunftperspektiven", 110 ff.
[50] Gibson, *A Social History of French Catholicism*, 153.
[51] Bonomi, *Under the Cope of Heaven*, 113-114.
[52] As Schneider, "Feminisierung der Religion" emphasized.
[53] Blaschke, "The Unrecognized Piety of Men"; Schneider, "Feminisierung der Religion".
[54] Kalyvas, *The Rise of Christian Democracy*; Righart, *De katholieke zuil in Europa*.

place in it as well.[55] Their engagement, however, also implied that clergy and laity would soon compete for who would take the lead.[56]

Late nineteenth- and twentieth-century Catholicism in Europe indeed shows an increasing tension between clergy and laity engaged in the public sphere as politicians, entrepreneurs and militants of fraternities and social movements. But their engagement offered the laymen a way to act as Christians, which seriously qualifies the argument about a quantitative 'feminization', as this only focuses on participation in Christian rituals or involvement in religious congregations - illustrative of the 'modern' nineteenth-century approach of narrowing down the definition of religion to personal spirituality and rituals.[57] Studies about feminization, however, ignore the existence of social and political Catholicism, which developed gradually from the mid-nineteenth century onwards, receiving a boost since the 1890s, among other things because of the encyclical *Rerum novarum*.[58] In the twentieth century, social and political Catholicism evolved into one of the major socio-political forces that shaped the typical European welfare states in countries such as Germany, Austria, Switzerland, Italy, Belgium, the Netherlands, Luxembourg, and to some extent also France.[59] This offered men, and some women, plenty of opportunities to express their faith in a different way. Within Protestantism it is difficult to identify similar developments, as Protestants, especially Lutherans, engaged in social and political action as Christians much less than Catholics did, and even less in confessional associations.[60] However, Catholics as well as Protestant politicians did support the states and in particular offered religious legitimacy to nationalist movements, associating nationalism and religion: Christian churches turned nationalist and nationalisms religious.[61] Nationalism then, in Blaschke's eyes, offered a source of masculine identity to Protestants.[62]

Another way of doing so was by offering 'masculine' examples, such as heroes. In this respect, Tine Van Osselaer and Alexander Maurits observed the very martial tone of Christian heroic stories in such divergent contexts as Catholic Belgium and Lutheran High-Church Sweden.[63] Most heroes were men, as were saints in the Catholic Church, though women also could be cited. Classical examples of Christian heroes are military men (such as the Zouaves in the Catholic case) and missionaries, though the first Christian hero of course was Christ himself - the images of Christ presented as ideal show a remarkable history of their own. The ideal of Christ shows the prevalent ideals very well, and in the later nineteenth and first half of the twentieth century obedience and sacrifice constituted a crucial component of that ideal, even if one was

[55] Schneider, "Feminisierung der Religion".
[56] See esp. Kalyvas, *The Rise of Christian Democracy*.
[57] See references in note 35.
[58] Lamberts, *Een kantelend tijdperk*.
[59] Van Kersbergen and Manow, *Religion*.
[60] See e.g. with regard to Christian labour Heerma van Voss et al., "Between Cross and Class".
[61] McLeod, *Secularization*, 216-247, esp. 286. See in particular Schulze Wessel, *Nationalisierung der Religion*; Haupt and Langewiesche, *Nation und Religion in Europa*; Smith, *Chosen Peoples*; Van der Veer and Lehman, *Nation and Religion*; Hastings, *The Construction of Nationhood*.
[62] Blaschke, "The Unrecognized Piety of Men"; Werner, "Studying Christian Manliness: An Introduction".
[63] Van Osselaer and Maurits, "Heroic Men and Christian Ideals".

quite well aware that this did not correspond to prevailing ideals of masculinity in the wider society. This was no doubt even more the case with gentleness, which also was a central heroic quality in Catholic narratives, though it belonged to the longing for a 'complete' or 'whole' man in the nineteenth century, certainly in Germany.[64]

One may wonder incidentally if scientists could be Christian heroes and examples. Science no doubt belonged to the masculine sphere, and science was believed to undermine Christianity. However, relationships between churches and science varied. Liberal Protestants, particularly German Lutherans, embraced the modern values and ideologies and developed a very positive attitude towards science, but for conservative Protestants and Catholics things were more ambiguous. They rejected attempts to reconcile science and religion if that meant giving up basic aspects of the traditional doctrines and interpretations. However, Catholic, Protestant conservative and even Fundamentalist Churches and denominations did try in different ways to develop their own scientific institutions and practices, and emphasized rationality, looking for ways to reconcile science and faith.[65] In nineteenth-century Germany, for example, Catholics apparently were eager consumers of scientific literature; there was no difference in this respect between Catholic and liberal subcultures.[66] It would be interesting to know if scientists were given a place in the popular Catholic counteroffensive. If so, it would seriously compromise one of the basic dimensions of the feminization thesis, the formation of an anti-intellectual counterculture.

MASCULINE SPACES, IDENTITIES, STRATEGIES

However, such representations also need to be qualified. On closer examination it appears that far more complex ideals of masculinity existed within the churches and denominations than the classic hegemonic masculinity model suggests. No example illustrates this better than ultramontane Catholicism. Indeed, in her critical assessment of gender stereotypes Sophie Heywood remarked with regard to Catholicism that power no longer resided in the divine and hence that the Church was no longer the place where power resided. Hence the Church actually tried to 'masculinize' the semantics of religion, using manly metaphors and associating religion with nationhood. Heywood in this respect emphasizes the strongly manly, even military language of French ultramontanism.[67] As ultramontanism originated in reaction and defence, it is no wonder that it also had features usually associated with virility: it intended to mobilize for a fight. In other confessions too, roles and representations of manliness existed that were supposed to appeal to ideals of hegemonic manliness that domi-

---

[64] Van Osselaer, "'Heroes of the Heart'". See also Kessel, "The 'Whole' Man".
[65] The literature is endless. Bowler, "Christianity and the sciences" gives a short state of the art of the literature. See also Graf, "Le politique dans la sphère intime"; Borutta, "Antikatholizismuse".
[66] Zalar, "The Process of Confessional Inculturation", 132-134.
[67] Heywood, "Les 'petits garçons modèles'", 210. Heywood incidentally uses these arguments to disqualify the concepts of feminization and masculanization altogether. On male semantics see Werner's volume *Christian Manliness*.

nated the secular, 'bourgeois' society in the nineteenth and twentieth centuries.[68] At least in Europe, this period was characterized by fierce struggles between churches and chapels, confessions and secularists, which offered plenty of possibilities for developing and emphasizing virtues and semantics that particularly appealed to men, and that offered possibilities for 'manly' roles.[69]

Obviously Heywood's qualification of ultramontane Catholicism stands in blatant opposition to the (qualified) presentation of ultramontane piety as softer, more 'feminine' in comparison with the Tridentine Church mentioned earlier.[70] The difference in appreciation comes particularly to the fore with regard to the cult of the Sacred Heart, which is seen as both an example of *"la religion au féminin"* and manly due to its stress on the defence of country and religion, and an alternative to the obviously more sentimental Marian devotion.[71] Actually the two visions do not absolutely exclude each other: as Tine Van Osselaer demonstrates with regard to the Belgian Sacred Heart movement, instead of a 'masculinization' or 'feminization', particularly in the later nineteenth century, the Catholic Church actually developed different strategies and discourses appealing to various audiences that cannot be reduced to a simple binary opposition based upon gender distinctions considered without history and context (chapter 6).[72] Derek Hastings and Irmtraud Götz von Olenhusen even established a clear link between the early development of ultramontanism and (especially quantitative forms of) Catholic feminization.[73] Olaf Blaschke as well as Tine Van Osselaer observed in this respect that the men's apostolate not only appealed to men to engage in public life, but also to show their piety, by taking communion and by confessing.[74] Thus the conclusion must be that many masculinities existed within confessional milieus.

The Catholic cleric, however, demonstrates that the question of multiple masculinities with regard to Catholicism raises even more issues. Manliness, Paul Airiau informs us, was mainly confirmed through sociability, at the inn - the most common gathering place for men in the nineteenth and twentieth centuries - which increasingly appeared as forbidden territory for clerics. Changes in the appearance

---

[68] Schmale, *Geschichte der Männlichkeit*, 227-230. On the concept of hegemonic masculinity (and its critics) see Connell and Messerschmidt, "Hegemonic Masculinity"; Dinges, "'Hegemoniale Männlichkeit'"; Connell, *Masculinities*.

[69] Blaschke, "The Unrecognized Piety of Men". On the confessional and ideological struggles see Id., *Konfessionen im Konflikt*; Hellemans, *Strijd om de moderniteit*; McLeod, *Religion and the People of Western Europe*.

[70] Cf. supra, note 18-19.

[71] Fouilloux, "Le catholicisme" and Menozzi, *Sacro Cuore* strongly emphasize its 'virility'. Compare Busch, *Katholische Frömmigkeit und Moderne*; Blaschke, "Fältmarskalk Jesus Kristus"; Jonas, *France and the Cult of the Sacred Heart*; Gibson, *A Social History of French Catholicism* (who nevertheless strongly emphasizes the nationalization of ultramontanism though in his treatment of the cult of the Sacred Heart).

[72] Van Osselaer, "'Une oeuvre essentiellement virile'".

[73] Hastings, "Fears of a Feminized Church", 41; Götz von Olenhusen, "Die Feminisierung von Religion und Kirche".

[74] Blaschke, "The unrecognized Piety of Men"; Van Osselaer, "'Une oeuvre essentiellement virile'"; Id., *The Pious Sex*.

and dress of priests have effectively been interpreted as a kind of 'feminization', or at least 'de-masculinization'. Examples of these changes include the long black *soutane* (cassock) which became common, and particular ways of behaving in public that are supposed to express 'a feminine sensibility', which includes the showing of emotions: tears became an instrument of apology. However, their hair was cut short, which in combination with a clean-shaven face stood for a 'rational virility'. Confession confirms the ambiguously gendered nature of the priests: laymen felt threatened by the information obtained through this sacrament, as it felt like it offered priests direct powers over women, undermining the authority of the married man as head of the family. In the imagination it moreover offered priests ways to live out sexual fantasies.[75] It also appeared that clerics and women had concluded some particular alliance against the married men, which may partly explain why the theme figured so prominently in anti-clerical literature.[76] Róisín Healy, however, has emphasized the contradictory images in Germany of Jesuits, who strongly appealed to the imagination of Liberal Protestants: Jesuits appeared both as manly, even extremely masculine and authoritarian, and as submissive and 'hence' feminine, in sum as *androgynous*. This ambiguity challenged Liberal ideals of masculinity, as they cherished the same values in other contexts: virility and rationality, but also obedience as soldiers, civil servants and citizens.[77]

During the culture wars that underpinned much socio-political action between the mid-nineteenth and the mid-twentieth century, the modern Catholic clergy were accused of being or becoming effeminate: it was a popular *topos* in anti-clerical rhetoric.[78] Their celibacy, abstinence, and vows of obedience made priests easy targets for such reproaches. However, calling others unmanly and emphasizing one's own manliness appears to be a general practice. Besides priests, laymen were also depicted as unmanly, because - so it was argued - they were obedient to both the clergy and to their wives, who were controlled by the clergy through the confessional. Those who were attacked emphasized their own masculinity by pointing out the courage they displayed in following their faith and the 'completeness' of the Christian ideals of masculinity, and contrasted it to secular men, 'incomplete' and prone to debauchery, gambling and drinking.[79] Emphasizing the 'wholeness' or completeness of confessional masculine identities of course also helps to make them 'normal', to de-emphasize the particularity of Christian ideals of masculinity.[80] This was neces-

---

[75] Airiau, "Le prêtre catholique: masculine, neutre, autre?"; Busch, "Die Feminisierung der Frömmigkeit", 214.

[76] Art and Buerman, "Is de katholieke man wel een echte vent?"; Id., "Anticléricalisme et genre".

[77] Healy, "Anti-Jesuitism in Imperial Germany", 159.

[78] Kaiser, "'Clericalism – that is your enemy!'"; Clark, "The New Catholicism"; Art and Buerman, "Is de katholieke man wel een echte vent?"; Hastings, "Fears of a Feminized Church"; Gross, *The War Against Catholicism*.

[79] Art and Buerman, "Is de katholieke man wel een echte vent?"; Id., "Anticléricalisme et genre"; Brown, *Death of Christian Britain*; Hastings, "Fears of a Feminized Church"; Kirkley, "Is it Manly to Become a Christian?".

[80] Likewise Anna Prestjan has shown that Lutheran remembrance texts of Swedish priests emphasized contemporary secular ideals of masculinity in order to show that clergymen were ordinary men with worldly interests. Prestjan, "The Man in the Clergyman".

sary indeed, as the alleged androgynous character of the priests, and particularly the stress on celibacy, also generated fears that it would jeopardize the health and future of the nation in Germany.[81] Remarkably, as Angela Berlis demonstrates in chapter 2, reproaches of 'unmanliness' were also used between Catholics,[82] in the dispute that led to the secession of the Old Catholics. Such negative images do reveal ideal images of manliness, but one should remain cautious, as they rather graft onto general stereotypes and aim at discrediting the others: the opposite of the negative is perhaps not necessarily the ideal one cherishes for oneself.[83]

Catholic priests increasingly appear to offer one form of masculinity. In nineteenth-century Belgian sermons, however, men were mainly depicted in their capacity as fathers, husbands and workers. The Catholic ideal was constructed through sets of binary oppositions and hierarchical relations, differentiating them from 'impious men' as well as from women.[84] Though the details vary, in essence these confirm the dichotomies Callum Brown observed in his assessment of Christian (mainly Dissenting) discourses on Christian men in Britain.[85] However there were other ideal images, as comes to the fore in the representations of Catholic heroes that were produced both for women and men. Priests could be heroes, but so could missionaries (male and female), saints - many of whom were female - and Zouaves. Each remarkably contained elements of both hegemonic masculinity - shall we call this 'virile'? - and elements often presented as 'feminine', such as humility, tenderness, and emotionality. Zouaves, for example, were portrayed as knights and soldiers (which they effectively were) but with a heart, which could be moved to tears.[86]

Sentimentality in this respect should not be confused with femininity, as Zouaves were anything but 'effeminate'. Likewise, as Olaf Blaschke argued, even the image of Mary can have different meanings, as "a symbol of motherhood and love, submissiveness and sympathy", but also as strong and combative, "even the one who crushes the (satanic) snake". This image reappeared forcefully in the late nineteenth and the twentieth century, for example with women fighting Communists in the Spanish Civil War as well as during the Cold War.[87] Incidentally, an emphasis on sentimentalism among men was not necessarily unique to Catholics.[88] Likewise, obedience was an important bourgeois value and not alien to working-class culture either: it is the concrete context that set Catholic values apart. This incidentally seems to refute the argument of Wolfgang Schmale that the religious revivals and church mobilizations also contributed, directly or indirectly, to the prevalence of hegemonic masculinity in

---

[81] Hastings, "Fears of a Feminized Church".

[82] Ibid.

[83] On masculinities and 'countermasculinities' see esp. Mosse, *The Image of Man.*

[84] Van Osselaer, "'A lot of women have good reason to complain about their husbands'".

[85] Brown, *Death of Christian Britain.*

[86] On the Zouaves see, apart from the contribution of Thomas Buerman in this volume (chapter 5), Harrison, "Zouave Stories"; Heywood, "Les 'petits garçons modèles'", 213; Viaene, "The Roman Question"; Guenel, *La dernière guerre du pape.* Heywood, "Les 'petits garçons modèles'", esp. 213 writes how Zouave stories were presented to young Catholic boys as heros to follow.

[87] Blaschke, "The Unrecognized Piety of Men".

[88] See e.g. the depiction of evangelical masculinity in Mosse, *The Image of Man,* 49; Blaschke, "The Unrecognized Piety of Men".

ecclesiastical milieus.[89] What happened is rather that different strategies of 'masculinization' and ideals of manliness were developed that partly coexisted, and partly succeeded each other.[90] How different ideals of masculinity could be is shown in the American South, the developing Bible Belt, where a Christian evangelical culture developed before the Civil War which associated masculinity, slavery and honour. This marked a break with the emancipatory and liberating message of earlier generations of evangelicals with their feet in the first and second 'Great Awakenings'.[91]

There is an increasing consensus that by the end of the nineteenth/early twentieth century Christian churches in Europe and the US had developed counterstrategies against the alleged feminization of Christianity - Olaf Blaschke refers to a strategy of 'remasculinization' around 1900.[92] According to Margareth Lamberts Bendroth "by the close of the 19th century, women suffragists and social reformers [in the US] had stretched the traditional boundaries of the feminine sphere to the breaking point. Their 'domestic feminism' elevated women as homemakers for the entire nation, responsible for both private and public standards of morality".[93] This provoked reactions among Protestant men, particularly as at the same time women's advances in the churches, particularly as preachers and educators, seemed to threaten male leadership positions. Fundamentalists in the US rejected the effeminate emotional expressions of piety and emphasized orthodoxy and doctrinal rightness, and denied women their status as the morally superior sex, making them morally and psychologically inferior.[94] Likewise, muscular Christianity in the Protestant Anglo-Saxon world tried to offer men a way to be Christian and manly at the same time by promoting sports. However, they apparently easily 'secularized', which actually seems to reinforce the feminization thesis.[95] Far more marginal, the 'Men and Religion Forward Movement' at the beginning of the twentieth century tried to reverse the tide of feminization: "The Women Have Had Charge of the Church Work Long Enough!"[96] They empha-

---

[89] Schmale, *Geschichte der Männlichkeit*, 153-154, 227-230; Werner, "Studying Christian Manliness: An Introduction".

[90] Blaschke, "The Unrecognized Piety of Men" offers a systematic overview.

[91] Sensbach, "Before the Bible Belt", 19; Lindman, "The Body Baptist" and Id., "Acting the Manly Christian".

[92] Blaschke, "The Unrecognized Piety of Men".

[93] Lamberts Bendroth, *Fundamentalism and Gender*, 6.

[94] "Gender stood at the heart of fundamentalist desire to be different. In the late nineteenth century the movement emerged in decisive reaction to conventional Victorian piety, demanding heartfelt conversion and a life of godly service. From the start fundamentalists doubted the sentimental faith in 'womanhood' that all but exonerated half the human race from the original sin of Adam. Evangelical Protestants of the previous century elevated women as the keepers of morality and assumed conversely that men had no natural aptitude for religion. Women maintained the private sphere of home, and by extension, church, while men managed the public world of business and politics, relatively free from moral entanglements. Fundamentalists, however, allowed no special favors when it came to sin." Lamberts Bendroth, *Fundamentalism and Gender*, 3. See also DeBerg, *Ungodly Women*.

[95] On muscular Christianity see chapter 4 by Hugh McLeod; Putney, *Muscular Christianity*; Hall, *Muscular Christianity*; Vance, *The Sinews of the Spirit*.

[96] Allen, *Rise Up, O Men of God*; Bederman, "'The Women Have Had Charge of the Church Work Long Enough'".

sized 'manly' metaphors and discourses, presenting Jesus as a master salesman. Nevertheless, the ideal of the Christian hero here remained one of personal sacrifice, in total obedience to the image of Jesus.

Similar observations have been formulated with respect to Catholic social movements, such as Catholic Action and the Leagues of the Sacred Heart, which employed manly metaphors such as that of the *miles Christi*, the soldier of God, or the master salesman.[97] These images and representations apparently show less ambiguity than those representing or relating to priests, but nevertheless the ideals of the Catholic man seem to not completely correspond to the dominant ideals of masculinity circulating in the secular society, among the bourgeois or workers. Obedience, sacrifice, an inclination to show emotion, charity, restraint, and an emphasis on the man as *pater familias* (head of the household) were still seen and represented as typical Christian and masculine values. Tine Van Osselaer therefore calls for caution when referring to so-called more 'masculine' representations of ideal men and heroes, as different images existed simultaneously.[98]

In some ways the twentieth century appears one where 'manly' values came to the fore in the Christian churches and denominations. World War I further increased the relevance of manly representations of Jesus. Catholic Action targeted particularly, albeit far from exclusively, men, and emphasized manly metaphors derived from the military (the *miles Christi*, the battle for Christ, etc.) or business world (the "salesman of Christ"). But the ideal images of Christian men still simply did not correspond to the ideal of hegemonic masculinity advanced, inter al. by Connel, and continued to include obedience and sacrifice as well as sentimentality and compassion.[99] Hence, as Emilio Gentile observed, Catholics rejected the personality cultus of fascists in Italy and Germany as "pagan statolatry".[100] Incidentally women were also represented in a militant, even martial mood, stressing their apostolic mission - i.e. also outside the domestic sphere - although obviously emphasizing the physical characteristics of virility and militarism less. Still French, Portuguese, Spanish and Italian Catholics particularly cherished the *dolorist* perspective that emphasizes sacrifice and suffering as closer to the image of Christ.[101]

Geoffrey M. Troughton, relating to New Zealand but I believe relevant for all Christendom, has observed that emphasizing Christian heroism could have paradoxical effects. Such images, especially of Jesus, appealed particularly to children, and cultivating them contributed to an 'infantilization' of Christianity and increasingly disqualified the religion as military values fell out of favour.[102] Still, far more than men, women remained attached to religions. Even in fundamentalist churches women proved 'unstoppable' and re-emerged as dominant figures because of their

---

[97] Van Osselaer, "Christening Masculinity?"; Blaschke, "The Unrecognized Piety of Men".

[98] Van Osselaer, "Heroes of the Heart".

[99] Id., "Christening Masculinity?".

[100] Gentile, "New Idols".

[101] Burton, *Holy Tears, Holy Blood*; Becker, *War and Faith*, on dolorism 24-31.

[102] Troughton, "Jesus and the Ideal of the Manly Man". At the Ghent conference *Dieu changea de sexe* Jan De Maeyer presented a paper on the infantilization. Unfortunately it could not be completed in time to be included in this volume.

involvement in religious education. One may wonder, though, why fundamentalist churches attracted women: was it because of the evangelical message of liberation or because it offered safety and stability?[103]

In contrast to the US, in large parts of Europe the position of Christian churches weakened after World War II, culminating in Northwestern Europe in an accelerated dechristianization and secularization, in which gendered changes surely played an important role.[104] That, however, will be the subject of another study.

STRUCTURE OF THE BOOK

When we originally launched the call for papers that generated the chapters collected in this volume, we hoped to be able to shed light on two issues that we initially identified as crucial, those of chronology and cross-denominational comparison. We indeed hoped that we would be able to look in more detail if and to what extent concepts of feminization and masculinization could be applied in different denominational contexts, in Europe and North America, taking into account a rather large time span. That, so we hoped, would enable us to see if similar dynamics were at work. As those who replied to the call for papers all concentrate on Europe and all but one deal with Catholics (including Old Catholics), it is only fair to admit that this book ultimately does not resolve either question. Instead, it raises fundamental questions about the utility and relevance of the feminization thesis, even if focus has shifted from women to men, as is the case in the majority of the chapters, and from the nineteenth to the twentieth century.

In the first chapter, Bernhard Schneider - who in 2002 published a seminal article in which he critically discussed the feminization thesis and proposed to distinguish several 'feminizations' - explores whether charitable activities were associated with feminine gender characteristics in Catholic poverty discourse. He points out that such attributions were rare in the first half of the nineteenth century since 'caritas' was perceived as a duty for all Christians and male religious were actively involved in these activities. Nonetheless, on some occasions, poor relief and sick care were associated with women albeit much less than one would expect and primarily in one specific perspective, that is in the elaborations on the Sisters of Charity of St Borromaeus in the 1830s-40s. The sisters' image, however, built not only on the 'angelic' and 'motherly' image of 'women in general' but also on more martial imagery and referred to, for example, the 'battlefield of secular life', turning them into almost 'genderless creatures'. Schneider highlights how the discussions on the sisters' activities and celibately state acquired political relevance in the second half of the nineteenth century, as they were compared against secular paid caretaking, linked to the women's question and the desirability of Catholic and Protestant feminine ideals. Connecting these characterizations to quantitative evolutions, Schneider points at the rise of female order members and female congregations in the nineteenth century

---

[103] Brasher, *Godly Women*; Lamberts Bendroth, *Fundamentalism and Gender*.
[104] Some assessments in Brown, "Secularization, the Growth of Militancy"; Id., *Religion and Society*; McLeod, "The religious crisis of the 1960s"; Pasture, "Religion in contemporary Europe".

and indicates that these congregations devoted themselves to charitable work. In spite of this exceptional presence of Catholic sisters in the social field, he nonetheless emphasizes that Catholic lay organizations have to be differentiated (women's Elizabethan societies did not dominate the field). Critical about the feminization thesis, he nonetheless recognizes the value of the concept in drawing attention to otherwise unnoticed phenomena. As regards Catholic caritas, he concludes that it did "display a strikingly frequent 'female face'" (*ein weibliches Gesicht*), a conclusion that he carefully puts into perspective and historializes.

It has often been observed that the term 'feminized' is not a neutral one. The terms 'feminized', or even worse 'effeminate', are frequently used to malign the non-female other in the nineteenth and indeed still also in the twentieth century. As we have already recalled, it was quite a common theme of secularists to denote Catholics. What is not well-known,[105] however, is that even within Catholicism these terms were used with similar purposes. Angela Berlis studies the role of gender discourse (i.e. 'attribution or denial of masculinity and femininity') in the polemic dispute between Old Catholics and Roman Catholics on clerical celibacy after the First Vatican Council when the topic became more prominent than in purely theological argumentations. Emphasizing the historical context of the debate - the *Kulturkampf* - she points out how masculinity constructions did not only differ between liberals and Catholics but also within Catholic discourse and served as a means for group differentiation and dissociation. The Old Catholic discussants, on the one hand, depicted (celibate) Roman Catholic priests as 'effeminate' (because of their submission to Rome), cold and egoistical Holy Joes with a far too important influence on women, while they referred to Old Catholic priests as 'real', 'complete' men who were independent of hierarchy and characterized by sensitivity and passion. Roman Catholic discussants on the other hand, accused the (non-celibate) Old Catholic priests of an addiction to women; in their opinion a *beweibter* priest could not be a real priest. Berlis' examination of the debate therefore points at another use of the concepts of feminization and masculinization, how 'feminization' meant 'defamation' and the 'masculinization' of one's own side aimed to prove one's superiority.

While emphasizing that psychological historians only propose to offer additional explanations, Jan Art draws on their analyses and on nineteenth- and twentieth-century sources in his assessment of the cult of the Virgin Mary, which he calls the "unequivocal symbol of the feminization of Roman Catholicism". He thereby links the cult's success to the 'Italianization' of Catholic devotional life in the wake of the Roman Question. More particularly, he builds on Michael P. Carroll's assessment of the cult and points out how the devotion to the Virgin was primarily promoted by celibate clerics, frequently from an Italian background and therefore not seldom characterized by a strong mother-binding (with *la mamma*). Depicting the popularity of the cult as "a symptom arising from that fixation with the mother type", he calls the 'androgyny' of the priest the potential result of this (unconscious) mother attachment; even though it might be considered the antipode of 'machismo', the other potential outcome. Art's assessment emphasizes the significance of religious men in the nineteenth century, subtly questioning the essence of the feminization

---

[105] See however Hastings, "Fears of a Feminized Church".

thesis, while furthermore pointing at some often underestimated dimensions of ultramontane Catholicism.

When one discusses men-oriented reactions against the alleged feminization of Christianity, Muscular Christianity is often invoked as an example. Whereas most of these discussions focus on the liberal Anglicans Thomas Hughes and Charles Kingsley, Hugh McLeod employs a broader perspective and adopts the term to describe Christians (of differing denominational background) who claimed that sports and physical exercise also had a moral, religious and social value. Gaining ground in the 1850s and 60s, its promoters were involved in a fourfold battle: they did not only face more conservative Christians, who opposed sport as immoral, they were also up against irreligious sportsmen (who rejected Christianity because it was 'effeminate') and less 'socially aware sportsmen', and they emphasized their manliness and strength against women. Although they broadened their goal at the end of the nineteenth century and tried to reach out to boys, women and girls as well, most of the Muscular Christians' concerns remained the same in the 1900s. The fundamental feature of Muscular Christianity was not "its muscularity or even its focus on masculinity" but its use of sports as a means towards "religious, moral and social ends", including creating a more harmonious society. The moral and religious ethos of the sportsman (most often a member of the gentry and aristocracy) and (lower-/ middle-class) Muscular Christian was therefore quite different and even though both regarded sport as manly and celebrated the strength and courage it required, the most innovative aspect of Muscular Christianity was probably its "attempt to promote sport while excluding gambling" (an "integral part of sports popular in the first half of the nineteenth century"). Muscular Christianity effectively illustrates that the scholarly discourse on the feminization of Christianity, in its different meanings, only covers part of a far more complex reality.

Thomas Buerman further expands the already lengthy gallery of ideal Christian men addressed in the previous chapters as he assesses the different ideals of Christian masculinity concerning the papal Zouaves, real 'soldiers of God'. Presenting the Zouave as "the synthesis between the unreligious man and the religious mother", he points out how the Belgian Zouave stories - while idealizing young Catholic men - also confirmed the stereotypical ingredients of the feminization discourse and how the conversion of the irreligious father "was more or less the major theme". Nonetheless, in emphasizing the younger (male) generation's religiosity and willingness for self-sacrifice (often stimulated by a pious mother), the Belgian authors of the Zouave stories also expressed their belief that "the present generation could be guided differently" and their "example could bring men back to religion". According to Buerman, this potential combination of "manly and womanly features" can explain the popularity of the Zouave movement and should incite us not to think "one dimensional of nineteenth-century Christianity in regard to gender".

In discussions about the feminization of Catholicism, the devotion of the Sacred Heart constitutes a contentious case. On the one hand, Tine Van Osselaer observes, it is often invoked as an illustration of *la religion au féminin* and refers to the high number of female devotees, the emotional and sentimental (so-called 'feminine') imagery and practices; while others stress its 'virility' and point at its militant image and emphasis on the defence of country and religion. Exploring the increased attention for men's involvement at the start of twentieth century, Van Osselaer shows how the Sacred Heart devotion, more particularly the affiliated Leagues of the Sacred Heart, was used effectively in the framework of a conscious clerical strategy to win back men to the church, not only for public roles but in particular for devotional practice. Still, even though these Leagues presented themselves as a men's movement and emphasized their 'masculine' character; women's Leagues developed as well and thereby incited the (Jesuit) leadership to emphasize separation and (gender) differentiation. So is it possible to assess the Sacred Heart devotion from a feminization/masculinization perspective? Van Osselaer calls for caution, as applying these concepts to a historical reality easily carries the risk of attributing fixed features to the sexes and of ignoring the fundamentally cultural construct that gender is.

Marit Monteiro also concludes that Christian manliness appears as a "rather unstable and elusive category in nineteenth- and twentieth-century history". She reaches that conclusion after analysing different ideals of Catholic manliness - "repertoires" - among Dutch Dominicans roughly between 1850 and 1940. Her assessment reads as a poignant critique of the highly secularist and oversimplified notion of hegemonic masculinity, as for example in the work of the German historian Wolfgang Schmale, who argued that Christian ideals of masculinity retreated in front of the growing hegemonic masculinity associated with nationalism.[106] Following Donald Hall et al.'s research on muscular Christianity, she argues for the recognition of 'multiple masculinities' also with regard to religion, taking in account confessional differentiation. She emphasizes that Christian ideals persisted in the interwar years, and the numbers of clerics, constituting a particular form of masculinity, peaked. That was the case with the Dominicans, who cherished a very particular ideal of masculinity which combined monastic (contemplative) as well as clerical (active) elements with secular values reinterpreted and appropriated in a Catholic perspective. This constellation was obviously subject to change as Dutch society transformed, as a result of secular and confessional tensions resulting in pillarization (*verzuiling*), among other things, which considerably increased the public clerical activities of the Dominicans. The Dominicans' changing roles in society (and also of the Catholic community in society) however led to a questioning of the balance between action and contemplation, decisiveness and passivity, and their (tacit) association with masculinity and femininity. Moreover, the patriarchal mode of manliness lost its appeal on a younger generation that fell back to ('virile') monastic features of Dominican identity. But aside from the shifting repertoires that undermine any notion of unchanging ideals of masculinity and femininity, Monteiro's assessment also reveals that discourses and power relations were and remained deeply gendered.

In several ways, Marieke Smulders continues Monteiro's chapter. She concentrates on the Catholic boys' culture at a minor seminary in interwar Holland which trained young boys to become true Dominicans. The closed environment of a Catholic boarding school offers a unique venue to study ideals of masculinity. Smulders confirms an observation made by Louise Bienvenue and Christine Hudon about a tension existing in Canadian Catholic boarding schools between a more 'virile' masculinity in the 'outside' world, typical for modern hegemonic masculinity, and

[106] Schmale, *Geschichte der Männlichkeit*.

the (clerical) daily role models representing a more 'feminine form' existing inside, but nuances this by observing that elements of the outside world penetrated the walls of the Dutch school, resulting in very complex patterns of masculinity made of partly contradicting ideals derived from the clerical and monastic imaginaries of the pupils' teachers (which, as Monteiro shows in the previous chapter, were also subject to change) as well as sports heroes and youthful self-confidence in their role as future priests. In sum, this type of Christian masculinity was, according to Smulders, "of a rather ambiguous nature".

Marjet Derks pushes the conclusions of Van Osselaer, Monteiro and Smulders one step further, blatantly stating that "the masculinization and feminization of religion are not valid concepts and offer no adequate means for analyzing religious history". She reaches that conclusion after studying three related conversion movements for Catholic women, the Ladies of Bethany, the Women of Nazareth and the Grail Movement, which each displayed very different views on femininity. Although in one respect they could be used as an argument in favour of qualifying Dutch Catholicism as being 'feminized', they actually undermine the concept. Indeed, whereas these women's organizations encouraged women to engage in the public sphere in defense of the Church and by doing so 'feminized' Dutch Catholicism in quantitative terms, in different ways, they also stimulated ideals inspired by stereotypical masculine ideals, such as a strong physicality and militancy - should one then speak of a 'femasculinization', Derks wonders in the case of the Women of Nazareth. Following the Dutch historian Paul Luykx's criticism on pillarization and more generally referring to the philosophical work of the Belgian-French philosopher and psychoanalyst Luce Irigaray on the culture of difference, she pleads for an approach that avoids homogenizing concepts but emphasizes differentiation instead. In her case studies she demonstrates the ambiguity of gender relations in Dutch Catholicism and warns for a reduction to the stereotypical dichotomy.

The same ambiguity and impossibility of calling something masculine or feminine returns in Michael O'Sullivan's rich and complex chapter in which he investigates whether German Catholicism still displayed 'feminine' features after World War I, also questioning the alleged 'masculinization' of Catholicism between 1918 and 1938. He observes that the Catholic Mothers Organizations during the Weimar Republic effectively cherished an ideal of feminine domesticity and piety, the dominant bourgeois utopia. However, Catholic Action, while restricting the agency of both men and women to the benefit of the clerical hierarchy, by contrast offered some new venues of leadership for these women. They even adopted political functions as they used maternal themes to demand greater equality. Nazism moreover put the responsibility of the survival of Catholicism on their shoulders, which forced the Catholic mothers to rise up to the challenge and function as the (moral) core of the Catholic world. While men abandoned church affiliated organizations *en masse*, Catholic youth associations responded to a new focus on masculinity and promoted strongly muscular values for young Catholic males, including a strict morality. They were successful, and generated spillover effects as comes to the fore in increased male participation in pilgrimages, at least until Nazism virtually and literally eliminated the symbolic (and physical) space for Catholic masculinity. In the meantime, images of Catholic piety and femininity circulated in some Catholic girls' associations that did not correspond to the bourgeois ideal of feminine piety and domesticity, for example as young girls openly displaying their piety were also preparing for professional careers. This occurred in subtle ways in the Marian Congregations (*Jungfraukongregationen*), and far more clearly in the *Heliand-Bund* (in ways strongly reminiscent of the activities of the Women of Nazareth and the Grail movement analysed by Marjet Derks).

CONCLUSIONS AND PERSPECTIVES

So shall we conclude then, with Marjet Derks, that the concepts of masculinization and feminization should be put in the dustbin of history, like secularization theory (though secularization theory at least is not dead as yet)? Perhaps. One should nevertheless concede that the so-called 'feminization thesis' has in a relatively short time profoundly shaped the new social and cultural history of Christianity.

Whatever objections may be expressed today, it has re-evaluated the role of women and uncovered hitherto ignored aspects of American and European history. The fact that more women than men went to church is not a new insight. The idea that ignoring things religious as being unworthy of much attention actually *implied* that one considered 'the things that really matter' as done by men and women's interests as easily ignored, was (and still is) quite confrontational. Moreover, by initiating new research perspectives in Europe it has helped to uncover surprising parallels between denominations on both sides of the Atlantic. The potential to transgress these spatial and denominational boundaries was not the least of its qualities: comparing Catholics and Evangelicals on the two sides of the Atlantic, let alone seriously considering transatlantic parallels, still dazzles more than one historian, but it can be a most rewarding venture - at least if one remains cautious and attentive to the differences.[107]

The feminization thesis as it was initially formulated also drew the attention to hitherto largely ignored or misunderstood phenomena such as religious revivalism in the nineteenth and twentieth centuries, including pilgrimages and apparitions of the Virgin. To a large extent it then meshed with the 'anthropological' (rather than 'cultural') turn of historical research in the 1980s and 1990s. This anthropological turn did not so much introduce anthropological methods and theories into the historical discipline, but mainly focused on the 'history of small things', daily life and magic. Especially the recognition of the continuing relevance of magic and mysticism, as in Maria apparitions and miraculous healings, challenged standard interpretations of modern history.[108] It contributed to the realization that the history of Christianity was part of a far more general transformation of society, perhaps even a constituent element of modernity - while many still consider both religion and domesticity as

---

[107] In this respect it is useful to remind the conclusions of Carroll, *American Catholics in the Protestant Imagination*, who uncovered and criticized the Protestant bias in research on religion in the US.
[108] See in this respect the pioneering studies of Blackbourn, *Marpingen;* Harris, *Lourdes* and Gibson, *Social History*.

pre-modern[109] - or, rather, the recognition of the existence of multiple and 'alternative' modernities also in European history.[110] This is one reason why the feminization thesis seemed an alternative to secularization as a master narrative. However, recent research on mystic experiences also seriously complicated the emerging consensus on the meaning of feminization, leading to the recognition of 'many femininities'.[111] It also revealed the particular worlds of women, e.g. in convents, where very different power relations existed than in the 'outer' world. But, as Claude Langlois argues with regard to the Catholic Church, such analyses also seriously question the validity of a representation of the modern Church as exclusively male dominated.[112] From quite different perspectives Bernhard Schneider, Marjet Derks and Michael O'Sullivan give additional substance to this argument as well.

Focusing on males and masculinity also shows more divergences than the first studies on the feminization of Christendom suggested. Including men in the analysis actually provokes reappraisals of the feminization thesis itself. Paradoxically, the first gender-oriented studies produced an overly one-'gendered' image, and even antagonized and decontextualized gender differences.[113] Some of the early conclusions were no doubt overstated. It became obvious that within Christendom, even within different denominations, different ideals and representations of femininity and masculinity co-existed, succeeded each other, competed and interacted, and that a simple masculine-feminine dichotomy is inadequate.[114] From that perspective, the chronology of the phenomena should be re-evaluated, because divergences increasingly reappear between regions as well as between denominations: European and American patterns in some respects seem more divergent than they appear at first sight. Also, concrete representations of ideal masculinity and femininity diverged within Europe and within denominations - in this volume Thomas Buerman even shows how images of Zouaves in Belgium and France in the 1860s did not overlap entirely. Therefore a reappraisal of the different representations of and for men and

[109] Van Osselaer and Pasture et al., *Households of Faith*. In both historical sociology and feminist writing, women only become 'modern' as they 'enter the public sphere'. See e.g. Adams, Clemens and Schola Orloff, "Introduction: Social Theory, Modernity", 47. Domesticity remains mostly unnoticed in studies about modernity. It is sometimes, however, discussed in studies about modernism, e.g. Huyssen, *After the Great Divide*. Heynen made the strongest case for considering domesticity as utterly modern: "Modernity and domesticity". Obviously there are quite different ways to approach the modernity of women and the simple dichotomy presented here does not do justice to the variety of positions. For an overview of different feminist positions see Freedman, *No Turning Back*; Offen, *European Feminisms*; Taylor Allen, *Feminism and Motherhood* and Felski, *The Gender of Modernity*. On domesticity in American culture see the insightful monograph of Lamberts Bendroth, *Growing Up Protestant*; Christie, *Households of Faith*; also McDannell, *The Christian Home*. As regards the modernity of religion this idea has slowly penetrated socio-historical scholarship through the works of Clark, Bayly and others. But the author that best understands this is undoubtedly Hellemans. See e.g. his "Die Transformation der Religion"; Id., "How Modern is Religion in Modernity?".

[110] Orsi, "Abundant History".

[111] E.g. Langlois, *L'autobiographie de 1895*; Id., *Le désir de sacerdoce*; Dauzet, *La mystique bien tempérée*; Maitre, *Mystique et féminité*.

[112] Langlois, *L'autobiographie de 1895*.

[113] Warne, "Making the Gender-Critical Turn".

[114] Roussel, "Roman Catholic Religious Discourse".

women is necessary. Since churches followed different strategies in their dealings with modern society, more attention should go to the places where gender roles are articulated and propagated, such as schools and pulpits.

Two more conclusions come to the fore. First of all, concepts such as feminization should not be used in an absolute sense but conceptualized and historicized. The discussion is quite different if the term is used to indicate an increase in women participating in religious rites or referring to changed views of piety. But as Ann Braude signalled already in 1997, even in quantitative terms the terms should be well defined and it should be clear what is meant. Especially when one refers to feminization with regard to changes in piety and culture, one easily runs into trouble, as there is no fixed standard of femininity or masculinity. The task of a gendered approach is precisely to unravel the different ways gender is culturally constructed and defined. Doing so has uncovered many 'masculinities' and 'femininities', and many 'feminizations' and 'masculinizations'. But it has also proven revealing, as Angela Berlis and Thomas Buerman demonstrate in this volume (following Jan Art, Derek Hastings, and others), that gendered criticisms were often used by adversaries - that ultramontane Catholicism was attacked for being 'effeminate' for example is not without significance. In this respect, the terms also played a role in processes of identification and distancing, but they may also help in discovering deep anxieties about gender identity.

Secondly, it can be concluded that the churches (in this volume largely the Catholic Church) developed different strategies to reach their potential public, as Tine Van Osselaer has illustrated so well. Very different ideals of masculinity and femininity co-existed, as the Belgian Zouaves studied here by Thomas Buerman, the 'Muscular Christians' of Hugh McLeod, the Dutch case studies by Marit Monteiro, Marieke Smulders and Marjet Derks, as well as Michael O'Sullivan's article particularly demonstrate. But the androgynous nature of priests - a term coined by Róisín Healy - points at something else too, a fundamental uneasiness with sexuality. Jan Art has suggested some interesting perspectives in this respect, but the subject no doubt is far from exhausted.

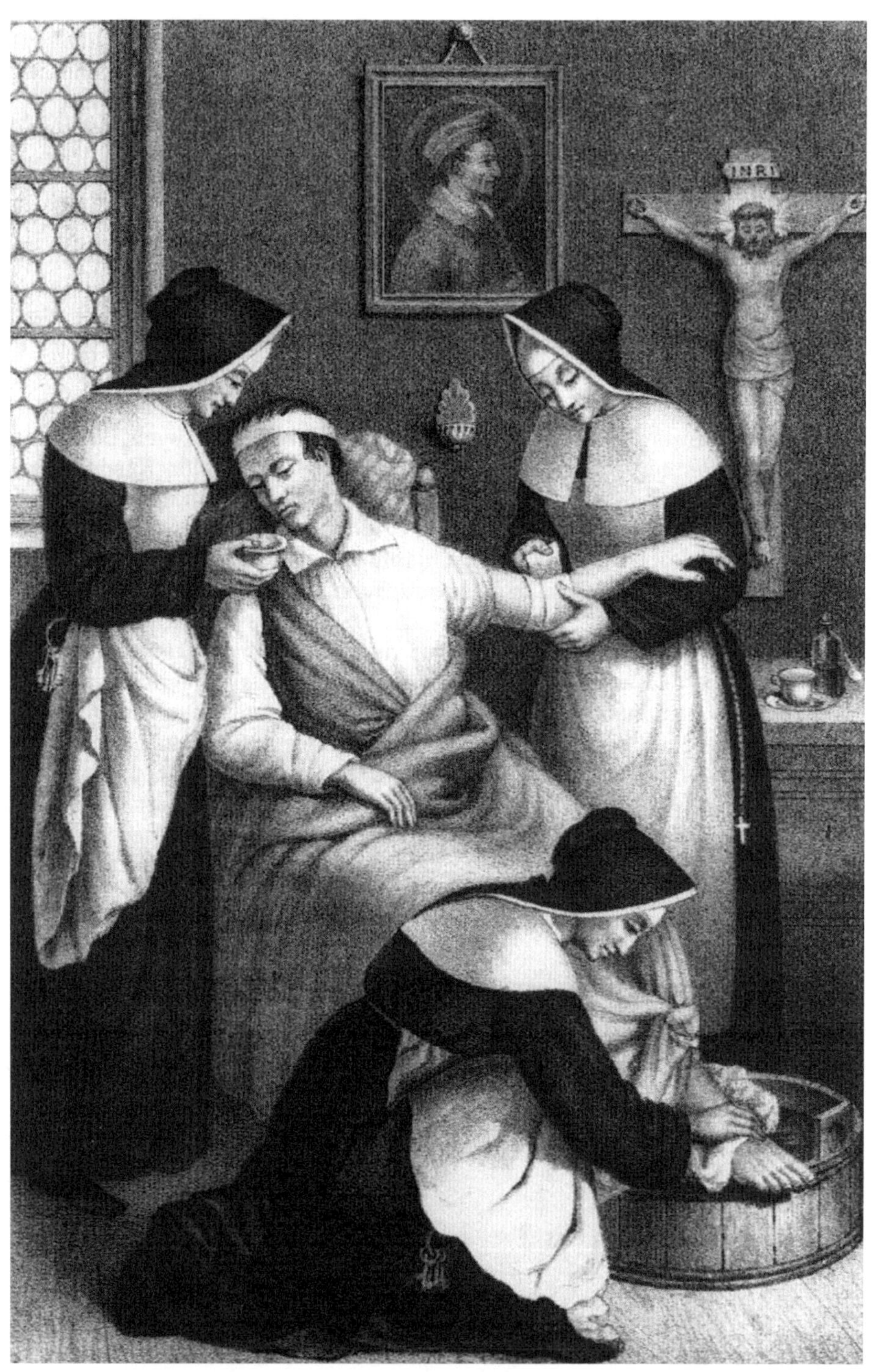

'Die Caritas trug ein weibliches Gesicht'. Sisters of Mercy in the hospitals of Trier and Koblenz.
[*C. Brentano*, Die Barmherzigen Schwestern in bezug auf Armen- und Krankenpflege. *Mainz, 1857[2]*]

THE CATHOLIC POOR RELIEF DISCOURSE AND THE FEMINIZATION OF THE CARITAS IN EARLY NINETEENTH-CENTURY GERMANY

BERNHARD SCHNEIDER

When one intends to investigate "Christian Feminization and Masculinization in Europe" - as was the subtitle of the original workshop in which a first version of this text was discussed - one should certainly include taking a closer look at German Catholicism. In doing so, I would like to follow up on my current research project within the special research area *Fremdheit und Armut* (Strangeness and Poverty) at the University of Trier.[1] This project investigates the Catholic poverty discourse[2] in Germany as well as its contribution to the construction of a Catholic identity following secularization until the middle of the century.[3]

With regard to the question of a feminization of the Caritas in the nineteenth century, it is also possible to consider current everyday experiences. Today, many women still work in social professions, although they usually only predominate in less well-paid positions, for instance, as geriatric assistants or nurses. Regarding the history of social work, these everyday observations correspond with women's socio-charitable efforts being connected to both the development of women's non-domestic employ-

---

[1] www.sfb600.uni-trier.de

[2] Here, the term discourse applies to a complex of linguistic output, which appeared at a certain time and place, and which systematically organizes a certain subject matter. As a product of society, the discourse itself is subject to certain rules and describes the domain of 'what may be said'. The limitation to linguistic output is due to the project's concentration on written sources, which does not mean that a discourse in general only contains linguistic output. For an introduction into this discussion, cf. Landwehr, *Geschichte des Sagbaren*, 97-102.

[3] The discussions on identity terminology cannot be taken into consideration at this point. It should merely be noted that, within my project, the term is not understood in the essentialist sense of the word, but as a construction that is based on processes of negotiating attributions to oneself or others. For an introduction cf. Pyka, "Geschichtswissenschaft und Identität"; Wagner, "Fest-Stellungen".

ment and the development of the women's liberation movement.[4] This connection is also identified in descriptions concerning the history of the women's movement. Thus, a recent instructive overview of women's history and the history of the women's movement states that, for many middle- and upper-class women of the nineteenth century, the commitment to the poor and oppressed was "the preliminary stage and vehicle of efforts towards their own gender".[5] Furthermore, there was a close relationship between women's 'deeds of love' and religion, allowing for the recognition of "a widespread feminization of religion".[6] By drawing on the religious dimension in order to "demonstrate the effect and value of social intervention by women in particular", religion should not have opposed the process of female consciousness, but should rather have proved beneficiary. This touches on a further historiographic dimension of the question, i.e. the discussion on a feminization of religion, which achieved a certain attention since Barbara Welter's propositions of the 1980s.[7]

Against this background, the following investigation will cast an eye on German Catholicism and place a greater emphasis on the first half of the nineteenth century. The discussions regarding the feminization thesis not least consider the possible chronology of this alleged process - a controversial issue and by no means a clarified subject.[8] As far as this is concerned, a closer look at the early nineteenth century might help to examine whether a possible 'feminization of religion' in the German context occurred directly at the beginning of the nineteenth century.[9]

Following a brief look at the feminization thesis, a more extensive chapter directed at the discourse history will question whether and to what extent the Catholic poverty discourse actually documents elements of a feminization process within the given research period. Finally, I will illustrate the practice of Catholic poor relief and pose the question whether this practice substantiates a feminization of the Caritas.

BRIEF NOTES ON THE FEMINIZATION THESIS

Some statements made by contemporaries along with other observations gave reason to speak of a 'feminization of religion' occurring in the nineteenth century. I have critically analysed and dealt with this thesis as well as its variants elsewhere.[10] At this

---

[4] For an overview, see Wendt, *Geschichte der sozialen Arbeit*, 467-518.

[5] Bock, *Frauen*, 156. In a non-German context, cf. e.g. works by Lewis, *Women's Welfare*; Id., *Women and Social Action*.

[6] Bock, *Frauen*, 160.

[7] See, in particular, the editor's introduction in this volume as well as the most recent research report by Van Osselaer and Buerman, "Feminization Thesis".

[8] Ibid., 515-518.

[9] In this connection, the term 'German context' points to the fact that Germany as a nation-state did not yet exist during the period of investigation, and loosely refers to the German-speaking lands including major parts of the Austrian Empire (those that were part of the Old German Empire until 1806, i.e. for the most part the German-speaking *Erblande*) not included in the new nation-state during the founding of the new German Empire under Prussian supremacy in 1871. As an overview, see e.g. Siemann, *Vom Staatenbund*.

[10] Schneider, "Feminisierung der Religion".

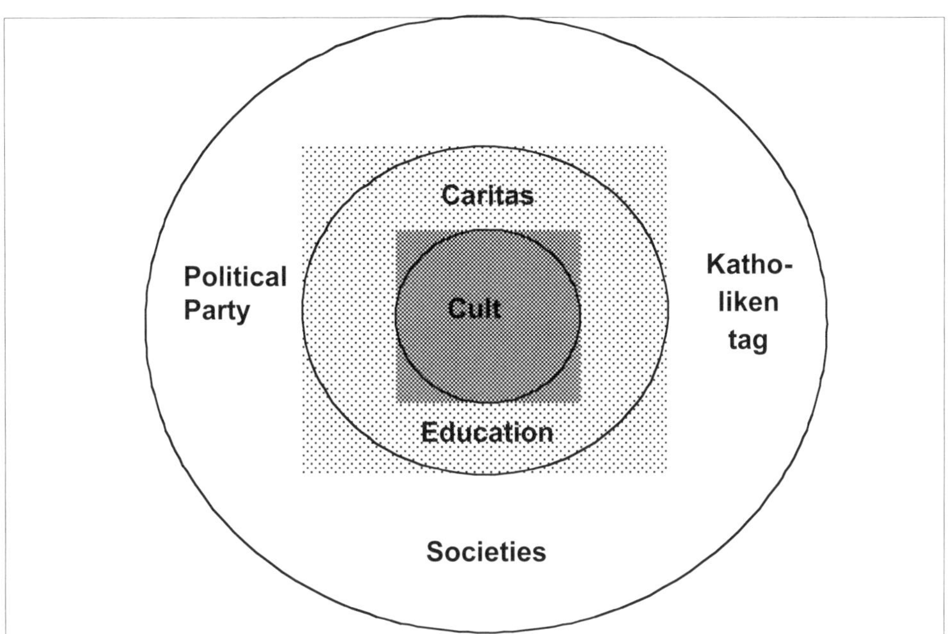

point I shall only deal with this discussion insofar as it touches the central question of this article, i.e. it is related to a 'feminization of the Caritas'. One of the critical points of the feminization thesis is that it is frequently encountered in a rather general and far-reaching, demanding form. By contrast, I take the view that the feminization thesis should be limited in its range. Furthermore, we should distinguish whether there are areas of 'feminization' of varied intensity, which would diverge denominationally and regionally.

According to my observations, a graphic model that uses concentric circles can be helpful to describe circumstances for German Catholicism. This model serves to illustrate that an area of maximum feminization (church attendance and receipt of sacraments, pilgrimages and membership in purely devout sisterhoods) is followed by areas with a high yet less intensive feminization, which could also include the Caritas domain.[11] This assumption will be investigated more closely.

THE CATHOLIC POVERTY DISCOURSE AND THE FEMINIZATION OF THE CARITAS

For its analysis of the Catholic poverty discourse this research project evaluates 44 Catholic and two Protestant periodicals, a long series of sermon works (53 Cath., 8 Prot.) as well as 40 prayer books.

Following our results so far, it is certain that these sources revealed a considerable involvement with the social needs of mankind. We were able to collect 4000

---

[11] A more detailed explanation: Ibid., 143.

relevant references, which differed significantly with regard to the kind of source and the given statements.[12] Roughly speaking, there are two diverging partial discourses: a liturgical-paraenetic and a pastoral, practical-political discourse. Within the liturgical-paraenetic discourse, found particularly in prayer books, sermons and many pastoral letters, poverty is a very general phenomenon of misery and suffering, presented as a time-indifferent social constant. From a reservoir of traditional biblical references a traditional theology of poverty unfolds due to the use of traditional religious semantics. Poverty and poor relief are strongly individualized and revolve around individual failure (sin) and the virtues of charity and mercy. The pastoral, practical-political poverty discourse is significantly more specific, analyses manifold causes of poverty without losing track of religious and moral deficiencies as essential factors. At the same time they often develop detailed concepts of poor relief or describe suitable implementation attempts. Some differences, which cannot be taken into consideration at this point, appear in internal Catholic 'camps' between the followers of the late Enlightenment, which existed during the first half of the nineteenth century, and the ultramontanes.

THE POOR RELIEF SITUATION IN GERMANY IN THE NINETEENTH CENTURY AND THE ROLE OF THE CATHOLIC CHURCH

During the first half of the nineteenth century, subsistence crises still existed in Germany, which created the overall 'age of poverty' that according to Karl Heinz Metz preceded the 'age of security' that emerged in the course of the nineteenth century.[13] The years 1770-72, 1816/17 and 1846/47 are particularly known as the times of classical famine crises. Due to the incipient industrialization these classical famine crises were accompanied by new economic depressions. These, however, did not intensively affect the broader German population until the second half of the nineteenth century.[14] The seemingly unstoppable and continued impoverishment during the first decades of the nineteenth century assumed such massive forms that contemporaries germanicized an English term for this new and threatening phenomenon: pauperism.[15]

Institutional pillars of Catholic poor and sick relief, monasteries/convents and in part foundations, which perhaps could have countered this poverty, had already been lost on a large scale during the secularization process. This gave impetus to the already observable trend of communal and state dominance with regard to poor relief. Until the mid-nineteenth century and to some extent later on, the birthplace-related 'home principle' constituted an essential characteristic of the poor legislation.[16] Every community or town was to take care of its own poor. The fundamental

---

[12] A detailed description of the research concept and first results are presented in the following volume: Schneider, *Konfessionelle Armutsdiskurse* (editor's introduction; articles by Michaela Maurer and Ingmar Franz).
[13] Metz, *Die Geschichte*, 13-14, 45-46.
[14] Concerning the upswings, cf. the classic study by Abel, *Massenarmut*.
[15] Cf. Schulz, "Armut".
[16] Regarding the legislation in brief: Ibid., 402-404. As an overview: Schaffer, "Staatliche Neuordnung".

distinction was therefore made between 'native poor' and 'poor stranger'. In 1842, the Prussian Kingdom broke with the previously dominant home principle in its poor legislation which, however, remained valid in other German states. In Prussia, the responsibility of supporting the poor was transferred from the birthplace community to the residential community.

So far, relevant research is largely lacking in terms of the actual involvement of the church in public relief through its official representatives (priests) or its significance in charity associations. They were frequently involved in the communal poor councils, and sometimes even did their file keeping.[17] In Austria, the parish poor institute formed the major part of public poor relief from the late eighteenth until the mid-nineteenth century.[18] Whether we can justifiably speak of a marginalization of denominational poor relief in the nineteenth century, as has been done in significant earlier research[19], is therefore in need of more detailed analyses.

DISCOURSES ON POVERTY, SICKNESS AND THE ROLE OF WOMEN

As several studies, including those on German areas, have shown, more and more constructions of gender differences emerged in the course of the nineteenth century, in which the different 'natures' of women and men frequently recurred.[20] These differences also appeared in theological discourses[21] which, however, also contained objections.

One of them came from the famous Viennese theologian and cathedral preacher Johann Emanuel Veith.[22] For Veith it was a self-evident fact that women display a more truthful devoutness than men. He rejects any references (known to him) to the female gender character which declared devoutness as a female virtue predicated on the natural weakness and emotional orientation of women. In fact, he emphasizes the strength of the female gender by means of a line of ancestors of holy women, a strength that was based on their faith in God. In this article he does not refer to the Caritas at all. However, with his rejection of the contemporary gender anthropology[23] he repudiates a stylization of women who were 'naturally' inclined to "compassion and tears".

In his fourth sermon on the 'Caritas', Veith not only mentions several charitably active women in Church history, but stresses the fact that Christian women proved themselves "so frequent and manifold" in the succession of Mary as "heroes and

---

[17] This was the case in areas west of the Rhine, where the poor legislation was still that of Napoleonic times, as well as in Bavaria and Nassau. Cf. Gatz, "Kirchliche Mitarbeit", 58. For Bavaria: Eder, *Helfen*, 63-66. For Nassau: Blum, *Staatliche Armenfürsorge*, 63 ff.

[18] See Scheutz, "Demand and Charitable Supply".

[19] According to Schulz, "Armut", 402. More detailed account in Sachße and Tennstedt, *Geschichte der Armenfürsorge*, 227-229 (just some short remarks describing Catholic Charity as an aspect of private welfare).

[20] See, e.g. Frevert, *'Mann und Weib, und Weib und Mann'*.

[21] Wagner, *Die himmlische Frau.*

[22] Veith, "Woran liegt es", 738. Regarding *Nathanel* cf. a more detailed account in Pesch, *Die kirchlich-politische Presse.* Concerning Veith cf. as an introduction: Weiß, "Veith".

[23] See Honegger, *Die Ordnung der Geschlechter.*

caretakers of holy love [*Caritas*]".[24] As evidence he cites female congregations who were active in the mission and the Sisters of Charity who would work away from home dealing with epidemic diseases. His full-blooded praise is also directed at charitable women's associations, which were established everywhere among the secular classes. These associations did not donate money, but rather called on the poor in their accommodations in order to help them in their physical misery and 'moral squalor'. Thus, he is not afraid to refer to them as angels and to regard them as a symbol of a better future.[25] His sometimes imprecise formulations suggest that he recognizes a particular vocation of Christian women therein.[26] With this, Veith refers to institutionalizations of female charity, which need to be presented more thoroughly within the next section of the study at hand.

The current literature stresses, and with good reason, the fact that fields of employment were strongly influenced by gender constructions. Sabine Braunschweig claims that "the definition of women's labour and men's labour cannot be based on work contents" and that "an association to 'traditional' female or male tasks is either constructed when required or vehemently disputed". This follows popular gender stereotypes, which in turn can be modified, shifted or altered by 'new associations'.[27] Low social status and a low income are the most significant structural features of female professions, which Braunschweig considers a given, particularly with regard to the nursing professions. The "ability to care, the knowledge, but also psychological qualities were not evaluated as skills, they were considered part of the female gender character"[28] and therefore justified the low salary and the lack of recognition of specific professional qualifications. At the same time it should be noted that representatives of the early women's movements wanted to extend the sphere of female action by returning to a specific female tradition of poor relief and sick care, thus wanting to reclaim the poor relief territory which had been taken over by men.[29] Against this background, this chapter shall investigate whether charitable activities within the Catholic poverty discourse were coupled with the female gender, whether sick care in particular was constructed as a female activity, and to what extent connections to religious dimensions were established.

SICK CARE AND THE FEMALE GENDER CHARACTER

Claudia Bischoff cites what she calls the controversy over whether men or women possess a special aptitude for charitable functions, particularly with regard to the care of the sick. She refers to a number of contemporary articles, which would have ulti-

---

[24] Veith, *Charitas [!]*, 84-111. Quotation on 109.

[25] See ibid., 110.

[26] He speaks of a "profession of Christian Women" on 109, however, he refers to the old meaning of the word, which implies a "vocation".

[27] Braunschweig, "Introduction", 20. See also Bischoff, *Frauen in der Krankenpflege*. The book is tendential and corresponds to the critical reservations towards an exaggerated "victim perspective" regarding women, in Eckkart and Jütte, *Medizingeschichte*, 286-293. An annotated source book: Hähner-Rombach, *Quellen*.

[28] Braunschweig, "Introduction", 22.

[29] Examples in Bock, *Frauen*, 161 ff.

mately decided this controversial issue "in favour of women".[30] In the Caritas sermon mentioned above, Johann Emanuel Veith does not attribute charitable actions to the female gender character in general. And he is not alone. It should be noted as a rather important initial result that, in general, these kinds of attributions rarely occurred in the context of the Catholic poverty discourse in the first half of the nineteenth century. An initial explanation for this could lie in the assumption that certain matters can be taken for granted and need no discussion. In contrast, it is impossible to assume that there existed such a general perception of gender constructions in the time under investigation, particularly since men were in fact active in sick care during the early nineteenth century. We shall return to this issue at a later stage. A further explanation results from the biblical and Christian tradition, which, as is generally known, calls upon every Christian to practice charity. This sets boundaries, although by no means impassable, to any form of one-sided attribution.

One of the few texts with a clear gender attribution manages to harmonize one with the other: "Every Christian is entitled to deeds of Christian love; serviceable care however is an activity best suited for women".[31] Catholic authors were also faced with the fact that male members of religious orders were charitably active and thus also engaged in sick care. Even within this special territory, it was difficult for authors to pursue such polar constructions.

The few scripts that use the female gender character as an argument are all the more worthy of note. In 1832, one author states in the *Breslauer Zeitschrift für katholische Theologie*, an important mouthpiece of the anti-ultramontane circles in German Catholicism, that most people generally agreed that "the female gender is more suited to attend to the sick than the male".[32] A comparable statement, despite a deviant church-political and theological orientation, can be found in one of the most important Catholic periodicals, the *Katholik*[33]: "Over the centuries experience has also shown that only the female gender with its singular sensitivity, its warmer sympathy for the suffering of others, its patience and cleanliness is exclusively suited for nursing the sick."[34] This is a passage taken from the text in which the (suspended) Protestant theologian Johann G. Bartholmä had his say in favour of the Sisters of Charity in 1838.[35]

In 1833, the founder of such a female congregation and future Archbishop of Cologne, Clemens August Droste zu Vischering, used a rather similar wording in his book on the Sisters.[36] He asks the rhetorical question whether "women or men

---

[30] Bischoff, *Frauen in der Krankenpflege*, 78-92; quotation on 79.

[31] Sintzel, *Geschichte, 19*.

[32] *BZKT*, 5 (1832), 55. Regarding the history of the Catholic press in Germany until 1848 cf. Pesch as well as Schneider, *Katholiken auf die Barrikaden?*, 44-94.

[33] With regard to the *Katholik* as the fierce apologetic mouthpiece of the strictly Catholic so-called Mainz circle cf. ibid., 63. The journal appeared on a monthly basis, from 1844 onward it appeared three times a week for a few years and was directed at an educated audience, especially the clergy.

[34] *Katholik*, 25 (1845) 149, 691.

[35] See Bartholmä, *Die barmherzigen Schwestern*. Bartholmä converted to Catholicism shortly before his death in 1839. I owe this information to Eder, *Helfen*, 90 ff.

[36] Droste zu Vischering, *Ueber die Genossenschaften*, 15. This passage is also quoted and discussed in Schaper, *Krankenwartung*, 147.

were generally more suited to nurse the sick", and answers tersely by referring to the general existing consensus that favoured a 'female care'.[37]

None of these authors had a more detailed justification for their assumptions. In another book on the Sisters of Charity, Michael Sintzel proposes a justification insofar as he draws on 'nature', which according to him had enriched the female gender far more.[38] Furthermore, as an insight from "the study of the soul" he elaborates that

> women are far more capable of executing piety, which is oriented towards the hospital service, than men, because women combine their greater ability to devoutly seize the smaller means of life with their even greater skill of morally devising these as opposed to the more outwardly and generally understanding man. ... Indeed, with regard to the sick, women possess a greater strength of moral disposition and persuasion than men, because they have the greater gift of affiliating to an alien individuality by entering into it. In particular, women come closer to the sick and primarily the poor sick by their mental communication. Women possess more of the necessary humility, not humiliated by the care of the poor, while the self-confident strength of man expresses pride. ... Men lack the naturally protected shamefacedness, which establishes an important moral effectiveness; ... men lack that strength of austerity for quiet concealed purposes, which women are so capable of, following an appropriate ascesis. Furthermore, men do not subordinate to that certain form of obedience, which receives the commandment from above without scrutiny and which willingly executes the rich service of thousands of encounters on a small scale. Finally, men lack the form of love committed and devoted to the neediness of strangers, which applies such an immeasurable sacrifice without the prospects of great successes in the outside world by displaying a unique readiness for equable, single and small needs. ... Man is a natural egoist. The woman, however, remains alien even with regard to her self-love. She is the vestal of love.[39]

This explanation closely follows contemporary constructed gender images[40] and applies them to a specific area, that of relief care.

The more specific question whether women should also nurse men or whether this should be reserved for male nurses, is answered by Droste zu Vischering to the effect that women would be permitted to do so, whereas the care of women by men was prohibited.[41] The famous doctor and member of the Munich Görres circle, Johann Nepomuk Ringseis, commented in the renowned and, in German Catholicism, favourably received *Historisch-politische Blätter* (HPB) that despite some counterarguments, "also with regard to the care of sick male patients, preference of female attendants

---

[37] Droste zu Vischering, *Ueber die Genossenschaften*, 15.
[38] Sintzel, *Geschichte*, 19.
[39] Ibid., 282.
[40] In addition to Frevert, '*Mann und Weib, und Weib und Mann*' and Bock, *Frauen,* see also: Habermas, *Frauen und Männer*; Schmid, "Weib oder Mensch".
[41] See Droste zu Vischering, *Ueber die Genossenschaften*, 16.

over male attendants" is superior beyond any doubt.[42] There are in fact voices, which as a matter of course are describing organized care according to the gender principle.[43]

THE SISTERS OF CHARITY AND THE FEMALE GENDER CHARACTER

The unambiguous context of all quotations put forward here is the Sisters of Charity caring for the impoverished sick. This is exactly a focal point of the Catholic discourse regarding the poor and sick relief, and closer to the discourse of the 1830s and 1840s. It is distinctly noticeable that, from 1831 onward, this partial discourse entered the overall discourse on Catholic poor relief and fundamentally influenced it following the publication of Clemens Brentano's book on the Sisters of Charity of St Borromeo.[44] Within the Catholic press, hundreds of writings[45] of different lengths and styles (brief news, reviews, elaborate article series) dealt with this topic, even beyond the ultramontane-oriented organs. Furthermore, a series of books and brochures was published on the Sisters of Charity.[46] Even the Protestant *Evangelische Kirchen-Zeitung* (EKZ) took notice of the topic.[47]

By contrast, male charitable congregations (Brothers of Mercy) hardly appear in the Catholic poverty discourse of these decades. There are only very sporadic incidences of their being included in any deliberations. For example, in the *Historisch-politische Blätter* the hope is set on the actions of the Sisters rather than on the Brothers of Mercy to solve the poverty problem. This is justified with the thought that male mercifulness has its place in dangerous individual situations (e.g. on the St Bernard Pass), i.e. not in everyday poor relief.[48] Other authors do not deny the merits of the male hospital orders in the past. However, they take for granted that the female species is generally better suited for the care of the sick and poor, which would also have been the opinion of the majority of contemporaries.[49]

---

[42] *Historisch-politische Blätter*, 24 (1848), 102. This journal was the mouthpiece of the influential Munich circle around the Catholic publisher Joseph Görres, who would contribute articles himself or temporarily work in the editorial staff. It appeared every fortnight and was directed at well-educated circles, also those outside the clergy. With its circulation of almost 2000 copies, it had one of the largest coverages of Catholic journals in the first half of the nineteenth century. The Munich circle united late Romantics and the ultramontanes. Concerning the journal cf. as introductory reading Schneider, *Katholiken auf die Barrikaden?*, 62, 77-83.

[43] Cf. Sintzel, *Geschichte*, 13-15, here a contemporary doctor is quoted following this argument.

[44] Cf. Brentano, *Die Barmherzigen Schwestern*. Concerning the Sisters of St Borromeo in Germany cf. Gatz, *Kirche und Krankenpflege*, 268-300 (see also older literature there).

[45] In her unpublished thesis Annika Morbach managed to determine 187 thematizations in seven ultramontane journals between 1828 and 1850. Morbach, *Der katholische Diskurs*, 54 ff.

[46] In addition to the abovementioned thesis by Morbach, an initial analysis of the material with a different perspective was provided by my former colleague Bircher, "Religious communities".

[47] *EKZ*, 12 (1833), 137-150 (review of Brentano). However, in 1830 an article on the Sisters of Charity already appeared: *EKZ*, 6 (1830), 169 ff; 177-180. The *EKZ* represented the strict section of Prussian Protestantism. See Kriege, *Geschichte*.

[48] *HPB*, 21 (1848), 570.

[49] Cf. *BZKT*, 5 (1832), 55. Also Sintzel, *Geschichte*, 19.

The detailed characterization of the Sisters of Charity links the Catholic poverty discourse to the (civil) discourse on women in general. A closer look at the article titled "Über die barmherzigen Schwestern und deren Einführung in Wien" reveals the following characterizations. The "tender sex" in the shape of the Sisters of Charity practices "devotional love", demonstrates "perseverance, patience and faithfulness", exhibits "most tender compassion" and "unresting practice", is "helpful as an angel", performs "every service" and "accepts every effort" namely for the sake of Jesus, as it is the "heavenly-spirited virgins" who have the "courage to fight against the charms of the world" and who perform "deeds of Christian love" as "God-enthusiastic souls" by performing "wise sick care". They are characterized by "evangelical zealousness of love", "heroic sacrifice", "humility", "gentleness", "modesty", "abstinence", "pudicity" and "angelic purity" and thus honour the female gender to the highest adornment and at the same time demonstrate its dignity.[50] Other characterizations of the "ideal femininity" from Brentano's book enter the press such as "diligence", "orderliness and cleanliness" or "adeptness" or "wise housekeeping".[51] The conformance with essential elements of the civil ideal of women is unsurprising. However, it is again surpassed in a typical Catholic manner, as we deal with "tender virgins" and "pure brides" whose "treasure of adeptness" "emerges solely from sheer virginity" and who have "hands of angels".[52] The angel motif,[53] in particular, relativizes the 'normal' gender affiliation of the Sisters and practically transforms them into genderless beings. This is thus an increasingly common factor in explaining why the Sisters, in particular, would also be permitted to nurse men.[54]

By contrast, another connection to the general gender ideal also originates from the motif of 'motherliness'. One author argues in his article, which appeared in the *Katholik* and the *Sion* in 1836, thus reaching a large Catholic readership, that the Sisters of Charity's renunciation of the joys of motherhood enabled them to become "mothers of orphaned children".[55] In one of the many books on the Sisters this motherly action is very insistently and emphatically characterized: "The Sisters' love creates food, warmth and cleanliness for the sick; but it also does ineffably more! It brings comfort, it cautions, it guides around the evil paths, it encourages, yes it brings comfort, an image of heavenly love, like being comforted by one's mother." [...] "Give

---

[50] *Neue Theologische Zeitschrift*, (1832), 374-389, here 374, 381 ff. This journal, published in Vienna, was the scientific-theological mouthpiece for Austria with a strong apologetic orientation. Cf. Schneider, *Katholiken auf die Barrikaden?*, 59 ff. as well as Hosp, *Kirche Österreichs*, 285 ff.

[51] *Sion*, 1 (1832), 262 ff., 286 (article sequence with excerpts of Brentano's scripture). Complementary reading without a direct reference to Brentano is provided in: *Sion*, 6 (1837), 569-574, here 569 ff. *Sion* was a widespread church journal, especially in Bavaria, with a more popular orientation than the *Katholik*. It appeared between 1832 and 1875.

[52] *Sion*, (1832), 244, 285 ff., 294.

[53] From contemporary books see also Sintzel, *Geschichte*, 42 ff., 292; Buß, *Der Orden*, 46.

[54] Also Schaper, *Krankenwartung*, 148.

[55] Quoted acording to *Sion*, 5 (1836), 885-888, here 887. The article was taken from the *Katholik*, 16 (1836), 37-45. "Motherly care" is attested to the Sisters in *Süddeutsches Kirchenblatt*, 5 (1845), 53. Regarding the new mother ideal of the civil circle since the late 18th century cf. indications provided by Köser, *Denn die Diakonisse*, 77 ff.

me mothers for the poor sick, they are in need of motherly care!" [56] The relationships in these orders and congregations are stylized according to a family pattern, with the Mother Superior caring for her daughters like a mother.[57] In some respects, these and other similar statements concerning the "motherly ministration"[58] or "motherly care"[59] of the Sisters of Charity anticipate the concept of a 'spiritual motherliness', which underwent a major upturn particularly in the civil women's movement of the second half of the nineteenth century. It served not least to legitimize female employment in those areas, where an analogy to the 'natural' female activity as a mother (i.e. education and care) could be established. In this construction, activities at school or the hospital appeared as an extension of the 'natural' family. It also implied the entitlement and, to a certain extent, the right to participate in shaping society in a specifically female way and to provide it with warmth and elements of comfort, which were considered women's responsibilities at home.[60]

Even although we come across the term 'tender sex', any semblance of 'weakness' is eschewed with regard to the Sisters of Charity. They are spry and powerful young women and represent the counterpart to young men doing military service. The Mother Superior can be compared to a commanding officer, and the group of Sisters to a legion.[61] In 1848, a comparison is drawn in the *HPB* between the charitably active Sisters and the Prussian *Landwehr*, i.e. the military territorial defence force.[62] The typical gender discourse is also prised open by changing weakness into strength, as the alleged 'weak virgins' resist the Zeitgeist in their religiousness, while the seemingly enlightened strong men succumb to it.[63] In almost the same manner the women overcome the "inherent female tendency for beautiful clothing" by directing this energy towards decorating the churches.[64] The fierce missionary assignment that the Sisters carry out for God and Church across the world therefore culminates in its renewal: they clean up the "battlefield of secular life", collect and heal its debris and "religiously bury its corpses".[65] At this point, the offensive character of the ultramontane strategy is significant. Other statements describe the Sisters as the "bulwark of church"[66], thus assigning a more defensive-defending role to them.

[56] Reinkens, *Die Barmherzigen Schwestern*, 183.
[57] See e.g. Sintzel, *Geschichte*, 152 ff. or Brentano, *Die Barmherzige Schwestern (1852)*, 100 ff.
[58] Sintzel, *Geschichte*, 102.
[59] Ibid., 171.
[60] As introductory reading cf. Bock, *Frauen*, 129, 159; Wendt, *Geschichte der sozialen Arbeit*, 480 ff. A more detailed account is in Taylor Allen, *Feminism*; Sachße, *Mütterlichkeit als Beruf*, 110-116; Breitenbach, *Frauen*.
[61] *Sion*, 1 (1832), 251, 286 (extracts from Brentano). "Das gemeinsame Werk der barmherzigen Schwestern Jesu Christi bedarf eben so sehr rüstige, kräftige und von den Händeln der Welt unberührte Jungfrauen, als der Kriegsdienst der Könige solche Jünglinge auswählt." Brentano, *Die Barmherzige Schwestern (1852)*, 52. Cf. also Reinkens, *Die Barmherzigen Schwestern*, 7.
[62] Cf. *HPB*, 21 (1848), 571.
[63] *Sion*, 5 (1836), 887.
[64] *Sion*, 1 (1832), 308.
[65] Sintzel, *Geschichte*, 72.
[66] Reinkens, *Die Barmherzigen Schwestern*, XI.

*SISTERS OF CHARITY AS AN IDEAL OF CARE AND SECULAR 'PAID CARETAKERS'
AS ANTITYPE*

According to all the material presented so far, the Catholic poor relief does in fact appear as a women's matter. However, these are not just any women. The Catholic poverty discourse focuses on a specific type: the Sisters of Charity. This is particularly apparent in an argumentative pattern, namely the juxtaposition of the Sisters of Charity and paid secular care staff. The success story of denominational sick and poor relief by Catholic Sisters and Protestant deaconesses since the 1830s lets people forget the paid caretaker as a 'normal' salaried profession, which was taken up by men as well as women. As the recent example of the major Vienna General Hospital showed and proved in detail, the number of women among the 'caretakers' increased not least because of the worsening pay. This counteracted the original concept of a nursing care for men by men (and women for women).[67]

In the sources analysed, the Sisters of Charity represent the ideal, the paid staff represents the antitype, and without making distinctions between church or public facilities. This accords with the characterizations which project nearly all the bad human characteristics onto the paid staff: they strive for private advantages, neglect the impoverished sick from whom they can expect no reward, they embezzle all belongings, are uneducated, crude and clumsy, and act arbitrarily instead of maintaining orderliness.[68] They are accused of having resorted to the service as a form of "sheet anchor" for lack of other alternatives and not out of inner vocation.[69] As such, the service of love for the sake of Christ and divine reward is contrasted with paid service.[70] It is striking that the antitype frequently occurs in masculine terms, for instance in form of "paid guardians" who acted with the "corporal cane" and without any gentleness.[71] A letter by the Prussian President von Zerboni is repeatedly mentioned, which states that "in no institution with male employees who merely did their service out of duty" could he observe such positive work as with the Sisters of Charity.[72] Without playing down the deficiencies on the part of the paid caretakers, the structural problem is by all means identified: the low pay and the lack of security in case of sickness and age does not appeal to those of suitable character, but to those people from poorer backgrounds who have no other alternative.[73]

A very extensive article in the *Breslauer Zeitschrift für katholische Theologie* (*BZKT*) illustrates that it was not just simply a matter of a men-women dichotomy.

[67] Cf. Walter, "Krankenpflege", 30 ff. A more detailed account is in id., *Pflege als Beruf*. See also Schaper, *Krankenwartung*, 116-118. On pp. 53-63 Schaper also describes the work and living conditions of paid caretakers around the year 1800.

[68] Cf. *Sion*, 6 (1837), 571 ff.; *Katholik*, 25 (1845) 149, 691.

[69] *Süddeutsche Zeitung für Kirche und Staat*, 1 (1845) 15, 61 ff., here 61. Similar *Katholik*, 21 (1841) 82, XCVIII. Also cf. *Katholik*, 25 (1845) 149, 691.

[70] Cf. *Katholik*, 25 (1845) Supplement 11, 308; Reinkens, *Die Barmherzigen Schwestern*, X (Foreword by Dieringer).

[71] Cf. e.g. *Katholik*, 25 (1845) Supplement 11, 308; Reinkens, *Die Barmherzigen Schwestern*, X.

[72] *SKB*, 5 (1845) 21 (according to Brentano); *Katholik*, 25 (1845) 149, p. 692.

[73] The corresponding remarks by the Bavarian doctor and health care reformer Simon von Häberl are mentioned several times. Cf. Sintzel, *Geschichte*, 13-15; Bartholmä, *Die barmherzigen Schwestern*, 94 and Buß, *Der Orden*, 493-495.

The review of Clemens Brentano's text in 1832 already stated that it was "a general and loudly declared truth of experience that a care of the impoverished sick, which emanated purely from the purpose of Christian love and divine reward had large and significant advantages over the sick care that was assumed only with a temporary regard to a mundane reward".[74] The article mentioned above was published following year, with the title "Wird die im christlichen Geiste zu verrichtende Hospital-Kranken-wartung von Mitgliedern religiöser Ordens-Vereine besser besorgt, als von weltlichen Lohnwächtern?".[75] This question is also elaborately discussed in the various books on the Sisters of Charity already quoted here,[76] each with similar arguments, so that this article can be considered representative. The author, priest Joseph Sauer from Breslau, at first clarifies the position that the female gender is better suited, so that his further elaborations attempt to clarify the question of whether the clerical Sisters or the secular payment claimants deserved priority.[77] Though "most voices already opted for the former", this "judgement was not a general one".[78] As was to be expected, this extensive essay draws exactly this conclusion. It is achieved by the author developing a detailed requirement standard for a nurse, which comprises physical, technical, mental-characteristic and religious aspects. Measured by this standard, many women are unqualified to carry out this form of occupation.[79] Directed at the universally understood principle of human dignity – also of the impoverished sick, a topos which is remarkably and explicitly used by the author,[80] everything finally points in favour of the Sisters of Charity, because "true love of mankind and the altogether impartiality" cools down in the face of "temporary nutritional worries" and human dignity would no longer be taken into account, if "the deep religious feeling did not live within and guide the human being".[81]

These statements illustrate the extent to which the Catholic poor relief discourse was connected to the superordinate discourse regarding the position of religion and church in the post-revolutionary society in general as well as the discourse on the sense and non-sense of religious orders. These discourses and their requirements strongly influenced the poor relief discourse.[82]

The discourse on the Sisters of Charity was undoubtedly influenced by interests. In the Catholic sources analysed it clearly served to provide the Sisters of Charity with a competitive advantage over the secular competition by proving their suitability.

---

[74] *BZKT*, 5 (1832), 67-76, here 68.

[75] Ibid., 5 (1833), 45-72; 6, 6-45.

[76] See Buß, *Der Orden*, 460-493; Sintzel, *Geschichte*, 13-15, 53 ff., 117-119 etc.; Reinkens, *Die Barmherzigen Schwestern*, X, 78-83.

[77] Cf. *BZKT*, 5 (1833), 56. He also wrote a book on a charitably-active congregation of sisters. Cf. Sauer, *Die Elisabetherinnen*.

[78] *BZKT*, 5 (1833), 56. Voices in favour of well-educated secular 'sick caretakers' are also dealt with by Buß, *Der Orden*, 464-466, 492 ff.

[79] According to *BZKT*, 6 (1833), 15.

[80] Regarding this complex cf. my article: "Poverty need no longer despair...".

[81] *BZKT*, 6 (1833), 26 ff.

[82] Cf., on the Protestant side, regarding Fliedner's deaconesses' institution the information given by Köser that Fliedner and his wife Friederike were influenced by moral concepts of the bourgeoisie, but also by specific religious concepts of the circle around the awakening movement. Cf. Köser, *Denn die Diakonisse*, 83.

At the same time the Sisters also provided the opportunity to (re-)occupy important societal domains in secular and church institutions. However, the negative characterization of paid nursing personnel also existed outside of internal Catholic discourse. Catholic authors could repeatedly refer to secular authorities, as did the literature on the history of nursing.[83]

The political relevance of such discourses also receives a certain acknowledgement in the debates of the second half of the nineteenth century. In Austria, for instance, the argumentative patterns described were reproduced in the fight between liberals and conservatives in order to transfer the care of the sick to the Sisters of Charity as extensively as possible and to remove secular nursing personnel: "True care can only result from Christian love". As observed in the case of Austria after 1887, this discourse had developed "much more strongly than the discourse on the supposed 'natural' suitability of women for nursing".[84] On the other hand, the anti-Catholic liberal discourse before and during the *Kulturkampf* in Germany, which involved the development of female order members and charitably active Sisters to a negative type, needs to be taken into account. Their professional efforts were questioned and their charitable actions portrayed as sheer attempts to expand the realm of church influence and power.[85]

SISTERS OF CHARITY AND DEACONESSES IN COMPETITION

The discourse on best nursing personnel was related to a denominational conflict, one which grew considerably more severe in Germany during the first half of the nineteenth century. It is not without reason that the thesis of a 'second denominational age' was advanced in recent German research.[86] Even though it is possible to argue against a one-sided version of the thesis, there is no doubt that intensified denominational competition and polemics existed, particularly in view of the denominational press.[87]

Against this background this discourse gains its own form, as a significant number of Catholic periodicals attentively registered the emergence of 'Protestant Sisters of Charity' and vice versa, as the Protestant press would ask whether it was possible for German Protestantism to generate its own form of Sisters of Charity.[88]

---

[83] Cf. e.g. Schweikardt, *Die Entwicklung*, 42-45.

[84] Cf. Walter, "Krankenpflege", 33. The second attempt to enforce female order members is dated by Walter to 1887, after the first attempt rapidly failed following the concordat of 1855 due to the temporary political dominance of liberalism.

[85] Gross, *The War Against Catholicism*, 157-184, 209-224.

[86] See Blaschke, "Das 19. Jahrhundert"; id. *Konfessionen im Konflikt*. A critical account: Steinhoff, "Ein zweites konfessionelles Zeitalter?".

[87] Without being able to go into detail, I would like to refer to some sharp criticism of Protestantism as a spritual, revolution-promoting force, analysed in Schneider, *Katholiken auf die Barrikaden?*, 353-368.

[88] Cf. *EKZ*, 6 (1830), 169-171, 177-180. In conclusion, the article on the history of the Sisters of Charity poses the question: "should it not be possible that in terms of less confined forms, similar associations could be established among us?" Evidence is provided for Fliedner's efforts to establish a deaconesses' institution due to his specific preoccupation with the Sisters of Charity, particularly the Sisters of St Clemens in Münster, and his wording in the statutes. Cf. Köser, *Denn die Diakonisse*, 89 ff., 193 ff.

People were highly aware of the fact that the charitable profession of the Catholic Sisters of Charity had a substantial weight in the controversy about the right church and played an important role as an apologetic argument. Denominational conceptions of the female image and the gender roles involved are reflected in this partial discourse alongside conventional controversy-theological differences. This is evident in the various reactions to the suggestion made by a Protestant author who supported the Protestant efforts for an increased deaconry in the *Deutsche Vierteljahresschrift* in 1842. In addition to an improved organization of stationary and ambulant sick care he also emphasized the motive "to guide the physically and, more so, mentally-sad position of so many virgins who are denied the destined existence as a wife, mother and housewife."[89] Here, he argues against the background of the dominant Protestant female image directed to marriage and motherhood,[90] but which was proving increasingly difficult in the real situation of society (the so-called *Frauenfrage*, which means the question of women's rights and opportunities outside marriage). The Catholic answer condemned the incitement to establish a female Protestant poor-care association as a solution to the 'surplus of women'. Busy wives and mothers as well as younger women who still had plans to get married would not be able to meet the demands. By contrast, "how different" were Catholic Sisters of Charity who would abjure everything and serve Christ in form of the poor sick in an 'undivided' manner, i.e. without any other intentions or goals.[91] Here, the traditional Catholic fulfilment of the female role becomes apparent, i.e. the 'profession' as an order member, which is even more highly esteemed than marriage. At the same time Catholic voices would also agitate for an introduction of the Sisters of Charity. Even though convents were not care-providing institutions for 'needy daughters', a religious order in these times would nonetheless be a shelter and tower of strength for the 'countless virgins' who lived the vow of poverty, celibacy and obedience due to bitter hardship.[92] Given the mentioned suggestions, the *Sonntagsblatt für katholische Christen* - published in Münster and distributed across Northwest Germany as a popular weekly paper - voiced the fear that due to the many young women who had no marriage or motherhood prospects, the Protestant institutions would be used as care institutions and that these women would be "degraded to being common nurses who can usually be acquired for money".[93] This again not only confirms the above-mentioned dichotomy as a main perspective, but it constructs, as in the case of the *Sion*, a divide between a Catholic and Protestant poor relief, which is not openly stated yet clearly recognizable to the reader. Therefore, the *Sion* could even predict that attempts to establish church institutions of "serving love" within Protestantism would contribute to "elucidate Protestants on the instability of their churchly position".[94] Even where people were willing to acknowledge the merits of the deaconesses' institution[95] founded by

[89] Quoted according to *Sion*, 11 (1842), 803-808, here 803.

[90] Concerning its development cf. Gause, *Kirchengeschichte und Genderforschung*.

[91] See *Sion*, 11 (1842), 804, 811 ff.

[92] *Sion*, 12 (1843), 89-94, here 93. The background consists of the government's refusal to permit settlements of the Sisters of Charity in the Kingdom of Württemberg.

[93] *Sonntagsblatt für katholische Christen*, 1 (1842), 220-225, 243-251, here 251.

[94] *Sion*, 11 (1842), 814.

[95] Most recently detected in the study by Köser, *Denn die Diakonisse*.

Theodor Fliedner, they would still concede a higher status to the Catholic Sisters of Charity. The deaconess may be a good nurse, but unlike the Catholic Sisters she will not be fully dedicated to her service, because with her "icy bible piety" she particularly lacks the Sisters' "invisible mysterious magic", radiated by the "brides of Jesus Christ, those virgins eternally affianced and bonded to the lord Jesus".[96] The Catholic ideal of virginity, which people recognized in the Sisters of Charity, is therewith proof of Catholic superiority.[97]

PERCEPTION OF FEMALE POVERTY?

Finally, it should be pointed out that there is a large void within the Catholic poverty discourse with regard to women's poverty. To our current knowledge the real circumstances of poor women were not of interest, since specific forms of female poverty are hardly recognized or mentioned in the different sources reviewed. This is even more so surprising, as research concerning the history of poverty was able to prove for Early Modern Times as well as the nineteenth century that the poor relief supported an exceptionally large number of women.[98] In this respect, Relinde Meiwes' observation that poverty was not a theme of the Catholic social reformers of the early nineteenth century applies to a broader circle of media and authors.[99] However, a specific group of poor females mentioned in the reviewed corpus is that of the poor widows[100], a classical topos from biblical times on the one hand, and a mirror image of early-nineteenth-century reality on the other. For instance, the detailed analysis of the poverty statistics of Münster/Westphalia revealed that 60 per cent of poor people supported by public poor relief in Münster were women. Not only were they more heavily represented than men, but, with 63 per cent, widows were by far the largest group among them.[101] The only other group of impoverished females, which is repeatedly mentioned in the reviewed sources, is identified as the 'fallen girls' who were accommodated in the 'houses of mercy' run by the Sisters of the Good Shepherd.[102] This particular case not only shows the indeed exceptional practical form of a femini-

---

[96] *Katholik*, 29 (1849) 137, 548. Also refer to *Katholik*, 25 (1845) 108, 502 or *SKB*, 5 (1845), 57.

[97] See also *Sonntagsblatt für katholische Christen*, 9 (1850), 89 ff., where the lack of this distinctive Catholic feature (virgin status) was held responsible for the "unfruitfulness of facilities for the care of the sick and poor" in Protestantism. See also Buß, *Der Orden*, 198: "Daher ist diese Frucht der Wohlthätigkeit dem die Gültigkeit der Gelübde verwerfenden Protestantismus versagt. Diese mag analoge Associationen erzeugen, aber die Höhe religiöser Congregationen in gelübdlicher Bindung erreicht er nicht."

[98] Fuchs, *Gender and Poverty*. From a German perspective: Köppen, *Die Armut*.

[99] Cf. Meiwes, *Arbeiterinnen des Herrn*, 276 ff.

[100] Cf. for instance a sermon held by Sebastian Winkelhofer on the seventh Sunday following Whitsun. Sailer, *Sebastian Winkelhofers*. Also the pastoral letter for Lent by the bishop of Chur in 1830, quoted in *Katholische Kirchen-Zeitung*, 2 (1830), 158.

[101] Glöe, "Frauenarmut", 264. With regard to the confined poor relief in Münster cf. the contentually and methodically productive study by Dethlefs, "Frauengeschichte".

[102] Cf. e.g. *Sion*, 6 (1837) Supplement 11, 81-85; *Nathanel*, 5 (1849), 57-59; *Katholik*, 20 (1840) 78, 187 and 27 (1847) 82, 333-335 (pastoral letter by Bishop Laurent); *Katholische Sonntagsblätter zur Belehrung*, 4 (1845) 46, 373-376.

zation of the Caritas in the sense of charitable work by women for women[103], but also displays a further element of a Catholic femininity construction in the polarization of the 'female sinner' and angel-like virgin. In actual fact, the reports in the reviewed material are consis-tently characterized by this form of black-and-white depiction.[104]

FEMINIZATION OF CARITAS? A GLANCE AT THE PRACTICE

More recent research has pointed out an international phenomenon under the term 'feminization of the clergy' or canonically more correct under the term 'feminization of church personnel': namely the emergence of numerous new female congregations or the large increase of women in religious orders and congregations.[105]

In the first half of the nineteenth century, eleven new women's congregations were established in the German-speaking area.[106] During this period neither male schooling staff nor male nursing communities came into existence, while seven of the eleven female congregations were devoted to sick care, the others to school education.[107]

In the Prussian kingdom, for which the basis is statistically most certain, the 'feminization of the church staff' accelerated in the further course of the nineteenth century. By 1907, almost two thirds of the 'church staff' were female order members or members of female congregations (64 per cent).[108] In the middle of the nineteenth century, there had still been an infinitesimal number of women, while the number rapidly increased to almost half of the 'church staff' by the time of the *Kulturkampf*. The frequently quoted gender-neutral 'rise of religious orders' following the Revolution of 1848 is therefore more accurately a 'rise of female congregations'. The male religious orders and congregations thrived to a far lesser extent.[109]

The new congregations, however, devoted themselves to charitable work and dominated in the extensive fields of ambulant and stationary care. By the end of the nineteenth century, 600 Sisters worked in the ambulant poor and sick care in the archbishopric of Cologne as opposed to 33 Brothers. In all Prussia 1403 Sisters

[103] Concerning the Sisters of the Good Shepherd and their settlements in Germany cf. Albert, "Ordensleben", 194 as well as Meiwes, *Arbeiterinnen des Herrn*, 82.

[104] Cf. *Nathanel*, 5 (1849), 57-59: the Sisters are "angels of mercy", the others are female penitents. The eternal virgins have preserved their sexual purity, the most valuable commodity of the female sex, others must first regain their honour and virtue by means of a penitent life.

[105] di Giorgio speaks of a "feminization of the clergy" in "Das katholische Modell", 196 ff. Regarding Germany a detailed account is provided by Meiwes who rightly speaks of a "feminization of church personnel". Regarding France cf. the classic study by Langlois, *Le catholicisme au féminin*. Regarding Belgium see Tihon, *Les religieuses*.

[106] Cf. as a source basis, Albert, "Ordensleben", 188 ff. I corrected his data for the diagram. The congregations in Metz and Strasbourg were not included and the first settlement of the Sisters of St Borromeo from Nancy in Saarlouis (1810), overlooked by Albert, was newly added.

[107] See Albert, "Ordensleben", 188 ff., 199.

[108] The world clergy provided for 27 per cent, the male orders for 9 per cent. Source: *Kirchliches Handbuch.* vol. 2: *1908/09*, 277, 407-454.

[109] Cf. Meiwes, *Arbeiterinnen des Herrn*, esp. 74-88. In 1855, 579 women and 397 men lived within orders and congregations in Prussia. By 1872/73 there already were 8011 women and 1037 men (ibid., 77). The following diagram is based on Meiwes, *Arbeiterinnen des Herrn*, 77.

practised sick care in 148 hospitals, while only 33 men worked in four hospitals. Of 47 Catholic institutions aimed at the education of impoverished, dissolute children, 34 were run by female congregations.[110] With regard to nursing there is also a substantial overrepresentation of denominational nurses (Sisters of Charity and Protestant deaconesses). In 1887, there were 8271 nurses active in Prussia, of which only 12.5 per cent were men. The denominationally organized employees accounted for 29.4 per cent Protestant and 52 per cent Catholic, which did not correspond to the denomination proportions of Prussia (only 40 per cent of the population were Catholic). Among the Catholic nurses only 289 were in turn Brothers, i.e. just under 7 per cent.[111]

Could there be more evident proof for a 'feminization of the Caritas'? Hardly, because for many Catholic women these numbers implied the conquest of a new occupational field with increased professionalization with a substantial social acceptance. It made models of living and organization available that male-dominated civil organizations did not offer.[112]

For a long time, however, the organized charitable dedication of Catholic women outside the congregations remained rather limited. Georg Ratzinger, the author of the Catholic standard work concerning the history of the Caritas, the first edition of which appeared in 1868 and the second in 1884,[113] generally advocated the "intervention of the female world" "into the charity domain". From this intervention he expected a "most wholesome effect", since "women's practical view regarding all issues of domestic life" could help eliminate many deficiencies of the poor. However, he links this indication with the complaint that "the educated and propertied women of today" lacked the awareness "not only to be indebted to the poor and helpless with parts of their outward fortunate assets, but also with their personal abilities".[114] With the so-called Elisabethan Societies the local charitable commitment of Catholic lay women actually developed into a clear denominationally structured form after 1840.[115] As stated on the third *Katholikentag* of 1849, which insistently recommended them, the women within these Societies were supposed to pursue their "profession" to "lead the way in true Christian love".[116] They were expected to restore the Christian status in the so-called disrupted family lives by means of home visits and their influence on the impoverished women.[117] The development of the Societies was immense, but by the turn of the century there were only approximately 500 local Societies in the

[110] Evidence provided in: Ibid., 283-286.

[111] Cf. Schweikardt, *Die Entwicklung*, 107.

[112] Cf. Meiwes, *Arbeiterinnen des Herrn*, 270. Concerning the momentum of women's professionalization of socio-charitable efforts regarding the deaconesses cf. also Köser, *Denn die Diakonisse*, 207. However, she also expounds on the relationship of *praxis pietatis* and profession in terms of the development of 'sick care' as an independent employment field.

[113] Ratzinger, *Geschichte*. Some information on the author (a great-uncle of the current Pope) is provided in the preface.

[114] Ibid., 575. This passage is also discussed by Meiwes, *Arbeiterinnen des Herrn*, 274.

[115] With regard to these, cf. Kall, *Katholische Frauenbewegung*, 23-71; Lüttgen, *Die Elisabethvereine*.

[116] *Verhandlungen*, 36. Regarding these so-called 'Catholic Days' (*Katholikentage*), first held in 1848 and still held in Germany today, see von Hehl und Kronenberg, *Zeitzeichen*. Concerning the *Katholikentag* of 1848/49 see Scheidgen, *Der deutsche Katholizismus*, 440-492.

[117] See *Verhandlungen*, 36.

FIGURE 1
FOUNDATION OF NEW FEMALE CONGREGATIONS IN PRUSSIA

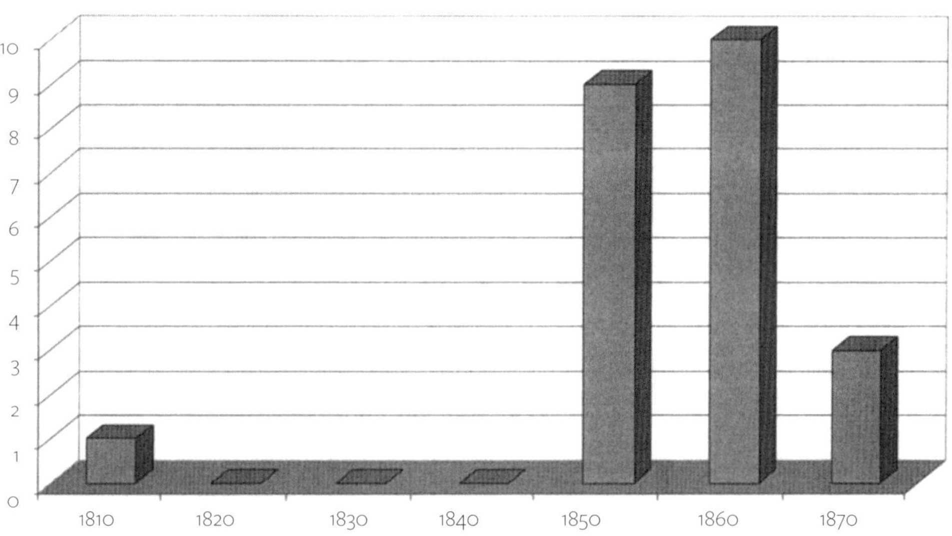

FIGURE 2
NUMBER OF NEW ESTABLISHMENTS OR FIRST ESTABLISHMENT
IN THE GERMAN-SPEAKING AREA

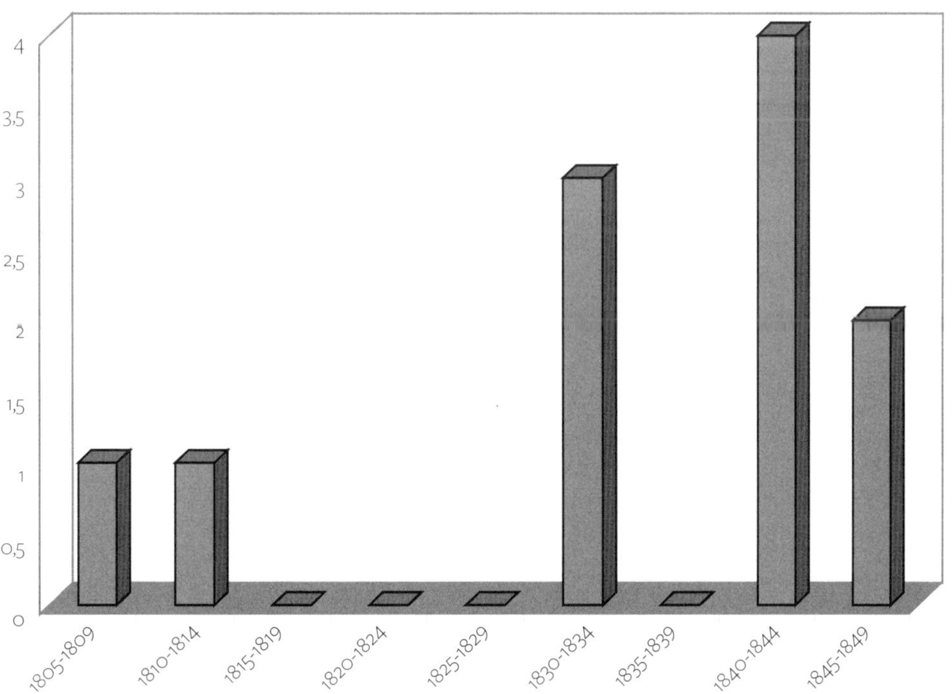

German Reich, while the number of male Vincent Conferences, which were founded almost at the same time, reached almost 700.[118]

FEMINIZATION OF CARITAS? AN INTERIM RESULT

This article began with my critical thoughts on the feminization thesis and its overrating in parts of the literature. Without merely wanting to negate its value, it seemed and still seems appropriate to me to differentiate more thoroughly, for instance according to subject areas. In 2002, I suggested speaking of e.g. a 'feminization of Caritas' rather than of a 'feminization of religion' or just a 'feminization of Catholicism'. The analysis in this article of the many sources concerning Catholic poor relief and health care in the first half of the nineteenth century and the assessment of the practice in the second half of the nineteenth century gives reason to even further delimit and differentiate a more modest thesis of a 'feminization of Caritas'.

1. First of all, it needs to be noted that: "Initially, Catholic women did not contribute to the formalized process of poor relief".[119] This means that they did not take part in the communal poor councils, for instance, which were responsible for the public poor relief. Women could even be excluded from voluntary work as principals of a municipal poor district.[120]

2. In the first half of the nineteenth century, the attribution of the female gender to sick and poor relief emerged in the Catholic domain, but, according to our sources, to a lesser degree than expected. The need remained to prove this on an argumentative level. That men were capable of nursing was not generally disputed, not least due to the existence of male nursing orders.

3. The constructed connection between Sisters of Charity and care turned out to be much closer. Although the Sisters of Charity represent the female gender in the many characterizations of them, they are at the same time transgressing and developing into almost genderless creatures or into beings who also bear 'masculine' attributes.

4. Furthermore, an observation made by Silke Köser regarding the Protestant institutions of deaconesses also recommends caution concerning the Catholic domain. Even although these had been unions of women, they were subject to a male administration and male sovereignty and there was little room for an independent organization of life.[121] By contrast, the Catholic female congregations were subject to a female administration and it was women who, as founders, contributed with their own ideas. However, it should not be forgotten that men had an extensive influence on the congregations as confessors, spiritual principals or bishops to an extent that the foundation history could be formally rewritten. This also befell Margaretha

---

[118] Cf. *Kirchlichen Handbuch*, vol. 2, 22-225.

[119] Meiwes, *Arbeiterinnen des Herrn*, 274.

[120] Concerning the development of poor relief and the poor legislation in Germany, cf. once more Schulz, "Armut und Armenpolitik". Women in Münster were not allowed to participate in poor relief, not even in voluntary positions. Cf. Dethlefs, *Frauengeschichte*, 145 ff.

[121] Cf. Köser, *Denn die Diakonisse*, 40.

Flesch ('Mutter Rosa'), the foundress of the Franciscan Sisters of Waldbreitbach. This woman, from a poor background and beatified in 2008, only laboriously managed to establish a nursing congregation on the outskirts of the Trier diocese against a male-clerical resistance. Even in her lifetime she was deprived of the leadership at the instigation of the spiritual rector and for decades denigrated as the foundress of a downright *damnatio memoriae*, while rector Konrad Probst directed the congregation with the help of some submissive Sisters before her very eyes and against the original intentions.[122]

5. The charitable associations also need to be differentiated. By no means did the Elisabethan Societies dominate the field of charitable associations, as the comparison to the parallel organization of the St Vincent Conferences already shows. However, in charitable mixed-gender associations the prevalence of women could be substantial, as revealed by a recently published study concerning the Seraphisches Liebeswerk, a Catholic association for child welfare, on a local level. Women were the most important key influencers on location, recruited members and handed out the association journal. More than two thirds of the members were women. When the powerful local division of this association in Krefeld went about recruiting Caritas helpers for the new community charity aid in 1911/12, 46 women came forward and not a single man.[123]

Moreover, male clerical control still prevailed in all these associations. In the case of the Seraphisches Liebeswerk, this was not only due to the close relationship with the Capuchin order, as male laymen participated in the directive organs. In 1921, two women became members of the board for the first time. It seems almost absurd that a vigorous conflict erupted regarding the presence of women at board meetings, since they took place in the conclave area of the Capuchin order. Rejected at the door at first, the ladies later received a special permit.[124]

6. From a chronological perspective the practice during the second half of the century can be considered a successful implementation of what was desired for the Sisters of Charity in the Catholic discourse of the first half of the century: Catholic Sisters were exceptionally present in the social field, far outside the internal realm of church facilities.

In terms of the analysed discourses on poor and sick relief and the charity practised it is impossible to claim in conclusion that God 'changed gender'. However, given all the necessary restrictions, the fact that the Caritas in Germany displayed a strikingly frequent 'female face' should finally be acknowledged at this point.

---

[122] Cf. the detailed reconstruction by Kracht, *Leidenschaft*.
[123] Cf. Henkelmann, *Caritasgeschichte*, 94, 110 ff., 291.
[124] Ibid., 111, 314.

Ignaz von Döllinger was a leading Old Catholic figure and vehemently opposed to the infallibity (Unfehlbarkeit) of the Pope, represented in this caricature as an infant.
[Woodcut by Tomassichl from Klein, 1871; Utrecht, Museum Catharijneconvent]

CELIBATE OR MARRIED PRIESTS?

POLEMICAL GENDER DISCOURSE IN NINETEENTH-CENTURY CATHOLICISM

ANGELA BERLIS

Throughout history, we have known of many conflicts within the Church and of the tendency of the parties involved in such conflicts to malign each other or brand each other as heretics during the course of the dispute.[1] This would often occur when one party would popularize stereotypes of the opposing party. Polemics in unstable times are nothing new in the history of the Church; polemical treatises have often been used in such times, in order to pointedly develop theological positions.[2] What insights have they yielded, however, with regard to the historical understanding of a certain period?

During and after the Reformation, for example, the Pope was often regarded as the Anti-Christ. Stories and caricatures of indecent secular and regular clergy were then and later on an element of an anti-clerical and anti-monastic tradition.[3] In the nineteenth century Catholics protesting against the First Vatican Council (1869-1870) and against the new dogmas of the infallibility and juridical supremacy of the Pope battled it out, often with heavy verbal attacks, with those who supported these dogmas.

Both sides, at times, called each other "New Catholics", in order to clarify that it was the other side that had introduced the innovations. The Old Catholics were bad-mouthed by the Roman Catholics as "Anal Catholics", "Nay Catholics", "Neo Pagans" or as "Neo Protestants".

The polemic dispute between Old Catholics and Roman Catholics following the First Vatican Council has been depicted many times. This contribution will bring to

---

[1] With thanks to Prof. Dr. Jan Jacobs (Tilburg) for his critical commentary on earlier versions of this article and to Joanne Lyons for the translation, made possible with the generous support of the Royal Dutch Academy of Sciences (Koninklijke Nederlandse Akademie van Wetenschappen).
[2] See, for example, de Kruif and Meijer Drees, *Het lange leven van het pamflet*; Bagchi, "Poets, Peasants, and Pamphlets".
[3] Cf. van de Sande, "Decadente monniken en nonnen".

the fore the role that the gender discourse[4], i.e. the attribution or denial of masculinity and femininity, played in the conflict. I will describe the construct of masculinity and femininity as a field in which disputes are battled out.

The following will firstly give a more detailed description of the historical context: the background to the emergence of the Old Catholic movement, its early development, and its relations to the 'Church of Utrecht'. Particular focus will be given to the Old Catholic movement's matters of reform, which also involved the question of celibacy. Secondly, I will give an overview of how a polemical gender discourse was woven into the conflict between the Old Catholics and Roman Catholics after the First Vatican Council. Feminization of the opposing party will be given primary focus here. I will then focus these more general observations on masculinity and the perception of priesthood, by concentrating on two texts that emerged in the 1870s from the ultramontane and Old Catholic camps. In both texts the issue of celibacy forms the focal point. Finally, I will summarize my observations and demonstrate how both sides claimed true masculinity for themselves.

THE OLD CATHOLIC MOVEMENT AND THE DISCUSSION ABOUT CLERICAL CELIBACY

In the months and years following 18 July 1870 – the day the new Vatican dogmas on the infallibility and juridical supremacy of the Pope were announced – a protest movement was formed in Germany and in other German-speaking countries. The movement named itself "Old Catholic" because the members wished to remain part of the Church as it had been before the First Vatican Council's innovations and because they recognized in the historic Church of the first thousand years the guiding principles of their ecclesiastical essence.[5]

Between 1871 and 1873, Old Catholic associations and congregations were formed and three congresses were held in Munich (1871), Cologne (1872) and Konstanz (1873). At these congresses strategic decisions were made, plans for church reform were formed, 'ecumenical' aims towards the reunion of churches were envisaged,[6] and considerations were made for a church organization for excommunicated Catholics.

Not only German delegates attended the congresses, but also Old Catholics from Switzerland, the Habsburg Empire, and the Netherlands, guests from Anglican, Evangelical, and Orthodox Churches. Due to their widespread effects and especially their objectives, these congresses had a great impact on Old Catholicism as a whole.

---

[4] Three aspects play a role in the discussion of 'gender': historicity of gender, the construct of gender, and dominance. With regard to the latter, the concern is - for Heide Wunder - "wie 'Geschlecht' immer wieder neu definiert wird, um eine erste gesellschaftliche Ordnung durch eine jeweils neu zu verhandelnde Verbindung von Unter- und Überordnung, aber auch von Gleichheit, herstellen zu können." Cited in Dinges, "Einleitung: Geschlechtergeschichte - mit Männern!", 10.

[5] Cf. for the following Berlis, *Frauen im Prozeß*, 319-370.

[6] In 1874 and 1875 the so called 'Bonn Union Conferences' were held, organized and presided over by Ignaz von Döllinger, which were in line with decisions made by the Cologne congress to form a committee for contacts with Orthodox and Anglicans. See: Oeyen, *Die Entstehung*; Neuner, *Döllinger*.

In the following I will focus on Germany and will first summarize the key points of the developments there.

In 1873, the Old Catholic movement in Germany established its own bishopric, encompassing the entire German Empire: clergy and lay people elected a bishop, who was officially recognized in several German states as a 'Catholic bishop' and who was consecrated by a bishop of the venerable Church of Utrecht. The latter, also called the 'Roman Catholic Church of the Episcopal Clergy' (*Rooms-Katholieke Kerk van de Bisschoppelijke Cleresie*) and known today as the Old Catholic Church of the Netherlands, had emerged in the eighteenth century from a schism between Rome and Utrecht. In the nineteenth century this Church had endured a difficult internal crisis.[7] In its dispute with Rome, the Church of Utrecht had always emphasized its continuity as Roman Catholic Church of the Netherlands and had ensured no changes were made to any aspect of its doctrine or practice. While this Church at the time was seeking, above all, to avoid any changes, it was now faced with the reform-bent, German-speaking Old Catholics, which was to lead to considerable tensions, especially with regard to the question of celibacy.[8]

The German-speaking Old Catholics regarded themselves - even after becoming a Church - as a Catholic reform movement, which sought to do away with certain abuses that had gradually emerged in the fields of cult and church law. They also sought to emphasize the responsibility of lay people and their right to elect vicars and bishops, and later to introduce the use of the vernacular in the liturgy. From the start, the issue of clerical celibacy was disputed. Some Old Catholics considered the abolition of celibacy a part of the reform package, whilst others did not. The debate for and against intensified between 1872 and 1878 and became a standing item of the Synod, which convened annually from 1874 onwards. In this debate the spectrum of viewpoints within the German diocese became visible; though delegates agreed unanimously that compulsory celibacy was an ecclesiastical law and was the cause of many grievances, opinions on the opportunity and urgency of abolishing this church law varied greatly. In the end, in 1878, it did not come to the abolition of compulsory clerical celibacy, but to a general dispensation from rule. The decision of the fifth Synod (1878) was a compromise between the large majority in favour of the abolition of celibacy and the small, but substantial, minority against it (including, for example, Ignaz von Döllinger[9], the *spiritus rector* of the movement, and Franz Heinrich Reusch, the vicar general who resigned from office over this issue). The Synod's decision enabled clergy who wished to marry to continue their work as married priests. Of

---

[7] See: Schoon, *Van bisschoppelijke Cleresie tot Oud-Katholieke Kerk.*

[8] See for detail: Berlis, "Einde aan een kaste". On the response of the Dutch bishops to the dispensation from celibacy in the German Old Catholic bishopric, see ibid., 55.

[9] Ignaz von Döllinger (1799-1890) in 1823 became Professor of Church History and Church Law in Aschaffenburg, and in Munich in 1826-1890. Besides his activity as political commentator, Döllinger published many academic works and supported the cause for freedom of theological-historical study. From 1869 he was vocal – anonymously at the time – against the infallibility of the pope and became the *spiritus rector* of the (Old Catholic) opposition movement. He was excommunicated in 1871. Döllinger is included among the most significant church historians of the nineteenth century. On Döllinger, see: Bischof, *Theologie und Geschichte*. See also the review of this book by Huppertz, "Auf dem Weg"; Id., "Ignaz von Döllinger".

the 56 clergy in office at the time of this Synod, 17 married. By 1886 half of the German Old Catholic clergy were married (27 of 54).[10]

A more detailed presentation of the arguments for and against compulsory clerical celibacy and of the debate's development must be omitted here for lack of space.[11] In order to place this debate within its historical context, it is good to note that the discussion of the celibacy issue within Old Catholicism forms part of the wider discussion of celibacy as it took place in the (Roman) Catholic Church, primarily in the early nineteenth century and prior to that. Since the second Lateran Synod under Pope Innocent II (1139) there has been an unaltered ecclesiastical law within the Western Church: the ordination of priests constitutes a distinct obstacle to marriage, i.e. priests cannot marry.[12] This law has not remained unchallenged, however. The Reformation was certainly the most significant attack on this law - celibacy became a point of distinction between confessions. Nevertheless, the Reformation was not the only challenge to the law. During the course of church history, movements against celibacy have come and gone - not to mention the many forms of violations of the celibacy law that existed.[13] With regard to the nineteenth century, on which this article focuses, the Roman Catholic priest Winfried Leinweber depicted in his thesis *Der Streit um den Zölibat im 19. Jahrhundert* ("The fight for celibacy in the nineteenth century") how there was extensive literature on celibacy towards the end of the eighteenth century, yet a "gradual depletion" (a *langsame(n) Erschöpfung*) of the same from the mid-nineteenth century.[14] According to Leinweber the question of celibacy "cascades over into the Old Catholic movement"; in it, many priests had found "eine praktische 'Lösung'" ("a practical solution").[15] After Leinweber, celibacy remained unquestioned within the Roman Catholic Church at the end of the nineteenth century, and it was only again 'contested' in Reform Catholicism or in the modernist movement of the early twentieth century.[16]

THE POLEMICAL GENDER DEBATE IN THE OLD CATHOLIC/ ROMAN CATHOLIC CONFLICT

Up until 1870 various streams co-existed within Catholicism, i.e. more liberal Catholics alongside ultramontanes who became a stronger force within the Roman Catholic Church after the 1850s. One effect of the First Vatican Council was that a polarization emerged, which I have termed 'internal confessionalization' in my doctoral thesis

---

[10] Cf. von Schulte, *Der Altkatholizismus*, 649.

[11] This will follow in a more extensive study.

[12] Leinweber, *Der Streit*, 3. For the text see Mirbt and Aland, *Quellen*, nr. 573, 298: ". . . statuimus, quatenus episcopi, presbyteri, diaconi, subdiaconi, regulares canonici et monachi atque conversi professi, qui sanctum transgredientes propositum, uxores sibi copulare praesumpserint, separentur. Huiusmodi namque copulationem, quam contra ecclesiasticam regulam constat esse contractam, matrimonium non essse censemus. " Mansi, *Sacrorum conciliorum*, 21, 526.

[13] See, for example: Tacke, *Wir wollen*; Flüchter, *Der Zölibat*.

[14] Leinweber, *Der Streit*, 6.

[15] Ibid.

[16] Ibid., 7.

Frauen im Prozeß der Kirchwerdung (1998).[17] I chose this term because both parties continued to regard themselves as 'Catholics':

> The First Vatican Council signified a breach, but not a complete termination of the spiritual-religious sense of belonging that [Old Catholic] men and women had to the Catholic Church.[18]

In the initial phase, the Catholics of both trends differed only a little, due to their Catholic socialization and liturgical practice. The effect of their attitudes towards the Vatican dogma, however, could be likened to a sharp sword slicing through silk. Any divergent devotions and ritual practices (e.g. devotions to the Virgin Mary) gained greater importance in the light of the differing viewpoints on the new dogma. These divergent practices became visible distinctive traits, revealing how far removed the two parties were from each other.

In the Old Catholics' view the supporters of the Vatican were blinded and loyal to the Pope to the point of utter dependence. A closer look reveals that the Old Catholics accused the ultramontane Catholics of rendering religion effeminate. The feminization of the 'enemy' is a common rhetorical strategy employed to weaken the other party.[19] In the eyes of the Old Catholics, the ultramontanes had offered no 'manly' resistance to the new dogmas but had subjugated themselves to the dogmas in an unmanly and faceless way by sacrificing their intellect (*sacrificium intellectus*). In their religious practices, too, they were perceived to behave effeminately: they fostered sweet devotions to the Sacred Heart of Jesus and to the Immaculate Heart of Mary, which would be unthinkable in Old Catholic circles. It is not surprising, then, that the Old Catholics did not only take a stand against the new Vatican dogmas, but were also vehemently against the dogma of the Immaculate Conception of Mary, which had already been pronounced by Pope Pius IX in 1854.[20] They observed, in this dogma, a forestalling of the papal claim to power, which became formalized in 1870. While it is clear from the Old Catholics' theological assertions that they rejected the Marian dogma for biblical, ecclesiological and tradition-related reasons, the Old Catholic press shows that their critique went well beyond the purely theological level and that, on top of everything, the dogma was regarded as the focal point of ultramontane devotion.

Marian apparitions, such as in Marpingen and elsewhere, added fuel to the fire for Old Catholic authors. In 1876, Mary appeared to three eight year-old girls in Mar-

---

[17] Berlis, *Frauen im Prozeß*, 570.

[18] "Das Erste Vatikanum bedeutete einen Bruch im, aber keine völlige Unterbrechung des geistig-religiösen Zugehörigkeitsgefühls der [alt-katholischen] Frauen und Männer zur Katholischen Kirche". Berlis, *Frauen im Prozeß*, 632.

[19] The foundation for this lies in the concept of binary opposition. Thus socially marginalized sections of the population were "häufig als effeminiert bezeichnet, weil dadurch ihre benachteiligte gesellschaftliche Position zementiert werden konnte" (often described as effeminate, in order to confirm their disadvantaged social position). Hödl regards the portrayal of others as effeminate as part of a discrimination strategy. The criteria for femininization were variable. Cf. Hödl, "Performative Beiträge", 142-143. See also Boyarin, *Unheroic Conduct*, 271-312.

[20] This concerns the doctrine that Mary had been conceived by her mother without original sin. On the Old Catholic response cf. my article: Berlis, "Maria".

pingen, a village in the Saarland region.[21] The apparition strongly resembled the one in Lourdes (1858).[22] Soon Marpingen was described as 'the German Lourdes'. For a few years, masses of pilgrims travelled to the place. In his important study of this event, British historian David Blackbourn has indicated the *Kulturkampf* as a background to this. The Old Catholic press at the time (similarly to the Evangelical press) reacted sharply against it and simply dismissed such apparitions as superstition and *Muttergottesschwindel* ["Mother of God spin"].[23]

This type of Marian devotion with its stock of passive metaphors and its theological appeals for atonement was befitting of the societal roles attributed to women.

The Old Catholics disassociated themselves from ultramontane Catholicism in all its expressions.[24] Women, thereby, at times became the personification of that from which male Old Catholics wished to distance themselves. This is clear from a closer study of the first three Old Catholic Congresses (1871-1873). Women were excluded from participating at these congresses.[25] An analysis of the congress reports, however, reveals that, though women were physically absent, they were very much present in examples or metaphors.[26] For many speakers at the congresses there was nothing worse than the ultramontane woman who, in the confessional, was entirely dependent on the priest, thereby relinquishing her entire family to ultramontanism. Women were regarded here as the instrument of the Roman Catholic clergy - this was an utterly prevalent image in liberal middle-class circles and was argued, for example, by the French writer Jules Michelet in his book *Du prêtre, de la femme, de la famille*, which was translated into several languages.[27]

However, attempts were also made in Roman Catholic polemics to devalue the Old Catholic movement by using women. Women were made the measure for the Old Catholics' lack of piety (from an ultramontane perspective). At one point, for instance, it is pointed out that there were Old Catholic women who would rather read the illustrated family paper *Die Gartenlaube*[28] (Garden Shed) than go to confession or

---

[21] On Marpingen, see: Blackbourn, *Marpingen*.

[22] See Harris, *Lourdes*.

[23] *Katholische Blätter. Organ des Schweizerischen Vereins freisinniger Katholiken*, 4 (1876), 247 ("Muttergottesschwindel") and 5 (1877), 5.

[24] This is demonstrated by the numerous Old Catholic publications on the theme, cf. for example Goetz, *Der Ultramontanismus*.

[25] According to current law, women were not permitted to take part in meetings that were termed 'political'. In 1871 the situation in Munich was very tense, as a result of which the preparation committee decided to exclude women from participating in the congress. This decision, incidentally, was not undisputed, as it was understood that it would eliminate the possibility to inform women of Old Catholic aims and interests. This precautionary measure served to pre-empt dissolution of the congress, which would certainly have been sought by the ultramontane side. After the Munich congress, lectures on the Old Catholic movement were held especially for women. Cf. Berlis, *Frauen im Prozeß*, 257-264; for the ultramontane reaction to this, see ibid., 356.

[26] Ibid., 319-370.

[27] Cf. Michelet, *Du prêtre*.

[28] This weekly newspaper, which was founded by the radical liberal Ernst Keil in 1853, was intended for a middle-class readership and reflects the middle-class code of norms and values. In the era of the *Kulturkampf*, the paper supported the Prussian politics. Therefore it is not surprising that the *Gartenlaube* was reviewed as follows by the ultramontane press: "There can hardly be any other paper that combats Christianity so energetically and that has such intense hatred of the

take the sacraments:[29] according to Roman Catholic polemics, Old Catholic women presented themselves more as middle-class liberal rather than strict Catholic.[30]

Closer study has shown that these images of each other were only a limited representation of reality - reality, of course, revealed a much wider spectrum of religious practices. For example, in 1874 the first Old Catholic Synod had prepared a commentary on auricular confession, aimed against abuse of this practice. The ultramontane press immediately regarded this as an abolition of the sacrament of penance.[31] However, many Old Catholic women in the Rhineland continued, as evidenced, to go to confession just as they had previously done (the case was different in the liberal Grand Duchy of Baden). Such statements, especially those with a polemical background, must be seen as belonging to the discourse of disassociation and of masculinity which aided the shaping and founding of one's own identity.[32]

This short exposition shows that Roman Catholic and Old Catholic men were in agreement on one point: both groups were of the assumption that, on a religious level, women were able to influence their husbands and other family members. On both sides, however, women were exploited. On the one hand, a woman was regarded less as an independent agent, and more as an 'instrument' being used by a third party. On the other hand, each group would involve and include 'good' women in parallel to the women of the other side who were thus defamed as 'bad', and they would thereby domesticate these women (by binding them to their own group's code of conduct). The distinction between 'good' and 'bad' is thus accompanied by a code of behaviour against which not only 'bad women' are held to account, but also 'good women'.

The conflict between Old Catholics and Roman Catholics following the First Vatican Council took place amidst the period of the *Kulturkampf*. A few years ago

Catholic Church" [Original: "Es gibt kaum ein zweites Blatt, welches das Christenthum so energisch bekämpft, die katholische Kirche so intensiv haßt."]. *Deutsche Reichs-Zeitung*, 7 (31 March 1878), nr. 89. The editor of the *Gartenlaube* published, in return, a few reports on critiques from ecclesial (not only ultramontane, but also orthodox-Protestant) circles of the *Gartenlaube*. In the eyes of its critics the content of the *Gartenlaube* was a 'fine poison' (*feines Gift*), which was "not suitable for a Christian housewife". See *Gartenlaube*, (1873), 738.

[29] See Berlis, *Frauen im Prozeß*, 355. The *Gartenlaube* of 1874 includes poems and images that take up the theme of "Women and confession". See *Gartenlaube*, (1874), 150-151 ("Am Beichtstuhl") and ibid., 398-399 ("Gang zur Beichte"). It appears that ultramontane authors also read the *Gartenlaube*, as they knew about church critique (of the Roman Catholic Church) that was found within. Old Catholics such as Döllinger (see above, note 9) or Loyson (see below, note 42), however, had good press coverage in the *Gartenlaube*. Cf. *Gartenlaube*, (1870), 144 (Döllinger) and (1869), 715-716; (1872), 668 (Loyson).

[30] The German word for 'strict Catholic' is *strengkirchlich*, which indicates an ultramontane ecclesiastical viewpoint.

[31] Cf. *Beschlüsse*, 50-53. The Synod strictly maintained the sacrament of penance, but at the same time named the abortive developments in the practice of auricular confession, such as renewed confession of sins at a repeated confession (the so-called devotion confession) and the practice of questioning by the father confessor. The Synod, instead, maintained that believers should be led "nach ihrem eigenen Gewissen zu handeln" ["to act according to their own conscience"] (ibid., 51). The Synod explicitly emphasized the importance of accounting for the various individual needs and situations (ibid., 53). See also Berlis, *Frauen im Prozeß*, 337-342.

[32] See the contribution by Stobbe who, however, disregards the aspect of the masculinity debate: "Konflikte um Identität".

Michael Gross identified the centrality of gender in the *Kulturkampf*. He pointed out that leading liberal politicians regarded the Roman Catholic Church as female and the State as male.[33] Gross claims that a huge fear of women and of the women's movement plays a role in the background of the *Kulturkampf*, especially the fear of their presence in the public realm or in public debate.[34] However, in his interesting book Gross has overlooked the fact that there was a discussion not only *between* (political) liberals and the Roman Catholic Church, but also *within* Catholicism itself. It was not Catholicism itself that was regarded as feminized, rather Roman, ultramontane Catholicism. Old Catholics and liberals agreed on this interpretation (many male Old Catholics, incidentally, were members of the national-liberal party). The gendered rhetoric, which according to Gross was typical of *Kulturkampf* rhetoric, is also partly found in the conflict between Old and Roman Catholics. One can conclude that the gender discourse serves the mutual differentiation of various groups from each other, also of groups within Catholicism.

Masculinity is defined, or distinguished, in relation to women.[35] The construct of masculinity helps to express, accentuate and structurally anchor the distinctions *between* the genders. The following will take a further look at the distinctions and disassociations *within* a gender by discussing the masculinity discourse and perception of the priesthood as reflected in two popular texts with polemical undertones. These texts, both originating from the 1870s, do not focus on the theological perspective of the priesthood; rather they reflect the people's perception and expectations of Catholic priests. The one text is written from a Roman Catholic, the other from an Old Catholic perspective.

THE MASCULINITY DISCOURSE AND PERCEPTION OF THE PRIESTHOOD

In 1873 the narrative *Priesterthum oder Hochzeit?* (Priesthood or marriage?) by A. Franke was published as the first in a series entitled "Der Zeitgeist: beleuchtet für das katholische Volk" ("The spirit of the age: clarified for the Catholic people").[36] No further details could be found on the author, who was presumably resident in Bavaria.[37] His narrative was addressed to "the Catholic people", for whom this "contribution to an understanding of several contemporary questions" (as it was subtitled) was written.[38] The story takes place in a public house in a small, rural town, where various

[33] Cf. Gross, *The War Against Catholicism*. Gross refers here to the professor of Roman law and representative of the German Protestant Union, Johann Kaspar Bluntschli (1808-1881). Bluntschli pointed out that in modern European languages, the Church is grammatically feminine whereas the State is grammatically masculine (cf. ibid., 201).

[34] See Planert, *Antifeminismus*.

[35] This signifies the concept of hegemonic masculinity. See Connell, *Masculinities*. Cf. the seminal discussion by Dinges, "Hegemoniale Männlichkeit".

[36] Franke, *Priesterthum oder Hochzeit?*

[37] He did write a further text in the above series: Franke, *Nicht nach Canossa!*

[38] The other narratives in this series also deal with current issues or events in the time of the *Kulturkampf*, e.g. von Schaching, *Ein gefangener Bischof*; Frei, *Clara*. Twelve issues were found in the library catalogue (*Karlsruher Virtueller Katalog*).

gentlemen fall into discussion at the table, whilst an extensive Marian procession passes by in the street outside. The little town is a place of pilgrimage in Bavaria and it is the eve of the festival of Mary's birth (8 September). The gentlemen exchange the hopes they had initially placed in the Old Catholic movement and its most important leaders. Those that are named are:[39] Ignaz von Döllinger, Johann Friedrich[40], Friedrich Michelis[41], Père Hyacinthe Loyson[42] and Alois Anton[43]. A civil servant, who is a proponent of the ultramontane position and of the Roman Catholic people and who, in the course of the discussion, will persuade his fellow drinking partners of his conviction, brings his critique to the following point: the Old Catholics speak of infallibility but their concern thereby is actually about marriage.[44] The civil servant tries to demonstrate that the Old Catholics are not only against the dogmas of 1870, but are also fighting against "the inner essence of Catholicism".[45] As 'evidence' he points to the Old Catholic critique of the dogma of the Immaculate Conception (1854) (for him this is apparently part of the essence of Catholicism!) and uses this critique against them. Whoever dares "to rip out a single jewel from the crown of God's mother" will turn the people against him: "It is especially here that our people's feelings are so heartfelt and true as they will always recognize a false belief with utmost certainty, if it dares to involve the Lord's mother".[46] Criticism of Mary, criticism of papal infallibility – in this civil servant's eyes the Old Catholics are teachers of false doctrine. His further criticism is directed against the Old Catholic clergy whom he regards as irresponsible, practically faithless priests.[47] This is demonstrated by the Old Catholic clergy's alleged "addiction to women" (*Weibersucht*[48]): "They wanted to have women or they

---

[39] The choice of names indicates a focus on the southern German (esp. Bavarian) and Austrian context of the text. Prominent personalities from Rhineland are not named. Friedrich Michelis, who is mentioned, is the only leader from the north, though he was known to be an itinerant preacher. The Frenchman Loyson often spent time in Munich in the early 1870s and had attended the Old Catholic congress at Constance in 1873.

[40] Johann Friedrich (1836-1917) was professor of church history in Munich from 1872 and later professor in Bern, Berlis, *Frauen im Prozeß*, 111. At the Cologne congress in 1872 Friedrich had spoken out against adopting the abolition of celibacy into the resolutions. He remained unmarried and an opponent of marriage for priests until his death.

[41] Friedrich Michelis (1815-1886), professor of philosophy in Braunsberg, Old Catholic vicar in Freiburg: Ibid., 103.

[42] Charles (Hyacinthe) Loyson (1827-1912), former Carmelite, Old Catholic vicar in Geneva, founder of the Église catholique gallicane in France: Ibid., 204. In 1872, he married Emilie James, daughter of Mr. Amory Butterfield, widow of Edwin Ruthwen Meriman.

[43] Alois Anton (1822-1878), Old Catholic vicar in Vienna, pioneer of the Old Catholic movement in Austria: Ibid., 122. In 1874 he married his long-term girlfriend Anna Srnec. Cf. Nippold, *Die Einführung*, vol. 3, 390.

[44] Franke, *Priesterthum oder Hochzeit?*, 10, 11 ff.

[45] Franke, *Priesterthum oder Hochzeit?*, 14: "das innere Wesen des Katholizismus".

[46] Ibid., 17. "Ich bin der Ueberzeugung, daß wir beim katholischen Volke sehr schief ankommen, wenn wir es wagen, einen einzigen Edelstein aus der Krone der Gottesmutter herauszureißen. Gerade darin fühlt unser Volk so tief innig und wahr, daß es eine Irrlehre am sichersten immer dann erkennt, wenn sie an die Mutter des Herrn sich wagt."

[47] Ibid., 14.

[48] The German *Weib* has more derogative connotations than 'woman'.

wished to cover up their earlier wrongdoings in the new apostolate."[49] In short, "Old Catholicism is and remains skirt hunting of the dirtiest kind"; it is concerned more with petticoats than with theology.[50]

Even the Munich church historian and *spiritus rector* of the Old Catholic movement, Ignaz von Döllinger, does not escape criticism. Döllinger was a known opponent of the abolition of celibacy and the civil servant cannot claim that he would have violated the vow of celibacy.[51] Nevertheless, Döllinger becomes - probably because of his important role within Old Catholicism - a target too. Döllinger is placed in the proximity of women, who are always termed pejoratively as *Weiber* in the narrative: He is depicted as a "woman's theologian" (*Weibertheolog*) and has developed "his theological opinions in the presence of wenches".[52] Döllinger's conversational partners are no longer men such as Johann Adam Möhler, Joseph Görres or Ernst von Lasaulx (famous Catholics of the time, all deceased by then)[53], but crazy women in private conventicles (*Privatzirkeln*[54]). Döllinger in fact is not only placed here in the proximity of women, but is also transferred from the public sphere into the private sphere.

These feminized Old Catholic priests, who do not even appear priestly in their behaviour or their clothing, are contrasted in the narrative with the men of the gentlemen's circle, especially the civil servant, who are true men, full of "manly convictions and manly deeds".[55]

At the end all gentlemen return to Roman Catholicism, the last one while standing before a statue of Mary at the entrance to his home. It is clear to readers of this narrative that it is, in the end, Mary who calls the men home from their 'false' Old Catholic ways. The claim is clearly made that the thousands of pilgrims outside must be considered "our people's response to the Old Catholic movement".[56] Finally, the civil servant, despite his attraction to the daughter of one of the gentlemen, chooses the path of priesthood.

In summary: the construction of masculinity within a gender group occurs likewise by disassociation from other men who do not belong to the same group. With regard to priests, this differentiation is made visible in their relationship to women (sexual or not). In short: a "be-womaned priest" (*beweibter Priester*) can no longer be a real priest.

---

[49] Ibid., 22. "Weiber wollten sie haben oder ihr früheres schlechtes Leben durch das neue Apostolat decken."

[50] Ibid. Der "Altkatholizismus ist und bleibt eine Weibergeschichte der schmutzigsten Art".

[51] On Döllinger's attitude see: Berlis, "Seelensorge".

[52] Franke, *Priesterthum oder Hochzeit?*, 23. About Döllinger the civil agent says: "daß er in seinen alten Tagen gewissermaßen ein Weibertheolog geworden ist; daß er während der letzten Jahre in Privatzirkeln sich darin gefiel, in Gesellschaft von Weibern seine theologischen Ansichten zu entwickeln. Man muß diese überspannten und verrückten Weiber kennen gelernt haben, um es zu wissen, wie sie sich des gelehrten Freundes annahmen; man muß sich erinnern, wie sie am Tage seiner Excommunikation ganze Körbe von Blumenbouquets in sein Zimmer schleppten. Ich glaube, daß Döllinger vor seinen Weibern sich viel mehr genirt hat, seinen Irrthum zu widerrufen, als vor dem Papste."

[53] All who are mentioned belonged to the famous *Görreskreis* in Munich, the circle around the historian and political commentator, Joseph Görres (1776-1848), an important representative of German political Catholicism.

[54] See note 52.

[55] Ibid., 27. "Mannesueberzeugung und Mannesthat".

[56] Ibid., 12.

The second example, which I would like to expand on here, comes from an Old Catholic author. It is the *Denkschrift des Propstes von Mogilno* (Memoir of the Provost of Mogilno) by Josaphat Sylvester Suszczynski (* 1827)[57], which appeared in 1876 at the height of the Old Catholic debate on celibacy. In this *Memoir* the author presents the reasons for his marriage. Suszczynski's change of direction towards the Old Catholic bishopric caused a great sensation due to his high ecclesial position. He had already married Anna Rosalie von Gajewska in 1875.[58]

In contrast to Franke's narrative, this concerns personal, autobiographical reflections of the former provost, in justification of his move. Suszczynski goes on the assumption that "in general, the clergy will only become independent of the hierarchy, when the clergyman becomes a *complete man*."[59] The man has a right to marry. For Suszczynski, the virtues of the husband are conceivable for a clerical husband: "the sacrificial dedication to one's kin, the faithful practice of domestic duties, the mutual loyalty, honour and love".[60] True heroism "of selfless devotion to the church" is not only demonstrated in the renunciation of marriage. Suszczynski claims it is also found in "confronting immoral prejudice with all one's strength and by combating the superstitious belief of the masses in the semi-magical character of the priesthood with regard to celibacy."[61] Suszczynski also makes a plea for achieving "male freedom" in the area of overcoming clerical celibacy. The realization also became accepted among the people that "a righteous priest's marriage is better than such a Holy Joe cleric's life!"[62] Suszczynski regarded a Holy Joe cleric (in German: *Pfaffe*) as a "shepherd of souls, concerned only with himself", while in his eyes a priest was a shepherd "who devotes himself to the good of souls."[63]

Suszczynski is concerned that priests should learn to "regard themselves as free, complete men, who voluntarily enforce the gravity of their duties towards the church community by taking on the great responsibility of family duties."[64] The opposite is the alleged freedom of the Roman Catholic priest with his "artificially cold flame of a monk's zeal", the "blind allegiance to church laws and church hierarchy".[65] In contrast, the Old Catholic priest presided over the church community "not only in the

[57] Suszczynski, *Denkschrift*.
[58] The church marriage was consecrated by the Old Catholic parish priest Johannes Matthias Watterich on 19 September 1875 in Basel (Switzerland). Cf. *Katholische Blätter*, 3 (1875), 40, 318.
[59] Suszczynski, *Denkschrift*, 6: "Selbstständig aber wird der Clerus gegenüber der Hierarchie im Allgemeinen nur, wenn der Geistliche ein *voller Mann* wird."
[60] Suszczynski, *Denkschrift*, 6: "die opfervolle Hingabe für die Seinen, die treue Uebung der häuslichen Pflichten, die gegenseitige Treue, Ehre und Liebe".
[61] Ibid., 33: "einem unsittlichen Vorurtheil mit aller Kraft entgegentritt und den Aberglauben der Menge an den halb magischen Charakter des Priesterthums in Bezug auf Ehelosigkeit bekämpft."
[62] Ibid., 35: "besser eine rechtschaffene Priesterehe als solch ein Pfaffenleben!"
[63] Ibid., 5, note: A Holy Joe Cleric is "der auf sich allein bedachte Seelenhirte", a priest is "der für das Wohl der Seelen sich hingebende" shepherd.
[64] Ibid., 38: "als freie, volle Männer betrachten [zu] lernen, die sich den Ernst ihrer Berufspflichten gegen die Gemeinde freiwillig noch durch die so schwer verantwortliche Uebernahme von Familienpflichten verstärken."
[65] Ibid., 38: "Er unterhält im besten Falle in sich das künstlich kalte Feuer der Mönchsbegeisterung, … die ihm den blinden Gehorsam gegen die Kirchengesetze und Kirchenoberen als das Ideal der christlichen Vollkommenheit erscheinen läßt".

spirit of a true father", but also committed himself "in a special covenant of loyalty to wife and child" and faithfully fulfilled "the full duties of a man as any other in the community".[66] The relationship between priest and community also differs: whereas in Roman Catholicism the bishop's favour on the priest counts for more than the favour of the congregation, and the church members are regarded as sheep, in Old Catholicism the "marriage between pastor and congregation" is shaped by the equality of lay and clergy.

As the historian Martina Kessel has demonstrated, Germany of the nineteenth century is permeated by this longing for the 'complete man'.[67] The integration of sensitivity, passion, a sense of community and an ability to love are requested of such a 'complete' man, i.e. a combination of 'female' and 'male' aptitudes, in the private and public realm. Sexuality was also part of a 'real' man.[68] As we saw with Suszczynski, the 'Holy Joe cleric' is regarded as an egocentric shepherd of souls, while the priest is the shepherd who cares for others, has fatherly traits and proves himself a 'complete man' in all aspects of life - in his relationships with the church community, with the bishop and in family life. With respect to this characterization the priest or Holy Joe cleric is not only characterized in terms of pastoral care, but also in terms of manhood.

The sharp distinction between 'priest' and 'Holy Joe cleric' (*Pfaffe*) is also found in texts of other Old Catholics, for example in one of the most influential texts during the Old Catholic debate on celibacy, published by the Old Catholic lay leader Johann Friedrich von Schulte in the same year as Suszczynski's *Denkschrift*.[69]

To further clarify the polemical distinction between *Pfaffe* and 'priest' the following observation by Róisín Healy may be of assistance. She recently drew attention to the fact that the polemic against certain Orders, in particular against the Jesuits (a polemic which as it happens was also commonly found in German Old Catholicism), was not least connected to the fact that the Jesuits were regarded as androgynous.[70] On the one hand, a Jesuit was a man of deeds, feared by others; on the other hand, a Jesuit

---

[66] Ibid., 38-39: "Der junge altkatholische Priester vielmehr gewöhne sich vor Allem an die Idee, dass er einst nicht blos der Gemeinde im Geiste eines wahren Vaters vorstehen, sondern sich auch noch durch ein specielles Band der Treue an Weib und Kind binden und die die vollen Pflichten des Mannes *wie jeder andere in der Gemeinde* treu erfüllen wolle".

[67] Kessel, "The 'Whole' Man". She speaks about the "ganzer Mann (the whole, well-rounded, but also 'real' or 'proper' man)", ibid., 2.

[68] Ibid., 8-11.

[69] See von Schulte, *Der Cölibatszwang*, 96. Schulte's text is a treatise concerning church law and history, in which the masculinity discourse is raised in a far less direct way than in, for example, Susczynski. Schulte's view on the relationship of priest and pastor completes Susczynski's account. Schulte expressed his hope that "nicht das Priesterthum, wohl hoffentlich aber das Pfaffenthum" ["not priesthood as such, but hopefully Holy Joe clericalism"] would stand and fall with celibacy (ibid.). With this he meant that clergy were accustomed to "als eine höhere, zum Herrschen bestimmte Menschenklasse zu betrachten" ["regard themselves as a higher class of people who were meant to rule"] who considered the foundation of the family, church community and the state as an annoyance to be suffered (ibid.). For real church reform, the priest should "wieder als Mensch, Bürger, Patriot fühle[n]" ["once again feel himself to be a human, citizen, patriot"] (ibid.). For Schulte's position in the discussion of celibacy see: Berlis, "Johann Friedrich von Schultes Stellung".

[70] Cf. Healy, "Anti-Jesuitism in Imperial Germany"; Id., *The Jesuit Specter in Imperial Germany*.

was also perceived to be a slave subjugated to papal authority: "it was the Jesuit's ambiguous sexual identity that made him seem particularly threatening".[71]

In reference to the views of 'Holy Joe cleric' and 'priest' it should then be noted that the Holy Joe cleric is not a real man (he is more androgynous, which was perceived negatively in the nineteenth century), whereas the priest who practices his job in all freedom and with care is a real man. If he is able, in addition, to practice care privately, he is even more of a real man.

What can be concluded from these two texts by Franke and Suszczynski with regard to the gendering, the feminization, of the opposing party? In the ultramontane discourse mentioned above, the non-celibate priest is associated with the female world and is, thereby, infected by the feminine (feminized). In the Old Catholic discourse mentioned above the non-celibate priest becomes the symbol of real manhood, with all male virtues (including freedom, loyalty and courage, as well as care for the weak, etc.).

SIX THESES AND SUGGESTIONS FOR FURTHER RESEARCH

1. British historian Hugh McLeod speaks of the feminization of religion as a result of men abandoning the church.[72] Catholic laymen had rejected other (clerical) men's claims to have authority over them.[73] It is perhaps the legally-rooted responsibility of Old Catholic laypersons[74] at all levels of church leadership, from parish to diocese, that offers an explanation and that provided a safeguard against a potential exodus of men from the Old Catholic church.

The strong presence of men in the public debate around the First Vatican Council shows that they very much felt responsible for religion and religious questions and apparently saw it as a 'male' duty to lead the religious-theological battle against ultramontanism.[75] One of the weapons used on both sides was feminization and defamation of the opponent and the masculinization of the own side to prove its superiority.

[71] Id., "Anti-Jesuitism in Imperial Germany", 163.

[72] The theory of the feminization of religion was first put forward by American Barbara Welter and has, in recent years, been adapted critically for European Christianity as well. Cf. for example Schneider, "Feminisierung der Religion". Schneider points out, among other things, that there is a need for more precision of what is meant: feminization of church staff, feminization of believers (and of voluntary work), feminization of piety, discursive feminization. Cf. also the recently published overview by Van Osselaer and Buerman, "Feminization Thesis".

[73] McLeod, "Weibliche Frömmigkeit".

[74] In fact, laymen, since women were only given the active and passive right to vote in the German Old Catholic Church from 1920.

[75] After the end of the *Kulturkampf*, from the 1880s onwards a "familiarization" of Old Catholic parishes took place (cf. Berlis, *Frauen im Prozeß*, 631-634). Women created their own space in which they contributed to parish life (women's associations). As they remained within contemporary gender roles, these actions did not bring about any role conflicts and therefore did not question the leading public role of men (cf. ibid., 633). It was only at the start of the twentieth century that this changed to a greater extent as women began to demand more co-responsibility on a parish level and eventually from 1920 made their entrance into parish leadership (from the mid-1960s into leadership on a diocesan level). Cf. Berlis, "Der Bund".

2. In the conflict between Old Catholics and Roman Catholics a number of differing notions and expectations of the office bearer were at stake. The central significance of the priest is not surprising, since the Catholic understanding is that a congregation can only be regarded as Catholic in the fullest sense if it has a priest (who is under a bishop) to preside at the Eucharist. Besides this more theological view, a discussion took place, more or less explicitly, about what constitutes real masculinity and manhood and in what way the priest is a real man. The discussion of celibacy can therefore be regarded as an expression of a masculinity discourse. This contribution has shown that each party itself made claim to this masculinity, though with differing arguments and by differentiating itself from the opposing party. The ultramontane party defined Old Catholic priests as "addicted to women"; it can thus be concluded that they reasoned the masculinity of the celibate priest on the basis of his distance from women (including his male sacrificial readiness etc.). The Old Catholics, on the other hand, perceived the ultramontane celibate priests as 'feminized' due to their dependence on Rome, whereas they considered resistance against Rome to be manly.[76] At the same time the Old Catholics had the task of integrating new aspects – the priest's position as husband and father – as consistent with priesthood, into the traditional Catholic perception of the priest.

3. The discussion of celibacy became part of the discussion of the perception of priesthood – this incidentally not only pertained to the Old Catholic debate, but also to the entire nineteenth century.[77] The Old Catholic notion of priesthood reflects an ideal that simultaneously contains a contrasting image, from which the Old Catholics differentiated themselves: the priest was attributed a role in educating the people (against superstition) and was to be the "doctor of the soul", not "someone who scouts out family relations, or a political schemer".[78] The Old Catholic image of the priest, as is described at Synods and Congresses, and in the publications of laypersons and clergy, also includes the contemporary prevalent values and world views of men and manhood, partly inherited from the Enlightenment, partly bourgeois-liberal.[79]

4. That the discussion of celibacy took place amidst the polemical atmosphere of the post-Vatican council's ecclesiastical debates and during the *Kulturkampf* may

[76] This is, incidentally, where gender and national discourse coincide, since Rome is not only observed to be a religious centre but also a foreign power. Roman Catholics were often (especially during the *Kulturkampf*) regarded according to the stereotype of "traitors to the fatherland" ("Reichsfeinde"). For a recent critical study see Dowe, *Auch Bildungsbürger*.

[77] See for this Leinweber, *Der Streit*, 393-431.

[78] This concerns a quote from a speech by Director Streng from Nuremberg, held at the 2nd public convention at the fourth Old Catholic congress (1874), where the speaker deals with the role of the priest at confession: the priest as "Arzt der Seele", not as "Auskundschafter von Familienverhältnissen und nicht ein politischer Intrigant". *Der vierte Altkatholiken-Congress*, 129.

[79] Incidentally, the external appearance of a priest also plays a role. For example, the 2nd Catholic (= Old Catholic) Synod of the Bern canton (Switzerland) in 1875 discussed the clergy's apparel. The liturgical vestments used for mass were not a problem. However, the Synod responding to one priest's request, declared a formal prohibition against wearing a cassock: "das unschöne *weibische Gewand*" ["the ugly *effeminate robe*"]. *Katholische Blätter*, 3 (1875), 43, 339-340. It would, furthermore, be interesting to relate the question of the differing forms of Marian devotion which were only briefly mentioned in this article more clearly with the perception of priesthood. Cf. further available studies for England: Engelhardt Herringer, "Victorian Masculinity"; Id., *Victorians*.

explain the severity of the confrontations. The reason why such significance was apportioned to this church disciplinary (and therefore resolvable according to simple canon law) issue only becomes clear, however, when it is understood that the discussion took place at an historical interface where differing opinions of the priest's relationship to ecclesial and state authority, differing perspectives on the role of modern science and the relationship to modernity collided. The gendering of the opposing party was an effective method of putting the opponent in his place, dismissing his views and even propagating varyingly gendered Catholicisms.

5. To start with we examined the historical insights gained from polemical texts and those gained from applying the gender perspective. The results can be divided on several levels.

In terms of methodology, the involvement of the gender perspective implies extending the perspectives with a new approach to the question. This has shown how fruitful it is to take a closer look at the use of 'feminization' or 'masculinization' as a tool for differentiation or even defamation, especially in situations of polemical debate. The question must always be asked as to who assigns whom which position, with which aim in the gender debate, and which contemporary connotations of masculinity and femininity play a role in this.

In terms of content, a new understanding of historical circumstances and interpretations of values are gained. Reviewing polemical statements and applying the gender perspective lead to an approach that, in any polarization, takes its starting point from the interrelation of the 'adversaries', rather than from their separation. On the one hand this means that Old Catholicism and Roman Catholicism are still perceived in their centrifugal and centripetal force fields, in which so-called attraction and repulsion can be explained as two sides of the same coin. These, then, no longer remain stuck on the expressions "We have *no* pope, *no* Mary, *no* celibacy...", which are so frequently heard on the Old Catholic side. Instead they allow us to recognize temporary models of response and behaviour that are today - within our different historical context - historically outdated. Placing a reform within its historical context and reviewing the polemical aspects of history can lead to a new awareness of a reform's essence whereby any polemic or disassociation loses emphasis. In the interdenominational discourse a historical contextualization of this kind could lead to a new valuation of certain issues that have, since long ago, been highly explosive. It could be a contribution to the purification or reconciliation of memory.

6. It is striking, that in a purely theological argument for and against clerical celibacy a gender discourse as the one discussed above is much more difficult to trace and to determine.[80] How can we explain this? It should be assumed that the gender discourse also plays a part in theological discourse on clerical celibacy, though in a more subtle way. It is probably the situation of conflict, the altercation that promotes gender discourse and uncovers it even in its caricatured expressions.

The inclusion of Roman Catholic and Old Catholic sources, historical interpretations, and perspectives in the study of Catholicism can, through comparative studies at least, shed great light on the importance of the gender discourse for the historical and contemporary character of religious traditions.

---

[80] See my inaugural lecture: Berlis, *Vergelijking*, 24.

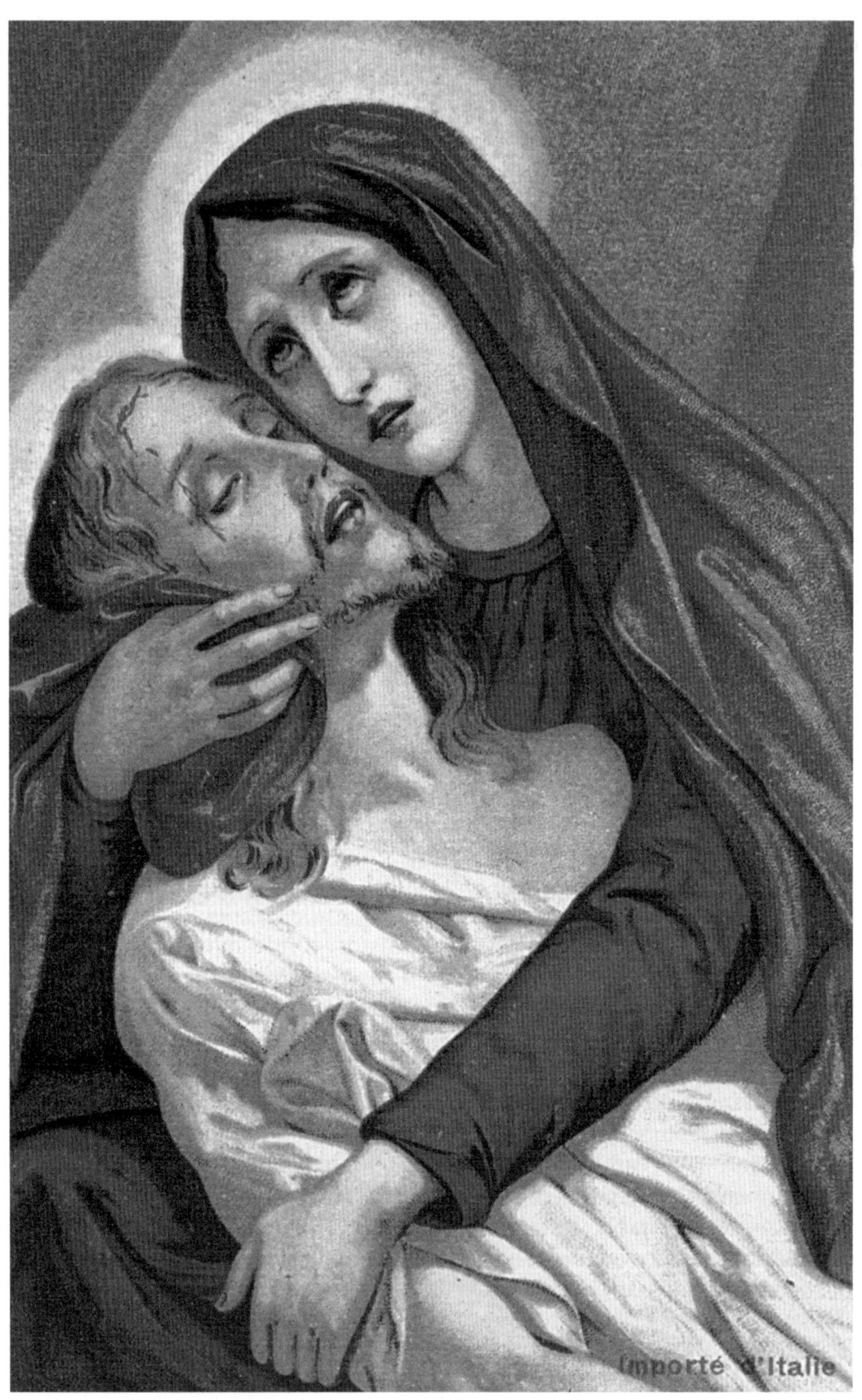

Devotional image of Our Lady and Jesus, imported from Italy, c 1900.
[Louvain, KADOC-KU Leuven]

THE CULT OF THE VIRGIN MARY, OR THE FEMINIZATION OF THE MALE ELEMENT IN THE ROMAN CATHOLIC CHURCH?

A PSYCHO-HISTORICAL HYPOTHESIS

JAN ART

If one extends Freud's ideas beyond the point where he himself drew the line, it may be said that to indulge in the study of history means to enter into a rivalry with past generations that have drawn the veil of secrecy over so many happenings that, nonetheless, have managed to exert their influence upon our minds.[1]

One of the clearest indicators of the expanding influence of the female element within Roman Catholic worship during the nineteenth century and the preconciliary twentieth century is the growing significance of the devotion offered to the Blessed Virgin Mary. The French historian Etienne Fouilloux points out that, as of circa 1850, there appear in the manifestations of piety clear Christocentric tendencies wherein, initially, the focus rests primarily either on the child Jesus or on Jesus Crucified, and, as of the twentieth century, likewise on the Sacred Heart, Christ the King, and the Consecrated Host. But surpassing all is the devotion offered to the Holy Mary that reached its pinnacle sometime during the first half of the twentieth century. One can only observe, says Fouilloux, that women, denied the priesthood, may find *una compensazione* in the figure of Mary, to whom are being assigned ever more attributes that, in the past, were the privileges of her son.[2] This increasing importance of Mary is evident not only in the pronouncements of the doctrinal authority, starting with the dogma of the Immaculate Conception in 1854 and that of the Assumption one century

---

[1] Vandermeersch and Westerink, *Godsdienstpsychologie*, 195.

[2] "Non si puo in effetti que sottolineare la convergenza tra pressione mariana e femminilizzazione del catolicesimo, di cui la prima parte del XX secolo segne egualmente l'apogeo: escluse dal sazerdotio [...] molte donne trovano una compensazione di qualche valore nella progressive attribuzione a Maria di tutti i poteri di suo figlio": Fouilloux, "Le due vie", 311. That the worship of the Blessed Mary may be seen as the index of the feminization within the Catholic Church was already pointed out in 1950 by Miegge, *La Vergine Maria*.

later, from the accredited epiphanies, the popular pilgrimage places, the countless congregations and devout associations that have made her name part of their title,[3] but also from the numerous publications about, and representations of, the mother of Jesus. When Savart discusses the devotional literature in France, he starts out with works dedicated to Mary: "if, paradoxically, we begin with Marian devotion, and not with those addressing themselves to Christ, the former is by far the premier *dévotion particulière* by the number of works whose publication it has involved". When he analyses a representative sampling of such publications, he can only draw the conclusion that "we almost see a transfer of divinity".[4] Likewise, the Belgian historian Jean Pirotte notes that amongst the 1131 devotional prints he analysed, some twenty-five percent were dedicated to Mary, one-third to Christ, and a mere half percent to God.[5] Mother and Son clearly leave the Father and the Holy Spirit far behind ... or should we, like Fouilloux, speak of Mary as "una specie di quarta persona della Trinità" - that is, a kind of fourth presence within the Trinity?[6]

Whoever can find an explanation for this steady advance of Mary worship will likewise immediately come upon some of the causes of the feminization of the Catholic Church. Even if one confines oneself to the literature that deals with the period following the Council of Trent, a brief exploration will already spawn a host of likely motivations: Mary becomes one of the driving forces of the Counter-Reformation and is strongly propagated by the Jesuits in their battle against Protestantism and, later on, Jansenism; Mary has long been the object of popular religious worship and the church hierarchy in the nineteenth century will therefore not hesitate to take advantage of her popularity to the benefit of ultramontanism; epiphanies and miracles constitute 'proof' that rationalism and science are not the end of all things and that the supernatural does, in fact, exist; the Catholic Church will take advantage of this devotion to Mary in order to reinforce and enhance its influence and power, sometimes aided in this by governments that consider her an instrument for social control and the impetus towards the forming of a national identity; the figure of Mary is represented in a certain manner and propagated as the paradigm of the ideal female in order to support the patriarchal dominance[7]... all plausible and *rationally* argued incidences that, nonetheless, tend to ignore one important fact. The remarkable aspect of this phenomenon, which as of the years 1930 will also - once again - run

---

[3] De Fiores, "Marie (sainte vierge)".
[4] Savart, *Les catholiques*, 592, 609.
[5] Pirotte, "Le paradis", 83: during the period 1926-1950, it is Mary who is most frequently depicted (28 per cent), more than Jesus (26.7 per cent).
[6] Fouilloux, "Le due vie", 305.
[7] A few titles amongst the many: Châtellier, *La religion*; Id., *L'Europe*; Warner, *Alone*; Perry and Echeverria, *Under the Heal*; Carroll, "Previous Explanations"; Bethouart and Lottin, *La dévotion* (especially the contribution by Lottin, Hilaire, Boniface and Langlois); Boss, *Empress*, 156-186; Corrado Pope, "Immaculate and Powerful".

into reactionaries within the Church,[8] is that it was made possible by the clergy, and, thus, by males.[9] Popes, cardinals, monks, friars, pastors and the like are, indeed, the active propagandists of devotion to the Blessed Virgin Mary and favour assigning ever more quasi-divine attributes to the 'Queen of Heaven'. How was this possible? Some authors believe that it also has to do with the fact that during that period the Catholic Church was led primarily by Italians and the devotion to Mary was propagated by priests and clerics, and, thus, by celibates. The latter point is being adduced to suggest that, aside from the rational argumentation, *unconscious* stimuli may also have been at work. In what follows, we examine to what extent this contention is being supported by historical and psychological research.

ULTRAMONTANIZATION = ITALIANIZATION = FEMINIZATION?

That something was happening to the devotions during the second half of the nineteenth century did not escape the notice of the well-informed church observers. "It seems to me that true and solid piety is being harmed by all the new romantically named devotions springing up on Belgian and French soil, and which instead of the serious and profound devotion of our ancestors, are elevating a certain vague, hazy, sentimental, *effeminate* religiosity..." (our italics) writes Jean Kockerols, the leader of the Belgian Redemptorists, in 1869 to the nuntius. "Sometimes statues of the Blessed Virgin or the saints, placed over the tabernacle, are more splendidly lit than the Blessed Sacrament", affirms a second witness. "The worship of the Blessed Sacrament is neglected in many places [...] Too much sentimentality, too much *devozioncelle*", to which Mgr. Cartuyvels, Vice-Chancellor of the University of Leuven, adds, "The imagination gives itself a strange course as regards devotions, devotional books,

[8] Fouilloux, "Le due vie", 331-333 reports that as of the 1930s, Northwestern European Catholic middle classes spoke out against "un soprannaturale troppo addizionato d'acqua di rose" and pleas were made for a "minimalismo mariano" (see also the contribution by Monteiro). "Si va profilando un "cristianesimo d'urto", adulto e *virile* (our italics) che numerosi intellettuali e militanti auspicano nelle chiese del nord-ovest d'Europa". Savart, *Les catholiques*, 610-611 reports a few lay voices during the nineteenth century. "Some" in the words of one of these authors, "see in the Mary devotion 'a prejudicial abuse of the honour of Jesus Christ, to the glory of God, and, which they don't always add, to the dignity of man'".

[9] "Car ces cultes sont produits, définis et diffusés par des clercs, seuls détenteurs de la parole et de la plume au sein de l'Eglise. Sous l'influence des femmes? Cela reste à démontrer. A destination des femmes? C'est difficilement contestable [...] D'où l'intérêt d'étudier la littérature la [=la dévotion à Marie] véhiculant [...] en sachant qu'elle renvoie autant aux idées reçues du clergé qu'aux mentalités de celles à qui elle s'adresse". Fouilloux, "Femmes"; Mc Sweeney, "Catholic Piety", 208: "The devotional impetus and, in particular, the Marian revival, came not from masses but from the Church authorities under the personal guidance of Pope Pius IX"; Corrado Pope, "Immaculate and Powerful", 182-183: "Pius [IX] and his immediate successors advocated new or renewed devotions that emphasized the affective rather than the rational or ethical aspects of faith."

religious imagery.''[10] As regards the latter, Cartuyvels' opinion is supported by Jean Pirotte's studies of the devotional prints in the Walloon province of Namur that in the nineteenth century saw wholesale distribution by, among others, the clergy. In spite of attempts to elevate the prints onto a higher plane until sometime well into the twentieth century, *l'académisme dévot* will maintain their preponderance. Yet, an indignant contemporary, Léon Gautier, "catholique convaincu et agissant", had already written in 1875, "A characteristic common to all these miserable images is sickly sentimentality [...] Might these printmakers [*imagiers*] by chance be female [*imagières*]? Certainly, everywhere one senses the invisible presence of women [...] These people are afraid of men, and have chosen not to paint them any more [...] And yet, what we lack most is virility. Truthfully, we have no more men. Thus, stop making 'baby Jesuses' and show us the Word made man, in his virile splendour."[11] Pirotte looks upon the ongoing success of this *mièvreries* [sickly sentimentality] as both symbol *and* cause of a larger movement of feminization of religion and quotes Gabriel Lebras, who detects in it one of the reasons of male absence during church services: "the virility of a good many uncultivated men is not comfortable with the sentimental canticles and little devotions saddening the sanctuary."[12]

It is remarkable as well that Pirotte, like Cartuyvels, also points to "a tender piety *à l'italienne* [our italics]"[13] and implicitly holds Italian influence responsible for the sentimental 'feminine' character of these devotions. The ultramontanism and centralism characteristic of nineteenth- and early twentieth-century Catholicism did, indeed, bring in its train an 'italianization' of the devotions.[14] Sabina Gola, who on the basis of the *Bibliographie nationale* investigated what was generally being published in Belgium between 1830 and 1880 about the politico-religious state of affairs in Italy, writes that she was struck by the proportionally large number of translations into French and Dutch of religious works authored by Italian ecclesiasts.[15] First and foremost are the Jesuits, followed by the Redemptorists as close seconds with their widespread dissemination of the writings by and about Alphonsus Liguori, for instance, via their sermons on the Redemptorist Mission. Likewise, the growing numbers of travellers to Italy promoted the spread of Italian devotions, including the worship of

[10] "L'imagination se donne une étrange carrière en fait de dévotions, de livres de piété, d'imagerie religieuse". Mgr. Cartuyvels in Art, "Documents", 452, 456, 484, 508. Boutry, *Prêtres*, 505; Launay, *Le bon prêtre*, 108.

[11] Pirotte, *Images*, 114. Other voices and initiatives in that sense with Pirotte, "L'empreinte", 134-136.

[12] Pirotte, *Images*, 19-20, 160-161.

[13] Ibid., 31.

[14] Bruley, "La romanité", 60-61: "Alors, pourquoi ne pas désigner, simplement, les 'ultramontains' sous le nom de 'romains' [...]? ...la romanization des pratiques religieuses a souvent été, de fait, une 'italianization' notamment dans les formes de dévotion."

[15] Gola, *Un demi-siècle*. Savart, *Les catholiques*, 77-78 reports the importation of Italian works into France, but this is only on a modest scale compared to what is brought in from Belgium (especially from Casterman), and wherein one can find a lot of Italian works translated into French (82 and 88-89).

Mary.[16] Despland writes about France that the "Old gallican, somber, austere piety recedes before Italian smiles. Mary is now called Madonne, again in imitation of Italian ways"[17] while in the Anglo-Saxon Protestant anti-papist writings this Italian influence is being criticized: "*Italian* Marian images were most often invoked as evidence that Roman Catholics were pagan idolators."(our italics)[18]

Amongst the few authors paying attention to the italianization of Catholicism, Michael P. Carroll figures as one of the most voluble.[19] Between 1523 and 1978, the Pope was invariably an Italian native, while most of the College of Cardinals and the leaders of the Curia also were for a very long time born and raised on the peninsula. They were hardly inclined to oppose the dissemination of the culture in which they were raised.[20]

According to Carroll, Italian devotions were now characterized by the central place that is accorded to Mary and the saints, by the multiplicity of names used in her invocations and – to which one may add – by the fact that also males have no reluctance to range themselves unabashedly on the side of the Mary Cult.[21] In his various writings, Carroll attempts to find an explanation for the phenomenon, turning, aside from anthropological, sociological, and historical, especially to psychoanalytical insights. In search of an explanation for the success of the Mary Cult well into the twentieth century, Fouilloux refers to a basic Freudian insight, the longing of men to the purity of the mother.[22] It is likewise the universally known central place of *la mamma* within the Italian family fabric that invariably returns as a motif in Carroll's works and is fingered as the deeper cause of the devotion to Mary. At the risk of inflicting severe injustice upon a thesis that in the course of many years has been

---

[16] About Italian devotions in Belgian travel accounts Viaene, *Belgium*, 271: "More importantly, some crucial revivalist devotions, such as the sentimental piety towards the Virgin [...] had their roots in 18th-century Italy". An example of such an eulogy on the Italian devotional practices: "La piété". Also the homeward bound 'Zouaves' must have played their part. See also Sanfilippo, "Du Québec" and Buerman, elsewhere in this volume.

[17] Despland, "A Case".

[18] Engelhardt Herringer, *Victorians*, 99. According to Heimann, *Catholic*, one ought not to exaggerate the Italian influence in English Catholicism.

[19] "Italianization" delivers only a few hits on the Internet, in contrast to the multiple "romanization", but rarely with respect to the nineteenth-century Church history. Carroll, *The Cult*; Id., *Catholic Cults*; Id., *Madonnas*; Id., *Veiled Threats*. Cholvy and Hilaire, *Histoire religieuse*, 154-165, 177, 179 pay also attention to the Italian influence on the ultramontane devotion, something that in 1985 "bien des historiens ont ignoré ou mal décelé" (163).

[20] Chadwick, *A History*, 551-552 expresses the same opinion when he notes that "Latins" have a better chance of beatification or canonization than others: "It might be affected because the Congregation of Rites consisted almost entirely of Italians and a majority of the cardinals in those days was always Italian, as were the popes, and the kind of sanctity most easily preferred was likely to have a 'romance' feel about its expressions of fervour or about the achievement that were possible".

[21] Something that was noticed by the nineteenth-century travellers to Italy: "Alors même qu'en France afficher, surtout chez les hommes, une foi un peu ostentatoire entraîne le ridicule et les sarcasmes, à Rome, la dévotion à la Vierge et aux saints s'affiche ouvertement dans toutes les classes, *aussi bien chez les hommes que chez les femmes*, sans susciter la moindre remarque désobligeante" (our italics) Amalvi, "Le Mythe", 117, following a travel account from 1890.

[22] Fouilloux, "Le due vie", 311.

remoulded, refined, revised and adapted, Carroll's main premise comes down to the fact that in the Oedipal phase, crucial for Freudian disciples, the father figure remains 'absent': the child grows up in a "father-ineffective family". This absence does not necessarily have to be physical, as it suffices that the mother, not the father, incarnates the authority within the family. The latter, also as a result of socio-economic circumstances, is (and would have been) the case in numerous (especially Southern) Italian families. The 'normal' initial attachment of the son with his mother, his identifying with her, would within that context be insufficiently held within bounds and stymied during the Oedipal phase, that is to say, it would ineffectively be followed by the second stage in the resolution of the Oedipus complex, namely the identification with the father, precisely because of the latter's weak psychological presence. The boy receives inadequate motivation to identify with the 'weak' father and remains stuck inside his childhood attachment to his mother. Only later on, when he comes to understand that by so doing he fails to assume the expected gender role, is this machismo behaviour over-compensated, without, however, being accompanied by the disappearance of the childhood bond with the mother, with all of the unconscious guilt feelings occasioned as a result. This then represents a repressed attachment that, at least according to Carroll, would find its manifestation via the Mary Cult.[23] This, in a nutshell and greatly simplified, forms one of his main themes.[24] Luisa Accati arrives via a different route, and without having read Carroll, at the same observation: "As a consequence of this [Italian and Catholic] structure sons do not develop (or develop only with great difficulty) the ability to take over certain selected aspects of their fathers' identities and behaviour and to translate them into an idiom of their own, at the same time rejecting other aspects which are less suited to their character. Instead, they feel a repugnance in identifying with their fathers."[25] Robert Orsi, in his penetrating study on the Italian immigrant community in New York, describes "Italian Harlem was a private matriarchy [...] Mothers dominated the life of the home [...] The source of the oldest son's authority was his close relationship with his mother [...] Oedipal rivalries raged right on the surface of the life of the 'domus' [...] Competition between father and son is total. There can only be one victor: either the father withdraws, or he fights back and expels his rival from the 'domus'".[26] From these authors we retain the sense that, in Catholic contexts, males that were raised inside a family situation dominated by the mother are more likely to turn into fervent Mary

---

[23] This is Carroll's approach from 1986: Carroll, *The Cult*, 49-74. In 1992, a still further developed (Kleinian) version follows, in id., *Madonnas*, 138-161.

[24] The thesis brings to mind what a namesake of Carroll, John Carroll, argues in his *Guilt*. Also with this author, the "Mother-dominated family" figures as the central element, albeit in a different context. According to this moralistic sociologist, the – in his view – sad situation prevailing within the Western society is brought about by the gradual fading away (since the Romantic period) of the – originally Puritanical – patriarchal family featuring strong-willed fathers and like sons. He connects with the reasoning of the other Carroll in the sense that, within Italy, Puritanism never developed into a factor to define culture there.

[25] Accati, "Explicit Meanings", 252; 254: "the Italian family is matricentric". Italy is said to remain today the country where sons keep living with their mothers longer than anywhere else, the so-called "mammoni", cf. *Der Spiegel*, 6 July 2006.

[26] Orsi, *The Madonna*, 131, 133, 118-119.

worshippers and that such situations are more prevalent in Italy than elsewhere. It would be interesting – albeit not easy – to examine to what extent non-Italian male Mary disciples passed through an analogous psychic prehistory.

CLERICALIZATION = FEMINIZATION?

The males that disseminated the Mary Cult throughout the whole of the Catholic body were not only Italian. They were also clerics, and their views were very favourably received abroad by their soul-brothers, priests, and religious groups. Pirotte quotes the testimony of a well-informed source that attributes the success of the sentimental devotional prints to the ready acceptance they enjoy amongst the Christian masses, "the Christian people, *headed by the clergy*, [who] unconsciously recognize themselves [in the prints] and take pleasure in them" [our italics][27]. More specifically, it is the devotion to Mary, elevated to the "Queen of the clergy" that burgeons mightily within the clerical community.

Psychologists have concluded that the family background of priests and clerics in general does, indeed, display a great resemblance to what Carroll characterized as being a typical Italian phenomenon. Karl Guido Rey, in his *Das Mutterbild des Priesters*, based on a survey amongst (candidate) priests that counted 265 usable responses, talks about "The mother as the main drive for the priestly vocation" ("Die Mutter als Hauptantrieb zur priesterlichen Berufung") and "The vocation enhancing effect of the father image being religiously indifferent or negative" ("Die berufungsfördernde Wirkung des religiös indifferenten oder negativen Vaterbildes")[28]. There is question of a poor father experience ("mangelhafte Vatererlebnis") as a result of the physical or affective absence of the father figure, which, in its turn, may be brought about by the fact that he is pushed away from his parental role through the behaviour of the mother ("dass er durch das Verhalten der Mutter aus seiner väterlichen Rolle verdrängt wird"). The author does not hesitate to conclude that "the archetype of the priest appears to be of androgynous nature" ("Der Archetyp des Priesters scheint androgyner Natur zu sein").[29] The similarity with the "father-ineffective" (M.P. Carroll) or "mother-dominated" (J. Carroll) family is striking, as is the androgyny as antipode to the machismo, that other possible answer for the (unconscious) mother attachment. We find the same idea with Jakob Crottogini, *Werden und Krise des Priesterberufes,* in this instance a non-psycho-analytically inclined researcher: "Within the family the most crucial importance is the religious attitude of the mother."[30] Marc

[27] Pirotte, "L'empreinte", 136.
[28] Rey, *Das Mutterbild*. The surveyed respondents grew up and worked during the preconciliary period.
[29] Without, however, attributing to this any pejorative connotation. Rey, *Das Mutterbild*, 109, 140. About the "origine bisexuelle de nos vécus religieux" and "La loi du père et sa fonction", see de Saussure, "Questions"; Zock, "The predominance". About the 'feminine nature' of the Roman Catholic priesthood in the eyes of the anti-clerical opinion, see Art and Buerman, "Anticléricalisme et genre". About clerical identity in historical perspective: Monteiro, "Mannen Gods".
[30] Crottogini, *Werden*, 268: "In der Untersuchung hielten wir uns strikte an die Methoden der empirischen Psychologie".

Oraison writes at the start of the 1960s: "In one of France's major seminaries, during rather informal psychological examinations, the specialist who had been called in found that at least 70 per cent of the young people (average age 21) psychologically speaking, did not have a father: either he had died, was ineffectual and not very 'present', or ill and infirm."[31] And, not surprisingly, Drewermann, a far less non-controversial author, also spends time on the extensive Mary Cult practised by the clergy: "There is no monastic rule, no instruction for priests or no papal address, which would not come to speak about the promotion of monastic chastity and celibacy, as with inner necessity, of devotion to the Blessed Mother".[32] To him, there can be no doubt about the link that exists between "Chastity requirement" [...] "mother fixation" [...] and Catholic Marian devotion. One may agree or disagree with his views on such a link, yet its existence is affirmed by nearly all researchers and could well be an explanation of the other fact that the generally married Protestant ministers are by no means given to the – in their eyes exaggerated – veneration of the Mary figure as are the Roman Catholic clergy.[33] Consequently, André Godin, in his 1994 overview of the psychological literature on the theme, can point out as one of the acquired insights that those called are stimulated by a *mobile inconscient*: "the prevalence of a maternal image [...] as a motif of the celibate".[34]

To what degree are these psychological insights confirmed by historiography? Gender-oriented historical research has abundantly demonstrated that throughout the nineteenth and until well into the twentieth century, the ideal female deployed her talents within the private sphere, whereas the public domain was the province of the male. This separation fluctuates, depending on class, country, religion, and time frame, but, nonetheless, appears broadly characteristic of the era.[35] The Roman Catholic Church also holds to this conviction, and, confronted with declining male involvement in Church matters, emphasizes the major role that has to be played by women, and certainly by mothers in the religious education of their offspring. Fathers only get interested – if they get interested at all – in their sons once these reach seven years of age or older. "It is rare, in a biography of a 19th-century man of the church, that the vocation is not linked principally to his mother's faith", writes Geneviève

[31] Oraison, *Le célibat*, 178.

[32] "Es gibt keine Ordensregel, keine Priesterunterweisung und keine Papstansprache, die im Zusammenhang mit der Förderung mönchischer Keuschheit und Ehelosigkeit nicht wie mit innerer Notwendigkeit auf die Verehrung der Gottesmutter zu sprechen käme". Drewermann, *Kleriker*, 499-525, here especially 504-505.

[33] Ibid., 512. On Drewermann's importance for religious historical recording, see Art, "Kerkgeschiedenis na Drewermann".

[34] Godin, "Psychologie de la vocation". See also Dittes, "Psychological Characteristics"; Rulla, *Structure psychologique*; Godin, *Psychologie*; Sipe, *Celibacy*, 83 and *passim*; Art, "Mannen als bruiden". An opposing interpretation in Vigneron, *Histoire*, 103.

[35] See Van Osselaer and Pasture, eds, *Households of Faith*. Langlois, "'Toujours plus pratiquantes'", does point out, in fact, that this is a phenomenon probably happening at all times but that manifests itself more strongly during certain periods than others. Accati, "Explicit Meanings", 242 points to the significance of the question if it pertains here to a dominant Catholic or to a dominant Protestant context. Recently, M.P. Carroll has devoted an entire volume to the 'Protestant' bias that is alleged to characterize and distort North American research into religion: Carroll, *American Catholics in the Protestant Imagination*.

Gadbois in her article with the telling title "'Vous êtes presque la seule consolation de l'Eglise'. La foi des femmes face à la déchristianization de 1789 à 1880".[36] Paul Seeley in turn believes that the answer to explain the reason for the continuation of a small but active male elite within the *bonne société* of Lyon is to be sought in the very strong maternal and weak paternal input into the education of these 'hommes d'oeuvres'.[37] Jean-René Chotard, who at one time was himself a student at a preparatory seminary, describes in penetrating fashion the bond that exists between mother and son and the link with the absence of the father.[38]

But it is particularly in the writings of the clergy itself that the close ties between the mother, Mary, and the priesthood are revealed. Some texts create in the outsider the impression that there is question of identification with Mary (or a striving for it), thus, for instance, in the text of Jean-Claude Colin († 1875), founder of the Society of Mary: "Let them [the Marists] perpetually keep in mind that they, on the basis of a merciful election, belong to the family of the Blessed Virgin, mother of God [...] But if they want to be and become the sons of the immaculate Mother, they must breathe and radiate her own spirit, namely that of humility, self-abnegation, profound connection with God and ardent love for one's neighbour; in all ways they must think, feel and act like Mary, since otherwise they would only be unworthy, degenerate sons".[39] Mary as a sublimated mother figure finds forceful expression in the words of the priest Poppe, who evoked her with *Moeke* (more or less a diminutive of 'mama').[40]

The contributions published in the specialized editions of preparatory seminary superiors, *Le recrutement sacerdotal* (1900-), are amongst the most explicit texts on the topic. Aside from the many contributions dedicated to the role that can be played by the mother, even including the responsibility she bears during the blossoming of a budding priestly calling, the journal also repeatedly discusses the place occupied by Mary within the spiritual life of the seminary student and the priest.

"Our little seminarian, torn from his family to live the Seminary's austere boarding school, will suffer in his heart from this emotional isolation."[41] He will need to find a mother, "a real living mother, if an invisible one, and one close to him, who will console him in the dormitory when his heart is heavy and while he, completely

---

[36] Gadbois, "Vous êtes", 315. See Langlois, "Le temps", 238 and 247-248.

[37] Seeley, "O Sainte Mère".

[38] Chotard, *Séminaristes*, 92, 141-144.

[39] "In mente perpetuo teneant se esse, delectu gratioso, de familia B. Mariae Dei genetricis... Si ergo vere filii huius almae Matris sint et esse desiderent, ipsius spiritum se spirare debere sentiant, spiritum, videlicet, humilitatis, propriae abnegationis, intimae cum Deo unionis et ardentissimae charitatis erga proximum; ut Maria cogitare, ut Maria sentire et agere debent in omnibus, aliter enim non essent nisi indigni et degeneres filii." Quoted by De Fiores, "Marie (sainte vierge)", 470, from the Constitutions of the congregation. This author emphasizes the "dimension mystique" of the text.

[40] And was for that reason reprimanded by his spiritual superior. See Van de Velde, *Priester Poppe*, 41, 44-47: "Moeke, moeke liefste moe/spreek toch weer uw kindje toe..." Also M.J. Chirion (1797-1852, founder of the 'Sainte Marie de l'Assomption') invoked Mary as "Maman": Keselman, *Miracles*, 226 n. 44. Amongst Italian immigrants "Mary was called 'Mamma'". Orsi, *The Madonna*, 226.

[41] "Notre petit séminariste, arraché à la vie de famille pour vivre dans l'internat austère du Séminaire, souffrira, dans son coeur, de cet isolement affectif". Duperray, "La Dévotion", 208.

moved, is saying the rosary", writes abbé Duperray, spiritual director of the *Petit Séminaire de Charlieu* (Loire) in 1937. He substantiates this contention with quotes garnered from a survey amongst his disciples: they are dreaming "of tomorrow bringing about the reign of Mary, my good heavenly mother" (208). "In the evenings, before going to sleep, I converse with my heavenly mother, in the same way I converse with my earthly mother" (209). The young seminary student sees Mary as the substitute for the spouse he will never have: "My quite sensitive heart reclaims the pure, sweet, delicate affection that is feminine affection. This is what Jesus is proposing for my renouncing everything, including the affection of a wife, to follow him and become a priest. It's fortunate that the Blessed Virgin was there. Isn't she capable of providing the feminine influence I badly needed? But of course! [...] She is in heaven, no doubt. Yes, but it's a real living reality with a heart of flesh like mine" (211-212). What is experienced as devotion during one's time as a seminary student grows, in the eyes of the Jesuit priest F. Charmot, into identification during adult life.[42] "The priests carry on with the maternal function of Mary [...] [playing] in effect, with regard to the Eucharist the role of a mother who generates and makes grow the body of Jesus Christ" (121). When laymen may then count already on the special grace and favour of Jesus ("Jesus verily 'marries' them"), "the priesthood enters into an even greater initimacy with Him [...] Jesus communicates to him a divine maternal power, more than a participation in divine life, [...] In him [the priest] has, by the virtue of the Holy Spirit, the birth of Christ as did the Virgin Mother." And thus: "The virginity of the priesthood must imitate that of Mary, since its functions extend and complete those of the Virgin Mary [...] A priest is above all a virgin. He is the continuation of Virgin: what a privilege!" According to Accati, this pertains to a belief that harkens back to the apologies of the priesthood that were written during the seventeenth century in reaction to the attacks by the Protestants, such as, the *Traité des saints ordres* by J.J. Olier (1608-1657). According to her, the bond between mother/Mary and son/Priest emerges as a consequence of the Counter Reformation and forms the basis of clerical power.[43] Whatever truth there may be in this latter opinion, for the nineteenth and preconciliary twentieth century, the texts written by clerics that establish the bond between mother, Mary, and chastity are there for the taking. To what degree this also holds true for the prior period needs to be investigated.

---

[42] Charmot, "Le prêtre". "Marriage to Christ was, of course, limited to women. There is some evidence that an analogous relationship of males to Mary as wife was also important, at least in the training of the clergy." Keselman, *Miracles*, 99.

[43] Accati, "Explicit Meanings", 242-243; Ibid., 241: "The Counter-Reformation Roman Catholic Church embodies nothing less than this principle [the son identifying with his mother]. It is a group of celibate men (i.e. men who remained tied to their mothers), who do not share the power which husbands and fathers wield, but instead manage the potency of women." Besides, ibid., 242: "The Oedipal dependence of a son on his mother is not an invention of Freud's, but a social relationship constructed over the course of four hundred years by the Catholic Church (especially by the Jesuits). What Freud found was the product of this long labour by unmarried men who became ever more devoted sons".

CONCLUSION

To answer the question why the Mary Cult, unequivocal symbol of the feminization of Roman Catholicism in the nineteenth and the preconciliary twentieth century, was particularly propagated by males, psychologists refer to the psycho-biography of the actors. Absent fathers are said to be characteristic of the Italian family situation as well as of the prehistory of many of the clergy – including non-Italians. The possible resulting incestuous ties with one's mother and unconscious guilt feelings could be translated into either a Latin machismo or an androgynous complementation of the gender role. The Mary Cult could be interpreted as a symptom arising from this fixation on the mother figure. A brief exploration of the historical literature and of a number of printed sources does not contradict this hypothesis but, nonetheless, can only confirm it up to a point. The central role of the mother in the Italian family is affirmed by Accati's and Orsi's studies on Italian-American families, while, likewise, other anthropological studies point to the special nature of the mother/son relationship in the Mediterranean region. There cannot be any dispute about the italianization in Catholic devotional life that followed in the wake of the Roman Question, whereby 'Mary' morphed more and more into the figure of the 'Madonna': the question remains, though, how deep this penetrated – nonetheless deep enough to elicit reactions, also from within the Church community. That the manifest interest of the clergy in Marian devotion could be related to the absence of the father figure appears to be confirmed *a contrario* by the studies and printed sources that illustrate the importance of the mother for passing on and maintaining the Catholic tradition and the burgeoning and safeguarding of a priestly calling. For adolescent, isolated students at the (preparatory) seminary, Mary fulfils the role of a surrogate mother, while some adult priests indeed do identify themselves with her – and thus with the mother figure. For 'some', aside from the fact that in this case, as so often happens in cultural history, no truly undisputed causal connections can be proven, the question remains as to how general, both in time and place, the aforementioned pattern really was. Nonetheless, it seems highly probable that it happened.

Historians are mostly sceptical vis-à-vis psycho-historical explanations – the 'absent father' is, indeed, a *topos* – if not a *deus ex machina* – in quite a body of psycho-historical literature[44], which is really not very surprising given the focal importance that is accorded to the Oedipal phase by adherents of Freud.

On the other hand: psychologist historians only aim at proposing *additional* explanations and adducing and accounting for factors that relegate other approaches to the sidelines. They tend to draw attention to recurring scenarios, without wishing to imply, however, that no other psychological prehistory is possible and that no factors other than unconscious stimuli or motives could play a role in elucidating the phenomenon of the large-scale clerical devotion to Mary. Their approach deserves, for what concerns an understanding of the feminization symptoms within the Roman Catholic Church, greater attention than what thus far has been the case.

---

[44] He would also be held responsible for the receptivity of the German population towards Nazism: Loewenberg, "The Psychohistorical Origins".

 The muscular Christian's fists were in the service of 'the weak'. Tom Brown's first defence of the new boy, George Arthur, who is being bullied by some of his dormitory mates because he goes down on his knees to say his prayers before going to bed.
[*Engraving by Arthur Hughes and Sydney Prior Hall in Thomas Hughes's* Tom Brown's School Days *(ed. MacMillan, London, 1898, 185)*].

THE 'SPORTSMAN' AND THE 'MUSCULAR CHRISTIAN'

RIVAL IDEALS IN NINETEENTH-CENTURY ENGLAND

HUGH MCLEOD

In Thomas Hughes' novel, *Tom Brown's School Days*, the classic text of 'muscular Christianity', the villain Flashman and his clique are described as "fast sporting young gentlemen".[1] At first sight this might seem surprising as the novel is famous (or, in the eyes of some readers, infamous) for its extended accounts of football and cricket matches, bare-knuckle boxing and many other forms of sporting encounter. Moreover, to call someone a 'sportsman' was for many people of the time the highest form of praise. Hughes clearly could not object to Flashman's interest in sport. The critique focused on four main points. First, Flashman was a bully: he used his physical strength to inflict pain on those weaker than himself. Second, he was a coward, as he flinched from confronting those who were stronger. Third, he was a gambler. And fourth, he ate and drank too much, with the result that he was sometimes drunk, and even when sober was less fit than he should have been. The second point was gratuitous. Courage was a virtue greatly prized by 'sportsmen', and in branding Flashman as a coward Hughes could not claim to be making a fair criticism of the behaviour of sportsmen in general. The first point is maybe nearer to the mark. On the one hand the ideal of the sportsman was closely linked to the ideal of the gentleman: courtesy was as important as physical prowess, and he was expected to behave with special consideration to social inferiors. On the other hand the concern of 'sportsmen' for physical strength and daring was always threatening to become an end in itself, over-riding any attention to gentler virtues. However the third and fourth points come closest to pinpointing the differences between 'sportsmen' and 'muscular Christians'. Drinking and gambling were essential parts of the sporting culture of the aristocracy and gentry; and the ability to 'take one's drink', together with the willingness to

---

[1] Hughes, *Tom Brown*, 180.

take risks by making large bets were among the chief ways in which masculinity was measured.

In fact there was also a working-class sporting culture, largely distinct from though sometimes overlapping with that of the upper classes, in which very similar values were prevalent. While the term 'sportsman' was generally used to describe members of the upper and upper middle classes, it might have been equally aptly applied to many working men. In this article I will look at the forms of masculinity associated with 'sportsmen' of both the working class and the upper/upper middle classes, before going on to look at the ways in which 'muscular Christians' offered forms of masculinity that were partly old and partly new, and examining the relationship between the older and newer versions. 'Muscular Christianity' was a term invented by a journalist in 1857 to describe the ideals propagated by writers like Thomas Hughes and Charles Kingsley. The latter disliked the term, but it stuck, and indeed remains in use today. (During the last month I have read in one paper that the new Australian Prime Minister, Kevin Rudd, is a 'muscular Christian', and in another that 'muscular Christianity' was to blame for British imperialism.) Rather than concentrating, as some of the standard literature does, on Hughes and Kingsley,[2] I shall be using the term to describe those Christians, increasingly numerous in the second half of the nineteenth century, who claimed that sport, and physical exercise more generally, were not only fun, but had moral, religious and social value, and should be actively promoted by the church. Hughes and Kingsley were liberal Anglicans associated with the Christian Socialist movement. But as 'muscular Christianity' came to be more widely accepted, it was adopted by those of other religious denominations and other theological or political persuasions, so it should not be stereotyped by exclusive association with any one religious or political agenda. On the contrary the pervasive influence of 'muscular Christianity' in later Victorian and Edwardian Britain arose from the fact that it was adopted by people whose religion and politics were in most respects quite different. In the latter part of the article I will show that the increasing professionalization of sport in the late nineteenth century was bringing in its train new versions of masculinity which drew on both of these older traditions while being fully compatible with neither.

---

[2] Vance, *The Sinews of the Spirit* does so sympathetically (and also discusses their longer-term influence). Hall, *Muscular Christianity* does so in a more hostile way.

THE GENTLEMAN SPORTSMAN

The word 'sportsman' began to be used in the eighteenth century to describe a gentleman who devoted large amounts of time to participating in and/or watching and betting on sporting events. So far as participation in sport was concerned this meant above all fox-hunting, which in the eighteenth century became a major part of the life of the English aristocracy and gentry. Many gentlemen more occasionally played cricket, though it had not yet acquired the semi-sacred status as symbol of all things English and embodiment of all national virtues which it enjoyed in the later nineteenth century. Men of these classes also bred or owned race-horses and there was some 'gentlemen jockeys' who rode these horses, though more often the jockeys were men of plebeian origins. 'Sportsmen' would bet on anything and everything, and often the betting was on individual encounters arranged ad hoc. However by the later eighteenth century horse-racing, cock-fighting and boxing were emerging as major spectator sports in which considerable sums of money were at stake and of which betting was an integral part.

The arrival of highly organized and commercialized sport was signalled by the establishment in 1792 of the *Sporting Magazine*. A number of similar journals followed, the most famous being *Bell's Life in London*, founded in 1824, which would appear to have been directed at the upper- and middle-class sportsman but covered a very wide range of sports. The paper's own reporters specialized in detailed accounts of horse races and boxing matches, but it also gave considerable space to narratives of fox-hunts, sent in by participants. More plebeian sports such as dog-fighting were covered too, as was chess. As the *Sporting Magazine* pointed out in an early issue, "we profess ourselves sportsmen not moralists",[3] and the sporting papers took little notice of the ethical, religious or humanitarian objections to many of the sports practised. Indeed they frequently ridiculed such objections. Fox-hunting could be very time-consuming. During the season, from November to April, many hunts were out four or five days in the week, and some of their members aimed to miss as few hunts as possible. Sporting gentry had very close relationships with their horses and dogs, and intimate knowledge of the distinctive characters of each. They also took a close interest in the breeding of horses and dogs, so that even when not actively involved in a sporting event a lot of their time was spent in the stables and kennels. In the case of boxing, devotees of the sport would travel considerable distances for a big match, often at short notice, since the sport increasingly acquired a cloak-and-dagger element, which became an important ingredient in the mystique surrounding it. From about 1820 magistrates in many part of the country were trying to suppress bare-knuckle prize-fights. These were often staged close to county boundaries, so that the contestants could cross into a different jurisdiction if the authorities in the place initially chosen tried to stop the fight. Information about the chosen location was therefore passed by word of mouth rather than being openly published, and fights might relocate two or three times before a safe site was found.

It is true that 'sportsmen' might also be responsible landowners or pursue successful political or military careers. However, for many 'sportsmen', sport was

---

[3] Harvey, *The Beginnings*, 36.

the most important thing in their lives. This meant that the qualities most generally admired in a man were physical strength and courage, together with dexterity and skill. These qualities were most obviously manifested on the hunting field or in sporting encounters. But it was also reflected in the betting which was integral to most sports. A sportsman took risks. Fox-hunting was a dangerous sport, in which many participants were seriously injured or even killed in falls from their horse. The risks involved in betting were less lethal, but the sportsman's trust in his own judgement and his courage in the face of possible consequences were reflected in his willingness to wager large sums, sometimes on strange and improbable bets. Violence was intrinsic to most of the sports practised at the time, and acceptance of, indeed enjoyment of this violence was seen as one of the marks of a true man. Thus *Bell's Life* in 1851 devoted an editorial to ridiculing the Surrey magistrates who had held a meeting "at which a great deal of ladylike horror was expressed at prize-fighting". *Bell's* praised prize-fighting as "intended to supplant delicacy with resoluteness and vigour", they attacked the "maudlin sensitiveness of the critics", and claimed that if bare-knuckle were banned, the lower classes would start fighting with knives, like foreigners.[4]

The object of many of these sports was to kill another creature, and in many of the others the participants themselves risked death. Revelling in death took its most extreme form in rat-killing, where spectators took bets on the number of rats a dog could kill within a given time. Here the victims had no chance at all. In the many sports which involved shooting at birds or chasing small animals with dogs, the intended victim had at least some chance of escape: the excitement lay not only in the spectacle of death, but in the skill of the man with the gun or the relative speed and skill of the dogs and of the hare or rabbit. More complex were the emotions surrounding fox-hunting, where the thrill of the successfully executed kill mingled with respect for the fox who had provided a particularly exciting chase or who made good his escape. Indeed fox-hunters were sometimes described as fox-worshippers. The need to preserve foxes so that they could be hunted led to a particular contempt for those 'vulpicide' farmers who simply went out and shot the foxes whom they regarded as a threat to their livestock. Indeed, as James Obelkevich showed in a pioneering exploration of fox-hunting rituals, these had a quasi-religious dimension.[5] Thus the 'blooding' of a novice hunter with the brush of a fox could be seen as a form of baptism. The Cleveland Friendly Society, a club for sporting gentry founded in 1722 had an initiation ceremony in which the new member "shall first publicly lay his right hand on a hunting horn and declare himself no enemy to cocking, smocking, fox-hunting and harriers". Clergymen were excused from the word 'smocking' (a term for sex) and from laying their hand on the hunting horn.[6]

In those sports which took the form of a fight between presumed equals, severe physical injuries were normal and death was always a real possibility. This was true of prize-fighting, one of the most popular sports of the early nineteenth century, but also of cock-fighting and dog-fighting. These three sports had a lot in common. Afficionados took a keen interest in the physique and appearance, as well as the diet and

---

[4] *Bell's Life in London*, 5 January 1851.
[5] Obelkevich, *Religion*, 40-44.
[6] Fairfax-Blakeborough, *Northern Turf*, 69.

training of the contestants. They were admired for their ferocity, courage and skill, but above all for their 'gameness'. The defeated man or animal was praised as warmly as, or even more warmly than, the victor if he showed willingness to go on fighting, even in the face of severe punishment. Indeed, some of the same concerns were transferred to the appreciation of what was arguably the most popular of all the spectator sports of the period - certainly the only blood-sport which interested women as much as men - namely public executions. *Bell's Life in London* described these in considerable detail, and often in a fashion not dissimilar to the ways in which boxing matches were reported. Thus the reporter frequently commented on the physique as well as the demeanour of the condemned man or woman and, without the word being used, respect was shown to the victim who died 'game'. Thus in 1836, when many crimes other than murder were still potentially liable to the death penalty, the hanging in Surrey of a burglar named Harley was described as follows:

> The culprit was a fine athletic man and in a state of ruddy health. He was dressed in a ploughman's frock, round which a coil of rope was fastened. He did not express any fear; but his restless unsettled gaze, his flushed cheek, and his short breathings, which were painfully audible, proclaimed his agitation. He walked with a steady step paying marked attention to the admonitions of his religious adviser. In arriving at the foot of the scaffold, he ascended the steps with a rapidity which seemed to indicate a wish for a speedy termination of his sufferings. The fatal noose having been put round his neck, and the cap drawn over his face, he begged the chaplain to let him join with him in prayer. He seemed extremely penitent; but his deportment was equally removed from hopeless despondency or extravagant enthusiasm. An immense crowd, extending to the commencement of the lane, assembled to witness the execution, which appeared to have little effect on them, as they were indulging in uproarious gaiety all the time.[7]

While, as indicated above, there were 'sporting parsons' - many of them the brothers and cousins of sporting gentry - there was an anti-clerical edge to the sporting culture. It was most evident in the first half of the nineteenth century, when bishops, concerned with the pastoral effectiveness of their clergy, were trying to take them out of the hunting field, and when ministers of religions were leaders of campaigns to suppress cruel, brutal or immoral sports. Obelkevich quotes sneering references to the "men in black coats" in the correspondence of some Lincolnshire gentry. *Bell's Life* seemed to enjoy stories which put the clergy in a bad light. Thus, under the headline "A Tipsy Parson", they thought it worth reporting that a London clergyman had been fined for being drunk and disorderly, and they reprinted exposés by other papers of clerical abuses.[8] As devotees of the Prize Ring they naturally resented the fact that clergymen were usually at the head of attempts to stop these fights. A typical story concerned a fight planned to take place near the Oxfordshire village of Enstone in May 1836. "The worthy parson" of that place persuaded the magistrates to stop the

---

[7] *Bell's Life in London*, 17 April 1836.
[8] Ibid., 4 January 1846, 3 and 31 January 1836.

fight, but acquiesced when the pugilists, their supporters and spectators moved to a new location on the Worcestershire border - "his Reverence retired in all the pride of Christian meekness, delighted at having shoved the nuisance, as he called it, from his own door to that of his neighbours".[9] Occasionally one gets hints of a more generalized critique of religion. Thus a former *Bell's* reporter who wrote a history of prizefighting in 1880 made sarcastic references to the fact that Bendigo, a champion of the 1830s, later became a Methodist preacher:

> There is a clearer psychological connection between fighting and fanaticism, pugnacity and Puritanism, than saints and Stigginses can afford to admit and the facile step from preachee to flogee of parsons of all sects and times needs no citations from history to prove.[10]

However, *Bell's* generally advocated a highly Erastian form of Protestantism, in terms of which the need for religion and a church was assumed, and the main concerns were to ensure that it was under firm state control, and to nip in the bud any tendencies towards sacerdotalism. Obelkevich goes further and detects among the Lincolnshire gentry and among fox-hunters more generally a drive to 'desecrate' Christian rites and sacred places.[11] Thus, as well as demonstrating the parallels between Christian and fox-hunting rituals, he highlights the special thrill that sporting gentry derived from a kill executed in a churchyard or in the grounds of a ruined abbey. Here he seems to me to go further than the evidence supports. As already noted, fox-hunting, like a number of other sports, incorporated quasi-religious elements. Yet in borrowing some of the resources of Christianity, it did not necessarily challenge or replace the older faith. In fact one of the sporting gentry quoted by Obelkevich was a devotee of the Oxford Movement as well as of fox-hunting. Maybe it was precisely because of his experience of and commitment to ritualistic Christianity that he was able to derive a frisson from sporting ritualism that his less devout neighbours would have missed.

Insofar as the sporting sub-culture challenged Christianity and the churches it did so indirectly and implicitly by fostering very different values. First, the sporting world was essentially a male world, whereas the majority of church-goers were women, and in spite of the male leadership of the churches and chapels, women could even reach positions of prominence in some branches of Nonconformity, such as the Quakers and the Methodist sects. Even conservative Christians recognized that women could potentially be mobilized for good causes. Thus in 1845 when Derby Borough Council was faced with two rival petitions, one calling for the reintroduction of the Derby Races and the other opposing the Races, the leading advocate of horse-racing tried to ridicule the rival petition by claiming that a quarter of the signatories were women.[12] Women were indeed beginning to be seen on the hunting-field in the 1840s, though still very rarely, and many women attended race-meetings. But boxing and cock-fighting, not to mention dog-fighting and rat-killing, were men's sports.

[9] *Bell's Life in London,* 15 May 1836.
[10] Downes Miles, *Pugilistica,* vol. 3, 3-4.
[11] Obelkevich, *Religion,* 40-44.
[12] *Derby Mercury,* 26 February 1845.

Moreover, ways of thinking and behaving flourished within the sporting world that would have been completely taboo in the religious world. In its milder forms this might simply mean a relaxed and tolerant conviviality, which potentially conflicted with the 'seriousness' and moral earnestness which pervaded the religious world in the first half of the nineteenth century, even if a degree of gradual relaxation later became possible. Here there are signs of a growing separation in the years around 1800 as the religious world became more militantly 'serious' and sections of the sporting world became more ostentatiously unserious. Thus the historian of the northern Turf, Fairfax-Blakeborough, notes that in the eighteenth century Races Week in York had been the occasion for parties in the town-houses of the gentry in Micklegate. But "there was a growing feeling among sportsmen at this period [about 1800, though the date is not precisely stated] that there was greater freedom, less ceremony and more hilarity possible when they met and dined and wined at an inn than at private houses".[13] The most obvious area of conflict between religious ethics and the sporting sub-culture lay in the heavy drinking which for many sportsmen was an essential part of their masculinity. It should be noted however that while religious moralists objected to drunkenness and to the drinking of spirits, teetotalism was rare before the 1830s and was initially adopted mainly by members of the more plebeian denominations, such as the Primitive Methodists, as well as by many political radicals. A more fundamental area of conflict lay in the double standard of morality which was taken for granted by many men of the upper and upper middle classes, while being condemned by Christian preachers. For 'serious' Christians much of the conversation at places where 'sportsmen' met was immoral, and while this may often have been no more than talk, for some sportsmen skill in seduction was as important a test of their masculinity as the drinking, betting and feats of horsemanship. In the early nineteenth century the hunting capital of Melton Mowbray became a mecca for a section of the sporting gentry who would rent a house for the season, and who became noted according to Itzkowitz for hard riding, dare-devil feats, heavy drinking, and patronising prostitutes, dog-fights and cock-fights.[14]

Douglas Sutherland's biography of Hugh Lowther, 5th Earl of Lonsdale (1857-1944), offers an unusually vivid and detailed portrait of a sporting aristocrat of a somewhat later generation but with many similar interests and values. Lowther was to play an important role in the transformation of the discredited sport of prize-fighting into the more respectable modern sport of boxing, and he is remembered through the 'Lonsdale Belts' worn by British boxing champions. As a young man in London in the 1870s and '80s Lowther belonged to a "brash, hard-living set of young men who put hunting above all else". The quality they most admired was 'bottom', reflected in feats of drinking and seduction, "gambling for more than one could afford (always provided one paid one's debts)", and above all by sporting achievements.[15] He "worshipped physical fitness and virility in men. For him life was a matter of the survival of the fittest".[16] "If Hugh had any Gods in his life, certainly one of them was

[13] Fairfax-Blakeborough, *Northern Turf*, vol. 3, 46-47.
[14] Itzkowitz, *Peculiar Privilege*, 42-49.
[15] Sutherland, *The Yellow Earl*, 21-22.
[16] Ibid., 29.

the eccentric Squire Osbaldeston." The latter died in 1866, but some forty years later a biographical dictionary of British sportsmen described him as "still a household word in the sporting community, famous for nerve and resourcefulness".[17] A Master of Fox Hounds, a cricketer and a successful steeplechase jockey who had fought a duel over a racing dispute, he has was best known for making and usually winning outlandish bets, the most famous being that he could ride 200 miles in ten hours. (He was less successful in his racing bets, where his net losses were said to have totalled £200,000, forcing him to sell his ancestral home.) As with many sportsmen, some of Lowther's closest relationships were with his dogs. Appropriately enough the frontispiece of Sutherland's biography shows the earl surrounded by dogs, and when travelling by train he booked two compartments, one for himself and one for the dogs. Like many upper class sportsmen, Lowther in the middle and later years of his life led a double life. As a "conventionalist" who "flouted convention" he was happy for his wife to rule supreme in their West End home, where only guests acceptable to her were admitted, but he met fellow men of the world and talked about racing, boxing and their extra-marital liaisons at the Pelican Club - though on one occasion discretion lapsed so far that he got into a fight in Hyde Park with another sporting gentleman, who was pursuing the same woman as himself.

In his later years, Lowther seems to have developed an interest in his Cumberland and Westmorland estates and the welfare of those working on them, and to have gained popularity by holding open house on the occasion of the annual Grasmere Sports, as well as becoming the subject of a huge local folklore. However, for most of his life he saw these estates simply as the necessary means for the financing of his several homes, his cars, his yachts and his horses. He was the kind of lord around whom legends clustered and he inspired fascination and a degree of respect, but perhaps not affection. Bluff man-to-man exchanges were his forte in dealing with tenants and workers on his estates, but his patience with anything that might be deemed in the slightest degree impertinent or inappropriate was very limited.

However the ideal of the 'sportsman' could also embrace gentler virtues. When people referred to a sportsman "of the best kind", they were likely to be thinking of a person of exemplary manners and consideration, as well as a high sense of responsibility. Thus, according to *British Sports and Sportsmen*, Lord Glasgow (1792-1869) was "not only a thoroughly good sportsman, but a British nobleman of the highest type", as exemplified not only by his kindness to horses and dogs, but by his generous support for good causes of all kinds. James John Farquharson (1784-1871) was famous for his courtesy to social inferiors, and for his patience and tolerance. As a Master of Fox Hounds "he never gave way to those outbursts of coarse and vulgar abuse on which some masters rather pride themselves" - even when his favourite hound, "Wrangler", was fatally kicked by a horse. The 5th Earl of Portsmouth (1825-1891), as well as being a race-horse owner and Master of Fox Hounds, was "a thorough country gentleman of the old school, with full knowledge of the duties and obligations of his position". "He lived all his life among his own people: at the country places, where he dispensed a magnificent hospitality", he was "a practical farmer and breeder",

---

[17] *British Sport and Sportsmen, Past and Present*, vol. 1, 17-18; see also Osbaldeston, *Squire Osbaldeston*.

"he built churches and schools" and "was a broad-minded man with the most genial nature". Some biographies of 'sportsmen' also mention that their hero had friendly relations with clergymen and was himself a regular church-goer.[18]

THE POPULAR SPORTSMAN

While the 'sportsman' was usually assumed to be a man of the higher social classes with sufficient leisure to make sport the main business, or at least a major business, of his life, there were also many men of other classes and especially working men who shared similar interests and some of the same values. Alan Metcalfe in his invaluable study of the recreations of Northumberland miners in the period c 1860-1914[19] argues that for many of them sport was the biggest thing in their lives, though the time which they could devote to it was necessarily very limited. Cock-fighting had once attracted men of all classes, though after it was banned in 1849 it survived mainly as a working-class sport, necessarily pursued in secrecy and often in remote locations. Some popular sports were similar to those of the upper classes, but with subtle differences. Miners coursed rabbits rather than hares, and shot pigeons, rather than grouse. Many of the sports pursued by Northumberland miners were, however, distinctive to the north-east as well as being followed exclusively by working men, for instance potshare bowling. Big changes were underway in the later years of the nineteenth century as regional sports declined in the face of sports that were organized nationally and practised in all regions, most notably association football - though football soon became a mainly working-class game, thus continuing the strong element of social segregation in the playing and watching of sport, even as the old regional differentiation was breaking down.

Miners and gentry largely played different sports, but these were underpinned by an ethos that was in many ways similar. Betting was intrinsic to nearly all of the miners' sports, and most events were accompanied by drinking, certainly after, but often during the play. Many of the sports involved contests between and/or the killing of animals. And the qualities most admired in a man were similar to those most admired in a dog - strength, speed and skill, combined with 'pluck'. Indeed Metcalfe argues that until the rise of football, one-to-one contests were the favoured form of encounter, in which the qualities of the individual man or dog could be fully tested, and the spectators also pitted their own judgement against other spectators in the bets they made on the likely outcome. Metcalfe relates this to the realities of life down the pit where the most prestigious job, that of the hewer, depended on physical strength, and where masculinity was on permanent trial. The prosperity of the miner's family depended on his 'masculine' qualities of strength, endurance and courage. This was also the basis of the privileges which men claimed within the home. To fully justify this argument, however, a comparative study of sport in mining communities would be necessary. Certainly team games were popular among workers in other parts of

<hr>

[18] Ibid., 12-13, 24-25, 160; Richardson, *The Life*, 26, 160.
[19] Metcalfe, *Leisure*, 67.

England, even before the rise of association and rugby football, and 'masculine' qualities were often on full display, albeit in different ways.

One example is that of the various forms of street football played on Shrove Tuesday in many parts of England, but often under threat in the mid-nineteenth century from modernizing town councils which regarded them as a 'nuisance'. Among the most famous was that in Derby, suppressed by the Town Council in 1845, though there were subsequent attempts to revive it, sometimes leading to fights between players and police, and to arrests.[20] By 1884 street football was 'heritage', and a local paper published the reminiscences of a well-known player, William Williamson, nicknamed Tunchy Shelton, who was by then living in an alms-house.[21] The game started in the Market Place and the aim was to get the ball into one of the goals, placed at opposite ends of the town. The teams represented respectively St Peter's parish and All Saints' parish, though the latter was taken to include other smaller parishes on the north side of the town. The players were unlimited in number. On Shrove Tuesday there was a general holiday in the town and crowds of avidly partisan spectators would line the streets or look out from windows. A lot of the play took place in the river Derwent, and the only known fatality was a man drowned in the river. However, lesser injuries were frequent. Shelton had broken his ribs on one occasion and they had never fitted properly since. Shelton's account highlights the familiar qualities of strength, willingness to take risks, courage in the face of injury, and ability to take one's drink, together with anecdotes about memorable characters and incidents, while also adding an element of intense local patriotism. His father had been a St Peter's man. Shelton himself "would have gladly died rather than give up St Peter's and so would many another and some have died for it. All the lads and lassies were either St Peter's or All Saints and the women were worst of all." He once had a fight with a man who said he had turned his coat. "I would not have turned my coat to save my life and would not do so now." However the intense will to win that was expected of the true footballer was modified by the need for chivalry to injured opponents. In its more extreme forms it could also lend itself to humour: Shelton recalled that Bob Yeomans, a 'queer chap', had once carried the ball through a sewer, coming out filthy.

For the working-class sportsman, as much as for his upper class counterpart, sporting events were a drama, replete with incident and with larger-than-life characters, recalled whether over a pint pot or a glass of port for years afterwards, and with humour playing an essential part. The adoption of nicknames was part of the dramatization, and this spread into prize-fighting and into the working class sport of pedestrianism, where the assignment of a nickname was an important mark of an athlete's reputation - though the nickname was sometimes placed in quotation marks by those who wished to claim that this reputation was inflated. Sporting gentry also used a sporting slang. Thus in *Bell's Life*, boxing was "milling" and those who attended prize-fights were "milling coves". The fighters hit one another on the "nut" or the "gob" and a really good hit made "the claret flow". In part, knowledge of the jargon was simply a certificate of bona fide membership of the group. But it also reflected the

---

[20] The best account is Delves, "Popular recreation". See also Hudson, *The History*.
[21] Derby Local Studies Library, manuscripts, BA796.33: "Tunchy Williams interviewed".

sportsmen's self-image, and the ways in which they distinguished themselves both from women and from those of their own sex who were likely to make dull companions, or who might actually want to spoil their fun. Religious zealots of all kinds and clergymen in particular were believed to be prominent among these "killjoys" and "canting hypocrites" and many verbal missiles were hurled at these enemies of sport. When in the 1830s the vicar of Wednesbury led moves to stop the annual bull-baiting, an enraged bull-baiter complained to a journalist "I say it's a nation shame. He gets his fun from sorm singing, and whoy can't he let us have our fun."[22]

THE CHRISTIAN SPORTSMAN

Thomas Hughes would have accepted at least some of these points, and his 'muscular Christianity' was partly directed at sportsmen who thought religion was not manly, as well as at religious people who thought that sport was not Christian. There were parts of the ideal of the 'sportsman' which those like Hughes could willingly embrace, although they clearly rejected other aspects. In fact the concept of the 'sportsman' included a spectrum of values and ways of behaving, some of which overlapped with those of the 'muscular Christian', while others were very different.

Hughes fully shared the 'sportsman's' delight in physical contests of many kinds and in closeness to nature. *Tom Brown* is full of blow-by-blow narratives of sporting events as well as of fishing and bird nesting. And while anxious to distance himself from "the brutal exhibition of men battering one another for money", he shared the fascination of so many of his contemporaries with fighting: "it is no good for Quakers or any other body of men to uplift their voices against fighting. Human nature is too strong for them, and they don't follow their own precepts."[23] Hughes would have agreed with those 'sportsmen' who declared that fighting was natural and it was fun. But the characteristic Hughesian note lay in the higher purposes to which this fighting instinct should be put:

> From the cradle to the grave, fighting, rightly understood, is the business of life, the real, honestest business of every son of man. Everyone who is worth his salt has his enemies who must be beaten, be they evil thoughts and habits in himself or spiritual wickedness in high places, or Russians or Border ruffians, or Bill, Tom or Harry who will not let him live his life in quiet till he has thrashed them.

In particular, the 'muscular Christian's' fists were in the service of women and children and 'the weak' generally. The most famous scene in *Tom Brown* is that where the hero comes to the aid of the new boy, George Arthur, who is being bullied by some of his dormitory mates because he goes down on his knees to say his prayers before going to bed. Tom's physical bravery and healthy instincts are of course praised, but

[22] Reid, "Beasts and brutes", 15.
[23] Hughes, *Tom Brown*, 282-283.

the equally important point is that the physically weak may be morally stronger, and moral strength is what counts for most - though the perfection of manhood is the combination of moral and physical strength. Physical strength combined with moral weakness might merely produce a bully. Moral strength and physical weakness might mean a person with the best of intentions but incapable of doing what was needed in a crisis. A typical day in the life of a 'muscular Christian' might include saving someone from drowning, running a five-minute mile in order to fetch a doctor, or coming to the aid of a woman who was struck in the street.[24] Moreover, Hughes, like Kingsley, was a fervent patriot. "I take it for granted", he wrote in a religious periodical, "that every man who reads this Magazine will come forward [in the event of war], and give his goods, his body, his life if necessary, for the old country and her women and children."[25]

Speakers at the Church Congress, an annual gathering of Anglican clergy and laity at which issues of contemporary concern were discussed, offer a view of some of the arguments for 'muscular Christianity' that were being more widely canvassed at the time. In 1869 the Congress considered "The Recreations of the People" and similar themes were again chosen in 1874, 1877, 1878, 1880 and 1892. The first of these discussions was opened by the Rev. J. Erskine Clarke, vicar of Battersea, a mainly working-class district of London, who wanted the church to be more active in recommending and indeed supplying legitimate recreation, while continuing to condemn harmful recreations. He unreservedly approved of cricket, rowing, athletics, as well as gardening and participation in the volunteer movement. He gave more guarded approval to dancing, which was good in itself, but often pursued in unsavoury dance-halls. This was where the church could play a role by holding dances, concerts, and other entertainments in a healthy atmosphere. The theatre was good in principle, but often associated with "drinking and licentiousness". In fact any form of amusement that was associated with drinking or gambling was harmful, and his speech was devoted as much to condemning the bad as commending the good.[26] Other speakers placed the stress more heavily on commending the good, and on ridiculing the negative approach of many clergy. For instance the Rev. J.C. Chambers, in the most comprehensive assertion of the recreational imperative, presented his vision of a 'merry England', in which the parish club would stand at the centre of the recreational life of each parish. He condemned all amusements which "encourage barbarity" or involve gambling, but he equally condemned the asceticism which had alienated many men from the church:

> Parson killjoy, it seems to me, would have more influence with his men and lads, if he were known to countenance their cricketing and boat-racing, their wrestling and their racing, their glees and their theatricals, and if he were not entirely taken up with the idea of cramming them with good tracts and books.

[24] Hughes, "How to be bodily strong in a town", 2.
[25] Ibid., 5.
[26] *The Official Report of the Church Congress*, 1869, 118-128.

> All that tends to health of mind and body is a handmaid to moral and religious
> culture.

He wanted to see parishes providing facilities for rifle-shooting, drilling, gymnastics, cricket, football, concerts and theatricals.[27] The Rev. William Glaister, a curate from Nottinghamshire, welcomed these ideas on behalf of the younger generation of clergy, and went on to enthuse about the many virtues that could be learnt through playing cricket. Indeed he attributed the high level of morality in Nottinghamshire to the large number of cricket clubs in the county:

> The best local Board of Health is a cricket ground, and the best moral club
> a Cricket Club, ten times better than all those clubs which call themselves
> 'Young Men's Christian Associations' and the like, which are not very invigor-
> ating either to the mind or muscle.[28]

A Hull vicar, the Rev. John Scott, provided a gym for the boys in his Sunday School. (He thought that there should be gyms for girls too, though as yet he had not attempted to do this.)[29]

'Muscular Christianity' was still controversial in the 1850s and '60s, though it was gaining ground fast, especially in the Church of England. (The Nonconformists would follow in the 1870s and '80s.) Those who wanted the churches to be actively involved in the promotion of sport were engaged in battles on three fronts: against more conservative Christians, who saw sport as being at best a waste of time, and as potentially sinful, or at least something that could lead Christians to sin, through its bad associations; against irreligious sportsmen, who rejected Christianity because it was 'effeminate' and/or 'puritanical'; and against less socially aware sportsmen who saw sport as being purely for their own pleasure, rather than something that could be socially beneficial.

Already in 1858 the first annual conference of the Young Men's Christian Associations (YMCA) of Great Britain and Ireland discussed "Recreation and the Duty of Young Men's Christian Associations Respecting it". Much of the discussion related to recreation in general, though some speakers referred to sport or to specific sports. The main speaker was Dr J.H. Gladstone, who admitted that recreation "may be pushed to an extreme, and perhaps, is so by a section of the English Church which has acquired for itself the ridiculous reputation of teaching 'Muscular Christianity'". However, he believed that YMCAs should provide recreation and many of his arguments would become very familiar in the following years: recreation was a necessary part of a balanced life; it was healthy; it enabled people to work more efficiently; "people will amuse themselves wickedly if innocent amusements are not provided"; it could be a good means of attracting recruits to the movement. Above all those who opposed healthy amusements were "modern Manichees". In the subsequent discussion three speakers, one of whom specifically recommended cricket, clearly favoured the inclu-

[27] Ibid., 133-134.
[28] Ibid., 142-144.
[29] Ibid., 141-142.

sion of recreation in the YMCA programme, while only one speaker was definitely opposed, but three seemed to have reached no clear conclusion.[30]

In the years following sport did become an increasingly important part of YMCA life (in spite of the aspersions of the Rev. William Glaister). At its inception in 1844 the Association's objectives had been strictly religious, but by the early 1860s the Manchester branch was also holding social gatherings and had a Society of Arts, as well as a considerable educational programme. At this stage its aim was "Promoting the Improvement of the Moral and Spiritual Condition of Young Men". However, by 1873 this remit had extended to embrace "the religious, moral and social welfare of the young men of Manchester and its neighbourhood", and it offered "facilities for Intellectual Improvement and Social Intercourse". A cricket club had been set up in 1871 and by 1873 there was also a Swimming Club and an Excursion and Rambling Club. In 1875 the relevant section of the programme was headed "Recreations of a manly and healthy character". The gymnasium, opened in 1876, was said to be the best in Manchester. In the opening ceremony the president "trusted that that part of the Association's premises would not become too popular to the exclusion of the other parts. The great object of the institution was to promote Christianity among young men: but there was no objection to a little muscular Christianity". 1876-1877 was indeed a boom year for the Manchester Association with over a thousand new members and associates joining (the latter, the majority, being men "of good moral character" but not church members).[31]

In the course of the 1880s clubs were also formed for cycling, football, athletics and lacrosse. There were similar trends in Birmingham, where by 1880 the Association aimed to promote "the Religious, Intellectual, Social and Physical Welfare of Young Men". They too had a gym and they claimed to encourage "all such manly and healthful pursuits as will tend to improve the physique of the members and associates, and make them the better fitted for active business life". The place of sport in the YMCA reached a high point in the early twentieth century. The Birmingham Association's new headquarters, opened in 1904, included "the most up-to-date gymnasium in the midlands" and at this time the *Birmingham YMCA Record* was devoting six of its twenty pages to sport.[32]

Many other Associations were building grandiose new premises at this time. A souvenir booklet marking the opening of a new Leicester headquarters in 1901 recalled that the association had collapsed in 1870, when "it could not afford very attractive rooms ... . It had no gymnasium and only a small library." A revival in 1883, following the visit to Leicester by the American evangelist D.L. Moody, led to improved premises with a gym as well as active support for foreign missions - "The Christian side of the Association has never been allowed to drop into the background." But, while stressing their spiritual work, they also noted that:

---

[30] *Report of the First Conference*, 33-45.

[31] University of Birmingham Library, YMCA Archives, A27: Annual Report of the Manchester YMCA, 1860-1863, 1873, 1875, 1877 [henceforth YMCAA].

[32] Ibid., YMCAA, A47: Annual Report of the Birmingham YMCA, 1880; *A Tale of Two Buildings*.

> Young men must have plenty of outlet for their physical energy, and it is
> the province of the YMCA to provide such an outlet, to the accompaniment
> of healthy moral surroundings, thus athletics are fostered in liberal fashion.
> A splendid new gymnasium is provided in the basement of the new buildings,
> and it has been fitted up in such a manner as to make it one of the best gymna-
> siums in the provinces. A competent instructor (Mr C.R. Robson) is engaged,
> and nightly many young men participate in the pleasures of organised muscu-
> lar exercise.[33]

There were also opportunities for cricket, rugby, soccer, hockey, cycling, chess and
draughts. The winter programme for 1906 included a photo of Mr A.R. Yapp, who was
holding meetings for 'Men Only': "Mr Yapp is a Young Man's Man. A friend called him
'A mass of masculinity!' He stands well over 6 feet, and as his photograph suggests, is
proportionately broad. His messages are characteristically broad, straight and manly
in presentation."[34] Many of the typical concerns of 'muscular Christians' remained
the same in the 1900s as they had been in the 1850s, though by this time they faced
much less opposition from fellow Christians, and they had become more uninhibited
in their claims for the moral as well as the physical benefits of sport. They continued
to revel in physicality, in muscular power and in bodily efficiency - and in this they
would have been at one with the 'sportsman'. But they always insisted that physical
efficiency was not an end in itself, but that it made for greater efficiency at work - and
not only in business, but in religious work too. Muscular Christians also had a continuing need to refute the claim that Christianity in general and the YMCA in particular
were unmasculine. The prominent Congregational preacher, J.H. Jowett, addressing
the Birmingham YMCA in 1907, welcomed the ways in which the Y had broadened its
remit since the time of his own youth:

> In the past the YMCA had been associated in the public mind with a flabby,
> emasculated piety. Goody-goody young men could not do the work of the
> strong Son of God. He wanted young men of strong will, clear head and fervent
> will to get hold of other young fellows. They could do it better than the clergy
> or ministers because they were not paid to do it... . It was not their business, it
> was a crusade.[35]

But their longest running controversy was with those Christians who wanted a clear
separation of the 'spiritual' from the 'secular', and who argued that sport, and indeed
most other forms of popular recreation, belonged to a worldly sphere which was no
concern of the church - and which Christians might be best advised to avoid altogether. In 1860 the Sheffield Broad Churchman, Rev. Samuel Earnshaw, was deplor-
ing the fact that some over-zealous Christians placed prohibitions on things never

[33] Ibid., YMCAA, A49: Leicester YMCA Souvenir, 1901, 3-7, 11.
[34] Ibid., YMCAA, A49: Leicester YMCA Prospectus of Winter Work, 1906.
[35] Ibid., YMCAA, A47: Annual Report of Birmingham YMCA 1907.

condemned in the Bible, including sport and the theatre.[36] In 1907 Canon Denton Thompson, addressing the same meeting of the Birmingham YMCA mentioned above declared:

> It was Christianity that sanctified the whole of life. That idea was well represented in the YMCA building by its reading rooms, study room, play room, and smoke room, all under the same roof as the room where they held religious meetings.[37]

Many of these arguments could as well be used in support of women's as of men's sport. As mentioned above, the Anglican Church Congress frequently debated the church's responsibilities in the field of recreation, and in the earlier years the focus was mainly on the needs of men and boys; but in 1892 several speakers also emphasized the needs of women and girls, and for the first time one of the main speakers on this topic was a woman, Miss Stuart Snell, the manager of a gymnasium in Kensington.[38] By the end of the nineteenth century some YMCA branches were providing sporting facilities for women or sponsoring activities in which both sexes took part. Thus the Leicester YMCA hosted "Ladies' Drill and Gym" on Thursday evenings and "Ladies' Physical Training" on Fridays. The cycling club at the Birmingham YMCA included "Ladies' Days" in its programme, and its *Record* gave an account of one such, which turned into an 80-mile run.[39] The *Northamptonshire Nonconformist*, a journal published in the later 1880s and '90s by the young men of College Street Baptist Church, Northampton, included a sports column, "Thews and Sinews", which sang the praises of sports of all kinds for women as much as for men - provided they did not involve gambling or cruelty to animals.[40] And indeed as early as 1861 Thomas Hughes was recommending the benefits of physical exercise for both sexes - although in practice all of his efforts seem to have been channelled into sport for men.

The most fundamental feature therefore of 'muscular Christianity' was not its muscularity,[41] or even the forms of masculinity embodied by its adherents, but its use of sport not only as something to be enjoyed for its own sake or as a source of status, but also as a means towards religious, moral and social ends.

Christian educationalists valued sport as a school of 'character'. A classic example was Edward Thring, headmaster of Uppingham School from 1853 to 1887, who was one of the most energetic and articulate promoters of public school sport.[42] Thring

<hr>

[36] Wickham, *Church and People*, 152-153.

[37] University of Birmingham Library, YMCAA, A47: Annual Report of Birmingham YMCA 1907.

[38] *The Official Report of the Church Congress*, 1892, 301-319.

[39] Birmingham YMCA Record, October 1904; University of Birmingham Library, YMCAA, A46, A49: Leicester YMCA Prospectus of Winter Work 1905.

[40] McLeod, "Thews and sinews".

[41] On this see also Gill, "How muscular was muscular Christianity?"

[42] Here my main source is the highly detailed and broadly sympathetic account in Tozer, *Physical Education*. A more critical popular account by Winner, *Those Feet*, argues that Thring was obsessed with the dangers of masturbation, and promoted sport in order to focus the boys' thoughts on things other than sex.

who, like all the headmasters of major public schools in his generation, was an Anglican clergyman, was the first to appoint a teacher of gymnastics and fencing (in 1860), and in 1857 he had made sport compulsory. Swimming, skating and rambling were practised mainly for fun; gymnastics for training the body; athletics for building the competitive spirit; but most important of all were cricket and football, because they placed the needs of the team before the desires of the individual player and because they taught the lessons "never cheat, never funk, never lose temper, never brag". Thring sometimes referred to sport in his chapel sermons, praising "the joy of strength and movement" and also courageous acceptance of defeat.

The "sporting parson", a figure often derided in the era of church reform of the 1830s and '40s, became a new role-model for Christian youth in the later part of the century. But where his Georgian predecessor had typically been a "hunting parson" at home with the gentry and large farmers of his own and neighbouring parishes, the late Victorian and Edwardian "man's man" was a cricketer, footballer or boxer with a special mission to young men and teenage boys of the working class. One boxing parson, the Rev. A. Osborne Jay, vicar of Holy Trinity, Shoreditch, a very poor district of London, even gave his name to a teenage gang, "Father Jay's Boys", which achieved notoriety when one of its members was killed in a fight with a rival gang in 1892.[43] A footballing parson, Rev. Llewellyn Gwynne, was centre-forward for Derby County in the 1880s, before going on to be Bishop of Khartoum and then Deputy Chaplain General during World War I. Gwynne's relatively modest educational record made it very unlikely that he would have been appointed to an English see, but his footballing prowess made him ideal for a missionary bishopric and for a leading role in ministry to the armed forces. Sportsmen were especially valued as military chaplains, as achievements on the football or cricket field were seen as the best means of securing the respect of the men.[44] But from the 1870s a growing number of clergy, first Anglican, but then Nonconformist and Catholic too, were providing sporting facilities for the young men and boys (later for young women and girls too).[45] Often they participated enthusiastically themselves.

THE PROFESSIONAL SPORTSMAN

It is well known that many of the top football and rugby teams of today originated from church teams founded in the latter part of the nineteenth century.[46] For instance, Aston Villa grew out of a cricket club established in the early 1870s by the members of a Wesleyan Young Men's Bible Class. Everton began in 1878 and also grew out of a cricket club - in this case one founded by the minister of St Domingo Methodist New

---

[43] McLeod, *Piety and Poverty*, 155.
[44] Snape, *Clergy under Fire*, 186, 188-189.
[45] In the Lancashire cotton towns in the 1920s around half the cricket and football teams were based on a place of worship, and well over half the teams playing rounders (an exclusively female sport) and tennis, table tennis and hockey (sports played by both sexes). See Williams, "Churches, Sport and Identities".
[46] Lupson, *Thank God for Football*.

Connexion chapel. Southampton ("The Saints") started as St Mary's Young Men's Association Football Club. It was founded at a meeting in 1885 chaired by the sporting curate of St Mary's Anglican church. According to St Mary's parish magazine, "All connected with [the Young Men's Association] are believers in muscular Christianity, and think that the advantage of strong developed limbs, a supple frame, and a quick eye cannot be overestimated." Northampton rugby club (also known as "The Saints") started in the 1870s as Northampton St James, its founders being members of the Mutual Improvement Association at St James' church. And one could go on and on with further examples.

However, as these and similar clubs rose in sporting importance their links with the churches that founded them often became more tenuous. The Football Association permitted the payment of players from 1885 and Aston Villa was among the first teams to go professional. To maintain their position as the top team in the Midlands, and soon as one of the top teams in England, they had to recruit outstanding players (often from Scotland) regardless of religious affiliation. Moreover, they had to keep winning. There were similar trends in rugby, where in 1895 the Northern Union, which favoured payments to players, broke away from the strictly amateur Rugby Football Union. Cricket, which had never banned professionalism, uniquely mixed amateurs and professionals ("gentlemen" and "players") at the top level, though the superstar of late Victorian sport, W.G. Grace, was a "shamateur", who earned more in "expenses" than top professionals did in wages.[47] The biggest earning professionals in this period were jockeys, though modern boxing was rising out of the ashes of the disgraced sport of prize-fighting, and offered professionals the possibilities of large earnings during their usually brief careers.

Many aspects of professional sport were alien to 'sportsmen' and 'muscular Christians' alike. Most obviously, since professional sport was all about winning, anything else could be sacrificed to further this end. W.G. Grace was particularly notorious for sharp practice, including the intimidation of umpires.[48] In football and rugby it was alleged that the need to win at all costs had led to an increase in violent play.[49] Moreover football and rugby teams soon became bound up with the identity, indeed the 'honour', of the surrounding community. Intense rivalries developed between neighbouring teams, resulting sometimes in fights between rival fans or attacks on players and referees.[50] As professional sportsmen emerged as popular heroes and role-models and professional teams became the chief focus of local patriotism, older ideals of 'fair play' or of the 'gallant loser' became largely outmoded. Admittedly an outstanding player could gain extra credit for magnanimity and 'clean' play, but these qualities were worth nothing if he did not keep on scoring goals or hitting runs. Moreover, the idea of sport as part of a balanced life in which the physical took its side beside the intellectual and the spiritual, and play took its place beside work, no longer fitted with a world where for some very prominent people play had become work, and where for many of their followers sport, rather than being one part of a balanced

[47] Rae, *W.G. Grace*, 102-104.
[48] Rae, *W.G. Grace*, 191-193.
[49] "The football slaughter".
[50] Maguire, "Images of manliness".

life, had become the meaning of life. Masculinity certainly remained a key aspect of the sporting professional. He was admired for all the qualities of physical strength, combined with dexterity, endurance and courage, which had marked the sportsmen of earlier generations. Some were, like W.G. Grace, physically formidable, and derived some of their charisma from their presence. But the second most successful batsmen of the later Victorian era, Bobby Abel, was notably undersized and derived his popularity both from his skill as a grafter and from his modest personality. The essential point was that both delivered the goods, and went on doing so season after season. Abel, who came from an impoverished working-class background was all too aware that being a professional sportsman was a very precarious way of earning a living and that only by constant practice and careful study of his own mistakes and failures could he retain his place in the team, elbowing out the many other talented players who were vying for his place.[51] Abel also recognized the advantages of a disciplined life-style. But professional sportsmen, like other professional entertainers, lived on a knife-edge, and heavy drinking was frequently their means of reducing the tensions inherent in their way of life.[52] The contrast with muscular Christianity was particularly stark, as religiously motivated propagandists for sport saw it as the antidote to the temptations of the pub. 'Sportsmen' were often keen drinkers, but for them beer or wine (depending on the social class of the drinker) were aids to conviviality rather than a way of coping with stress. Professional sportsmen were unlikely to be anti-clerical or irreligious in the way that some 'sportsmen' were, and indeed some were personally devout, but their religion was of little relevance to their performance on the field - though it might be important to their supporters, insofar as the community whose honour the football team or the boxer was championing might be defined in religious rather than geographical or national terms. However, the fact that they were Catholic, Protestant or Jewish made little difference to the way they played, as opposed to the interpretation that others gave to their victories and defeats.

THE SECULAR SPORTSMAN AND THE MUSCULAR CHRISTIAN

'Sportsman' and 'muscular Christian' were agreed in regarding sport as 'manly' and in celebrating the strength, the skill and the courage displayed in many different sports. They gained great pleasure both from playing and from watching, and they also made claims for the benefits of sport for society and nation. However, the moral and religious ethos associated with these two sporting sub-cultures was quite different, and they often had different ideas as to the kind of social benefits they were expecting. This was partly a matter of social class. The 'sportsman' was typically a member of the gentry or aristocracy and able if he wished to enjoy far more leisure time than was available to other classes. He expected and usually received deference. Some of the sports practised by these classes, such as shooting and yachting, excluded all but

[51] Kynaston, *Bobby Abel.*
[52] Collins and Vamplew, *Mud, Sweat and Beers*, 104-105.

the very rich, while others, such as fox-hunting involved a somewhat wider section of the rural population, though anyone below the ranks of the well-to-do farmer was unlikely to be on horseback. The 'muscular Christian' was more likely to belong to the middle class or lower middle class and to be committed to the gospel of work. Sport might indeed be the part of life that was dearest to him, but it was likely to be limited to Saturday afternoons and sometimes weekday evenings, and it was often justified by the claim that it enabled one to work more efficiently - not a claim made by 'sportsmen'. Muscular Christians also believed that sport could promote social harmony - though in this case it was the fact that the clergyman or Christian employer participated on equal terms alongside their parishioners or employees that was intended to strengthen the bonds between them.[53] This more democratic style was also reflected in support by clergymen for the National Amateur Rowing Association founded in the 1890s to challenge the elitism of the Amateur Rowing Association, which excluded working-class rowers.[54]

But the biggest area of difference between 'muscular Christians' and other sports enthusiasts may have lain in attitudes to gambling. As suggested earlier, bets were an integral part of most of the sports that were popular in the first half of the nineteenth century, the only major exception being fox-hunting. Betting had of course attractions of many different kinds, but the most important was that it allowed the spectators to feel that they were not passive onlookers, but that they too were involved in a contest which depended on their skill and maybe their daring, though not their physical prowess. The most innovative aspect of 'muscular Christianity' - and the one that most often led its practitioners into conflict with other players and followers of sport - was the attempt to promote sport while excluding gambling. Gambling (often in combination with drink) came to be seen as the embodiment of all that was corrupt. Betting was dishonest, as it was a way of getting money without working for it; it led to crime, as those who had lost then stole; it meant hungry children as "the shilling that ought to have gone to the grocer's shop went on a horse"; it was addictive, as those once started on a gambling career poured more and more money into their craze. According to the prominent Congregationalist preacher, R.F. Horton, gambling was wrong in itself, whereas alcohol (the other main target of Nonconformist moralists) was not wrong if taken in moderation, and sexual immorality was "the misdirection or abuse of that which is not only legitimate but hallowed by God".[55] There were many rational arguments against gambling, but the depth of revulsion which it provoked in its critics led them often to resort to metaphorical language. According to one Methodist writer, for instance, betting was a "moral plague" that was "rapidly infecting every branch of the community, and invading the home and the church", and he included it together with other forms of immorality and crime among the "ulcers on the body, indicating a pervasive poison in the blood".[56] By

[53] Howat, *Village Cricket*, 15-17, 89-101, gives several examples of rural clergy, the earliest being in 1820s, who founded cricket clubs, including some who also played for the team.
[54] Lowerson, *Sport*, 100-101.
[55] These arguments are taken from Woodcock, "Betting"; see also Munting, "Social opposition".
[56] Woodcock, "Betting", 97.

contrast the images "muscular Christians" associated with approved sports, such as football, athletics, swimming, and above all cricket, were those of physical, mental and spiritual health - they were "vigorous", "sound" and "robust". They promoted "courage, presence of mind and self-reliance". They brought "joy", "animation", "a bounding pulse" and "a blithe heart".[57]

[57] These are taken from the paper by Colonel Onslow, "Physical Recreation", at the Church Congress in 1892.

Papal Zouaves illustrate the ambiguity of ideals of Christian manliness: courage and strength but also obedience, sacrifice and sentimentality.
[Cover of a song of the zouaves, Brussels, c 1870; Louvain, KADOC-KU Leuven]

LIONS AND LAMBS AT THE SAME TIME!

****

BELGIAN ZOUAVE STORIES AND EXAMPLES OF RELIGIOUS MASCULINITY

THOMAS BUERMAN

PONTIFICAL ZOUAVES AS IDEAL CATHOLICS

Within my PhD research, as part of a project examining the feminization of religion in Belgium, I spent considerable time seeking a suitable angle to tackle questions about the difficult relation between masculinity and religion in the nineteenth century. As it turned out, I settled on Catholic secondary schooling. While I was doing what historians do, mostly reading and looking for primary sources concerning one's topic, an interesting subject for looking into Catholic manliness suggested itself: the papal Zouaves. I understand that the link between Catholic secondary education and the soldiers of the Pope does not seem clear-cut. Working from the historical context, I will make the association explicit.

The papal or pontifical Zouaves were members of a corps of volunteers, originally Frenchmen and Belgians and later supplemented with other nationalities, formed in Rome for the defence of the pope between 1860 and 1871.[1] They were especially identifiable by their Arabian-cut crimson trousers. Their name and uniform were

---

[1] One extensive historical published study exists about the French Zouaves: Guenel, *La dernière guerre*, 196. In a study on the French devotion for Pius IX the Zouaves are discussed as a self-sacrificing movement in Horaist, *La Dévotion*, 54-59. Recently an extensive and wide article, which will be discussed in this contribution, has been published on a certain aspect of the French Zouave mobilization: Harrison, "Zouave Stories". For Belgium a thorough but of less scientific value local history is available: Goddeeris, *De Pauselijke Zouaven*, 429. In the literature on the *Risorgimento* the Zouaves are discussed obliquely and in religious history they are almost completely lacking. For example Coppa, "Italy", does not mention them. Brief reference can be found in Clark, "The New Catholicism", 22. The Zouaves received more attention in Viaene, "The Roman Question", 144-146; Viaene called the mobilization "The most spectacular aspect of Catholic mobilization on behalf of the pope [...]".

adopted from a French light-infantry corps created by Louis-Napoléon Bonaparte in 1852. During the wars of the Second Empire, the Zouaves earned themselves a name as an elite corps. Their bravery together with the easily recognizable uniform made them universally known and examples for soldiers and common people alike. The origin of this French corps and their exotic uniform lies in 1830 during the French Regency, when mercenaries from a Kabyle war tribe were organized into three French regiments and were given a uniform based on their local dress.[2]

After the Italian seizure of two thirds of the papal territory in 1859, it became clear that the papal army was not up to its tasks.[3] The Belgian prelate Xavier de Mérode was selected from the pope's entourage to reorganize the army. Together with the French veteran general Louis de La Moricière, appointed commander-in-chief, de Mérode decided to start building up an international corps of volunteers. Besides Austrian, Swiss and Irish divisions, French and Belgian volunteers were grouped together into what was called the Tirailleurs Franco-Belges. This pack of infantry-men consisted of 450 men, of which at least 183 were Belgians.[4] They took part in the battle at Castelfidardo where the papal army was defeated by the Piedmontese. Sixty of them met their death, plenty were wounded and the majority were imprisoned. The survivors were supposed to be repatriated when released from the enemy's prisons, but most of them returned to Rome.[5] These men were the basis on which on the first of January 1861 the battalion of pontifical Zouaves was formed.[6]

Between 1861 and 1870 these papal soldiers mostly undertook police actions consisting of border patrols in the reduced Papal States and operations that helped prevent the outbreak of revolutions.[7] The Zouaves' finest hour was when they fought Garibaldi and his volunteers on 3 November 1867 at Mentana and won. However, as with most of the events during the Risorgimento, the role of France was pivotal at Mentana. It was the French expeditionary force's reinforcement of the withdrawing Zouave army that landed the victory. In this case the new *chassepot* rifle used by the French made the difference and forced Garibaldi to retreat.[8] The importance or even indispensableness of the French troops becomes clear when the army of pontifical Zouaves came to its end in 1870. The Franco-Prussian war forced Napoléon III to recall his troops to France. The absence of these armed forces brought about Italy's annexation of Rome. After what has appropriately been labelled a simulacra resistance,[9] the Zouaves, on direct order of Pius IX, surrendered at the Porta Pia, one of the gates of Rome, and the Eternal City was taken.

The misfortune suffered by the States of the Church activated the religious zeal of Catholics. According to Bruno Horaist in his study on French devotion to Pius IX the defeat at Castelfidardo was apropos the enlisting essential:

[2] Petit, "Zouaves".
[3] For the ideological, political and religious aspects of the clash between the Catholic Church and Italian nationalism, see Coppa, "Italy", 233-249.
[4] Guenel, *La dernière guerre*, 29; Leconte, "Les Belges".
[5] Leconte, "Les Belges", 181.
[6] Jarry, "Zouaves".
[7] Ibid.
[8] Ganiage, "Mentana".
[9] Id., "Rome".

The crush of Lamoricière's small army at Castelfidardo wounded the sense of chivalry and national pride of the ultramontains. This defeat aroused the desire for battle, the hope of being heroes, in the young.[10]

Similar in-depth research into different aspects of the Belgian worship to Pius IX has not been done yet. Nevertheless it is clear that the events in the Papal States aroused numerous addresses, petitions and newspaper articles in Belgium devoted to the Pope and the fund-raising system of the Peter's Pence.[11] A recruitment campaign directed at young male Catholics involving books, plays, allocutions and published personal testimonies was set up. This recruitment discourse, which lasted for the whole period, had the desired effect: between 1860 and 1870 nearly 2000 Belgian men went to Rome to serve the Pope.[12]

The discourse was also introduced in schools and resulted in pupils entering the papal army. Exact numbers on the commitment of secondary schoolboys cannot be provided yet. It probably was not the prevailing standard as it is certain that the local ecclesiastic hierarchies did not advocate the recruitment of minors; the bishop of Bruges, for instance, expressed concerns about a possible exodus from preparatory seminaries and about making the cause of the pope into a *bambineria*, a case for children.[13] A recent study on Belgian Jesuit colleges assesses that the Jesuits in Belgium (as in the rest of Europe) devoted themselves greatly to finding new people to join the pontifical army. The small number of conscripts connected to the Jesuit colleges, 12 enlistments for 5 institutions, however suggests that the Jesuit recruitment efforts were not directed towards their own pupils. Probably parental objections to possible enlistments were decisive in reducing the propaganda for actual service whereas zeal for the pope's cause was titillated in different ways.[14]

On the other hand, therefore, it is interesting to note that the recruitment discourse prompted an image of the papal Zouave as an ideal Catholic male. The creation of Zouave companies for boys in schools appeals the most to the imagination. Zouave corps were established in several high schools during the nineteenth

[10] "Chez les ultramontains, l'écrasement de la petite armée de Lamoricière par les troupes piémontaises à Castelfidardo, blessa le sentiment chevalresque et l'orgueil national. Cette défaite aviva, chez les jeunes, le désir de se battre, l'espoir d'être un héros". Horaist, *La Dévotion*, 54. In an accompanying essay in the catalogue of the 2007-2008 exhibition "Héros d'Achille à Zidane" in the Bibliothèque nationale de France on French heroes through the ages the Zouaves are not included in the "Galerie confessionelle de héros zélés *ad majorem Dei gloriam*" but a short reference is made to the importance of hero worship of Christian knights for the determination of French Catholics to defend the interests of the Pope. Amalvi, "La construction".

[11] Viaene, "The Roman Question", 143-146.

[12] The first Belgian Zouave joined in Brussels on 17 April 1860 and the last one enrolled on 1 September 1870. Between these two dates 1963 Belgian men joined the pontifical Zouaves. See Stevens, "Een goudmijn".

[13] Bruges, Episcopal Archives Bruges: File minor seminary 1859-1869. On a controversy surrounding a possible conscription of minors for the papal forces in the city of Bruges see: De Smet, "Ronseling".

[14] Dusausoit, *Les collèges jésuites*, 708-709.

century.[15] The best example is the minor seminary of Roeselare where the Zouave corps existed from 1869 to 1960. Students who had been real Zouaves carried the corps during its first few years, leaving a body of descriptive literature for the following members to use in organizing their school society. The members of these corps received a military rank, dressed up in the fancy uniform and walked around with wooden weapons. On festivals they re-enacted battles. The members saw a school year as a military campaign.[16] The importance of this Zouave tradition and the lasting devotion to Pope Pius IX in the minor seminar of Roeselare can be seen in the festivities in 1929, organized to celebrate the Lateran Treaty and in honour of the real Zouaves and Pius IX.[17] Besides Zouave squads, the staging of Zouave plays in different colleges,[18] the composing of passionate speeches about Pius IX and his soldiers for literary societies[19] and the sending to Rome of expressions of support[20] all prove the carry-over of the Zouaves to secondary school boys. It is of course not surprising that these men served as an example. It so happens that they were men who were dedicated to their religion in anything but a noncommittal way. Besides, they belonged to an army, generally accepted as a feature of modern masculinity.[21]

The following quotation from Wiseman's *Fabiola*, cited in the Zouave novel *For Two Fathers*, which was part of the recruitment discourse, points to the sacrifice of life and thereby to the Zouave as a role model with a status of or even higher than a priest:

> Many a pious parent has devoted her infant son from the cradle to the holiest and noblest state that earth possesses; has prayed and longed to see him grow up to be, first a spotless Lévite, and then a holy priest at the altar; and has watched eagerly each growing inclination, and tried gently to bend the tender thought towards the sanctuary of the Lord of Hosts. And if this was an only child, as Samuel was to Anna, that dedication of all that is dear to her keenest affection, may justly be considered as an act of maternal heroism. What then must be said of ancient matrons, - Felicitas, Symphorosa, or the unnamed

---

[15] Known to me are corps in the minor seminary of Roeselare; Colleges of Sint-Josephs, Torhout; Sint-Amands, Kortrijk; Sint-Aloysius, Menen; Tielt and Moeskroen and the Jesuit college in Mons. For France Ruth Harris has noted that Père Emmanuel d'Alzon clothed his pupils at his Assumption College in Nîmes in the colours of the Zouaves. See Harris, *Lourdes*, 215-216.

[16] Roeselare, Archives of Roeselare minor seminary: Fund Zouave corps and Library of the Zouave students.

[17] Strobbe, *200 jaar dichters*, 330.

[18] In the different Jesuit colleges several plays about the Zouaves were staged, for instance *Pour le drapeau, épisode de la guerre pontificale (1860)*; *Le départ du zouave pontifical*; *La caverne d'Osinio, le zouave pontifical*, all three by Paul Lefevre, SJ, see Dusausoit, *Les collèges jésuites*, 660-683. *Pour le drapeau* was also performed in the minor seminary of Roeselare. Roeselare, Archives of Roeselare minor seminary: Library of the Zouave students.

[19] For instance the Literary Societies of the Jesuit college in Mons and the minor seminary in Sint-Niklaas have produced different pieces on the Zouaves. See Dusausoit, *Les collèges jésuites*, 646-647 and Sint-Niklaas, Archives minor seminary Sint-Niklaas: Logbook of the Literary Society, 1848-1888.

[20] Ghent, Episcopal Archives Ghent, Fund minor seminary Sint-Niklaas: Letter of Pius IX sent as an answer to the letter sent to him by the pupils of the minor seminary of Sint-Niklaas out of piety, 6 October 1860.

[21] Nye, "Western Masculinities".

mother of the Maccabees, - who gave up or offered their children, not one, but many, yea all, to be victims whole-burnt, rather than priests, to God?[22]

Martin Rutten, a seminarian in 1864 and later on bishop of Liège, was also convinced the Zouaves were paragons, as his words testify in a letter to his Zouave brother René Corneille Rutten: "Yes, the zouaves have a mission, a very great mission to fulfil; they are fulfilling it now, for example, perhaps, one day, with the sacrifice of their lives."[23]

Convinced of the importance of the Zouaves as examples for secondary school boys this article will analyse some works of the Zouave discourse and will try to determine how the Zouave as an ideal Catholic male was presented in these works.[24] One should keep in mind however that this discourse was formulated in a period and milieu that historiography has defined as feminized. At first glance there is no room in the feminization of religion thesis for the pontifical Zouaves or for a propagation of their engagement. The rationale behind this article is this contradiction between the scholarly narrative of a feminized church and these masculine Catholic heroes.

ZOUAVE STORIES PRESENTING RELIGIOUS MASCULINITY

The recruitment discourse will be analysed predominantly through *For Two Fathers* by Canon Servaas Daems.[25] The book can be seen as important for several reasons. First, because it is a work of fiction. Fiction leaves more space for the author to present the narrative. In this respect one could define *For Two Fathers* as a tendentious novel, which implies that the message is presented explicitly.[26] It does not mean, however, that the other works are more accurate. Second, the book has known several editions, three in Dutch (1868, 1898 and 1902), two in English (1869 and 1877), one in French (1870), one in Czech (1876) and one in German (1903). Third, the importance of the author - who became a member of the Royal Flemish Academy of Language and Liter-

[22] Wiseman, *Fabiola*, 11. Cited in Daems, *Voor twee vaders*, 57. Referring to the Maccabees was common in the recruitment discours. It can also be found in Cautereels, *De pauselijke zouaven*, 59 and De Corte, *Lijkrede*, 1.

[23] "Oui, les zouaves ont une mission, une grande mission à remplir; cette mission ils la remplissent maintenant [1864] par l'exemple, un jour peut-être par le sacrifice de leur vie." Martin Rutten, Letter to his brother, 7 February 1864, reproduced in: Id., *Lettres*, 39-40.

[24] The analysed works are: De Ségur, *Les Martyrs*; Terwecoren, *Ludovic de Taillart*; Van Hulsem, *Het pauselijk zoeavenleven*; *Bloemen*; Cautereels, *De pauselijke zouaven*; Daems, *Voor twee vaders*; De Becdelièvre, *Souvenirs*; De Corte, *Lijkrede*; Pruvost, *Notice*; Terwecoren, *Auguste Misson*. Numerous references to Belgian Zouave stories can be found among others in Gola, *Un demi-siècle* and Lorette, "Historiographie". For this article only Zouave stories have been selected which were published between 1860 and 1871. The works also had to be in a school library like that of the minor seminaries of Roeselare or Sint-Niklaas or at least had to have been reviewed in a Belgian Catholic pedagogical journal of the nineteenth century. Without claiming full proof these criteria contain the possibility of having been read.

[25] The book has been translated in English as *The Double Sacrifice*. I prefer to use the literal translation "For Two Fathers" of the original Dutch title *Voor twee vaders* as I have only read the Flemish version and as different fathers play an important role in the narrative.

[26] Suleiman, *Authoritarian fictions*, 7.

ature and was a much sought-after preacher to adorn retreats, especially in Catholic boarding schools and colleges - suggests that his work was known and possibly read in the Catholic milieus I am interested in.[27] I will discuss the Zouave image observed in the book and compare it with the other works in the recruitment discourse.

Daems formulates several motives for writing his book. First, he hopes to deliver writings that are not dangerous. This indicates once again the preoccupation of the church with the reading habits of her followers. But most of all the commitment of the Zouaves inspired him to act. According to himself, he does this best by writing a book. With this, Daems suggests something that is present in all Zouave discourse, namely that everybody should participate in Pius' battle. People should do everything in their power. Besides fighting, Daems sees praying as most essential. Third, the author wants to fill a gap in the Zouave literature. He refers to the Italian Zouave novel *Olderico, o lo zuavo pontificio* by Antonia Bresciani, in which according to Daems no mention is made of the Belgian contribution to the Pope's struggle.[28] Finally, he concludes with an appeal to the "brave children of Belgium" to "gather around the rock of Peter" (7). By doing this he links himself to the recruitment efforts. It is notable that he explicitly calls on children and not adults. Throughout his book Daems idealizes the youth as the real defenders of the Catholic Church. Strikingly, his introduction makes no gender difference. Only after introducing two of his main characters, a brother and a sister with the most appropriate names Joseph and Maria, does he make the gender difference clear. At a chapel praying for the recovery of their terminally ill mother, the girl urges the boy to pray more and harder. Joseph suggests that he has better means at his disposal, namely sacrificing himself for the pope: prayer is not the only weapon.[29] As the mother is miraculously cured, the author clearly suggests that Joseph's promise to join the Zouaves was most efficient. Joseph will band together with two other adolescents, his cousin Victor and friend Marten. Although Victor will not survive the endeavour, before he dies he gets enough opportunities to prove he is a good Christian and a good soldier. And when he finally passes away, he goes down in a blaze of glory.

This idealization of children and their sacrifices are themes that recur in other works by this author and are general features of Catholic youth literature in the second half of the nineteenth century.[30] The other texts in my selection equally emphasize youth although more exclusively boys. For example in a funeral oration in 1860, the priest Joannes-Baptista De Corte speaks of Belgian sons having children's hearts but manly courage.[31] Eleven years later a sermon delivered at the funeral of August De Rijnck, a Zouave who died from injuries sustained at the battle of Porta Pia, emphasized De Rijnck's chastity and virtue and his extreme youth when called to become a

---

[27] Weyns, "Daems, Servaas".

[28] This novel is discussed profoundly by Harrison, "Zouave Stories". The failure to appreciate the contributions of Belgians is a topos in all Belgian Zouave literature, from fiction to historiography, from nineteenth-century to contemporary local studies on individual Zouaves.

[29] Daems, *Voor twee vaders*, 16.

[30] Van Coillie and Ghesquière, *Uit de schaduw*, 92-97. In particular the story "Of Janneken and Mieken who went to Our Lady for food" in Daems's *Descriptions and Tales* [my translations], 1897, bears great resemblance to *For Two Fathers*.

[31] De Corte, *Lijkrede*, 11.

Zouave.[32] The priest Petrus Cautereels, who presents what he considers a pantheon of Zouaves in the third part of his book on the Zouaves, does the same. It seems that Cautereels' selection criteria were being young and having died on the battlefield or because of sustained injuries. For example, Cautereels quotes the newspaper *Le Bien public* which stated that in the Zouave Carlos d'Alcantara, killed at the age of twenty in the battle of Mentana, one could see "[...] the vigour and resoluteness of a man coupled with the sweetness and open-heartedness of a child [...]".[33] In biographical works about certain Zouaves the authors also stress the youth of their subjects. In Ludovic de Taillart's biography written in 1862 by the Jesuit Éduard Terwecoren, his brother gave evidence that Ludovic was "a good child [...] of a rare tranquillity; and although he had an almost-feminine natural sensitivity, his resolute spirit never failed him for a moment: he shed not a single tear in front of his mother".[34] In their life story Alfred de Limminghe and Auguste Misson are presented as young pious boys, who lived an exemplary life but died too young. De Limminghe's biographer adds that Alfred's devotion was still lively and true.[35]

Being youngsters, the Zouaves were somewhat logically presented as unmarried. But strikingly, there was never mention of a fiancée, or even a girlfriend at home or a possible love interest in Italy. The Zouaves were innocent virgins. Their virginal state was embroidered with the support the papal soldiers received from their mothers. The above quotation from Wiseman's *Fabiola* is one of many references to mothers who have to be prepared to sacrifice their sons for the cause of the pope. Because of this, Anatole de Ségur dedicates his book to the mothers of the Zouaves who "[...] participated in the sacrifice by their abnegation, devotion and the heroic courage with which they accepted it".[36] Mothers clearly outshined a possible wife or marriage itself. The Zouaves are sons, not husbands. A contrast to this maternal bond was a non-believing father who tried to forbid his son's commitment. For the sake of completeness, since the whole family was discussed, girls stayed at home but contributed to the wellbeing of their brothers and that of the pope by praying a lot and with such dedication that it often had an immediate effect on the course of battle. The home is presented as a home front, which is only of smaller importance.

The use of children, in this case a boy, as ideals was common practice in all arts and ideologies. Hence one should see the representation of the Zouaves as young and dying heroes in the context of, for example, the creation of Joseph Bara and Agricole Viala as young champions of the French Revolution[37] and in the traditions of child saints. As Cautereels explicitly refers to it, the beatification of the young Johannes Berchmans in 1865 is the best example. These persons, or even better, personages not only increase the dramatic tension but also bring about cultural influence. According to Karen Sánchez-Eppler in a study on children's participation in the making of social

---

[32] *Bloemen*, 6.
[33] Cautereels, *De pauselijke zouaven*, III, 45.
[34] "[...] un enfant sage, [...] d'un calme rare; et, quoiqu'il fût naturellement d'une sensibilité presque féminine, sa fermeté ne se démentit pas un seul instant: il ne versa pas une larme en présence de sa mere" Terwecoren, *Ludovic de Taillart*, 7-8.
[35] Id., *Auguste Misson*, VII; Pruvost, *Notice*, 5, 9.
[36] de Ségur, *Les Martyrs*, 5.
[37] Burleigh, *Earthly Powers*, 75.

meaning in the nineteenth century, "The death of a child stands as the quintessential example of how the helplessness of any actual individual child can be converted into cultural influence. The power that adheres in the figure of the dying child may be used to enforce a wide array of social issues, and any reader of the nineteenth-century fiction can easily produce a list of the lessons - temperance, abolition, charity, chastity, and most of all piety - underscored by the death of a child."[38] The latter remark concerning de Limminghe is one of many indications in the texts that illustrate that the dying Zouaves not only stand for piety, but above all portray a pure piety in contrast to corrupted adults. Therefore one could say that the Zouaves are personages that symbolize an 'infantilization' of Roman Catholicism.[39] I would in this particular case and for different reasons add the adjective 'male' to this expression. Firstly, the Zouaves are men, secondly women have limited roles in the Zouave stories and thirdly, women's functions are consistent with what has already been determined within the feminization of religion theory. Women are presented as profoundly pious and are seen as passing religion down from generation to generation. But fourthly and most importantly, no real difference is made between younger girls and their adult counterparts. They are two of a kind. There is just one exception. Only in Cautereels' work one can find an unreligious woman. When discussing Garibaldi, the author presents Garibaldi's wife Anitta as as non-believing as her husband. But Cautereels suggests that her mixed race could be an explanation and surely presents her as an 'unwomanly' woman:[40] "She was brown of colour, like all the Creoles in the tropics, small in stature, heavily built and swift in her movements; she had an expressive face, fiery eyes, and broad shoulders like a man."[41] I would also claim that this male infantilization is part of the larger feminization thesis as the antipode is the same, namely the unreligious adult man.

Daems elaborates on manly irreligiousness by introducing anticlerical men at several points in the story. This is worked out explicitly in a chapter titled "How a freethinker ends". In it Victor's father Mr. Morren witnesses the last moments of a Freemason's life. The dying man, flanked by his brother and sister, his doctor and a friend, cries out that he wants to see a priest. As all three men are members of the *Solidaires* they refuse to comply with the last wish of their friend and brother.[42] The man turns to Mr. Morren: "Ah, Morren! cried he; a priest, a priest!... They want me to pass away without a priest!... [...] No, no! moaned the sick person. It is the death! I feel it burning deep down. A priest, quick! They don't want to call one, I can't die like a dog."[43] Only the sister, indeed clearly ashamed because she thinks a priest

---

[38] Sánchez-Eppler, *Dependent states*, 101.

[39] Infantilization of religion has not yet received much scholarly attention. It has been argued that it is part of an exceeding religious specialization, next to, among others feminization, in which children are seen as a separate target audience. It consists of e.g. the practice of children making their First Communion at the earlier age of seven years, the adoration of child saints and youth literature. See De Maeyer, "The Concept".

[40] This expression is taken from Mosse, *The Image of Man*, 13.

[41] Cautereels, *De pauselijke zouaven*, I, 79.

[42] According to Daems the *Solidaires* is a grouping that is allied to the Carabona, secretly helps the Italian republican cause and is antagonistic towards priests.

[43] Daems, *Voor twee vaders*, 243.

will not follow her into a notorious house of Freemasons, can be persuaded to find a priest. When the clergyman arrives, Mr. Morren and he are kicked around and out after witnessing the terrible death agony of the dying man who neither confessed nor received the last rites. Mr. Morren reflects:

> So it is then, how a Freemason ends!... Such is the fate that awaits you if you do not return to religion, to the faith of your younger years. [...]; the desperate death-struggle and the horrible rage of the wretched deceased deterred him and clot his blood in his veins, and the hideous face, immediately disfigured and turned black after death, stayed before his eyes and made his limbs shudder."[44]

With this description Daems lets Belgian current events slip inside his narrative, as starting in the late 1850s civil burials were becoming recurring manifestations of anticlericalism that were at the heart of the culture wars in Belgium.[45] Daems' disturbing take on a Freemason's last breath was probably a reaction against the most illustrative example of a Belgian civil burial. In December 1862 Freemason Pierre-Théodore Verhaegen, founder of the liberal Université Libre de Bruxelles, died and under the terms of his will did not have a priest at his deathbed, did not receive extreme unction and was carried to his grave with a big politically charged funeral procession. His devout Catholic family was consternated and the ultramontane journal *Le Bien Public* called the manifestation "une orgie maçonnique.[46]

Daems' rendition of the dying freethinker distinctly contrasts with his account of the departed Victor, who had a soft radiance of blissfulness and a joyful smile on his face.[47] And in his chapter "How a Zouave dies", a title that in a way mirrors Daems' section under discussion, Cautereels chronicles that Zouaves lose their lives with patience in suffering and resignation and with endurance and submission to God's will.[48] Similar accounts are given in the studied eulogia. De Corte tells about a child who is mortally wounded by a bullet, makes the sign of the cross and departs to heaven with a sweet and laughing face.[49] De Rijnck's published tribute includes a description of his funeral service in which the observer notices that the open casket made it possible to see that De Rijnck's face remained expressive and full of power. In contrast to Daems' anticlerical personage, death did not leave marks on August De Rijnck.[50] The same physical dissimilarity is stressed in a journal article reporting on the battle of Mentana in 1867: "Next to this brave [Zouave] lay garibaldists; [they] died, one could see it in the features of their face, with slanderous talk on their lips and despair in their soul. What a difference! How beautiful is the death of a Christian soldier!..."[51] Almost identical utterances are made by the Zouave Théodore de

---

[44] Ibid., 250-251.
[45] Witte, "The battle".
[46] Ibid.
[47] Daems, *Voor twee vaders*, 274.
[48] Cautereels, *De pauselijke zouaven*, 83-94.
[49] De Corte, *Lijkrede*, 20.
[50] *Bloemen*, 4.
[51] "Veldslag van Mentana".

Turck de Kersbeek whose letters are reproduced in Terwecoren's work on Auguste Misson: "Auguste died gently and happily. A smile of faith, piety, love and happiness seemed to animate his still, pallid lips, which had kissed the cross of salvation so effusively."[52] According to Pruvost, de Liminghe died with the same quiet forbearance. The Jesuit adds that this is characteristic of the chosen few.[53] This establishes that the acceptance of death has everything to do with the fact that the Zouaves are prepared to sacrifice themselves. Perpetual evidence can be found in the texts. As just one example, Auguste Misson stated "What better thing could have happened? I will never die in better circumstances. To die defending the faith is the best thing in the world."[54] Sacrifice is the ultimate motivation in the Zouave stories. Clearly the reason behind it will have been the possibility to imitate Christ. That this sacrifice not only consisted of fighting becomes clear when one sees the description of Misson's life, and certainly in Cautereels. It is mainly the resignation with which the Zouave dies that proves his martyrdom. Again, this is elaborated most explicitly in Daems' novel.

Daems does this by focusing on the male generational rift between Victor and his father. Victor, inspired by his nephew Joseph and their mutual friend Marten, wants to join the Zouaves. As a minor he has to receive permission from his parents. Victor's mother is pleased by his intentions, but as a freethinker, Mr. Morren refuses to let his son endeavour in what he calls "foolishness, preposterous foolishness! [...] zealotry, [...] fanciful."[55] This row is central to the book. Joseph and Marten receive their parental permission without any problem. As their fathers are deceased, Joseph and Marten only need the consent of their mothers, who are to say the least fairly enthusiastic. It is striking that in *For Two Fathers* and in other stories by Daems, the fathers of Catholic families have passed away. If patriarchs are still alive, they are unreligious. Daems does not provide a single religious male adult protagonist. Personal motives may have lain at the basis of this narrative or it could well be that Daems uses a strong symbol for the feminization thesis, the religious man is death.

But once again it turns out that the male infantilization is merely a part of the feminization. Mr. Morren attacks his wife more than his son: "But, he continued; my wrath is unreasonable: myself - I have myself to blame! I who gave full rein to your mother, to bring you up within her superstition! Yes, I can guess it! It shall be she, who, once again, has put this foolishness in your head."[56] Letting one of his characters speak this way, Daems shows that he is familiar with the anticlerical reproaches or fears that sons are more influenced by their mothers than their fathers.[57] Morren's accusations tie in with certain nineteenth-century French family conflicts that Paul Seeley has described and elucidated. Seeley found that a boy with the consent of his father was educated in the domestic sphere by his mother and thereby internalized religiosity. However it became crucial for the boy to renounce the values of his initial maternal socialization later in life. Whenever this rupture did not occur, the

---

[52] de Turck de Kersbeek, *Letter to his father.*
[53] Pruvost, *Notice*, 77.
[54] Terwecoren, *Auguste Misson*, 27.
[55] Daems, *Voor twee vaders*, 42.
[56] Ibid., 43.
[57] Art and Buerman, "Is de katholieke man wel een echte vent?", 28.

boy received scorn from society and came into conflict with his father because of an ideological commitment identified as unmasculine.[58] However, in the rest of Daems' narrative one finds the Catholic author's solution to this division between male adolescents and adults.

Victor's father can only be persuaded to grant his permission when he witnesses the physical state into which his son enters because of his refusal. And when Victor finally leaves for Rome, like Joseph he makes a deal with God. Like Joseph, who will fight to give thanks for the physical recovery of his mother, Victor will fight for the mental state of his father in the future. Victor has to pay a higher price for his reward than Joseph as he dies. Daems might be suggesting that a physical recovery is more easily attained that a mental one. In this struggle the women in the story help Victor. As Mr. Morren's secularist friends are no longer willing to talk to him because of the engagement of his son, Morren is condemned to talk more than usual to the womenfolk in his house, namely his wife, his sister-in-law and her daughter, being the mother and sister of Joseph, who all try to persuade him to join them in their prayers in particular and their religion in general. They can only bring Mr. Morren into doubt. It is Victor's commitment, fighting spirit and sacrifice that changes his mind. When Mr. Morren and the rest of the family are reunited around Victor's death-bed, Morren reveals that he has become a believer. The father cries out that his son has sacrificed himself for the well-being of his father. "Victor, sweet Victor! He cried between sobbing; it's over: you have conquered!... I believe, my Lord, I believe just as my Victor!"[59] At this moment we also see that the name Victor was not randomly chosen. The name comes from the Latin *vincere*, which means conquering. He is not only victorious on the battlefield; he also wins the mind of his father. Victor is fighting for two fathers: for the rights of his religious father, the pope, but also for the mental state of his natural father. To the well-informed reader, Daems suggests the end of the book by using this name from the beginning, a rhetorical device that underlines Daems' message of an inescapable fate for religious and irreligious people alike.

The sacrifice for the pope in general and in particular for one's own family shows that the Zouave is presented as the synthesis of the unreligious man and the religious mother. This dichotomy between man and woman is particularly present in the fictional work. A similar narrative is discussed in Hugh McLeod's *Secularization in Western Europe, 1848-1914*,[60] and a recent and similar convert was Tony Blair (following the faith of his wife and children). The Zouave as saviour is present in all works. Thanks to the Zouave, religion passes not only through the mother from generation to generation but also via the young Zouave from one sex to another. Women lack something crucial to defend the pope, in Rome as well as at home, namely being a man. Zouaves can infuse manliness into religion. Therefore a male infantilization of religion is necessary to bring the men back to religion. *For Two Fathers* can be seen as a coming-of-age novel but backwards. As Daems is from the educational sector this could show that there was some awareness that men probably left church after their education. But the belief also existed that the present younger generation could

[58] Seeley, "O Sainte Mère", 875, 889-891.
[59] Daems, *Voor twee vaders*, 267.
[60] McLeod, *Secularization*, 124-125.

be guided differently and their example could bring men back to religion. These youngsters possessed a quality essential to manliness, specifically the will to defend a greater cause. Most importantly for religion they could do more than just praying, namely they could fight. They had "the heart of a lamb in the body of a lion".[61]

ZOUAVE STORIES AND THE FEMINIZATION OF RELIGION

Recently two other authors have written about Zouave stories, although French ones. The first author, Sophie Heywood, studied the oeuvre of the Comtesse de Ségur, a French Catholic author of children's literature who in some of her books presents pontifical Zouaves as models for Catholic men.[62] Heywood finds these ideal pious men to be combinations of a virile religion based on militancy and combativeness and a sensitive, romantic piety. According to her this combination was not perceived as problematic and was even in conformance with social norms. Any conclusion that would suggest otherwise is for Heywood based more on "a modern vision of masculinity than any wish on the part of the Comtesse or the ultramontanes to feminize men".[63] In this article I have however tried to establish that there is not as much incongruence between the Belgian Zouave titles studied and the feminization thesis. For the most part male unreligious adults are antagonized against believing wives and children. The conversion of the father to Catholicism is more or less the major theme in the Belgian works. In the texts the young men get opportunities to prove they are good Christians as well as good soldiers and in doing so receive the means they need to do their conversional duty. Hence the Zouave is presented as the synthesis of the unreligious man and the religious mother.

In the sources of the second author, Carol E. Harrison, no mention is made of fathers.[64] Harrison wrote an extensive article based on a large and varied sample of French Zouave stories, a term she introduced. These French texts focus exclusively on the mother-son relationships. As the French and Belgian texts show many similarities this difference is important. Since irreligiousness is the core issue here, this dissimilarity might be explained by a disparity in French and Belgian anti-clericalism. During the 1860s the secular-clerical conflict was already at its height in Belgium.[65] In France, by contrast, the maturation of republican anti-clericalism only began in the 1870s with the end of the Second Empire and the onset of the French *Kulturkampf* in 1877.[66] Therefore French Zouave stories produced after 1870 should be studied to see if the Catholic father also becomes a literary trope in French stories. If so, this would make it possible to deduce even more that the Zouave narratives should be seen as confirming the feminization thesis. Some studies particularly emphasize the gendered nature of anti-clerical attacks on worshippers and see this as a result of

---

[61] Daems, *Voor twee vaders*, 40.
[62] Heywood, "Les 'petits garçons modèles'".
[63] Ibid., 216.
[64] Harisson, "Zouave Stories", passim.
[65] Witte, "The battle".
[66] McMillan, "'Priest hits girl'".

the feminization.[67] The recurring conclusion in these studies is that Catholics were scorned as being effeminate. Therefore the Zouave narratives in Belgium are (and in France might be) Catholic reactions against these accusations. For now, Harrison agrees that these narratives present a Catholic paragon consisting of supposedly incompatible characteristics such as a childlike purity or an emotional spirituality and soldierly virtue.[68] According to Harrison, however, men and women who followed this model intentionally broke societal norms, although with a reason. "Repetition of the Zouave story, with the ritual evocation of physical and spiritual suffering that ran through all of its variations, generated a powerful vocabulary for Catholic men and women who hoped to produce militancy out of self-denial, individual suffering, and private anguish."[69] For Harrison the Zouave movement gave men and women alike a certain agency.

The antagonism touched upon by myself and Harrison suggests that the Zouave stories were formulated in a society that linked women with religion and identified religiosity with womanliness. This article, Heywood and Harrison nevertheless agree that the Zouave movement as a devotion gave Catholics the opportunity to combine manly and womanly features which could explain its popularity in the second half of the nineteenth century. Therefore one could conclude that with regard to gender, nineteenth-century religiosity was not as one-dimensional as it has sometimes been evaluated.

[67] Healy, "Anti-Jesuitism in Imperial Germany"; Verhoeven, "Neither Male or Female"; Gross, *The War against Catholicism*, 186; O'Malley, *Catholicism*, 117; Wheeler, *The old enemies*,106; Hastings, "Fears of a Feminized Church"; Art and Buerman, "Anticléricalisme et genre".
[68] Harrison, "Zouave Stories".
[69] Ibid., 305.

The Sacred Heart devotion strongly appealed to men. Hundreds join a manifestation of devotion in the village of Lauwe (Belgium), 1927.
[Louvain, KADOC-KU Leuven]

'FROM THAT MOMENT ON, I WAS A MAN!'

IMAGES OF THE CATHOLIC MALE IN THE SACRED HEART DEVOTION

TINE VAN OSSELAER

The exclamation "From that moment on, I was a man!"[1] is doubtless not the most frequently used description of a religious conversion. Still, in an article published in 1936 in the Flemish *Messenger* of the Sacred Heart *of Jesus*[2], this phrase perfectly covered its central theme, the blending of masculine and Catholic identity. This discourse on 'masculine Christianity'[3] will be the central theme of this article. More specifically, the focus will be upon the discourse on men and masculinity in the Sacred Heart devotion.

This cult offers an interesting case for studying gender roles as there is some discussion on how to define the devotion; some scholars consider it 'feminized' whereas others emphasize its 'virility'. While supporters of the 'feminine' interpretation refer to the great number of female devotees and its emotional and sentimental (so-called 'feminine') imagery and devotional practices,[4] scholars such as Étienne Fouilloux stress the 'virility' of the Sacred Heart devotion and allude to its militant

[1] *Bode*, January (1936), 32.

[2] *Bode van het Heilig Hart van Jesus* was the Flemish edition, the French edition *Messager du Sacré Coeur de Jésus*, was also read in Belgium. "Van Bode".

[3] See for example: Arts, "Mannelijk Christendom"; "Mannelijke vroomheid".

[4] Busch, "Die Feminisierung der Frömmigkeit", 209-210. Harris also pictures the cult as typical of "*la religion 'au féminin'*". Harris, "Les miraculées", 287. The attraction of the cult on French women was also noted by Smith, *Ladies*, 109. "I see no evidence to support Michael P. Carroll's assertion of the maleness of the Sacred Heart." Jonas, "Anxiety", 64. (On Carroll's *Catholic Cults*, 132-153.) He believes that the image of the Sacred Heart was created for a generation that was no longer satisfied with a God defined in strong patriarchal terms. The image of the Sacred Heart would remain in conflict with this more conventionally depicted patriarchal God and figured more as a supplement than a substitute. Jonas, "Anxiety", 73, note 70.

image and emphasis on the defence of country and religion.[5] German authors as Olaf Blaschke and Norbert Busch point at a '(re-)masculinization' of the 'feminized' cult at the start of the twentieth century. They thereby refer to the increasing attention for men's involvement expressed by changes in the cult's organizations and focus at the start of the twentieth century.[6] In these differing analyses of the cult's 'feminine' and 'masculine' character, 'feminization' and 'masculinization' mostly denote the nature of the devotion (and changes in this nature) and the target group.[7] This article will not offer an opinion on this discussion about the characterization of the cult since the countries and epochs studied in these analyses are too diverse. Rather, it aims to reassess the term 'masculinization' through an analysis of the discourse of a Belgian men-oriented movement associated with the cult of the Sacred Heart.

Even though the cult of the Sacred Heart was very popular in Belgium,[8] no detailed study exists of the ideal/real male and female images that were disseminated in the Belgian devotion. This article will focus on the (ideal) image of the Catholic male promoted in the Leagues of the Sacred Heart, which originally were all-male movements, but soon became women's movements as well. It will study the strategies used by the men's movement to present itself as 'masculine' and to differentiate itself from the *Apostolat de la Prière* that was depicted as 'feminine'. The analysis will mainly focus on the 1930s, a booming period for the Leagues[9] and the years in which the debate on women's Leagues reached the central board of the men's movement. This discussion offers interesting material on how the gendered ideals were formulated and how the Leagues presented themselves as a 'masculine' movement. A few references will be made to how the ideas trickled down into the non-gender-exclusive periodicals and organizations.

---

[5] "Autant le culte du Sacré-Coeur apparaît en effet viril, dans sa défense de la foi et de la patrie, autant le culte marial témoigne de la féminisation du catholicisme depuis le XIXe siècle." Fouilloux, "Le catholicisme", 194. Similarly, Daniele Menozzi remarks that Ramière, a Jesuit from Toulouse, end of the nineteenth century, saw the devotion as militant, "une dévotion de combat", "une dévotion éminemment virile" and pictures the cult as manly, conquering and connected to the Kingdom of Christ. Menozzi, "Un rêve", 142.

[6] Busch, "Die Feminisierung der Frömmigkeit", 216-219; Blaschke, "Field Marshall Jesus Christ", 10-17. On the image of men in the Sacred Heart Leagues in Quebec: Roussel, "Roman Catholic Religious Discourse".

[7] E.g. a more masculine image of Jesus, the importance given to the dogmatic content and the role of men in the development of the cult. Busch, "Die Feminisierung der Frömmigkeit", 205, 216-217.

[8] Belgium was the first country to devote itself to the Sacred Heart (on 8 December 1868) and would repeat that action in 1919 and 1943. Different types of devotion and associations were connected to the cult, e.g. fraternities, l'*Apostolat de la Prière*, dedication of the family to the Sacred Heart, the enthronement of the statue of the Sacred Heart, the coronation of the statue of the Sacred Heart and so on. Jacques Marx sees the following elements among the reasons for the success of the cult in Belgium: the return of Romanticism and the influence of the Jesuits and the boarding schools run by French sisters. Marx, "De cultus", 107; Gevers, "De 'belle époque'", 174; Rion, "Une illustration", 27, 32; Gabriëls, *De Bonden*; Quaghebeur, "De Eucharistische", 108.

[9] According to Gevers there was a peak in the devotion during the interwar period. Gevers, "De 'belle époque'", 181.

ORIGINS

Although there already had been a private devotion and confraternities of the Sacred Heart, it was only in the second half of the nineteenth century that Belgium saw a very virulent rise of the Sacred Heart cult.[10] Not only did the bishops in 1868 devote the country to the Sacred Heart, the 1860s also saw the development of a Belgian branch of the *Apostolat de la Prière* (1864 in Ghent and later on in Leuven) and a Flemish version of its periodical in 1869 (*Bode van het Heilig Hart*).[11]

The Leagues of the Sacred Heart grew quite spontaneously in the margin of this *Apostolat* and out of the initiatives that were taken for working-class men. They originated in 'movements of perseverance' organized for workers who had been on a retreat. These retreats had been held since 1890 (in places such as Charleroi, Lier, Alken and Ghent) in order to ensure the moral health of the workers and to strengthen them against the bad influence of socialism. To make sure that these men would keep to their Christian life when they came home, they were organized in a movement for perseverance in which they could find comfort and religious support. Some of these movements were affiliated with the *Apostolat* and were called the Leagues of the Friends of the Sacred Heart (1897), of which the members shared in the spiritual benefits that were conferred on the members of the *Apostolat de la Prière*. Around the turn of the century the name of the movement changed into the League of the Sacred Heart and its goal broadened.[12]

Although the perseverance movement was primarily aimed at working-class men, in 1909 the Belgian archbishop Mercier encouraged these Leagues to open up and to address the whole male population and not only the workers who had been on a retreat.[13] He thereby followed in the footsteps of Leo XIII, who in 1899 formulated the hope that Sacred Heart movements would develop that addressed all adult men, since it was men who held a prominent position in society.[14] The following years the Leagues became very successful as they developed a more general appeal, mass character and a firm central organization and structure. There was a clear task division: the central organization was in the hands of the Jesuits, the local administration was under control of the parish priest or his assistant priest and the activities of the movement were mainly carried out by the lay promoters.[15] Although the movement was primarily aimed at men, women's Leagues developed spontaneously and references

[10] This attention went parallel with the worldwide increased interest in the cult: the beatification of Margaret-Mary Alacoque (1864) and the *Syllabus Errorum* (1864) ended with a call for the Cult of the Sacred Heart. Busch, "Fromme Westfalen", 341.

[11] This happened under strong impulse of P. Toussaint Dufau. AFJ, COA 1/6: L. De Coninck, *Histoire de l'Apostolat de la Prière en Belgique*, offprint of the supplement of the *Messager du Cœur de Jésus*, May 1928, 1; Marx, "De cultus", 107-110; Gabriëls, *De Bonden*, 27-30; "Van Bode" 1-2.

[12] Van der Veken, *Handleiding*, 35-40; Gabriëls, *De Bonden*, 49-51; Quaghebeur, "De Eucharistische", 108.

[13] *Gods zegen*, 1909, 40-41.

[14] "Een wensch".

[15] "Algemeen Secretariaat"; Quaghebeur, "De Eucharistische", 108-109; Gabriëls, *De Bonden*, 54-70; Verheylezoon, *Handboek*, 130.

to them were made from at least 1911 onwards.[16] These women's Leagues triggered a virulent debate in the 1930s and the discussions they incited form an ideal means to study the gender ideology promoted by the Leagues. They offer interesting material showing how the central board[17] tried to define the Leagues of the Sacred Heart as a men's movement (arguments, accentuation of men's characteristics) and how they differentiated their creation from a women's movement that had used the men's Leagues as its model.

A 'MEN'S' MOVEMENT

Men were considered an important target group since their cooperation was depicted as a prerequisite for the maintenance of Christian society and because men's religiosity (or lack of it) in the interwar period was quite often considered a problem.[18] Men were depicted as rather reluctant towards religiosity as it was discursively feminized into 'a women's thing'. However, one should note that what was lamented was not men's lack of religion per se, but their neglect of Catholic practices (e.g. Communion). Men's religious involvement was considered particularly important as they held higher positions in society and as *patres familiae* had the authority over their families. As such they had an important influence on the (Christian) behaviour of their family members, especially on their sons' comportment.[19] Therefore, men's involvement could be considered more important than women's:

> When the man is a Christian, then the whole family is; the opposite is not true; when you have the women and the children, often the man still resists, is that not to be blamed on an ill-placed love of oneself, to not appear tied to the apron strings of the 'weaker sex'.[20]

[16] Hardy, *Practische wenken*, 14.

[17] The central office was installed in 1922 in Mechelen; later on the Flemish dioceses would also install diocesan offices. The Walloon office was installed in 1930. Quaghebeur, "De Eucharistische", 108-109; BME, II.4: Le Secrétariat des Ligues du Sacré Coeur d'expression française en Belgique 1930-1940; Les Ligues du Sacré Cœur dans les paroisses belges d'expression française 1930-1940.

[18] Van Osselaer, "Christening Masculinity?". Cf. Tihon: the Leagues of the Sacred Heart's aim was the mobilization of adult men "peu engagés jusqu'alors". Tihon, "Les mouvements", 171.

[19] AFJ, V.4: Letter about the Feast of the Sacred Heart in Roeselare, 1925; COA/4.7: Report of the work of the Leagues of the Sacred Heart by J. Hardy, Eucharistical Congress of Amsterdam 1924; AFJ, III.5: Extract from the *Messenger of the Sacred Heart*, April 1926, by Hardy; AFJ, IV.3: Reports about the mass action; Henvaux, "Le Problème", 150-155; "Waarom".

[20] "Quand l'homme sera Chrétien, toute la famille le sera; la réciproque n'est pas vraie; quand on a les femmes et les enfants, que de fois l'homme résiste encore, ne fut ce que par amour-propre mal placé, pour ne pas sembler être à la remorque du 'sexe faible'." AFJ, III.5: Extract from the *Messenger of the Sacred Heart*, April 1926, 193-199: "Les communions mensuelles et collectives d'hommes", by Hardy.

Apparently women's enthusiasm could not guarantee men's involvement. Thus references to the 'weaker sex' were best avoided in the development of the discourse of a men's movement. The affiliation between the Leagues and the *Apostolat* therefore turned out to be a problematic one. Although the successful men's Leagues originated within the *Apostolat*, by the 1930s the Leagues' leaders criticized the image of the mixed movement and lamented in their private correspondence its 'feminine', 'French-bourgeois' and 'old-fashioned' character. Although the *Apostolat* was a mixed organization and by no means presented itself as a 'women's' movement, it apparently struggled with this image and the feminine connotation was, most clearly, not considered a positive one.[21]

This negatively evaluated feminine characterization of the *Apostolat* points in the direction of an explicit differentiation between the genders. Accentuation and elaboration of gender characteristics had, primarily since the eighteenth and nineteenth centuries, become a central theme in discourse.[22] According to Aurora Morcillo, the discourse that emphasized this difference between the sexes "was revived throughout Europe in the first third of the twentieth century. New psychological and sociological arguments revitalized the already stale notion of biological determinism."[23] These characteristics were a common knowledge, strong and persistent enough to build a movement's discourse on, strong enough to maintain a gender exclusiveness of the all-male Leagues in the first years of their existence, but also influential enough to insist upon the creation of a 'feminine' version of the Leagues even after women had already developed their own Leagues along the lines of the men's movement. 'Men' were depicted as a delineated pole of a binary opposition with 'women' at the other end of it. According to the Leagues' discourse, men's and women's characteristics did not and could not overlap. Men were in need of an all-male movement with a 'masculine' character; mixed Leagues were not taken into consideration.

[21] AFJ, III.4: Letter by J. Zeij, S.J., 25 November 1933: "That in France and elsewhere, the Apostolat is regarded as 'feminine' is simply fatal." (Dat in Frankrijk, en elders, het Ap.d.G. vooral 'vrouwelijk' schijnt te zijn, is gewoonweg fataal."); a letter to J. Zeij, 8 March 1933 on the situation in Belgium: "In fact the Apostolat was too well known as a women's work." ("In feite was het Apostolaat des Gebeds te veel bekend als een Vrouwenwerk.")
[22] Wetterer, "Konstruktion", 126-127; Rutz, *Bildung*, 397. Schnell nuances the image of the eighteenth century as a turning point. Schnell, "Text", 18-19. On the importance of religion in legitimating gender order: King, "Religion", 71.
[23] Morcillo, *True Catholic*, 19.

MASCULINE AND CATHOLIC IDENTITY

'MASCULINE' CHARACTER

According to the Leagues' leaders in the 1930s, it was the explicit appeal to men that made the movement successful. Men were apparently flattered by the attention they received and showed it by flocking to this men's movement.[24] This all-male movement was noted in the rest of the Catholic world and in 1929 the pope addressed the pilgrims of the men's Leagues and expressed the wish that they would always 'preserve' the 'masculine character' of the Leagues. This quote did not only stress the importance that was given to male involvement, but would also turn into a favourite argument in the creation of gender-exclusive Leagues.[25] The 'masculine character' thereby did not only point in the direction of an all-male movement, but also at the 'masculine' definition of the features the Leagues had in common with the non-gender-exclusive *Apostolat*.[26] In order to achieve the best results, the Leagues' leaders tried to take into account 'masculine' characteristics in the organization and development of the men's movement. Not only were their members recruited by men, a guarantee for an adequate apostleship, but their membership tasks were also designed for the male persona.[27]

Once they had signed up, members of the Leagues shared some obligations, i.e. a morning prayer and rehabilitating Communion.[28] These tasks were not only described as fit for a man and his busy 'masculine' life, but were actually also presented as 'designed' to fit men's features. Men were, according to the Leagues' leaders, ruled by a worldly view, and in order to fight those prejudices their public activities, for example their collective Communion, had to be carried out collectively. This performance as a group represented a double benefit for the Leagues. Not only would the men's numbers impress the other churchgoers and eventually attract other men, but the members would feel more safe, connected and comforted when they stood shoul-

---

[24] "A l'origine, c.-à-d. entre 1910 et 1920 la grande particularité des Ligues était que c'étaient des Ligues d'hommes. Ce fut le grand succès. Jusqu'à présent l'apostolat commençait généralement par les enfants; puis il s'étendait aux femmes et enfin on demandait à celles ci de dire une bonne parole à leurs maris ou à leurs enfants pour également s'affilier à cette oeuvre eucharistique. Les hommes voyant qu'on n'osait pas les attaquer de front, se faisaient prier et en général ne répondaient pas à l'appel. L'originalité des Ligues a donc été d'attaquer les hommes en face et de front. Ils y ont été sensibles et ont répondu avec enthousiasme à l'appel." AFJ, I.2: Note sur les Ligues du S.C. pour femmes; III.5: Presentation of P. Meeus on the Congrès national de l'Apostolat de la Prière, Paris, April 1933.

[25] Van der Veken, "De mannen", 49; "Leve Paus Pius XI".

[26] Van der Veken, *Handleiding*, 163-164.

[27] Meeus, *Mannen- en vrouwenbonden*, 5.

[28] The Rehabilitating Communion is a Communion in which Christ's honour is restored and the sins committed by mankind (diminishing Christ's honour) are balanced through a public honouring of Christ's suffering. An all-male version had been introduced in Toulouse in 1875 under impulse of Henri Ramière. AFJ COA 1/6: L. De Coninck, *Histoire de l'Apostolat de la Prière en Belgique*, offprint of the supplement of the *Messager du Cœur de Jésus* of May 1928, 5; Van der Veken, *Handleiding*, 31.

der to shoulder with other men.[29] This Holy Communion made all men equal and improved the feeling of brotherhood among the members.[30] Since their presence had to be impressive, the men would not only flock together, but also sit, quite prominently, in front of the altar and not at the church's portal, the much-lamented favourite spot of a male churchgoer. The Leagues' leaders explicitly stressed the importance of this group activity, as they did not really think highly of men's religiosity, believing that without this collective Communion far too many men would keep away from this Christian duty.[31] Group activities such as the monthly Communion, public demonstrations and 'spiritual lectures' were organized in order to improve a community feeling, publicly demonstrated by the members wearing the same pin and men - whose capability to sing had been questioned - singing songs about their brotherhood.[32]

The morning dedication was also presented as especially fit for men. The prayer formula was "short", "masculine" and "striking" and therefore ideal for men who were not really drawn to long prayers.[33] So, although these tasks - the morning dedication and rehabilitating Communion - had also been part of the obligations of some of the *Apostolat* members, the Leagues gave them their own cachet and presented them as 'masculine'.

FE/MALE MOVEMENT

According to the Leagues' leaders, this men's movement inspired women with amazement, cooperation and above all, jealousy. Although women's first response had been astonishment,[34] they had soon got over the initial surprise and had contributed to the success of the men's movement by their enthusiastic response, urging their male family members to join the Leagues, sending them to the meetings and making sure they went to confession and brought their prayer books to church.[35] However, according to the central board, the success of the movement also incited some jealousy and before long, women developed their own Leagues.[36] This women's movement presented a difficult situation for the men's Leagues, as it challenged the self-implied 'masculine character' of the men's movement. The response of the Leagues' leaders was at first

---

[29] AFJ, IX.1: Note presented at the 28th Congrégation Générale à la demande du T.R.P. Ledochowski; AFJ, I.1: Hardy, J., Report on the Leagues of the Sacred Heart at the S.H. feast in Roeselare, 1925; "Waarom".

[30] Van der Veken, "De mannen", 49.

[31] "Het Pilatushoekske!"; "Onze Zondagmis".

[32] Van der Veken, "De mannen".

[33] Ibid., 49.

[34] Meesen, *La belle histoire*, 9; "De eerste Bondsmis".

[35] "Aartsbisdom Herenthout"; "Waarom"; AFJ, I.9: Report of the meeting of 11 February 1936. Cf. the remark of a commentator of the Leagues: "The nagging of the women has contributed more to the success of the operation than the authority of the priests." ("Het gezaag van de vrouwen heeft meer bijgedragen tot het succes van deze actie dan het gezag van geestelijken.") Van Haver, *Voor U, Beminde Gelovigen*, 199.

[36] At the Congress of Bruges in 1926 there existed already 250 women's leagues. Meeus, *Mannen- en vrouwenbonden*, 2. In the 1930s women's leagues existed in Limburg, Mechelen and West Flanders. AFJ, I.7: Letter May 1935, June 1935, November 1940; Meeus, "Mannen- en Vrouwenbonden", *MM*, June 1936, 2-3; Ibid., July 1936, 2-3; AFJ, I.9: Report meeting 11 February 1936.

denial, but pressed by the archbishop to take control of the central organization of the women's movement,[37] they decided not only to make a clear difference between the men's and women's movements, but also to do everything in their power to not let the women outshine the male Leagues.[38]

Women's Leagues were thereby considered a double problem: not only would they make the male members feel less exclusive; it would also not take long before the attention of the Leagues' leaders would only concentrate upon the female audience as it was more easy to please and almost effortlessly showed good results, in contrast to men, considered a tough audience.[39] The central board only consented to organize and control the women's Leagues, after years of refusal, because around the 1930s some of the clergy concluded that women needed this movement (just as much as men) and that the image of the more 'pious sex' was no longer adequate. However, it would be the archbishop who gave the final push in the central creation of the women's Leagues. As he publicly announced the need for a central organization of the women's Leagues, the Jesuits could no longer deny the request and had to give in. As they discussed this demand they realized that they themselves could profit from the control over the women's movement. By taking the central organization into their own hands, they avoided another religious order's taking charge of it and as the central board they could prevent the women's Leagues from becoming more successful than men's. [40] The board therefore reformulated its vision: the women's movement could be useful, but men's Leagues had to remain their priority.[41]

In order to preserve their masculine character, the Leagues' leaders created differences between the men's and women's Leagues. In their correspondence they very explicitly stressed the fact that the women's movement had to differ from the men's movement in appearance and content.[42] The most prominent demarcations between men's and women's Leagues were made along the following lines.

The first differentiation pointed at the rehabilitating Communion. Since the male members of the Leagues were obliged to attend a rehabilitating Communion once a month, so were the members of the women's movement. There was, however, a clear distinction made between the men's and women's movements. Women's rehabilitation would have less of a social character, since it was men and not women who represented society. Men, and in concreto men's Leagues, were therefore held responsible for the public rehabilitation and women for the 'private', i.e. familial, rehabilitation of Christ's honour.[43] This division was clearly made along the lines of the

---

[37] AFJ, I.2: Note sur les Ligues du Sacré Coeur pour femmes.

[38] "Onze Mannenbonden, waarop men terecht in ons land fier is, zullen er aan houden, hun roem waardig te blijven en zich niet te laten overtreffen door de Vrouwenbonden." "Vrouwenbonden".

[39] AFJ, I.9: Report of February 1936.

[40] AFJ, I.2: Note sur les Ligues du Sacré Coeur pour femmes; COA, 1.10: Note on women's Leagues, October 1931.

[41] AFJ, I.8: Letter to Mgr. De Wachter: "Are women's Leagues useful or necessary?" (7 September 1927).

[42] AFJ, I.7: Letter to Meeus by Verwimp, 15 June 1935.

[43] "Haar eerherstel heeft uiteraard minder een sociaal karakter, daar niet zij, maar wel de mannen, de aangeduide vertegenwoordigers zijn der Maatschappij." Meeus, *Mannen- en vrouwenbonden*, 5-6, 11; AFJ, I.9: Report meeting 11 February 1936.

archetypical distinction between the 'masculine' public spheres and the 'feminine' private spheres as they have been presented in the separate-spheres ideology.

Since women were not allowed to take part in the public manifestations of the Leagues (i.e. demonstrations, consecration of the flags), the division between public and private also played its part in the second difference between the two Leagues.[44] However, they were allowed to contribute to the success of these public manifestations by sending their husbands to them, reminding their male family members of these activities. They could support the demonstrations by making sure that their husbands had a nice dinner waiting for them once they got back and by showing a warm interest in the events of the day.[45] As a movement, the women's League might even be asked to cooperate in the organization of these public manifestations. More specifically, its help would be needed for tasks "along the line of their feminine character": i.e. "the decoration of houses and windows, the fabrication of flowers and the selling of signs".[46] Men apparently were the external representatives, the symbolic identification of the Leagues.

The third differentiation related to the Leagues' symbols. As one's identity is strongly based on external elements, women's Leagues had to have a different sign, song and preferably even a different name. However, the name League of the Sacred Heart, according to the central board, was too much connected with "churches full of men, with waving flags, demonstrations, dedications of parishes and communities, the processions at congresses and pilgrimages", and men would not like that unity to be touched. They would rather not share their name with any other organization, "however charming it might be".[47] The central board wanted to name them Margaret-Mary Leagues, because the name referred to the Sacred Heart devotion and also had something "specifically feminine".[48] However, the reaction to this name proposal was not unanimously positive. Other names were proposed, such as St Lutgardis League (named after a Belgian saint also connected with the Sacred Heart devotion) and Mary Leagues.[49] Their name was not the only element the men's League closely identified with; apparently their song was also an important expression of the movement's identity. The Leagues' song was considered a 'masculine' song and therefore not fit for a women's movement. Women's improvizations on the text (for example the replacement of 'sons' with 'daughters') were not only considered a musical blunder,

---

[44] AFJ, I.8: Note to Mgr. De Wachter: "Are women's Leagues useful or necessary?" (7 September 1927); COA, 1.10: Note on Women's Leagues, October 1931.

[45] Meeus, *Mannen- en vrouwenbonden*, 12-13.

[46] "(...) die op haar terrein gelegen zijn: b.v. de versiering van huis en vensters; de vervaardiging van bloemen, de verkoop van herkenningsteeken enz., enz." Meeus, *Mannen- en vrouwenbonden*, 12.

[47] "De naam Bond van het H. Hart is één geworden met die grootsche beweging, die de mannen enthousiasmeert, is één geworden met kerken vol mannen, met de wapperende vaandels, de optochten, de toewijdingen van parochies en gemeenten, de optochten bij kongressen en bedevaarten. Aan die eenheid laten de mannen niet gaarne tornen. Zij deelen hun naam liever niet met een andere organizatie, hoe sympathiek ze dan ook weze." Meeus, *Mannen- en Vrouwenbonden*, 8.

[48] AFJ, I.9: Report meeting 11 February 1936.

[49] AFJ, I.9: Report meeting 20 July 1936; Meeus, "Mannen- en Vrouwenbonden", *MM*, July 1936, 2. On Saint Lutgardis see: "De godsvrucht tot het Heilig Hart".

but were also regarded as not sufficient; women had better have their own song.[50] According to the board it would be preferable if women's Leagues were not only indicated by their own name and song but also by their own pin, which "women would be proud to wear". Apparently, there were even some discussions about adapting the mark of the *Apostolat* for this use, a rather ironic choice if one thinks about the (problematic) 'feminine' connotation of this movement.[51]

The fourth, and one of the most striking, differentiations between the men's and women's movements alluded to the organization of the rehabilitating Communion that the members of the League were supposed to attend once a month. In the opinion of the central board, men's exemplum would count for more than women's; therefore not all too much attention had to be paid to the Communion of the women's Leagues as a group.[52] In the men's movement, the leaders stressed the attendance of the monthly Communion on a specific day; in the women's Leagues the members were given various options. In their own reports and discussions they explained this flexibility in this way:

> For the women we use the pretext of difficulties in the household, to let them have the choice between the first Friday (requested by the Sacred Heart) and a Sunday different from the one of the men's Leagues. The outcome will be that; divided between two Masses to attend Communion, their number will be less impressive and the men's Leagues will make a better impression and we will use every opportunity to put the men's Leagues on a pedestal and in the spotlight.[53]

The Leagues' leaders and the movement's authors quite literally followed this strategy and presented this monthly Communion as they had planned it: in their booklets, women's instable life is lamented as they are offered flexibility. The public discourse on women's dual option therefore looked like this:

> For a lot of women it is not easy, even impossible, to commit themselves to attend H. Mass on a certain Sunday of the month. Various domestic occupations hold her back: making coffee, getting the children ready to go to church, and so on. From a utilitarian point of view a change is already required. The group

---

[50] Meeus, "Mannen- en Vrouwenbonden", *MM*, July 1936, 3. The text of the song was as follows: "Oh Heart of Jesus, we are Your sons, with a powerful will and strong in number. That we are and that shall we prove to be, everywhere." AFJ, I.3: Songtexts. Women's song is alluded to by Van der Veken, *Handleiding*, 179: J. Bogaerts wrote the text and the music was the congress song from Budapest.

[51] Meeus, "Mannen- en Vrouwenbonden", *MM*, July 1936, 3; AFJ, I.9: Report of 13 March 1939.

[52] AFJ, I.8: Note to Mgr De Wachter, 7 September 1927.

[53] "Pour les femmes nous prenons prétexte des difficultés de ménage, pour leur laisser le choix ou bien le premier vendredi (demandé par la Sacré-Coeur) ou bien un dimanche différent de la Ligues des hommes. La conséquence est que divisé en deux Messes de communion, leur nombre est moins imposant et la Ligue des hommes en est rehaussée et nous prenons prétexte chaque fois que la chose est possible, de mettre en épingle et en vedette les Ligues des hommes." AFJ, I.2: Note sur les Ligues du Sacré Cœur pour les Femmes (s.d.).

should not be demanded so strictly of the women's movement as of the men's movement.[54]

The differentiations that had been discussed by the Leagues' leaders were also published in the periodicals and in small booklets. In these editions the male and female movements were presented not as opposites, but as a complementarity.[55] Although the modifications in the women's movement (the pin, flexibility concerning the monthly Communion) were presented in discussions and publications as if they would better fit a feminine audience, they were also made to clearly differentiate men's and women's movements. Men would no longer have to feel embarrassed that women took part in their movement, as women's Leagues were clearly presented as part of another organization, a women's movement. No longer would women operate in the shadow of a men's movement that was so clearly defined as 'masculine' without presenting themselves as an (externally and internally) different organization. Apparently, this solution was also approved by the clergy. The priests were happy that the Jesuits took care of the women (and women did not have to turn to yet another religious order), but at the same time they were, according to the central board, delighted that men remained the main focus of the Leagues of the Sacred Heart.[56]

INCORPORATION OF A MASCULINE CATHOLICISM?

The importance of men's involvement was a common theme in the periodicals of the men's Leagues. Members were reminded of the fact that their "moral life was in greater danger" (than women's) and their "religious life" was "threatened to a larger extent". However, the meaning of their membership was not only based upon the moral support they could receive from these group activities and from this religious funding, but also on the fact that, as heads of the community life and as authority holders, they could represent society's rehabilitation of the honour of the Sacred Heart.[57] The Leagues' members were addressed as men, with their own (masculine) problems, duties and ideals. As Catholic men they combined multiple identities and were confronted with principles corresponding with the various aspects of this ideal masculine image. They were depicted as men, fathers, husbands, citizens, Catholics and apostles.

The Leagues' members were reminded of their duties as fathers and heads of the household. They were to make sure that no bad influences could trickle down into their family lives and into the souls of the members of their households. They ought

[54] "Voor vele vrouwen is het niet gemakkelijk, is het zelfs onmogelijk zich te verbinden om iedere maand op een bepaalden Zondag een bepaalde H. Mis bij te wonen. Allerlei huishoudelijke bezigheden weerhouden haar; koffie klaar maken; de kinderen gereed maken voor de H. Mis, enz. Uit utilitaristich oogpunt dringt zich reeds een zekere aanpassing op. De groep mag niet zo strikt geëischt worden voor de Vrouwen- als voor de Mannenbonden." Meeus, "Mannen- en Vrouwenbonden", *MM*, August 1936, 2.
[55] Meeus, "Mannen- en Vrouwenbonden", June 1936, 2.
[56] AFJ, I.2: Note sur les Ligues du S.C. des Femmes.
[57] "Waarom ik lid werd", *BB*, August 1937, 2.

to know what literature, fashions and movies were fit for their family.[58] Apparently, men were not always capable of meeting those prerogatives and could be called back to their duties as husbands and fathers by the Leagues' discourse. At any rate, this is the conclusion that can be derived from some of the letters preserved in the archives of the movement. One of them introduces a woman, signing as "Mother and wife of a Christian family" who saw her husband a changed man: "... he has become a promoter of the League of the Sacred Heart, which made his nature much softer ...", though he was not yet what he should be "... but his inclination to other women is not really fading well ...". She has great confidence in the power of the Leagues' leaders over her husband and hopes that they may make some remarks on the subject in their periodical. She is convinced that her husband will listen to them and remarks that he often tells other people to read that magazine and derive a lesson from it.[59]

These marital and family ideals return in the description of the death of an "exemplary member" of the men's movement. His life was a "model of Christian life and a loyal sense of duty", according to the *Bondsblad*. Although he was a fruit merchant and often had to go to Brussels on Sunday, he nevertheless always tried to attend Sunday Mass and take part in the group Communion of the League. He also tried to go to church during the week, and showed his sense of religious duty as a father. He did not hesitate to make his sons sit down with him in the evening to make them say the rosary with him and carried his suffering, after a deadly fall from a ladder, in a 'manly' Christian way.[60] In this description, the Catholic father not only combined his duties as head of the household and member of the League of the Sacred Heart, but also went to church and attended Mass. Since the group Communion was one of the central features of the men's movement and the Eucharist had become an important point in Catholic discourse and organizational life, this stress on an ideal member's Mass attendance was not very surprising.[61]

This interest in Mass attendance was stressed by the Leagues' cooperation in the action "Back to the Sunday Mass". Through intensive media campaigning they tried to get the Belgian population, and especially men, back to church and made them attend Mass. In the posters and folders, men could explicitly be addressed as fathers who had to set a good example to their children. The campaign protested against the empty chairs and the inattentive male presence at Mass. It promoted the use of a prayer book and advised lectures in which a detailed analysis of Mass promoted a better understanding of the ceremony. During the campaign the Leagues meditated

---

[58] "Zedenverwildering"; AFJ, IV.3: Letter from E.H. Pissens.

[59] The date stamp notes "17 JAN 1938". "Moeder en vrouw van een christelijk huisgezin" "... nu is hij ieveraar geworden van den bond van het H. Hart hij is ierdoor veel zachter van aard geworden maar een neiging naar andere vrouwen dat gaat er niet goed uit ...." "... want ik hoor hem tegen de menschen zeggen ge moet het lezen er staan soms goede dingen in waar ge veel nut kunt uit trekken." Another letter has almost the same content but in that case the writer asks them to mention their lesson in the sermons. No date is given there. AFJ, I.3.

[60] "Voorbeeldig Bondslid".

[61] See for example the founding of the Eucharistic Crusade (Eucharistische Kruistocht) for children. This Crusade also had its adult sections. Quaghebeur, "De Eucharistische". The central position of the Communion inspired a number of books concerned with men's Communion, e.g. Solvyns, *De Heilige Communie voor Mannen*; Lintelo, *De Heilig Communie der Mannen*.

on the best way to reach men and encouraged the use of slogans as "Using a Prayer book is not sanctimonious".[62] According to leaders of this action, the best method by far was the home visit. Those were considered very effective since one would not only talk to men, but - more importantly - by visiting people at home, one would also contact wives who would be keen on their husbands attending Mass, and who would make sure that their husbands would keep the promises they had made to the men involved in this campaign.[63]

The Leagues' members were not only addressed as fathers and practising Catholics, but also as potential voters. Although the Leagues did not have a political goal, and avoided every political connotation, the members were still reminded of their duties as Christian citizens. Since men were entitled to vote, they had to do their best as a voter or even a propagandist in order to defend the Christian interests in modern society. Although no League activities could be devoted to the elections - the Leagues had to remain apolitical - members were encouraged to pray within a family context for a 'positive' result of the elections.[64]

The promoters of the Leagues, the lay elite of the movement, were not only addressed in their men-only capacities as fathers and citizens, but also as apostles. The apostleship was a man's job par excellence, since the first apostles had been men and Christ had built his Church, counting on the help of men.[65] They were motivated to show courage, to battle, to suffer and to sacrifice. They not only had to defend, but above all they had to battle and conquer in the name of Christ.[66]

The masculine character of the men's Leagues was cultivated to such an extent that one entering the Leagues could say that he was depicted and addressed as 'a man'. Their physical manhood apparently was a unifying quality and any differences that may have existed between them (e.g. class) were dissolved by the monthly Communion that equated and elevated every man. Although these distinctions had been able to motivate the construction of various men's movements before, in the Leagues of the Sacred Heart they preferably did not play a part. The central board did differentiate between men, however, in its discussions on the non-practising of the men of Wallonia, the religiosity of men in the countryside, or in their analysis of various work spots, but most commonly men were addressed as men, with more characteristics in common than differences between them.[67] Not only were the members referred to in their men-specific identities as fathers and citizens, but the 'masculine' image of the Leagues was carefully constructed, preserved and externalized through monthly Communion and demonstrations. Even when the women's Leagues came into existence the 'masculine' character was not to be challenged, and a clear differentiation consolidated the idea that men's and women's Leagues were two different organizations. Men's Leagues presented themselves as a masculine version of the

---

[62] "Een kerkboek gebruiken is niet kwezelachtig"; "Terug naar de Zondagsmis. De tijden zijn rijp!".

[63] "Onze Zondagmis"; "Terug naar de Zondagmis!".

[64] "De Bonden en de aanstaande verkiezingen".

[65] Palau, *De Katholiek*, 106.

[66] AFJ, V.10: Report (book) on the Diocesan promoters Congress of Ghent 7.3.1937, 23. On these militaristic metaphors see e.g. Blaschke, "Field Marshall Jesus Christ", 12.

[67] "Uit het Walenland"; "Bij onze Waalsche broeders"; Meeus, "De Bonden van het Heilig Hart".

Apostolat,[68] although this mixed movement had never claimed to be a women's movement and the origins of the Leagues have to be placed within this movement. Still, by the 1930s the *Apostolat* had a 'feminine' reputation (maybe because the promoters were mostly and preferably women)[69] and attempts by the still-existing Belgian *Apostolat* cells (Antwerp, Ghent e.g.)[70] to contact the leaders of the Leagues were blocked. Still, although the leaders of the Leagues would not collaborate on an organizational level with these remaining cells, they did present themselves as part of the *Apostolat* and were presented as such in its publications.[71]

The ideas about differentiation between the sexes and the critique of men's religiosity also trickled into the *Apostolat*.[72] Its periodical, the *Bode van het Heilig Hart*, published some articles on the subject, e.g. the article on 'Masculine Christianity'. Since the editorial staff consisted mainly of Jesuits and this religious order was also in charge of the Leagues of the Sacred Heart, interaction would have been very likely. At least one Jesuit, Louis Verheylezoon, wondered in 1930 whether or not the *Apostolat* was fit for men. "In general", he began, "it is better to take on women as promoters of the *Apostolat* but if one wants to bring men together in a separate league it will be better to let men act as apostles." Although his stress on women as promoters of the *Apostolat* was quite along the line of the first draft of the organizational model by Toussaint Dufau, the first apostle of the *Apostolat de la Prière* in Belgium, this stress on an all-men's movement and its male apostles was not.[73] The passage clearly refers to the Leagues of the Sacred Heart, since the movement was regarded as the male branch of the *Apostolat* and he mentions it a little later. Apparently the attention paid to the advantages of a gender-exclusive movement (e.g. "men are more easily attached to an all-male movement that is designed especially for them") was a new feature, the result of increased interest in differentiation between the sexes, stimulated and externalized by the Leagues.[74]

---

[68] Van der Veken, *Handleiding*, 163; AFJ, COA 4.6: De Internationale Bond van het Heilig Hart.

[69] On its female promoters see e.g. AFJ.,III.2.; Verheylezoon, *Het Apostolaat*, 10-11.

[70] AFJ, III.4: Letter to Zeij (8 March 1933); COA 6.4: Letter from Hardeman to the Provincial Father.

[71] AFJ, III.2: Comment fonder l'Apostolat de la Prière, Toulouse, 1923, 14.

[72] The Leagues had their own periodicals: e.g *Bondsblad* (°1930); *Maandblad voor Xaverianen en H. Hartbonders* (1929); *Maandelijksche Mededeelingen over de Bonden van het H. Hart* (°1924, from 1935 onwards there was also an edition for women: *Bonden van het Heilig Hart Vrouwenbonden*); *Regnum Christi* (1931).

[73] Dufau, *Beautés*, 605-606.

[74] Verheylezoon, *Handboek*, 63-64, 110-130; AFJ, III.2: Verheylezoon, *Het Apostolaat*, 10-11. This edition in the archives includes a little note with remarks "all done by female promoters. Is the Apostolat only for women?" "What if there is a men's League? Or when a men's League is organised in a parish where such an Apostolat already exists?"; "Alles door ijveraarsters. Is ADG enkel voor vrouwen? [...] quid waar mannenbond bestaat?"; - quid waar mannenbond in parochie ingericht wordt waar zoo'n ADG bestaat?"; AFJ, I.9: Report of the meeting on 13 March 1935.

MASCULINIZATION?

The men's apostleship in the Leagues of the Sacred Heart has been described as part of a 'masculinization' of the cult of the Sacred Heart at the beginning of the twentieth century, but this phrase raises more than one question.[75] At first sight one could agree: the Leagues targeted men and cultivated a 'masculine' character. However, taking into account the spontaneously developing women's Leagues, one would also have to consider a renewed 'feminization' of the Sacred Heart devotion in this women's movement, a development parallel to the 'masculinization' of the men's League. Therefore, the term 'differentiation' seems to be a better description for this (Belgian) case since it indicates the (increasing) stress on the constructed difference between men and women and the (conscious) adaptation to 'natural' characteristics of both. For if one uses the term 'masculinization', one may all too easily follow the idea of a constant binary opposition with a permanent 'masculine' and 'feminine' character that would be imposed on historically, socially and geo-politically different discourses. 'Masculinization' can be a helpful term, but it may include too much the idea of a linear development from 'feminization' towards 'masculinization(s)'. The phrase very easily leads one into an essentialist view on 'masculinity' and 'femininity', and imposes it on a religious discourse without consideration for the contextual, historical flexibility of these very fluid terms. For what is there to say about the 'masculine' character, if women were attracted enough to develop their own Leagues in the shadow of this 'masculine' movement? Should we not think of the Leagues as a men's movement that could also attract women and did so to such an extent that differences had to be imposed on them, again?

[75] For Germany see: Busch, "Die Feminisierung der Frömmigkeit", 216-219; Blaschke, "Field Marshall Jesus Christ", 10-17.

With this triptych depicting the three stages of spiritual development leading towards the union with God, the Dominican painter Raymond van Bergen (1883-1978) engaged in a gendered debate on identity among the Dutch Dominicans.
[*Zwolle, Convent of Saint Thomas; © Stichting Kerkelijk Kunstbezit in Nederland, Utrecht*]

REPERTOIRES OF CATHOLIC MANLINESS IN THE NETHERLANDS (1850-1940)

A CASE STUDY OF THE DUTCH DOMINICANS

MARIT MONTEIRO

In 1923 the Dominican painter Raymond van Bergen (1883-1978) finalized a triptych depicting the three stages of spiritual development leading towards the union with God. Three friars posed consecutively for the panels reflecting the stages of purification (*via purgitativa*), illumination (*via illuminativa*) and union (*via unitativa*). These stages were originally introduced by the neo-platonic philosopher Pseudo-Dionysius (about 465-490). The Dominican Thomas Aquinas would later associate them with the spiritual progress of the soul.[1] Van Bergen's impressive work of art, measuring over two metres in width and about eighty centimetres in height, is preserved in the Convent of Saint Thomas in the Dutch town of Zwolle, where the painter spent nearly his entire Dominican life.[2] The triptych was exhibited in the first showing of Van Bergen's work in 1924 and was appreciated for its "softly well-disposed contemplative stillness and modesty", in contrast to "the ultra-subjective reproduction of things, which reveals the feverish artist rather than the object itself". According to a reviewer of Van Bergen's first retrospective, his portraits "guarded the inner secret soul of the human complex rather than exposing 'la nudicité de l'âme'".[3]

With the triptych Van Bergen engaged in the debate on identity among the Dutch Dominicans. It epitomized monastic life as an anchor of Catholic tradition in modern

---

[1] As explained by Maltha, *Theologisch Woordenboek*, 1661-1675.

[2] For his work see: Jacobs, *Beeldend Nederland*, 88b; van Deil, "Raymond van Bergen"; Vijverberg, "In memoriam Fons van Bergen". See also "Pater/schilder Raymundus van Bergen (95) overleden". I would like to thank Kees Brakkee O.P. for his help with the research on Van Bergen.

[3] "[D]e zacht-genegen contemplatieve rustigheid en ingetogenheid [en juist niet van] een hypersubjectieve weergave der dingen, die meer den koortsigen kunstenaar dan het ding aan ons onthult." His portraits expose "niet la nudicité de l'âme onversluierd [...], maar bewaren in eerbiedsvolle pudiciteit het zielsgeheim van een menschcomplex, dat in zijn samenstel hoogstens vermoed, niet geraden of ontdekt wil wezen". A.B., "Een monnik-schilder".

society. This reference to monasticism not only entailed gendered connotations, but it was rather complicated in view of the history of the Dutch Dominicans.[4] They were counted among the most influential religious institutes in the Netherlands, next to the Franciscans and the Jesuits. The Franciscans dominated in parochial pastoral care and outnumbered the Preachers by far. The Jesuits mainly competed with them in the domain of the intellectual apostolate. The Dominican community remained the third largest male religious institute until 1936, when it fell back to the fourth rank as new missionary congregations rose to favour with spiritually ambitious young men.

In their self-construction as high-profile Catholics, the Dominicans continuously shifted the emphasis from the clerical to the monastic dimensions of their identity, which in turn tied in with changing societal expectations of these men of God. At first glance, the continuous reassessments of Dominican identity between 1850 and 1940 seem to revolve primarily around contemplation and action, considered to be the key dimensions of Dominican life. A closer look reveals, however, that both aspects pointed at various repertoires of male religiosity that shed light on the gendered dimensions of processes of confessionalization since the mid-nineteenth century. The debates among the Dominicans on the fundamentals of their identity enable us to refine current concepts of Christian manliness that are still innately Protestant and tend to neglect the impact of denominational difference. Furthermore, these debates help to differentiate between forms or repertoires of manliness within Catholicism. This case study of the Dutch Dominicans elucidates that Catholic manliness in itself was by no means a stable or fixed category, but contained clerical, monastic, and secular manifestations of masculinity. These repertoires of Catholic manliness and their interplay reflected changes in the cultural and social meaning of religion starting in the mid-nineteenth century.

The Dutch Dominicans shared a particular characteristic of all male religious institutes in the Netherlands: due to the missionary nature of the Catholic Church in the Netherlands between 1581 and 1853, the clerical aspects of their way of life came to eclipse the monastic traits. The monastic reforms, in which these orders had invested at an international level since the mid-nineteenth century, could only partly redress this tendency. At first, the Dutch Dominicans merged monastic characteristics with current secular standards of masculine behaviour by underscoring the martial, even heroic features of their celibate life. They employed the monastic aspects of their way of life to emphasize its manly nature and to distinguish themselves thereby from the secular clergy.

Because of the process of pillarization (*verzuiling*), the monastic reform in the Dutch Dominican province only sank in partially. By the end of the nineteenth century the secular and regular clergy took the lead in the creation of an autonomous, self-reliant Catholic subculture which would enable the faithful to engage in modernity on the basis of Catholic principles. Similar processes of confessionalization took place in other European countries due to the separation of church and state, and entailed shifts in the public position and appreciation of the clergy. The Dominicans articulated both their status and their activities in the patriarchal terms that by then could be labelled hegemonic: men of God who would be good fathers to the offspring

---

[4] I dealt extensively with this question in Monteiro, *Gods Predikers.*

of the Church, depicted as their Bride. These articulations of Catholic masculinity mirrored the role of men as husbands and fathers and were essentially geared to consolidate the leading position of the clergy within the Catholic Church. Celibate masculinity required for priests was thus explicitly moulded according to the norms of manliness in secular society. These norms reflected in part the ideals of Christian manliness coined in Anglican circles, yet in a specific Catholic, celibate, translation that was - however chastely - sexualized nevertheless.

The case of the Dominicans indicates that this development should be interpreted in the context of the efforts of the Catholic Church to maintain a prominent position under liberal politics which made every effort to minimize the role of religion in the public domain. By re-shaping and strengthening the internal organization under clerical leadership, it faced up to common associations of Catholicism with a backward and essentially female confessional culture.[5] By the 1920s, however, the essentially patriarchal mode of this clerical leadership was being challenged by rebellious young Catholic intellectuals, authors and artists whose support the regular clergy in particular tried to rally. These young men put forth more radical versions of Catholicism, denoted as virile. In this vein, they publicly dismissed the patriarchal masculinity of the secular and regular priests as an expression of clericalism to which they firmly objected. The Dominicans, who were trying to win the favour of precisely these young, in part academically trained Catholics, reacted differently to this challenge to clerical authority. Various reassessments of Dominican identity illustrate not only their attempts to reconcile tradition and modernity, but also the generational differences in the ways the Preachers attempted to profile themselves as "men of their times". As good 'fathers' the members of the established generation attempted to safeguard the Catholic community from the harsh opinions and rash actions of the 'sons'. These 'sons' defied patriarchal patterns with virile repertoires of Catholic masculinity, falling back on the monastic features of Dominican identity, discarding 'the old world' and attempting to replace it by a new one: fervently Catholic in orientation and led by spirited Catholics who surpassed the established clergy in its evangelical ardour.

CHRISTIAN MANLINESS DIFFERENTIATED

This case study of the Dutch Dominicans puts current notions of Christian manliness to the test. In general, social and cultural constructions of manliness form a rather new domain of academic interest. Zooming in on the Dominicans as prominent representatives of the regular clergy in the Netherlands enables us to overcome the binary opposition between hegemonic and Christian manliness which has come to dominate the rather young field of research on religion and masculinity. In *Geschichte der Männlichkeit (1450-2000)* the Austrian historian Wolfgang Schmale, for instance, argues that the formation of nation-states during the nineteenth century entailed an eclipse of Christian definitions of masculinity by secular varieties. These hinged

---

[5] van Zuthem, *Heelen en halven*. See also van de Sande, "Decadente monniken en nonnen". Cf. also the argument Gross made for the German situation in *The war against Catholicism*.

upon able-bodied strength, rationality, independence and responsibility and gradually came to represent the dominant or hegemonic form of manliness.[6] This idea may fit in neatly with the master narrative of the secularization of society in the course of its modernization, but hardly holds up when analysing nineteenth- and twentieth-century conceptualizations of Christian manliness more closely.

The intellectual father of the notion 'Christian manliness', Charles Kingsley (1819-1875), preferred this term to the tag 'muscular Christianity', which originated in a review of his novel *Two Years Ago* (1857). In his introductory essay to the volume *Muscular Christianity* Donald E. Hall stresses that it was Kingsley's primary intention to unite physical strength and religious conviction and to define this union as truly masculine.[7] A closer analysis of Kingsley's work reveals his personal preoccupation with sexuality and his anxious attempts to reconcile his sexual identity, needs and passions with the prevalent prim standards of Christian virtue. His definition of manliness was not only inherently Protestant, but was in fact prompted by a rejection of Catholicism which he associated with the weakening of the proper social and gender relations.[8] Hall points out that the adherents of Kingsley's concept of Christian manliness were deeply troubled by complex contemporary questions regarding class, gender and nationality. The modernization of society and the process of industrialization profoundly changed social structures. According to Hall, the discourse on Christian masculinity formed a crystallization point in the ensuing shifts of power that involved class, gender and race in the nineteenth-century British Empire and essentially revolved around national identity.[9] Consistent attempts to Christianize masculinity by entwining moral and physical vigour thus not merely reflect the release of the religious fervour of white middle- and upper-class males, but also reveal the patriarchal web within which they continuously attempted to subject underprivileged men and women.

The elitist and essentially Protestant features of Christian manliness were by no means monopolized by Anglicans, but affected Catholics and their conceptions of gender and religion as well. Yet, according to the editors of the volume *Masculinity and Spirituality in Victorian Culture*, the dominant Anglican matrix of Christian manliness in Britain obscured alternative significant patterns of masculine religiosity.[10] Implicitly, they reject a general concept of Christian masculinity, pleading for the analysis of multiple masculinities in religion instead. The conceptual differentiation they propose hinges around class, ethnicity and sexual preference, but should, in my opinion, also include denominational differences.[11] The relevance of confessional differentiation is underlined by a recently published volume on Christian manliness in Scandinavia, edited by the Swedish historian Yvonne Maria Werner.[12] Werner

[6] Schmale, *Geschichte der Männlichkeit*.
[7] Hall, *Muscular Christianity*, [2006], 3-13.
[8] Engelhardt Herringer, "Victorian Masculinity".
[9] Cf. Rosen, "The volcano and the cathedral".
[10] Bradstock, *Masculinity and Spirituality*.
[11] Cf. Miller, "The (Re)Gendering of High Anglicanism".
[12] Werner, *Kristen manlighet*. See in particular her introduction: "Kristen manlighet i teori och praxis", 9-22.

herself elucidates Catholic varieties of Christian manliness in her contribution on Catholic missionaries,[13] whereas the German historian Olaf Blaschke draws attention to differences in masculine Christian repertoires between Catholic laity and clergy.[14] The contributions to this volume, moreover, generally point at the heightened impact of religion between 1830 and 1940, for women as well as for men. As such, they put the thesis of the feminization of religion in this time frame into perspective. As Peter Gay already pointed out in *Schnitzler's Century*, the nineteenth century was the era of Darwin *and* the Virgin Mary, of scientific progress as well as of heightened religious fervour.[15] He argues that the mental landscape of the middle class in Western Europe in particular revealed a tendency to scientification and declericalization of culture and society on the one hand, and on the other to modern mysticism, pilgrimages and revelations. The impact of the Industrial Revolution and science on the individual and collective meaning of religion and religious experience was shaped by differences in class, gender, age or location. It is for this reason that the historian Hugh McLeod proposed that religious transformations since the nineteenth century be defined in terms of pluralization rather than secularization, in order to allow for the inclusion of experience and perception in the re-conceptualization of religion.[16]

The relevance of this recent research for the analysis of Catholic repertoires of masculinity is twofold. Firstly, the findings in general contradict the thesis that Christian conceptions of manliness in general were slowly but surely pushed out by secular and hegemonic notions of masculinity. Although this contention, as mentioned before, seems to fit in neatly with general theories about the marginalization of religion in the process of the modernization of society, it obscures the tenacity as well as the malleability of Christian definitions of manliness and specific masculine patterns of religiosity. This calls, secondly, for refining the general concept of Christian manliness, taking into account different dimensions of identity as well as denominational diversity. For instance, the male religious institutes prospered in the Netherlands during the interwar period, when the level of vocations to the priesthood reached its peak.[17] Such findings weaken simplified assumptions regarding the marginalization of religion in general, and challenge the claim to a habitual relationship between modernity and hegemonic masculinity. The case of the Dominicans presented here, moreover, elucidates various repertoires of manly religiosity and religious manliness within the Dutch Catholic culture. A brief overview of their history illustrates that their self-conception traditionally reflected clerical and monastic aspects, whose mutual relations and gendered attributions and associations alternated as the circumstances changed over time.

[13] Werner, "Feminin manlighet? Katholska missionärer I Norden".
[14] Blaschke, "Fältmarskalk Jesus Kristus", 23-50.
[15] Gay, *Schnitzler's century*.
[16] McLeod, *Secularization*, 10-11.
[17] Dellepoort, *De priesterroepingen in Nederland*, 42.

CONSTRUCTIONS OF DOMINICAN IDENTITY

In 1910, the historian of the Dutch Province, Augustine Meijer (1857-1925), explicitly referred to the fact that Dominic or Domingo de Guzman (1170-1221) founded his Order as a mendicant order in reaction to the established religious institutes of the Benedictines and Cistercians that were firmly embedded in medieval feudal society.[18] As Francis, the other prominent founding father before him, had done, Dominic opted for an active, evangelical and personal spirituality. The apostolate of their respective foundations revolved around preaching and confession, capitalizing on the spiritual and pastoral needs of the inhabitants of the new towns in Western Europe. Contemplation and action, in the form of preaching, represented the fundamentals of Dominican life. Meditation and study were practised for the benefit of one's preaching, which was geared to the salvation of the faithful. The organization of the Order as well as its internal division of labour favoured structural opportunities for contemplation for the ordained members.[19] The motto of the Dominicans, *contemplari et contemplata aliis tradere*, expressed the functional relationship between the active and contemplative dimensions of Dominican identity.[20] To Thomas Aquinas the purpose envisaged by Dominic epitomized the apex of religious life: to contemplate and share the fruits of contemplation with others.

The monastic traits of the identity of the Dutch Dominicans, however, had become rather atrophied between approximately 1600 and 1800. Catholicism was suppressed in the Dutch Republic in favour of the Dutch Reformed Church as publicly privileged Church. As a result, convents were closed and the clergy formally banned from the country. Secular and regular clerics, however, clandestinely travelled round to administer the sacraments. By the middle of the seventeenth century an intricate system of paid tolerance of minority religions had come into being, which allowed for the development of stations where Catholic worship was maintained. These missionary stations mostly survived on lay patronage and shaped a particular Catholic culture that continued to determine parochial pastoral care long after these stations had become full-blown parishes again after the restoration of Episcopal hierarchy in the Netherlands in 1853.[21] Nearly a century later, the Dutch Dominicans acknowledged that their influence still depended upon the parishes, which provided income, an influential social network and vocations for the Order. By then, they also had several convents in the country as a result of the restoration programme of the Dominican Order under the leadership of its Master, Vincent Jandel (1810-1872). This programme put their attachment to the parishes as well as the actual identity of parish priests under severe pressure. Jandel put forth a set of reforms that met with approval of the Holy See and greatly emphasized monastic observance, not only to restore a rigorous discipline within the Order, but also to reconstruct its proper tradition.

In the broader perspective of Roman Catholic Church politics, the stress put upon monastic observance served as an instrument of internal confessionalization

---

[18] Meijer, *Studiën*, 4-8.
[19] Vicaire, "Dominique (saint)", 1526-1530.
[20] Barendse, *Thomas van Aquino*.
[21] Parker, *Faith on the Margins*.

aimed at the reinforcement of a uniform Catholic identity which buttressed the ultra-montane ideology.[22] Religious communities performed a key role in this process, as is illustrated by, for instance, the appointment of vicar generals of influential institutes such as the Dominicans.[23] Jandel's appointment was instrumental for the pursuit of administrative centralization envisaged by Pope Pius IX, as were similar appointments for the Benedictines (1850), the Redemptorists (1853) and the Franciscans (1856 and 1862).[24] The pope attempted to tie these religious institutes more closely to the Holy See, thereby enlarging his own sphere of influence. Jandel's programme of reform became synonymous with a strict observance of the rule and the constitutions of the Order.[25]

His programme of re-monasticization met with resistance, not only in his own country, France, but also in Italy and in the Netherlands. Objections were essentially rooted in the question of what was imperative for the Dominican identity.[26] As far as the Dutch province was concerned, Jandel's programme played into the hands of the Dutch provincial, John Dominic Raken (1798-1869), who regarded the strengthening of the monastic aspects of Dominican life as instrumental for the transformation of rather heterogeneous group of parish priests into a more uniform group of men religious. As parish priests, the Dominicans had grown self-reliant and had outgrown the convent life with which they had had at most a passing acquaintance in their formative years. Until the end of the eighteenth century they usually spent these years in a convent in the Southern Netherlands. After the closing of these convents in the aftermath of the French Revolution, such a convent training became an exception to the rule, reserved for the happy few of which Raken himself had been one, spending his years of religious and clerical training in Rome between 1818 and 1821. Without opportunities to cultivate the monastic dimensions of Dominican life, Raken had no doubt that they risked becoming clerics rather than men religious. Yet he was well aware that some influential fellow brothers had raised fundamental doubts as to whether the strict monastic observance was a Dominican characteristic at all. Some pointed out that a rigidly ascetic regimen could probably be more easily maintained by those brothers in other provinces who could indeed enjoy convent life, but not by the Dutch Dominicans themselves, as their pastoral duties severely challenged their physical constitution.[27]

Pressured by the master general, Raken managed to craft a compromise between the monastically oriented international reform programme and the parish-oriented Dutch Dominican culture. While the Preachers held on to 'their' parishes they also founded new convents, first in Huissen (1858), a small town in Gelderland, followed by the Convent of Saint Thomas in Zwolle (1901) mentioned earlier and the Convent of Saint Albert the Great in Nijmegen (1932). On an ideological level they

---

[22] Blaschke coined the notion *innere Konfessionalisierung* in "Der Dämon des Konfessionalismus".

[23] Cf. De Maeyer, *Religious Institutes*.

[24] Duffy, *Saints and sinners*, 234; cf. De Maeyer, "Introduction", 20-22.

[25] Walz, *Compendium*, 442-444.

[26] Cf. the debate between Jandel and Henri-Dominique Lacordaire: B. Bonvan, *Lacordaire-Jandel*.

[27] PAOD 8097b, Mk 1 en Mk 14: Letters of Th. Van der Heijden to provincial Raken, Nijmegen, 13 December 1848, 10 December 1848 en 30 January 1850. See also PAOD 8097b, Mf 14: Letter of Peter Sjoukes to Thomas Sjoukes, Amsterdam, 26 January 1851.

put explicit effort into the cultivation of a double identity: clerical and religious. The circular letters from the subsequent fathers provincial to their subjects testify to this effort. They associated a courageous, decisive attitude with the active and clerical dimensions of Dominican life, and a more submissive and receptive attitude with its contemplative and religious aspects. The Dutch Dominicans were expected to cultivate these characteristics equally. This, in turn, was presented as somewhat a hopeless aim, since the majority of them remained active as parish clergy. As such they partook in a clerical culture, which mirrored that of the secular clergy.[28] The particular way of life in the parishes became scorned, while the efforts the Dominican parish priests put into the cultivation of the monastic dimensions of their Dominican existence were depicted as heroic.

The circular letters reflect what specific religious masculinity was required for the Preachers. By their vows of obedience, chastity and poverty, they renounced the general social standards of self-determination, material wealth, and legitimate offspring for male adults of the middle class from which they themselves descended. The Belgian historian Jan Art has pointed out that living by these three vows required virtues which were essentially qualified as feminine, such as humility, obedience, self-renunciation and self-sacrifice.[29] Although this is certainly true, in the context of male religious institutes like the Dominican Order, the sacrificial character of religious life was directly associated with physical endurance and moral strength typified as masculine qualities. The capacity to live according to stringent internal discipline and to bow to hierarchical authority was denoted as 'manly'. Celibacy, on the one hand, set the Dominicans apart from lay men, joining them closer to God than any non-celibate man. Rigorous monastic discipline, on the other hand, set them apart from the secular clergy. This internal discipline was principally geared to one's obedience to God, as well as to his earthly representatives, the religious superiors. Martial terms were used in descriptions of their regimen of prayer, seclusion (often temporary) and fasting. Such descriptions not only underscored the pious militancy of their choice to become a priest and to contribute to a truly Christian society, but also the manly character of this endeavour.

This did, however, not solve the basic tension between the active (clerical) and contemplative (religious) dimensions of their identity. Around 1910 the Dutch Dominicans started to distinguish more clearly between *identity* and *position*. Their *identity* rested upon monastic fundamentals, whereas their *position* had mostly become intertwined with parochial pastoral care. The confidence in their superiority to the secular clergy remained untainted. This sense of superiority gradually trickled down their ranks. Within the international Order, however, the Dutch Dominicans with their parish responsibilities turned into the exception to the rule that the Preachers essentially were religious who kept their distance from activities which would frame them in the diocesan structures. The Dutch Dominicans clearly could not easily reconcile

---

[28] With one major difference: the master of the order insisted that the members who were engaged in pastoral care did not live all by themselves, as was customary for secular priests. Therefore, the Dominicans often lived in small groups (two to four) in the presbyteries of the parishes they administered.

[29] Art, "Mannen als bruiden".

their historically evolved responsibility for over ten, mostly inner-city, parishes with the monastic characteristics which the Order claimed and promoted internationally as Dominican.

CLERICAL LEADERSHIP OF THE CATHOLIC SUBCULTURE

Attempts to balance the contemplative monastic aspects of Dominican life with its clerical components proved to be rather fragile as Dutch society was reshaped along denominational lines during the process of 'pillarization' (*verzuiling*). Between 1890 and 1920, Catholic and (orthodox) Protestant politicians came to agree upon the principle of largely self-contained and self-supporting denominational subcultures or pillars (*zuilen*) as a means to advance their social and cultural emancipation while preserving the Christian character of society at the same time. For the Dutch Catholics, over a third of the entire population around 1900, emancipation went hand in hand with a religious revival in a largely separate subculture dominated by their own schools, newspapers, social, political and charitable organizations.

Historiographical evaluations of pillarization in general roughly vary from describing it either as an essentially conservative response to modernity employing modern means, as the Swiss historian Urs Altermatt put forward in his *Katholizismus und Moderne* (1989), or as a reflection of modernization of religion itself, as argued by the Belgian sociologist Staf Hellemans in *Strijd om de moderniteit* (1993).[30] In both theories the process of pillarization hinges upon fundamental changes in the relationship between religion and society under the influence of industrialization and urbanization in large parts of Europe. These developments undermined traditional patterns of behaviour, status and power related to agrarian society and entailed the dislodgement of the social, political and economic domains from the direct and indirect sphere of influence of the Church. This was exactly what the Church sought to prevent by designing an autonomous, self-supporting Catholic subculture which made it possible for Catholics to actively be a part of processes of modernization, albeit on religious principles which underscored its fixed and God-given nature. The Catholic subculture which came into being in the Netherlands was subdivided by gender, age and social status but, in contrast to largely similar subcultures in Germany and Switzerland, also highly clericalized.[31]

This pillarization process clearly fostered and strengthened the clerical dimensions of the identity of regular priests such as the Dominicans. Although the internal stability and the monolithic nature of the Catholic pillar in the Netherlands have been questioned, most forcefully by the historian Paul Luykx,[32] the domination of the Catholic subculture by the secular as well as the regular clergy is incontestable. While transforming into the organizational backbone of the Catholic subculture and contributing to the shaping of a distinct Catholic identity, the clergy extended its influence far beyond the actual ecclesiastical domain. Necrologies of Dominicans

---

[30] See also Hellemans's recent study: *Het tijdperk van de wereldreligies*.
[31] Cf. Righart, *De katholieke zuil in Europa*, 29-36.
[32] Luykx, *Andere katholieken*.

show us just how far their span of control expanded. Pastoral guidance evolved into extensive moral control exercised by priests who watched closely over their flock and stopped their parishioners to learn why they had missed Mass.[33] Interestingly enough, typologies of clerical authority and clerical manliness were moulded into the secular, patriarchal mode of masculinity of lay bourgeois men as dedicated, decisive husbands and fathers.[34]

Men of God were men of the Church, depicted as the Bride whom they could make bear fruit by preaching, administering the Sacraments, and tending to the pastoral needs of the faithful. The mystery of the motherhood of the Church, in other words, relied upon them.[35] This responsibility required a dedicated spiritual life, qualified as "manly and earnest".[36] Although they were celibate, men of God ought to be true men, who could prove their manliness by profiling themselves as strong leaders of the Catholic community, being compassionate pastors as well as competitive priests, militant and submissive at the same time. As they were exempt from military service - in contrast to their colleagues in Belgium, for instance - the Catholic subculture remained the privileged arena in which Dutch priests could prove their masculinity. While the older patterns of asceticism served to distinguish the Dominicans as regular priests from the secular clerics, by the 1920s they had gradually become aware that men were increasingly turning away from parish-based organized religion, and they now employed the exercise of a stringent asceticism to set the men of God apart from the female faithful and their religious practice. This decline was particularly manifest in the male membership of the Dominican Third Order. Moreover, it was proving increasingly difficult to attract and keep young, academically trained Catholics committed to the parishes or the apostolate beyond the parishes.[37] This awareness is mirrored in the describing and denouncing of parish-based religious practices as feminine.

The Dominicans were explicitly admonished to refrain from a piety that consisted of external "forms, practices and devotions" which was said not to go beyond the mere sensitive aspects of piety and which only induced sentimentality. Superiors insisted that their fellow brothers give up all devotions that were considered "weak and sentimental". Instead, they were admonished to lead a sincere, manly life, cultivating a piety without any sentimental tendencies.[38] The adjectives "sentimental" and "weak" undoubtedly referred to the female sex and were used to ostracize specific forms of piety by labelling them feminine. Apparently, the terms "piety" and

---

[33] As was said, for instance, of the Dominican Raymundus N.G. Orie (1863-1944). Hermans, "Em. Pastoor Orie".

[34] Cf. for similar gendering of clerical identity in the Protestant and Anglican tradition since the late nineteenth century Bos, "A Good Enough Parson" and Mews, "Clergymen, Gentlemen and Men".

[35] Stockums, *Priesterschap en ascese*, 262. Interestingly enough, such qualifications of religious leadership and inspiration were metaphorically denoted as forms of spiritual motherhood in the High Middle Ages, which was even ascribed to Jesus Christ. Bynum, *Jesus as Mother*.

[36] Cf. Stockums, *Priesterschap en ascese*, 178.

[37] PAOD 2574: Membership of the Third Order, including intellectuals and priests.

[38] PAOD 6393: Conferences during retreats (15 until 22 September 1937) 12, (25 July until 3 August 1940) 11. See also the criticism of Petrus van den Tempel O.P. in the apologetic periodical *Het Schild*, May 1931, cited by Van der Plas, *Uit het rijke roomsche leven*, 135-136.

"pious" had become tainted and were replaced with notions such as "contemplation" and "contemplative", which were contrasted with devotional patterns of religious practice. In Dominican circles *contemplation* was now described as an act of inner discipline, denoted as masculine, while at the same time representing a necessary check on the pastoral duties and the apostolate that were labelled as *action*. Yet, the Preachers could hardly ignore the fact that within the clericalized Catholic subculture it was precisely these forms of *action* that underscored the manly character of their presence.

Faced with an increasingly feminine presence in Church and with what they referred to as "the men's question", by the 1920s some Dominicans were also becoming aware that the clericalization of Catholic culture could potentially harm the spiritual prestige of the clergy. Catholic emancipation seemed to be complete with the settling of the long-lasting controversies over state funding of confessional schools in 1917 and universal suffrage in 1919. This political success started to compromise the prominent role of the clergy in the Catholic milieu. The Dominicans were not the only incumbents who had to face up to questions and criticism from young educated Catholics, whose support they actually tried to rally in their intellectual apostolate. In their case, the criticism induced them to reconsider the parameters of their identity as priests religious, bringing up old questions concerning the balance between action and contemplation, characteristics that were linked to connotations of decisiveness (action) and passivity (contemplation) which, in turn, were tacitly or overtly connected to definitions of masculinity or femininity.

RE-EVALUATIONS OF FAMILIAR PARAMETERS

A series of commemorations provided an opportunity for intensified reflections on Dominican identity. In 1921, the seventh centenary of Saint Dominic's death was celebrated, in 1923 the sixth centenary of Saint Thomas Aquinas's canonization, and finally in 1934 the seventh centenary of Saint Dominic's canonization.[39] The Preachers seized these opportunities to clarify and maintain their prominent role in the Catholic community and advance [maintain?] the position of this community in Dutch society. They not only had to deal with the criticism of lay intellectuals mentioned above, but also feared the indifference to Church and clergy of a growing group of Catholics.

In 1921 the philosopher Joseph van Wely attempted to reconcile the Order's tradition with modernity. He set out to defend the rationale of the Order by contextualizing Saint Dominic's foundation in the historical development of the religious institutes, as well as by pointing out the specific characteristics of the Dominican apostolate.[40] Van Wely was trained as a philosopher at the University of Fribourg in Switzerland

---

[39] These occasions were seized to make up for the fact that the seventh centenary of the foundation of the order in 1916 was celebrated rather modestly due to the outbreak of the First World War, even in the Netherlands that remained neutral. Walz, *Wahrheitskünder*, 142. PAOD 2775: Scrapbook of the Dutch Province I, 1910- May 1935, 78-79: "Zevende Eeuwfeest der Dominicaner-orde"; "Het zevende eeuwfeest der Dominicaner-orde".
[40] Van Wely, *Waar Sint Dominicus*.

and was considered one of the promising Dominican intellectuals of the Dutch province. He argued that the religious project of Saint Dominic formed the link between the classical mode of monastic life grafted onto the *stabilitas loci* on the one hand, and the more modern and mobile religious way of life promoted by Saint Ignatius of Loyola on the other. This evolutionary perspective legitimized the existence of the Dominicans as a semi-modern order. Their rationale, Van Wely pointed out, was to be found in the connection between contemplation (guaranteed by the monastic life) and action (expressed in pastoral and apostolic activities). He acknowledged that the Dominicans could not monopolize the motto *Contemplata aliis tradere*, which Saint Thomas had coined for all apostolic institutes.[41] Yet, this 'pronouncement' clearly reflected Saint Dominic's ideals, as well as the "characteristic properties of the Dominicans" who stated that their preaching should invariably be rooted in the plenitude of the contemplation advanced by their monastic way of life (*ex plenitude contemplationis*).[42]

While referring to the historical development of the Order and its characteristics Van Wely obviously accounted for the changing circumstances in which the Dominicans had to accomplish their specific calling. He self-critically remarked that it did not suffice to excel as proficient polemicists, skilful scholars, smooth preachers, or smart organizers. In order to capture the attention of the 'masses', the Dominicans had to express the "full Christendom which lives in us" in their sermons. They needed to be aware that they would not be judged by their words, but by their acts as well. In this vein they could and should contribute to bringing about "a new humanity" and "a new world".

Whereas Van Wely emphasized the necessity of a revival of religious vigour in a familiar patriarchal mode, preferably with regular clerics as the Preachers in the lead, a group of young friars in Zwolle focused on the more passive aspects of Dominican life instead, accentuating the need to lead a life of love and suffering. They did so in a collection of poems and essays brought out as a special edition of the Dominican periodical *De Rozenkrans* (The Rosary). The authors are of the same generation as the three young friars depicted by Van Bergen in his triptych, born around the turn of the twentieth century. Their contributions to the debate over Dominican identity in fact reflect the ambiguity of this painting, glorifying the decisive strength of Catholic tradition in modern society embodied by contemplative friars submitting to God's will. Postulating the resemblance between Saint Dominic and Christ, the contributors to the special issue of *De Rozenkrans* depict the founder of their Order alternately as a humble and meek man and a powerful warrior of God who fought heresy and enlightened the world with his apostolate. The heroic qualities ascribed to Saint Dominic clearly echo an older discourse articulated in the circular letters of the superiors during the first two decades of the twentieth century. More important here, however, is the emphasis young Dominicans put on the obedient and submissive atti-

---

[41] Thomas Aquinas, *Summa Theologiae*, II, 188, 6. Cf. Stockums, *Priesterschap en ascese*, 159.
[42] "[Dit] machtwoord [...] als uitdrukking van Sint Dominicus' idealen, als wedergave dus van onze Dominicaansche eigenheid [...] toch een bepaalden, wel omschreven zin, namelijk het Dominicaanse ideaal om de prediking te laten voortkomen uit de volheid of de overvloed van door de monastieke levenspraktijk bevorderde contemplatie". Van Wely, *Waar Sint Dominicus*, 13.

tude of Saint Dominic. According to them, he thereby testified to his personal insignificance, glorifying Christ and His willingness to suffer and even die for His faith. In the weight they ascribe to Saint Dominic's martial martyrdom the young friars were able to connect contemplation and action along different lines than Van Wely, yet with a similar outcome: a life of prayer would strengthen and prepare Dominic's sons for their main task: preaching. Yet, in contrast to Van Wely's argument they implicitly refuted his familiar, essentially patriarchal mode of the re-fashioning of Dominican life and challenged its clerical foundations.

Van Wely as well as the young friars each attempted to reconcile the tradition of their Order with the changing circumstances. The Dominicans hesitated to accommodate what they called "the spirit of the times". This expression proved to be short hand for modernity: everything that opposed and undermined the Christian character of society. As "men of their times" the Preachers set out to control this spirit, drawing inspiration and legitimacy from their tradition. They considered tradition to be the driving force of their religious life, which kept it in its proper track.[43] Concern for the tradition of the Order precluded disdain of the old and familiar in favour of the new and unknown, the Dominican Jan Sassen explained in *Het Klooster* (The Convent) in 1922.[44] The essentials of this tradition were, however, put to the test by representatives of the generation of the Dutch Dominicans who vented their vision on the fundamentals of Dominican life in the special edition of *De Rozenkrans* of 1921. Some of them proved to be susceptible to the viewpoints of their radical lay peers. To them, the clerical dimensions of the Dominican identity should be kept in check by the contemplative aspects, which were thought to foster the true internalization of faith to which their apostolate should be geared. This viewpoint revealed reservations within the Church regarding the leadership of clerics who did not meet these standards.

CLERICAL REPERTOIRES CHALLENGED

These young Dominicans could not easily slip into the patriarchal mode of Catholic masculinity which had become familiar to their older brothers and torch bearers of Dutch Catholicism. Most prominent among the latter were the professors of the Catholic University of Nijmegen, founded in 1923: the exegete Reginald Jansen (1879-1947), Jan-Benedict Kors (1885-1966) who held the chair in moral theology after 1928, and Peter Kreling (1888-1973), chair of dogmatic theology beginning that same year.[45] These Dominicans were educated during the struggle against modernism between 1908 and 1914. They inadvertently bore the stamp of a two-faced Catholicism: outwardly complacent, triumphant and sometimes even defiant, inwardly cautious

[43] Cf. in this respect the idealized images of tradition among converts to Catholicism, analysed by Luykx, *'Daar is nog poëzie'*. There are striking resemblances between Van Bergen's triptych and the oeuvre of the painter and Catholic convert Lodewijk Schelfhout, in particular his painting *L'évolution* (1913) (ibid, 130-134).

[44] Sassen, *Het klooster*.

[45] But also Weve (Tilburg), Molkenboer (lector in Nijmegen) and Welschen (since 1922 professor of Thomist Philosophy at the (public) University of Amsterdam).

and controlling. To Catholics of younger generations, they epitomized patriarchal clericalism rooted in unswerving neothomist schooling. Kors, for instance, was associated with various Catholic social and intellectual initiatives. Jansen literally seemed to embody the sturdiness of Catholic theology, "his massive head planted on his square shoulders", at the same time reflecting the masculine character of a neo-thomist training, expressed in his "tough, truly manly mind [...] without any little-ness, without sentimentality, professional, objective".[46]

Younger protagonists, by contrast, criticized the essentially clerical mode of Catholic masculine leadership, opting for what could best be termed as 'reactionary modernism'.[47] They strove to renew their personal faith and spirituality, not by ruling over the spirit of the times as older Dominicans had tried, but by actively resisting it as being materialistic and all too rational.[48] While developing a radical religious agenda, they took sides with young Catholic intellectuals who publicly questioned the clericalization of the Catholic community and criticized secular and regular priests for forsaking their actual vocation. Dominicans met with their disapproval as well, as the criticism of the ex-seminarian, journalist and author Anton van Duinker-ken (1903-1968) directed at Hyacinth Hermans O.P. (1876-1962) illustrates. In 1931 Van Duinkerken, well on his way to become one of the leading Catholic intellectuals in the Netherlands, painted an unfavourable portrait of this Dominican in an article entitled "The unrecognizable priest" ("De onherkenbare priester"). Hermans wrote for the influential, conservative newspaper *De Maasbode* and celebrated the 25th anniversary of his ordination that year. This newspaper then characterized him as "the least cleri-cal of all Catholic journalists [...] whom only a few people will have ever spotted in his Dominican habit". Van Duinkerken was outraged; he could not understand how this Dominican was honoured by *De Maasbode* for not being recognizable for what he actually was: a priest religious. Moreover, he attacked Hermans for admitting that he had become a journalist because he did not like the pulpit after all. Not only did the Dominican reveal his personal embarrassment over the actual goal of his life, as Van Duinkerken pointed out, but he was apparently unaware of the danger of the profes-sional confusion in the Catholic community, where priests spent their energy on jour-nalism or other professions, while neglecting their actual, pastoral duties. According to Van Duinkerken, these duties could not be performed by lay Catholics, unlike the activities with which the priesthood squandered its precious time. He scorned clerical efforts to engage the laity in pastoral duties in the parishes, for this would leave the faithful in the hands of pastoral amateurs.[49]

Van Duinkerken's philippic reveals the resistance to the clericalized Catholic culture young Dominicans had to reckon with. It was published in the periodical *De Gemeenschap* (The Community), founded in 1925 as a "monthly magazine for Catho-

---

[46] "Zijn massieve kop stevig geplant op zijn vierkante schouders" gepaard aan "een forse, echt mannelijke geest [...] zonder kleinheid sentimentaliteit, zakelijk, objectief". Cited in Monteiro, *Gods Predikers*, 281.

[47] Herf, *Reactionary Modernism*; Golan, *Modernity and Nostalgia*, xiii.

[48] PAOD 5865: Lecture of Rafaël Meussen, January 1928 in: Verslagboek Lacordaire-debatingclub XV, 55-57; PAOD 5867: Lecture of Pius Kok, 8 March 1931 in: Verslagboek Lacordaire-debatingclub XVII, 67-70.

[49] van Duinkerken, "De onherkenbare priester".

lic reconstruction" and as such it bore an anti-liberal, anti-individualist stamp.[50] This periodical was the main mouthpiece of the ideas of the French convert Jacques Maritain (1882-1973) in the Netherlands - in fact, the editors even contemplated simply naming their periodical *Maritain*.[51] Interestingly enough, the link with Maritain was strengthened by a Dominican, Casimir Terburg (1892-1968). In 1924 he published the Dutch translation of Maritain's *Art en scolastique* (1920). As an unwritten rule the editors of *De Gemeenschap* did not collaborate with priests, but they made an exception for Terburg. In late 1924 he became one of the regular contributors to the magazine.[52]

To young intellectuals in the circle of *De Gemeenschap*, Maritain's reconciliation of modern art and Catholicism served as a more general framework to merge modernity with what was perceived as religious tradition. In his provocative study *Catholicism in the Jazz Age*, the American historian Stephen Schloesser S.J. explains how Maritain employed Thomas Aquinas's theory of art in *Art en scolastique* to emphasize the importance of form in art as a means to visualize a deeper meaning intended by God. Using the scholastic notion of hylomorphism, Maritain mobilized this respectable tradition in order to glorify abstract modern art as *the* form of art which would transcend the mere imitation of nature by uncovering the internal and vital processes which animated nature in its very workings.[53] Schloesser's analysis not only sums up the agenda of an artistic avant-garde during the interwar years, but also clarifies its partially reactionary character. Moreover, his analysis explains the attraction of neothomism to dissatisfied young Catholic intellectuals in the Netherlands as it underpinned their efforts to bring about change in the hierarchical structures of the Catholic subculture. These structures had always been guarded as god-given, and were now challenged by new claims of new protagonists to true godly inspiration.[54]

The Dominican Terburg took it upon himself to explain Thomas's philosophy to a small group of these men, attempting to do what Maritain did: bridging the gap between Catholic tradition and modern culture.[55] He thus initiated laymen in a philosophical and intellectual mindset that had been reserved to its future elite within his own Dominican community. Only those friars who were destined for an intellectual or administrative career within the Order concentrated directly on Thomas's *Summa* during their training in theology. This thomistic empowerment inspired some of Terburg's listeners to more radical interpretations of their personal calling as Catholic intellectuals. Henri Bruning (1900-1983) was one of them and became one of the founders of the hypercritical periodical *De Valbijl* (The Guillotine, 1925) under which many a prominent priest was virtually executed. The editors of this radically religious, anti-democratic and anti-clerical periodical, which proved to be extremely short-lived, professed an uncompromising Catholicism, glorifying vigour and mascu-

---

[50] van den Haterd, *Om hart en vurigheid*.

[51] Sanders, "Maritain in the Netherlands".

[52] Id., "Dominicus in de *Jazz Age*", 51.

[53] Schloesser, *Catholicism in the Jazz Age*. Cf. Sanders, *Het spiegelend venster*, 261-263, 268-276.

[54] Ibid., 261-263, 268-276. See also Luykx, "Daar is nog poëzie".

[55] van der Meer de Walcheren, *Menschen en God*, vol. 1, 176. Cf. Kieft, *Het plagiaat*, 18-22, and Sanders, "Dominicus in de *Jazz Age*", 49 and 51.

line vitality, against the tide of the modern, secularized world, but also against established Catholicism which, in their opinion, was wrongly satisfied with the existing balance of power, because it offended the original intentions of the Gospel.

Terburg's conferences illustrate that he sympathized with more radical ascetic interpretations of Catholicism to counter the spiritual poverty and materialism of modernity.[56] Materialism and egotism separated man from God and this separation could only be undone by mortification, submission to God's will and by consistent prayer.[57] It is difficult to precisely assess Terburg's influence within the Dominican community. His ties with the dissatisfied young Catholics did, however, prompt the superior of the Dutch Dominicans in 1931 to forbid his censorship of yet another new, radical periodical initiated by some of the editors of *De Valbijl*, which by then had ceased publication.[58] Though respected, Terburg was somewhat of an odd man out in his own community. His non-conformism was exemplified in the pastorate he single-handedly set up for a group of caravan-dwellers. His ties with the aforementioned Bruning go back to Bruning's training at Saint Dominic's College, the minor seminary of the Order where Terburg taught Latin and Greek.[59]

During his school years Bruning also got acquainted with Raymund van Sante (1896-1946), a Belgian 'army man' with a strongly developed Flemish nationalist sentiment who had become a novice in the Dutch province in 1919. By 1931 Van Sante had become the key figure among a group of in part overzealous Catholic students who were attracted by his programme of religious renewal. This revolved around so-called lay core groups that were to co-operate with clerics prone to change in the spirit of the Gospel. Van Sante provided the thomistic underpinnings of their programme in a small study on authority (*Gezag*), in which he tried to turn the tables of authority, encouraging students to take it upon themselves to support the clergy, which he characterized as failing in its principal duties.[60]

SHIFTING REPERTOIRES

Needless to say, the proposed inversion threatened the hierarchy of the Dutch Roman Catholic Church, where lawful authority was synonymous with the control of the bishops over their priests, as well as with the power of these priests over the laity. The alliance Van Sante and Terburg forged with young Catholic intellectuals in the 1920s and 1930s proved to be extremely fragile.[61] Of more importance here, however, is that

[56] Terburg, *Het innerlijk leven*. See also Van den Haterd, *Om hart en vurigheid*, 40.

[57] Cf. Sanders, "Dominicus in de *Jazz Age*", 52.

[58] Catholic Documentation Centre, Nijmegen, Archives Henri Bruning, nr. 520: Letter of Bruning to Raymundus van Sante, 16-05-1931; Kieft, *Het plagiaat*, 25.

[59] See the chapter by Marieke Smulders (chapter 8).

[60] van Sante, *Gezag*; Catholic Documentation Centre, Nijmegen, Archives Henri Bruning, nr. 520: Letter of Bruning to Raymundus van Sante, letter of Bruning to Van Sante, 14 March 1934. I dealt extensively with Van Sante in Monteiro, *Gods Predikers*, especially 181-183, 203-212.

[61] Cf. my article "Catholic Intellectual Elites in the Netherlands: Fruitful and Vulnerable Alliances during the Interbellum", to appear in the Relins-volume on communities of communication, edited by Altermatt, Metzger and De Maeyer.

the opposition between the established clergy and educated lay Catholics also reveals diverging conceptions of Catholic manliness. The group with which both Van Sante and Terburg associated themselves embodied a mix of vital vigour denoted as virile and a mystical submissiveness. Their proclaimed mission in the Church demanded what they defined as manly decisiveness. Yet, they also had to acknowledge the fact that they were neglected by Church authorities on account of their lay status and youthful inexperience. They were well aware that their sometimes uncompromisingly radical conceptions of Catholicism were kept in check by patriarchal organizational patterns guarded by older representatives of the clergy. They tried to come to terms with this tension by identifying themselves with Jesus Christ who served as a model of identification as a martyr for his faith and religious convictions.

The Dutch bishops recognized Van Sante as one of the main instigators of what was branded as 'intra-church anticlericalism', and consequently he was exiled from the Dutch Dominican Province in the spring of 1933. In the same year, Terburg distanced himself from Bruning and his circle when Bruning published a booklet entitled *Onze priesters* (Our Priests),[62] which breathed the vitalistic discourse of the radical young Catholics. He argued that many Catholics would leave their Church not only because of the "feeble predications" of the clergy, but also because the priests did not live by the moral standards they preached. The fact that the youngest generation of Preachers proved to be susceptible to the essentially anticlerical agenda of Bruning *cum suis* explains why the Dutch provincial of the Dominicans launched a counteroffensive. In a series of conferences for Catholic students as well as the young friars that same year, Kors, who had been highly critical of Van Sante's opinion on authority,[63] and Kreling, who did not share Van Sante's views either,[64] attempted to restore the patriarchal authority of the clergy against their rebellious 'sons', condemning the uncurbed idealism and activism of the radical young Catholics as anti-intellectualistic and anti-clerical. Terburg did his share in defending the *status quo* by distancing himself to some extent from the young men whom he had initiated in the principles of Thomas. In May 1933 he dedicated a conference to the theme of prudence, of which the "men of action" and "many youngsters among us" seemed to have such a low opinion. The virtue of prudence, Terburg lectured, saw to it that men would keep time in their moral actions and would fulfil the purpose for which God had created them.[65]

Against the background of this controversy over authority, the exchange of views among Dominicans on the balance between action and contemplation was gaining momentum. By 1933, *action* could easily be mistaken for one-sided decisiveness that disregarded customary patriarchal patterns of authority and could therefore be branded as anti-clerical, whereas the notion of *contemplation* ran the risk of becoming stigmatized as passive and frail. On the occasion of the seventh centenary of the canonization of the founder of the Order in 1934 the parameters of Dominican

[62] Bruning, *Onze priester*.
[63] Private Collection, Berg en Dal, Archives Willebrord 21: Lecture by Kors on authority ("Het gezag"), 2 May 1934.
[64] Catholic Documentation Centre, Nijmegen, Archives Henri Bruning, nr. 520: Letter of Bruning to Van Sante, 14 March 1934.
[65] PAOD 8529: Lecture held on 14 May 1933 in Ubbergen near Nijmegen.

identity were once again pondered, this time, however, only by representatives of the established generation. While concentrating on the history of the reception of Saint Dominic they trod carefully, in order to position clerical energy and apostolic action well within the customary patriarchal order of things while avoiding the pitfall of passivity. As men of their times, Dominicans had to control the spirit of these times, for which they were excellently equipped, being clerically trained men of God, loyal to the Church. This patriarchal mode of manliness, however, lost at least some of its appeal among the young Preachers who wondered whether the changing times were not asking for a change in them, as they considered it their vocation not to control, but rather to understand the spirit of times.[66]

CONCLUSION

Christian manliness proves to be a rather unstable and elusive category in nineteenth- and twentieth-century history. Although the concept of a de-Christianized hegemonic manliness fits in smoothly with the secularization theory, Christian masculinity and hegemonic manliness did not entirely part ways after the middle of the nineteenth century. Recent research has discredited the secularization theory as the master narrative of religious change,[67] as this master narrative largely neglects the heightened impact of religion precisely in the century between 1840 and 1940. Instead of being pushed to the margins of society by modernization or new conceptualizations of humanity derived from the Enlightenment, religion in its denominational variance propelled various processes of confessionalization to which both women and men were party and which were essentially gendered. Whereas the feminization of religion has received due academic attention, research on processes of masculinization is still in its infancy. This research should, in my opinion, take inter- and intra-denominational differences into account when assessing the impact of gender in perceptions and meanings of religion and religiosity on an individual and collective level.

This article has aimed to contribute to this assessment by offering an analysis of Catholic repertoires of Christian manliness, focusing on the Dutch Dominicans between 1850 and 1940. They then represented one of the most prominent religious institutes; the patterns of clerical and religious masculinity they cultivated are probably valid for other male orders as well.[68] Over a period of almost a century these patterns reveal significant shifts. As missionaries within the boundaries of the Dutch Republic, the Dominicans came to cultivate the clerical dimensions of their identity. During the restoration of the Order from the mid-nineteenth century onwards, however, the monastic aspects in turn were stressed due to an international monastic reform instrumental to the revival of the Order. Though not uncontested in the Dutch province, which firmly held onto its parishes, the Dutch Dominicans employed the monastic traits of their identity in self-appraisals in order to distinguish themselves

---

[66] PAOD 5869: Verslagboek Lacordaire-debatingclub XVIII, 135-149, in particular 137 and 138.
[67] Cf. Cox, "Secularization and other"; id., "Master narratives". See also Brown, *The Death of Christian Britain.*
[68] Cf. de Kok, *Acht eeuwen Minderbroeders.*

from the secular clergy. During the process of pillarization between 1890 and 1920 their identity as men of God then became modelled after secular, bourgeois standards of masculinity. This patriarchal mode of manliness neatly supported the clerical leadership of the Catholic community.

Attempts to strengthen the sturdier, masculine traits of the clerical identity backfired once the process of pillarization reached its peak and Catholics came to question the clerical dominance outside the ecclesiastical domain. This clericalism was severely criticized by a new generation of educated Catholic men, who were not at all impressed by the spiritual heroism and innate virtue priests claimed on account of their (celibate) state in life and status as *alter Christus*. These Catholics set out to separate the spheres which had come together during the denominational segmentation of Dutch society. By 1920 the Dominicans saw themselves faced with the need to clarify their relevance in modern society. This triggered tentative reflections on the familiar parameters of their identity during the 1920s and 1930s.

These reflections are illustrative for the manner in which the Dominicans tried to reconcile tradition and modernity, thus profiling themselves as men of their times under changed conditions. These reflections not only circled around the well-known poles of Dominican identity, action and contemplation, but also reveal how these characteristics were gendered in the interwar debate over status and authority within the Catholic community. To the Dominicans, action was connected to the patriarchal pastoral span of control, kept in check by contemplation which guaranteed the prudence considered necessary. Young Catholic intellectuals who opposed the clericalized character of the Catholic subculture, however, glorified new conceptions of action, denouncing the patterns of action of the clergy as weak, effeminate and out of date. These 'sons' cultivated virile varieties of Catholic manliness that challenged the classical patriarchal order. Whereas the established generation of the Dominicans invested in an internal debate over the virtue of a well-balanced life of action and contemplation, this way of life was discarded as weak and ineffective, not only by representatives of the new lay intellectual elite, but by a few high-profiled fellow brothers as well. These Dominicans took up the ascetic traits of the monastic dimension of the Dominican identity in an attempt to regain some of their Order's authority within the Catholic community. They thereby attempted to chart the prerequisites of Catholic manliness anew in the gendered opposition within the weakened clergy, in need of help of the ascetic strength of lay and religious men guided by a more profound Christian spirit than most ordained men of God.

Circa 18-year old ... at Saint Dominic's College, Nijmegen, 1936. In this closed Catholic institution, masculine socialization was influenced by various ideals and images of men and masculinity that stemmed from the Catholic tradition as well as from Dutch interwar culture.
[Sint Agatha, Erfgoedcentrum Nederlands Kloosterleven, PAOD]

THE BOYS OF SAINT DOMINIC'S

CATHOLIC BOYS' CULTURE AT A MINOR SEMINARY IN INTERWAR HOLLAND *

MARIEKE SMULDERS

In 1927, the Dutch Dominicans opened a modern boarding school complex in the village of Neerbosch just outside Nijmegen, in the southeast of the Netherlands. It provided accommodation for an expanding group of minor seminarians. The original Saint Dominic's College, built in 1856 in the centre of Nijmegen, no longer met the standards of a modern educational institute, necessitating the move to the new college in 1927.

In 1930, in a brochure for the parents of prospective pupils, the Dominicans presented their institution as a modern school with the latest in technical equipment and facilities. Central heating throughout the building, clean and hygienic bedrooms for the boys, each with running water and a proper mattress were some of what parents could expect for their sons. The new building made the minor seminary fit for a new century. It offered plenty of room for the increasing number of boys who wanted to become priests. Its modern facilities made it possible for the Dominicans to compete with the Jesuits' Canisius College in Nijmegen and the minor seminary of St Alphonsus. St Alphonsus was an impressive building on a hill on the outskirts of the town, which had been christened 'Nebo' at the turn of the century, after an open-air museum, devoted to creating a reconstruction of biblical locations in the Holy Land, opened its doors opposite the hill. St Alphonsus was founded by the Redemptorists in Roermond, in the far south of the Netherlands in 1870 and moved north to Nijmegen in 1928. Both the Redemptorists and the Jesuits also presented themselves and their institutes as modern and well-equipped. The Jesuits of Canisius College even provided pupils with postcards showing the central heating system, to send home to impress family and friends.

* I am very grateful to Marjet Derks and Marit Monteiro for their critical reading and useful suggestions.

The 1930 brochure produced by the Dominicans assured the boys' parents that everything at Saint Dominic's was "aimed at making things as pleasant as possible for your boy, whilst at the same time maintaining his inner soul in a state conducive for him to answer his calling."[1] The relatively isolated position of the new building would help create a protective environment. The Dominicans understood that a priest's vocation was a fragile phenomenon which needed protection from the 'dangers' of modernity as they were depicted in grim terms among the Catholic clergy during the interwar years. A village just outside the city, therefore, seemed to be a more appropriate location for the new college than the heart of a modernizing Nijmegen.

Saint Dominic's was among the growing number of Catholic boarding schools and minor seminaries in the Netherlands during the first half of the twentieth century. Nijmegen, in fact, became the Dutch 'capital of Catholic education', especially after the Catholic University was established there in 1923. This institute for higher education attracted many students from the ranks of the clergy and religious population, and offered educational prospects for members of staff of minor seminaries in town. Between them, the Dominicans, the Jesuits and the Redemptorists attracted boys from all over the country, although the three schools recruited students from different areas and social backgrounds.

The Dominicans cultivated an identity of intellectual and self-assured priests, attracting many boys from middle- to upper-class Catholic families.[2] Saint Dominic's was to be the first Dutch minor seminary to meet the intellectual standards needed to obtain the official status of 'gymnasium' (grammar school), in 1950.

Unlike pupils from Canisius College, those from Saint Dominic's had expressed their wish to become priests. Officially, Saint Dominic's prepared students for the priesthood, but not necessarily for entrance into the Dominican Order. In practice, however, the school culture was very much geared towards shaping 'real Dominicans'. The boys were constantly influenced by their Dominican educators in their white habits and the College turned out to be a nursery for new recruits.

Transforming young boys into mature Dominicans was the central aim of education at Saint Dominic's. This homosocial boarding school environment, where pious and not-so-pious boys were turned into men of God, was not only marked by religious standards, but also revealed traits of a particular masculine socialization. This masculine socialization was reflected negatively by the fact that only boys could enrol, and also in a constructive and formative way as a fundamental dimension of the school culture. In this closed Catholic institution, masculine socialization was influenced by various ideals and images of men and masculinity that stemmed from the Catholic tradition as well as from Dutch interwar culture. This type of religious masculinity proved to be of a rather ambiguous nature.

However, before elaborating further on the concept of masculinity, this study will concentrate on the historiography of masculinity in the context of boarding-school education.

---

[1] PAOD 779: Brochure Saint Dominic's, ca. 1930: "Alles werkt er toe mede om het Uw jongen zoo prettig mogelijk te maken, doch hem tegelijkertijd in den zielestaat te houden, die hem het gehoor geven aan zijn verheven roeping licht zal doen vallen."
[2] Monteiro, *Gods Predikers*, 17-19; Dellepoort, *De priesterroepingen in Nederland*, 227.

FROM BOYS TO MEN – SOME HISTORIOGRAPHICAL AND CONCEPTUAL REMARKS

The making of young Catholic boys into educated men at institutions such as Saint Dominic's has not yet been the subject of serious historical research in the Netherlands. Catholic boarding-school histories appear mostly within the genre of memorial books.[3] Although sometimes very detailed and thorough, these works do not approach the history of such educational institutions thematically, but focus mainly on facts and details. Needless to say, these books hardly put the school history in a broader social or cultural perspective. Gender or aspects of masculine socialization are themes that are hardly ever referred to. A remarkable exception is Henk Kroon's semi-autobiographical *Pubers voor God* (Adolescents for God) that systematically analyses life at a diocesan minor seminary.[4]

Kroon, himself a former pupil, outlines various ambivalences of seminary life that touch upon identity and masculinity. He describes to what extent the ideal of collectivity pervaded school life, in line with the importance the Church itself attached to 'the collective', formed by the community of believers.[5] This emphasis officially accounted for the condemnation of so-called 'particular friendships' between two boys. The underlying notion was that, as future priests, boys needed to be equally available to and interested in every member of their 'flock'.[6] Yet, Kroon points out that the dangers associated with a homosocial school environment, a strong Catholic rejection of homosexuality, and a need for priests to be celibate, played an equally important role in establishing particular friendships.[7] Although Kroon's book is fairly systematic in its approach, it is not meant to be a scholarly evaluation. The same goes for Jos Perry's highly informative, but mostly journalistic book *Jongens op kostschool* (Boys at the boarding school), which also explores the day-to-day life of a Catholic boys' boarding school.[8] In her study of Dutch Dominicans, historian Marit Monteiro looks at the specific role Saint Dominic's College played, but focuses more on dimensions of masculinity in the internal religious regime than on views on the academic curriculum and school culture.[9]

Catholic colleges and minor seminaries have also been explored by French and French-Canadian researchers, who have studied the institutional history of schools, the religious education of boys, and their social backgrounds, but gender is not, or

---

[3] E.g. Struyker Boudier, *Vijftig jaar Nebo*; Starink, *Hoe wij slaagden*; Reul, *Het vierde Rolduc*; Wolfs, *Van oude en nieuwe schooljaren*; Wijfjes, *Het Stanislas*; Tromp, *Meer dan het geweest is*; Elgershuizen, *Een kroniek*.

[4] Kroon, *Pubers voor God*.

[5] Ibid., 107.

[6] Ibid., 132.

[7] Ibid., 183.

[8] Perry, *Jongens op kostschool*.

[9] Monteiro, *Gods Predikers*, 297-302.

is only in part the explicit motivation behind this research.[10] In this article, however, I am mainly interested in school culture and boys' culture as it took shape in those institutions, a theme which has been comprehensively explored by British and American sociologists.[11] Their studies often only *implicitly* refer to aspects of masculinity and masculine socialization. In my article I intend to bring gender to the fore as a relevant category of analysis. This is exactly what British historian Christine Heward did in her book *Making a man of him* (1988), in which she analyses a public school for middle-class boys.[12] In this study Heward explicitly connects boarding school education with the masculine socialization that boarding schools strived for. According to Heward, the collective school identity revolved around the construction of masculinity. The public school was a setting in which boys learned from other boys, and learnt how to become men.[13]

The shaping of the boys was mainly influenced by future career perspectives. To prepare pupils for their future role as men of the world, they were not only given appropriate knowledge of relevant subjects (including Latin),[14] but were also taught to function in a competitive hierarchy. The entire school organization was geared towards this competition. Sport, in particular, was regarded as functional in this respect, as matches between houses or schools illustrate. Yet academic achievements were also competitive, with annual prizes awarded for excellence.[15] Not only did it matter who excelled in sports or intellectual performance, but also who did not. The school environment provided a setting for a 'survival of the fittest' scenario at various levels, a daily struggle which caused the 'weak links' to leave.[16]

Heward discerns three phases in which respective headmasters link career perspectives with social and cultural concepts of manliness in the public school system. The first phase roughly consists of nineteenth-century ideals of discipline, order and Christian morals. This ideology was embodied by the 'Christian gentleman', for whom the daily religious practice was considered necessary and formative.[17] In the second phase, which started in about 1900, this ideal was replaced by the principles of 'mus-

---

[10] Galarneau, *Les collèges classiques*; Brelivet, *La Formation chrétienne*; Launay, "Essor ou decline". Two articles by the French-Canadian historians Bienvenue and Hudon on three Catholic colleges in French-speaking Quebec that focus specifically on Catholic masculine socialization; I will discuss their conclusions more elaborately later in this article.

[11] Wakeford, *The cloistered elite*; Cookson and Hodges Persell, *Preparing for power*; Walford, *Life in public schools*; Danzinger, *Eton voices*; Rich, *Elixer of empire*; Id., *Chains of empire*.

[12] Heward, *Making a Man*.

[13] Ibid., 80.

[14] For an interesting relationship between Latin as a school subject, elite formation and ideals of manhood, see Stray, "From monopoly to marginality".

[15] Heward, *Making a man*, 34; compare to Derks, "Modesty and Excellence"; in her comparison between a girls' and boys' college she convincingly shows that this aspect of competition and excellence was related to the male gender.

[16] Heward, *Making a man*, 193.

[17] Ibid., 80-81.

cular Christianity'.[18] This saw the virtues of the Christian gentleman combined with physical strength and sport. This image changed again during the interwar years. In this third phase, learning how to serve society became an important aspect of the masculinity cultivated in public-school education.[19] In all three phases, it not only mattered *what* the boys would be doing in their future lives, but *how* they would actually perform in their future careers. Heward's study details the impact of changing standards of masculinity and masculine behaviour on curriculum and school culture.

Her findings are pertinent to a minor seminary such as Saint Dominic's, yet only to a certain extent. Indeed, the perspective of becoming secular or regular priests did shape collective standards and the underlying notions of aspired identity. In daily life, this specific future perspective was embodied by the boys' educators, the Dominican priests and lay brothers. Yet, these men were not 'men of the world', and did not embody the general standards of manliness. They were bound to a celibate lifestyle and dressed in habits that more resembled a woman's dress than a man's suit. Thus, the masculine socialization of students was marked by a specific form of Catholic clerical masculinity.

These observations coincide with outcomes of research conducted by Canadian historians Louise Bienvenue and Christine Hudon.[20] In their article "Entre franche camaraderie et amours socratiques", they discuss relationships between Catholic college boys in the period 1870 to 1960. In "Pour devenir home" they focus on the masculine socialization of students from the same three classical Catholic colleges in Quebec between 1880 and 1939.

In this last article they note that a clear distinction existed between the masculine dimensions of Catholic culture within the schools, and what they call the 'virility' of the Quebec culture outside the college walls.[21] Within the colleges, students were confronted with daily male role models that clearly deviated from what was considered masculine in Quebec society at the time. Bienvenue and Hudon state that the boys tried to compensate for this difference in clerical manliness and worldly virility by subtly breaking the rules. Although only of a modest nature, such rebellious behaviour enabled the boys to develop a gender identity that coincided with the hegemonic masculinity of the 'real world'.[22]

One could rightfully question the conclusion that only students of Catholic colleges tried to strengthen their masculine identity by breaking the rules. However, Bienvenue and Hudon clearly point out that particular forms of masculine socialization in a closed Catholic environment deserve, and even demand, attention. This certainly applies to Saint Dominic's. The distinction Bienvenue and Hudon make be-

---

[18] Ibid., 81-82. On 'muscular Christianity' see also McLeod's article, chapter 4 in this volume; Hall, *Muscular Christianity*. On Catholics and the notion of muscular Christianity see e.g. McDevitt, "Muscular Catholicism" and especially Derks, "Modesty and Excellence", 12.

[19] Heward, *Making a man*, 82.

[20] Bienvenue and Hudon, "Entre franche camaraderie"; Id., "Pour devenir homme".

[21] For the influence of a virile masculinity in Dutch interwar society, see: Derks, *Heilig moeten*, 30-31.

[22] On the concept of hegemonic masculinity (and its critics) see Connell and Messerschmidt, "Hegemonic Masculinity"; Dinges, "Hegemoniale Männlichkeit"; Connell, *Masculinities*.

tween the virile culture 'outside the walls' and the more feminine form of masculinity found inside the schools, is also applicable to this minor Dutch Dominican seminary. Yet, the opposition between religious or clerical masculinity and worldly virility that Hudon and Bienvenue propose appears to be too strict. In daily life, both varieties seemed to have been complexly interwoven. Within the walls of a school like Saint Dominic's, they even merged, as will be pointed out later.

This contribution will argue that the Catholic identity of Saint Dominic's was influenced by the professional future perspectives of students, and that this had profound consequences for the ideals and masculine self-image of the pupils. At the same time, it will show that features of a more worldly, or even hegemonic masculinity, marked by modernity, penetrated college life, even though the Dominicans did their very best to safeguard traditional seminary culture from undesirable modern influences. They did so by carefully exposing youngsters to sports, modern film culture and popular music. At Saint Dominic's a specific boys' culture evolved, consisting of religious masculinity mixed with what boys between 12 and 18 outside the college considered to be fun or meaningful.

Obviously, this article will not interpret 'masculinity' as a fixed category. On the contrary. Masculinity is regarded as a constitutive element in the education and formation of the boys, to which students as well as educators attributed various meanings. As this analysis will show, Catholic boys were not only influenced by clerical and monastic ideals imparted by their instructors, but also by sports heroes and starry-eyed idealists who took it upon themselves to change the world with their manly passion. Religious and clerical definitions of manliness at Saint Dominic's blended with forms of hegemonic masculinity that dominated Dutch interwar culture.[23] As will be pointed out, virility, an essential feature of this hegemonic manliness, clearly affected the culture of Saint Dominic's.

This study explores these types of masculinity within the culture of Saint Dominic's in the so-called Rhetorica. The sixth-formers took their exams and were faced with choices over their future: entry into the Dominican Order, becoming a priest, or - seldom a preferred option then - a worldly career. The focus is on the class of 1936. The majority of the young men would enter the Order. They were supposed to become leading figures in the Dutch Catholic milieu. This specific Catholic and clerical future

[23] See also chapter 7 by Monteiro and the next chapter (9) by Derks, as well as Monteiro, *Gods Predikers*, 205-206. Monteiro describes what she calls the virile-polemic attitude of the generation of Dutch young Catholics who manifested themselves in the interwar years. This attitude was characterized by positively appreciated values such as creativity and energy that were presented as typically masculine, as opposed to feminine values with a negative connotation. In this respect she refers to an analysis by Dutch linguist Van Boven who speaks of "the virile generation of 1918". In her study on Dutch Catholic radical religious women *Heilig moeten*, Derks also refers to the virility that marked the interwar culture of the Netherlands. Derks notices that such virility was not reserved for non-Catholics, or restricted to men. While the nineteenth century in their eyes was seen as a time of a passive, feminine and weak culture, the twentieth century was seen as an era of activity and virility. Modern times were masculine. Derks, *Heilig moeten*, 30-31.

perspective had been the central and formative aspect of their seminary years. The exploration of the seminaries' culture is presented along three lines: sports culture, formal education and self-images of minor seminaries as presented in the school paper, *De Vlieger* (The Kite).

SAINT DOMINIC'S BOYS' CULTURE

A sunny day in a Dutch playground in 1936. The cheerful young men in the photograph (see illustration p. 156), about 18 years old, together formed the Rhetorica, which was the sixth and final year of the minor seminary. After completing the year, the students - if considered suitable candidates - could enter the Order. For the 11 boys in the picture, a future as a Dominican priest had by then become self-evident. Ten out of the 11 started their noviciate in September 1936. In the end, only five of them would remain in the Dominican Order for the rest of their lives.

Students of Saint Dominic's usually got in touch with the college through a Dominican priest from the parish where they lived, or through family members who had ties with the Dominican Order. This was the case with several of the Rhetorica students of 1936.[24] The 11 boys originated from different parts of the country, although more than half came from the west, where the Dominicans had several parishes. The boys also had varied social backgrounds, although most of the families can be categorized as middle-class. Jan van Vugt's father had his own grocery store, while Bertus van Elswijk's father was a carpenter. Dirk Jan Gomes's father was a merchant officer while Louis Ariaans' father was a policeman. Herman van Run's father owned some land, had his own drapery shop and worked as a town treasurer.[25] Social status, like other factors, such as having a rural or urban background, played a part in the formation of a social hierarchy among the boys.[26]

Although the two other Catholic boys' colleges in Nijmegen of that time, Canisius College and Nebo, had much in common with Saint Dominic's, the background of their pupils differed slightly. The Redemptorists seemed to have recruited pupils from mostly rural areas and a lower-middle-class background.[27] The six Jesuit Colleges in the Netherlands, by contrast, attracted more boys from upper-class families. This not only reflected the social composition of society at the time, but the colleges also prepared boys for the ranks of the social elite. In this respect, Saint Dominic's consciously or unconsciously opted for another pattern of recruitment, consistent with objectives that differed from those of Jesuit Colleges.

[24] Interview with Herman van Run, 10 July 2006.
[25] Remarks on his classmates by Herman van Run, August 2006.
[26] Interview with Herman van Run, 10 July 2006.
[27] Dellepoort, *De priesterroepingen in Nederland*, 226-228.

EDUCATION

In the 1930s Saint Dominic's was not yet an officially recognized grammar school. The education on offer was modelled on the curriculum of a grammar school, but in general the instruction level was not as high, and not all the teachers were qualified. This, however, did not mean that intellectual achievements, competition and discipline were not appreciated by the Dominicans. On the contrary, prizes were awarded annually to the best pupils in each subject and in each class. The Dominicans certainly considered themselves to be an intellectual order. Intellectual performance, stimulated by the system of awards, was considered an essential part of Dominican socialization.[28]

SPORTS CULTURE

Until the early 1920s, Dominicans at the college seemed to adopt the attitude that a future priest could do well without sports. In the latter years of that decade and the 1930s this attitude started to change. As the sports adventures of the 1936 Rhetorica students and their school mates reveal, by 1936 competitive sports had developed their own place at the Dominican minor seminary. This section shows how boys such as Rhetorica student Bertus van Elswijk experienced college sports, and how this popular feature of interwar culture was relatively smoothly incorporated into school culture.

Before the college moved into the new building outside Nijmegen, entertainment for the boys was limited to indoor activities, such as handicrafts, billiards, chess and music. This is not to say that the Dominicans underestimated the benefits of physical exercise, but the opportunities proved to be scarce as there was no room for such activities in the vicinity of the old school buildings. Therefore, in the early 1920s the students' physical exercise consisted mainly of walking tours around Nijmegen and occasional exercise in the courtyard.[29] However, not long after the school had moved, the spacious fields surrounding the new college building were converted into sports facilities.[30] Gradually, previously mistrusted sports such as athletics and football gained a better reputation and came to form an important part of the programme. In contrast with the more traditional walking tours, these sports made it possible for the boys to compete against each other, to excel physically and to obtain popularity among the other boys.[31]

---

[28] Monteiro, *Gods Predikers*, 18. Of course, the *religious* formation also was a constitutive part of this socialization. Without comprehensively examining this subject, the last section, dealing with the seminarians' self-image, will cover this further.

[29] Wolfs, *Van oude en nieuwe schooljaren*, 57.

[30] Ibid., 79.

[31] In Catholic circles competitive sports such as rugby, cricket (which became more popular in the nineteenth century after originating in Saxon or Norman times) and football, originating in the nineteenth century, were looked at with distrust at the beginning of the twentieth century. This was a consequence of the ambivalent Catholic vision on corporality, in which the body was seen as a temple of God, as well as a locus of sin and lust. Derks, "Modesty and Excellence", 11.

The elements of competition and the risk of physical exercise being given a higher priority than intellectual training explain the ambivalence of some religious institutes to sport. Religious orders running secondary schools had to deal with the rising popularity of sports among pupils. They had already had their doubts about physical exercise as part of the curriculum because it entailed a risk of putting the body over the soul. Moreover, schools feared that physical exercise would negatively influence the modesty and decency of the pupils. Relatively 'modern' sports such as cricket and football were seen as particularly threatening, for they stimulated competitiveness, a characteristic of modernity.[32]

Competition on the football field was appreciated differently by the Dominicans than competitiveness in intellectual matters. Their high appreciation of discipline and intellectuality that they hoped to stimulate by their system of prize-winning, probably made the difference here. However, by the 1930s the Dominicans had accepted that football and other modern sports were a suitable means of recreation for their pupils. They began to stress the positive influence that football had on the boys' physical health, instead of underlining the competitive element.[33] Of course, this did not prevent the boys from becoming aware of fierce competition when playing a match against a football team from one of the nearby Catholic colleges.

Although sports became increasingly important at Saint Dominic's, they did not define the boys' college culture as much as was the case at the nearby Canisius College of the Jesuits, where competition became the most constitutive element of school culture. Here, enthusiastic boys as well as younger staff members, who had become acquainted with a fanatic sports culture of the British Jesuit College in Stonyhurst, had built up a very popular and extensive sporting life at their school. The virtue of excellence, traditionally favoured by Jesuits, probably played an important role here.[34] Student Bertus van Elswijk, one of the boys from the Rhetorica of 1936, was a real sportsman who did not hold the other footballers at the college in high esteem because, in his opinion, they lacked a proper sports mentality.[35] Most boys on the football pitch only played the game because they detested the traditional school walk that was organized twice a week. The result of this 'negative mentality' was 22 players just trying to keep the ball to themselves, with no team spirit at all.[36] Bertus was not the only one who complained about untalented footballers at Saint Dominic's. In 1930 one of the boys criticized the 'crocks' on the Dominicus football grounds and

---

[32] Derks, "Modesty and Excellence", 11-12.

[33] PAOD 785: Concilium de Studiis, 1 October 1933. Derks explains that the ideal of the so-called 'muscular Christian' helped to accept modern sports culture in Catholic circles. See Derks, "Modesty and Excellence".

[34] Ibid. Sports became so popular at Canisius that in the 1950s a commission of Dutch Jesuit educators expressed concern about the position sports had taken, and feared that sport harmed the intellectual, more refined and sensitive students of the College who either did not want to or could not excel at sport. PANJ 913: Meeting Commissio de Instituenda Juventute, 20-3-1957.

[35] Written remarks on classmates by Herman van Run, August 2006.

[36] PAOD 6182: *De Vlieger*, 1935-1936, 42.

remarked that "our football club was founded for boys who want to play football and not for boys who do not want to walk".[37]

Nevertheless, the players who performed well on the field were admired by their schoolmates, and this boosted in-house spirits considerably. Their accomplishments, especially in matches against the Canisius College of the Jesuits in Nijmegen, drew the attention of the rest of the school. Players from the sport-minded Jesuit College were usually too strong for the boys from Saint Dominic's, but that only seemed to elevate the heroic status of the players who dared to fight the strong boys from Canisius College. The annual match against Canisius College was referred to in the school paper as "the great battle".[38] Victories were appreciated, losses were taken proudly if the boys from Saint Dominic's had played well. "Honourable defeats", wrote Van Elswijk in the school paper, did not harm the reputation of the college.[39]

Van Elswijk's thoughts on inter-college football, with his emphasis on team spirit, fair play and honour, seem to have been successful in reconciling the Dominican ideal of a harmonious community with the ideals of competition and excellence associated with football. However, there was no serious sports culture at Saint Dominic's during the interwar years. It was not until 1949 that the college prefect announced that from that point on, sports had to be actively practiced by *all* college boys, instead of being a hobby for a smaller group of sport fanatics.[40] This is not to say that enthusiasm for football was not a definite part of college life. Although not a central factor in the masculine socialization of the students, it certainly was one of the ways for boys to develop physical and mental strength. Thus, fanatic sportsmen such as Van Elswijk introduced a virile variant of masculinity to the school, allowing more subdued fellow students to be passively involved as supporters of the school's teams. This supporting of the College's football players strengthened the collective identity of the students at Saint Dominic's.

Clearly, the modern sports culture was simply something that could not be ignored by Dominicans. From the 1930s onwards, the interplay of fanatic footballers among pupils, and an enthusiasm for sport by several of their teachers guaranteed the institutionalization of modern football in this minor seminary.[41] Although it fitted in well with a pedagogical emphasis on competition, it collided with specific clerical standards of masculinity. In Saint Dominic's culture, therefore, sport was not given a central position. However, it did provide ample opportunity for teachers and pupils to merge a sporty modern masculinity with a clerical manliness, in which the collective and the team spirit played a minor part. They did so by connecting football to physical health, honour and team spirit, which helped to intensify the collective identity of Saint Dominic's.

---

[37] PAOD 6181: *De Vlieger*, 1930-1931, 32. Indeed, one of the former pupils who went to Dominicus College in this era admitted that he only played football because he hated the compulsory walks. Questionnaire completed by former Dominicus student Baars.

[38] PAOD 6181: *De Vlieger*, 1930-1931, 52.

[39] PAOD 6182: *De Vlieger*, 1935-1936, 108.

[40] PAOD 6186: *De Vlieger*, 1949-1950.

[41] Wolfs, *Van oude en nieuwe schooljaren*, 89-90.

SELF-IMAGES OF THE MINOR SEMINARIAN

As the school population moved to the new college in 1927, they started their own newspaper, titled *De Vlieger* (The Kite). Pupils formed an editorial board and one of the teachers functioned as a censor. The school paper provided a forum for exchanging opinions, but also for a discourse on school culture and the identity of the minor seminarians at Saint Dominic's. By 1929 readers were encouraged to write critically about "the characters of the Saint Dominic's boys", to see who they really were: "pious, hard workers, or dandies or lazybones?".[42] The articles show that ideals on priesthood and Dominican life were put forth as guidelines for the students' own behaviour. The editors linked modern and popular activities, such as football, with virtues such as honour and community life. They reprimanded undesirable behaviour or character traits such as vanity. For instance, boys who were too keen on following the latest hairstyles were corrected in a poem that ended: "And then something else, you poor things/ Do remind yourself why you are even here/ Becoming a priest, that is your vocation / So don't prance around like fashion dolls."[43]

Becoming a priest, of course, was why the boys attended Saint Dominic's. It was this definite future perspective that formed a constantly recurring theme in the school paper. According to the founders and first editors of the paper, its title, *De Vlieger* (The Kite), did not merely refer to its intended audience, the boys who generally loved to fly the kite, but also to their vocation as priests, for which the kite was said to be a proper symbol.

> Isn't our vocation up in the sky like a kite, above the lively city of our youth? Don't we all have one purpose, one and the same vocation, one and the same kite? There will be gusts of wind and storms. The kite may lurch to and fro... But we will have to take care then - while keeping the rope tight! - that it will not drop down on the bustling city of our youth![44]

This analogy directed the boys' eyes towards heaven and allowed them to visualize their perception of their proposed vocation as something (literally) to look up to, as an ideal that was almost unattainable. The culture at Saint Dominic's in the 1930s was clearly marked by this notion of the priesthood as a highly elevated and therefore almost unreachable ideal.[45] This theme runs throughout poems or stories of the boys about the priest celebrating the Eucharist, which reflect how the pupils saw their future as priests. In their minds, a priest was set apart from the community as a direct mediator between God and his people. "So highly elevated is the priest, that he may daily bear Christ's precious body, and even may command Christ to descend on the altar."[46]

---

[42] PAOD 6181: *De Vlieger*, 1929-1930, 43.

[43] PAOD 6181: *De Vlieger*, 1929-1930, 43. "En dan nog iets arme stumpers / Denk toch aan wat je hier komt doen / Priester worden, dat is je roeping, en / dan niet als modepoppen doen."

[44] PAOD 6181: *De Vlieger*, 1927-1928, 3.

[45] *E.g.* PAOD 6181: *De Vlieger*, 1930, 3 and 5; PAOD 6182: *De Vlieger*, 1935-1936, 16 and 19.

[46] Ibid., 19.

Some students, such as Herman van Run from the Rhetorica, romanticized the priesthood, depicting it as something that resembled the Holy Grail: desirable but unattainable.[47] Like most other seminarians, Van Run had been an altar boy in his parish church before coming to Saint Dominic's. While serving Mass, he had experienced standing at the altar and being part of a sacred ritual where bread and wine are believed to become the body and blood of Christ. As an acolyte he already felt "chosen" in a way. The boys remained ambivalent about becoming a priest. On the one hand, there was the exceptional status of the priesthood, while on the other the students continuously doubted their ability to reach such a status. They could picture themselves as future men of God, whom people would look up to, but were very aware that it was out of their hands whether they would indeed join the clergy.

Dominican fathers who led the college provided examples of this ideal of the priesthood on a daily basis, especially while performing their rituals during Mass and other religious gatherings in chapel. The Rhetorica also had the privilege of visiting the nearby Albertinum in Nijmegen, where young Dominicans studied theology while preparing for their ordination. The boys were impressed by the asceticism and religious fervour of these young Dominicans. In the school paper the inhabitants of the Albertinum were described as both ascetic and chaste religious men, as well as highly elevated priests who, with their monastic humility and hardiness on display, were shown to be truly pure and chosen men of God.[48]

Such discussions on priesthood and monastic identity seem to have been reflected in the internal debates among Dominicans in the interwar period regarding their specific identity as regular priests.[49] The pupils of the Rhetorica appreciated the monastic priest, whom they later hoped to emulate. Their idealized views of the chastity and purity required for this life revealed various and, at times, ambivalent dimensions of masculinity. For the demand of purity was made not only of young seminarians, but also of girls of their age. The discourse of celibacy, however, was connected to moral strength and the heroism of making a sacrifice. In school life the boys were constantly reminded not only of their shared ideal, but also of the price they had to pay. Their educators controlled their purity and chastity, trying to restrain the pupils from discovering and enjoying their own sexuality.

The debates among the Dominicans revolved around the clerical and the monastic dimensions of their identity.[50] Echoes of these deliberations reverberate through the school paper. In their appreciation of devoted and responsible priests who lived up to the high standards of their status, the boys criticized those less devoted and responsible: the hedonistic parish priest, to whom a good cigar and a drink were essential diversions from parsonage life. He proved to be the stereotype of an undesirable form of clerical masculinity. For many boys, the Dominican parish priest in their

---

[47] Interview Herman van Run, July 2006.
[48] PAOD 6182: *De Vlieger*, 1935-1936, 29.
[49] Monteiro, *Gods Predikers*, 302-314.
[50] See the contribution by Monteiro in this volume.

home town had been the first Dominican father they had ever seen, and they often thought highly of him. They saw him as a spiritual caretaker, a fluent preacher, a man of high social status.[51] But a parish priest could also be a fat, smoking and drinking type that played cards every night with colleagues from nearby parishes and did not come close to the ideal *alter Christus*.

The school paper warned boys who considered such men to be examples of the priesthood "what a priest actually is: an *alter Christus*, that he should completely forget himself, that his entire life and ambition ought to be directed to the salvation of souls, and therefore he must never be tied to alcohol, that would give him a pleasure which is beastly and unworthy of a priest".[52] Such examples confronted the boys with the fragility of their own future perspective as priests. They were asked "Would you not like to think of what *you* are going to become?"[53] The answer seemed to be given in active 'boyishness' cultivated by the pupils from Saint Dominic's, which comprised passion, idealism and manly activism.

Considering the discourse on unwanted aspects of clerical life and the emphasis on excessive drinking, it was no wonder the battle against alcohol was underlined as an integral part of the proper mentality of a Saint Dominic's boy. The school had its own temperance society, the *Kruisverbond*.[54] One of the active members was Rhetorica student Louis Ariaans. He asked his schoolmates to keep their promise to abstain from alcohol like 'real men' by not drinking during the holidays. He also urged other club members to participate actively in club work. But he sensed that most boys were not willing to invest actively in the anti-alcohol movement and criticized their attitude as passive and spineless.

> Boys, keep your ardour and be as active as possible as a member of the *Kruisverbond*. So be animated and don't be weak-willed as if you are a bunch of stick-in-the-muds. That does not suit you as boys, but even less as young fiery advocates of temperance.[55]

Passion, action and idealism were also preached in the first edition of the school paper, as the editorial board urged all boys to employ their boyish enthusiasm to write good and sound articles. A paper for boys that were equally striving for the same ideal should be characterized by happiness and fiery boyish passion. "Our boys' idealism wants to move forward, we don't want to stand still but we want to work as much as

[51] Questionnaires completed by former pupils of Saint Dominic's from the 1930s and 1940s. Van Dongen, Joosten, Van den Idsert and Willems.
[52] PAOD 6181: *De Vlieger*, 1929-1930, 117.
[53] Ibid.
[54] The *Kruisverbond* at Saint Dominic's was part of the Dutch Catholic temperance society which was established by Catholic priests at the end of the nineteenth century. Despite this clerical support, not all priests adhered to the ideal of temperance. The society was mainly supported by members of the Catholic upper middle classes. Men and women, boys and girls all had their own society branch. The temperance movement can be considered an attempt to refine and civilize the lower classes. Cf. Dols, *De geesel der eeuw*.
[55] PAOD 6182: *De Vlieger*, 1935-1936, 50.

possible on our education right now, in order to be able in later years, to work with greater energy."[56] The boys presented themselves as idealists in their school paper, combining all the youthful energy, religious fervour and idealism that they felt was necessary to become priests. Their shared enthusiasm bound them together and even seemed to bring them a bit closer to the seemingly unattainable priesthood. In the students' self-proclaimed idealism religious masculinity and youthful energy were united.

CONCLUSIONS

This analysis of Catholic boys' culture at Saint Dominic's shows that masculinity was a constitutive, though variable element of school life. By exploring three different areas of the boys' school culture, it has been shown which concepts of masculinity came into play in the relatively closed Catholic environment of a minor seminary during the interwar years.

The central objective of the education the Dominicans offered their students was the building of the character of prospective members of their order. The intellectual formation was therefore aimed not only at stimulating intellectual achievements, but on concentrating on discipline and competition as well. The humanities, especially Latin, were thought to help form the boys' characters and to initiate them into the clerical world of priesthood. Alongside this clerical form of masculinity, was a more 'feminine' and softer, nineteenth-century masculinity-ideal of the gentleman, made visible in the emphasis the Dominicans put on cultural education, specifically stressing classical music. This is not to say that elements of modern twentieth-century culture were completely banned by the school. Although placed in a critical Catholic perspective, aspects of a virile interwar world outside the school were highly appealing to the boys, and formed an integral part of school life, thanks to books, papers and excursions.

The college's sports culture was also influenced by this virile masculinity that characterized modern times. Although sports were not a core activity for all Dominican boys, they were nevertheless a popular element of school life. The fanatic sports lovers among the college introduced a muscular masculinity into the school. Those who did not or could not participate themselves could support the teams, and thereby become part of the collective and strengthen the collective college identity. For Dominicans this modern and virile element of school culture was not a threat, since they successfully 'framed' it in a more religious perspective that underlined the importance of teamwork and physical health instead of the need to win.

Apart from formal education and sports culture, this article has explored the boys' discourse on their identity and future state in life. Their self-image is reflected in their school paper, which reveals that the students' future as Dominican priests plays an essential part. In their perceptions of the priesthood, the boys merge aspects of clerical and monastic manliness, as their Dominicans educators at that time did.

---

[56] PAOD 6181: *De Vlieger*, 1927, 5.

In their opinion, priests ought to embody the humility and purity of their religion in order to reach the high expectations of their status within the Catholic community. In addition to writing about their future as priests, the boys from the Rhetorica of Saint Dominic's clearly cultivated their own boys' culture, in which their religious vocation merged smoothly with an energetic and virile spirit of boyishness.

FEMALE SOLDIERS
AND THE BATTLE FOR GOD

GENDER AMBIGUITIES AND A DUTCH
CATHOLIC CONVERSION MOVEMENT,
1921-1942

MARJET DERKS

> Male and female represent the two sides of the great radical dualism. But in fact they are perpetually passing into one another. Fluid hardens to solid, solid rushes to fluid. There is no wholly masculine man, no purely feminine woman.[1]

In 1937, Father Jacques van Ginneken S.J., an internationally famous and acknowledged psycholinguist and ethnologist who was also a religious radical, addressed a group of women. They were young and highly educated, some of them even to postgraduate level, and they were the leaders of the so-called Women of Nazareth. Van Ginneken had founded this conversion movement in 1921 and acted as its spiritual guide, even though his involvement was restricted after a series of collisions with the bishop of Haarlem, under whose diocesan authority the group fell, and with other members of the clergy. In a typical display of self-confidence, he looked back at the founding years, saying it was clear:

> [...] [that He meant me] to establish an apostolic lay order, that would bring the whole world back to His feet. But that contrary to the approach of Ignatius this would have to be a female order was clear to me from the very beginning. Because of my studies in ethnology and psychology, and last but not least because of my own life experience, I was convinced early on that until then the Church had exploited woman in a totally unsatisfactory way.[2]

---

[1] Fuller [US transcendentalist author & editor (1810-1850)], *Woman*.

[2] AG, 40: Jac. van Ginneken, *Wat ik met de stichting van de Vrouwen van Nazareth bedoeld heb*, [1937]: "[...] [dat Hij mij bedoeld] had een apostolische lekenorde te stichten, die de hele wereld terug zou brengen aan Zijn voeten. Maar dat dit, in tegenstelling tot Ignatius, een vrouwen-orde moest zijn, stond van den beginne af aan bij mij vast. Want dankzij mijn etnologische en psychologische studies, alsmede mijn eigen levenservaring, was ik er van jongs af van overtuigd dat de Kerk de vrouw geheel onvoldoende had geëxploiteerd."

The Women of Nazareth was a female lay association with roots in the Netherlands. During the 1930s its members travelled to Germany, England, Scotland, Ireland, the United States and Australia, turning it into an international movement that in time also attracted indigenous young women in the countries that it had spread to.[3] Wherever they went, they set up the Grail movement, a radical Catholic girls' movement which adolescent girls from the age of twelve years upwards could join. Although in most countries the movement remained elitist and fairly small, in the Netherlands it became the largest girls' movement ever.[4] Especially in the western part of the country, the Women of Nazareth and their movement were very well known among their contemporaries. Since the interwar period they have become an integral part of the collective *lieux de mémoire* of Dutch Catholicism. Photos and impressions of their actions have appeared continually in numerous historical overviews of Catholics in the twentieth century. This was partly due to the reputation of their founder Van Ginneken, who was one of the forerunners of Catholic emancipation and, although he was not uncontroversial, certainly stood out as an intellectual giant.[5]

The ambitious aim of the original group echoed the infinite goals of Van Ginneken. It can be summarized in a few words: the conversion of the world. They saw themselves as Christ's soldiers, battling in the public domain against a world which they perceived to be atheistic and materialistic, and fighting to restore 'Christian culture'. The young women who became Women of Nazareth devoted their lives to this religious cause, and set up the Grail movement as one of the instruments to achieve their goal. Theirs was a militant piety, an embattled form of spirituality that emerged as a response to a perceived crisis.[6]

Despite their struggle against certain aspects of modern society, these women did not see modernity as bad and certainly did not want to be excluded from it. Consequently, their conversion strategy did not consist of preaching hellfire and damnation. Quite the opposite: like their founder Father Van Ginneken, they embraced all the possibilities that the modern era provided and they applied all sorts of modern techniques whenever possible. In hindsight, they even labelled their strategy in a somewhat challenging fashion as 'dangerously modern' and themselves as "women of the twentieth century". They saw these as appropriate descriptions because, in their self-definition, they deliberately challenged mainstream Catholicism in order

---

[3] For the history of the Grail in the Netherlands see Derks, *Heilig moeten*, 236-324. For the history of the international Grail see Donders, *History of the international Grail*; Kalven, *Women Breaking Boundaries*; Brown, *The Grail Movement*; for a review, see Appleby, [Review].

[4] In 1935 the Grail consisted of 13,000 members, predominantly from the Haarlem diocese. They represented 23 per cent of all organized girls in the Netherlands. In 1937 there were more than 14,000. The popular socialist youth movement AJC had 8,630 members at the time. Donders, *History of the international Grail*, 22.

[5] E.g. Pijfers, *Het Katholieken Boek*, 192; Pijfers and Roes, *Memoriale*, 18, 20, 94-97; van Schaik, *Katholieken*, 22-23, 99; van der Plas, *Uit het rijke Roomsche Leven*, 2-3, 88-96; Rogier and de Rooij, *In vrijheid herboren*, 595-596.

[6] Armstrong, *The Battle for God*, xiii named this sort of spirituality as one of the core traits of religious radicalism, if not fundamentalism.

to firmly establish a more profound religious society within modernity.[7] It should not really come as a surprise that Van Ginneken's speech was filmed by a team from the Grail's own Film Council. In order to be seen and heard by larger audiences, the members had had training in professional film studios in Amsterdam and London and used their skills to produce all kinds of religious propaganda films and documentaries. One of them later confessed that she had even secretly dreamed of making a religious *Battleship Potemkin*.

In one respect, the Women of Nazareth seem a perfect affirmation of the so-called theory of the feminization of religion. In this debate, it is generally said that religion, and especially Catholicism, underwent a significant change during the modernization process by adopting and advocating more feminine traits. Not only was there a gradual but 'Great Divide' between men and women in religious attendance and loyalty to the church, with the latter becoming the more spiritualized and religious,[8] but religious practices, rituals and symbols also became more feminized. Religion and women were closely connected, both on a discursive level and in everyday life. In short, although this did not change anything within the hierarchy or affect hegemonic power relations, which remained restricted to men, the religious domain became a more feminized one.[9] We should take notice of the fact that 'feminization' here has a double meaning or covers two different developments. First, it means a more intense participation of women in religious practices, intense both in numbers and on a spiritual level. Second, it refers to those prototypical connotations of womanhood as soft, sweet, romantic, and restricted to the private domain of one's inner self or one's own home. Meanwhile we have to keep in mind that neither the concept of femininity nor of masculinity is natural, transparent or unproblematic. Both are socially constructed patterns of expectations, behaviour and discourse, defined within particular historical circumstances.[10]

Perhaps certain developments in the modern history of Dutch Catholicism can contribute to broadening these discussions. Focusing on the pre-war years in the Netherlands, it is possible to question whether we really can distinguish a 'feminization' of Catholicism. Without any doubt, the Women of Nazareth, who were active during these years, were very religious women. They sought to re-evangelize the world in a period when debate on modernity and religion was intense, but in a period which

[7] van Emmerik, *Gevaarlijk modern*; Donders, *Lydwine van Kersbergen*. I have therefore labelled the character of the Grail movement as "retro-modern": while aiming at restoration, they applied all sorts of modern means. E.g. Derks, *Heilig moeten*, 36-37.

[8] The 'great divide' is an expression used by Huyssen in *After the Great Divide* to indicate the growing division between modernism and postmodernism and the blurring boundaries between high art and mass culture.

[9] Schneider, "Feminisierung der Religion" gives an overview of publications on the feminization of religion debate. I would like to add the excellent study of Smith, *Ladies* who has pointed at this increasing entertwining of women and religion during the modernization process in Northern France. For more recent work i.e. Brown, *The death of Christian Britain*, 175-181, 193-198. Also: Art, "Mannen als bruiden", 35-48. For the opposite hypothesis, that of a masculinization of religion, see Werner, *Kristen manlighet. Män och religion*; Id., "Mannliness and Catholic Mission".

[10] Elaine Showalter points out the great variety of metaphors, myths and images that surround these concepts and the change within them. Showalter, *Sexual Anarchy*, 3.

also saw the emergence of secularization. Like their founder Father Van Ginneken, the Nazareth Women perceived women as the locus of true religious zeal. They also adopted a distinctive set of practices, rituals and symbols to emphasize their identity and quest. The question, however, is what the emergence of these women in the public domain implies with regard to the alleged feminization of Catholicism, and also what impact their feminized symbolic culture had.

As I want to point out in this article, the Women of Nazareth and the Grail movement - although consisting of women and girls who were religiously active - should not be perceived as a case for the feminization hypothesis. In fact, they might even be a reason to question the hypothesis as such. The mere presence of women in the religious realm was simply that, despite the number of women who became religiously involved and manifested this publicly. However, in terms of their self-understanding, the Women of Nazareth represented quite the opposite of traditional feminine values. They not only expressed themselves in a way that could be labelled as stereotypically masculine, but also nurtured certain values that go with the label, such as the cultivation of a strong physicality and militancy. They even appropriated some tasks which had traditionally been the preserve of the male clergy and adopted an accompanying attitude. So how *should* we label these women? Female certainly, but not epitomes of feminization - perhaps *femasculinization* would be a more appropriate concept to use in relation to them. In any case they should be looked upon rather as examples of the ambiguities within gender relations and of the complex symbolic meanings of gender within religion. They demand conceptual re-interpretation.

I will illustrate this first by outlining the societal and religious landscape in which the Women of Nazareth and the Grail movement came into being. Secondly, I will elaborate on the implicit and explicit masculine traits (i.e. masculine in the prototypical sense) of this female conversion movement. Finally, I will look into the clerical power relations that surrounded these women and eventually successfully undermined their influence and relative autonomy.

---

[11] Eksteins, *Rites of Spring*.
[12] Felski, *The Gender of Modernity*, 9. Also: Showalter, *Sexual Anarchy*, 1-18.

DUTCH CATHOLIC CULTURE AND THE RITES OF SPRING

Despite the Netherlands' neutrality during the First World War, international cultural transfer in its aftermath led to the 'birth of the modern age' there as well.[11] The modernization process that had taken off starting at the end of the nineteenth century became full blown. Cultural theorist Rita Felski has described the essence of modernity as "a modern secularized universe predicated upon an individuated and self-conscious subjectivity", although in reality, modernity resulted in a number of paradoxical effects: individualization and mass movements, democratization and totalitarianism, and secularization and religious identification.[12] Throughout all these processes, women appeared more and more in the public domain and existing boundaries between the sexes were the subject of debate. Felski and other theorists have labelled 'modernity' as an essentially gendered process. Gender and sexuality became central elements for modern culture, as became clear in the emergence of mass culture and in a range of other domains.[13] However, religion still remained an important force in both the public and the private realms. If gender was a central element of modern culture, what can be said about the complex interactions between modernity, gender and religion, for example, in Catholicism?

First, it is important to state that, while it may have been true that women were perceived as the crucial figures in religious upbringing, the *public* face of Dutch Catholicism in the interwar period was first and foremost a masculine affair. To a large extent it was defined and led by clergymen and laymen from the upper and upper middle classes. After years of legal and informal subordination and discrimination, Dutch Catholics had been successfully emancipated and they wanted to show this to the world. This resulted in numerous Catholic organizations, public displays, and speeches in high-flown language. These were the years of the so-called 'rich Roman (i.e. Roman Catholic) life'. There was an increasing discourse that, partly in reaction to feminism, stressed the role of women in religion (at least in the private sphere of the home and family) and promoted the development of a devotional culture that held 'feminine' traits. Despite all of this, most of the public displays of religious identity and zeal were dominated by men. Even though for the first time women could and would appear on the streets in religious demonstrations they were limited to minor roles. With the exception of whoever portrayed the Virgin Mary and held a prominent place, girls and young women marched in the parades and processions in restricted representations: as angels and virgin brides. Their mothers held no central place at all; they merely watched the parades and applauded.[14] The lengthy and episcopally approved book *The Catholic Netherlands* (*Het Katholieke Nederland*), published in 1913 to celebrate a century of increasing legal rights for Dutch Catholics, only praised 'sons' and, again with the exception of Mary, mentioned no women at all as 'Great figures'.[15]

---

[13] De Keizer, "Inleiding".
[14] Photobooks illustrate this observation, e.g. Pijfers, *Het Katholieken Boek*; Pijfers and Roes, *Memoriale*; Van Schaik, *Katholieken;* Van der Plas, *Uit het rijke Roomsche Leven.*
[15] Loeff, *Het Katholieke Nederland* [no page numbers].

However, while this image may have reflected mainstream Catholic culture, it certainly did not paint the whole picture. There was also an intense undercurrent of tension at the time that centred mainly around the discourse on modernity and religion. The tension led to a variety of reactions in which certain patterns can be discerned. There were groups that became outspoken critics of church rules and regulations, and of the existing pillarization that characterized the organizational system through which Dutch Catholicism tried to maintain its identity. Historian Paul Luykx has labelled those critics "Different Catholics", claiming that publications and behaviour that signalled such signs of religious rebellion were in fact much more widespread than has previously been acknowledged.[16]

By pointing to the existence of "different Catholics", Luykx made a plea for differentiation within Catholicism, thus implicitly referring to theories of difference. This type of theory shattered the presumed 'oneness' in culture and society and made room for various kinds of difference: repressed social groups and categories (women, blacks, homosexuals, mentally ill people) were recognized in their own right. It was also maintained that being 'different' is always defined *in relation* to the 'accepted', and is therefore critical of implicit standards of normality. Both notions are subjects of discussion here.[17] This can be seen as an appeal against monocultural and mono-theoretical thinking, and should be kept in mind when analyzing culture - including Catholic culture.

Luykx made it clear that the existence of a monolithic Catholic culture is a historical and sociological construction that does not hold. I tend to follow Luykx in this criticism, and especially in his deconstruction of Catholic culture and his emphasis on the interwar period as one in which socio-religions tensions became apparent. But unlike Luykx, I want to stress that gender played an important part in these tensions. Theories of difference have developed strongly within feminist studies and it is therefore a logical step to make explicit the combination of Luykx' notion of Catholic 'difference' with gender notions, and with differences within gender.

With this in mind, it can be argued that criticism of dominant Dutch Catholicism was thoroughly gendered. First it can be stated that Luykx' examples of differentiation mainly focus on male critics, such as political dissenters and intellectuals. Some intellectuals revealed themselves as religious radicals; radicalism was an important but unacknowledged characteristic of Dutch Catholicism in this period. There were articulate groups of radical conservative Catholics who aimed for the restoration of an idealized and imagined Christian past. The radicals were self-willed, often young and well-educated male writers and journalists, who were labelled collectively as the movement of "the Young Catholics" - although they were not really a homogenous group but rather a bunch of highly individualistic intellectuals (and semi-intellectuals). Without being anti-modernists per se, they criticized the dominant culture and articulated utopian notions and ideals. These were rooted partly in early Christianity

---

[16] Luykx, *Andere katholieken*, 9-41, see also the discussion in Luykx, "'Andere katholieken': een nieuwe visie".
[17] Irigaray, *Je, tu, nous*.

and partly in the perceived golden age of religion, the Middle Ages - and in this way represented a typical invention of tradition.

A second aspect that underlines the gendered nature of Catholic differences refers to the fact that "the Young" manifested themselves as strong and very masculine rebuilders of true Catholicism. Their complaint was that dominant Catholicism lacked vigour and strength. They can be typified by the word that Dutch literary theorist Erica van Boven used to define the literary circles of which these "angry young Catholics" were generally a part: they were *virile*, because of their overt display of verbal muscle and masculinity, and their rejection of lukewarm Catholicism as 'feminine'.[18] In this way they defined ideal Catholicism as masculine and rejected all notions of feminization, both on a symbolic level and in religious experience.

Thirdly, it is important to notice that religious radicals were not exclusively male, although the men are the ones that have been publicly acknowledged, both by their contemporaries and by historians.[19] Although the concept of 'gendered difference' does not necessarily imply that 'different' Catholics would have had to be women, it is important to examine their role in this matter, especially by looking at the public sphere. As was the case in early American religious radicalism, where women played an important yet unacknowledged role, also the role of women in Dutch radical Catholicism cannot be overlooked.[20] It was precisely within this radical Catholicism that women manifested themselves *as Catholic women* in the *public* sphere. The female conversion movements - as well as the Women of Nazareth there were also the Ladies of Nazareth, their 'sister movement', also founded by Father van Ginneken - were driven by comparable radical societal and religious ideals. They also strove for a masculinization of religion, but paradoxically did so under the umbrella of being the *apostles of a new and feminine era within religion*. To understand this, some light has to be shed on the theories of the founder of both conversion movements: the aforementioned Jesuit, Jacques van Ginneken.

[18] van Boven, "De viriele generatie van 1918"; also see Derks, *Heilig moeten*, 30-32, and Andeweg, van Boven and Meijer, "Een campobsessie met katholicisme", 57-67.
[19] Kieft, *Het plagiaat*, 11-138; Sanders, *Het spiegelend venster*; Joosten, *Katholieken en fascisme*; van Lieshout, *Onze onevenwichtige jongeren*.
[20] Lamberts Bendroth, *Fundamentalism and Gender*; Id., "Fundamentalism and Femininity".

VAN GINNEKEN AND THE RISE OF A CATHOLIC FEMININE ERA

Jacques van Ginneken (1877-1945) was the founder and *auctor intellectualis* of three radical conversion associations, the two women's associations already mentioned and one for men, the St John's Crusaders. He was a brewer's son who was raised in a family dominated by women (a strict mother, aunts and sisters). He became a member of the Jesuit order, an outstanding professor at the Catholic University of Nijmegen and an internationally famous linguist. In addition to his intellectual ambitions, he was driven by religious zeal and, like the "the Young Catholics", Father van Ginneken was very critical of church and society in Western Europe in the aftermath of World War I. Struck by what he perceived as a growing secularization in the larger cities, and by the moral consequences of the war, he became a critic of the rigid and often lukewarm Catholicism he noticed everywhere. In line with other radical Catholics, such as the French thinkers and lay Catholics Léon Bloy and Jacques Maritain, and several spokesmen of an international conversion movement, such as the English Cardinal John Henry Newman and writer G.K. Chesterton, Dutch journalist Pieter van der Meer de Walcheren and scholar Gerard Brom, Van Ginneken developed an ideal of a mythical, profound and vigorous Catholicism. He derived this ideal from early Christianity, which he perceived as the era of the martyrs. He thought that faith practices should not consist of meetings and shallow devotions, but that they should be passionate and militant. Medieval ascetic movements also inspired him, as he admired their devotion and suffering for a religious cause.[21]

Van Ginneken was an active proselytizer, arranging numerous lectures on Catholicism for non-Catholics and founding the Committee for the Conversion of the Netherlands (*Comité tot Bekeering van Nederland*) to coordinate all the activities that developed in this field from World War I onward.[22] Although all members of the committee were men, unlike most of his contemporaries Van Ginneken believed that women were the most suited to the role of militant combatant and converter. He also perceived women as the ideal devoted sufferers for such a new golden age of Catholicism. Although he tended to agree with the analysis of neothomist theorists like Victor Cathrein S.J. and Joseph Mausbach which attributed 'natural' qualities to women, he differed with them on what those qualities were.[23] According to Van Ginneken, women embodied a heroic and mystic religiosity that had characterized the formative years of Christianity. He substantiated this theory by referring to several strong women from the history of Christianity. Patriarchal influence, on the other hand, represented rational and technical dimensions that characterized religion in modernity and Van Ginneken argued that the twentieth century was predominantly masculine, not because of vigour or virility, but because of rationality and technol-

---

[21] For the (international) impact of converts to Catholicism from the turn of the century onwards, see: Luykx, *'Daar is nog poëzie'*; Derks, Nissen and de Raat, *Het licht gezien*; Pearce, *Literary converts*; Allitt, *Catholic converts*.

[22] van Ginneken, "Die Konversionsbewegung in Holland".

[23] Cathrein, *Die Frauenfrage*; Mausbach, *Die Stellung der Frau*; also see Salemink and Borgman, "Katholieken en de eerste feministische golf".

ogy. This called for a renewal of a heroic and mystic Catholicism. Although both men and women could embody this heroism and mysticism, in general women were best fitted for it. They had a natural disposition to give themselves up totally to a higher ideal, and, furthermore, possessed a superior capacity for suffering. In other words: according to Van Ginneken women embodied strength and virility, while men embodied a rational and lukewarm religion.[24]

This was why Van Ginneken founded his two women's associations for religious conversion. By constructing a female genealogy, Van Ginneken identified and legitimized those women he wanted to gather to save the world. They were 'chosen': "Didn't God make me write these lines especially for you, just for you, perhaps for only you?" he wrote in an article entitled "Call of awakening" ("*Wekroep*").[25] Such vigorously articulated convictions attracted a number of socially and religiously motivated young women, who were searching for a goal beyond marriage or convent life. The women were to take a leading role in the conversion of children and adolescent girls in the poorer quarters of the large cities. It was not to be women religious but lay women who would take this role, because the strict rules and regulations imposed on convents by the church prevented sisters from performing such a militant task in the world. And militancy was a precondition for the associations.

PLANNING WORLD CONVERSION: THE WOMEN OF NAZARETH

The first conversion association, the Ladies of Bethany (1919) consisted of young women, the majority of whom came from wealthy backgrounds (a precondition for entry, because Van Ginneken had more plans than money) and who had completed higher education. Their aim was to convert city children by means of a system of youth homes that provided clubs, entertainment and religious education. They recruited their potential converts by public performances and via house calls and their system gave them access to families in which priests were no longer welcome. This special access endowed their task with a heroic character and attracted several recruits. Within a few years, the women had opened homes in the four main cities of the Netherlands, which thousands of children attended. However, entertainment and religious education were one thing, and conversion another. Because of the complex road towards conversion, the time-consuming approach and the on-going financial difficulties, all the ladies' efforts resulted in only a few hundred baptisms during a period of more than twenty years. On the other hand, their name and fame were far greater than these quantitative results would suggest. Their clubs and modern methods of working embodied a new form of catechetics, youth work and social work within Dutch Catholicism.[26]

---

[24] Meerman and van Oostrum, "'Een groote vrouw waar vindt men haar!'".

[25] "Heeft God mij deze regels wellicht laten schrijven voor U, juist voor U, misschien voor U alleen?", quoted in: AG, 1: Jac. Van Ginneken, *Mij kwelt en prangt*. This title refers to the opening words of the article "Wekroep".

[26] For the history of the Ladies of Bethany, see Derks, *Heilig moeten*, 90-187.

This religious belligerence combined with a modern approach was even more thoroughly articulated by the second association, the Women of Nazareth (1921), even though they soon clashed with their 'spiritual sisters'. This association consisted of highly educated young women, some of whom had been students of Van Ginneken and had been recruited by him after finishing their studies. Four of them went on to complete their dissertations with Van Ginneken, and were therefore real forerunners. No more than a mere thirteen women did so before 1940 at the only Catholic university in the Netherlands in Nijmegen.[27] Their exceptional position, being so well educated and at the same time enthusiastic and religiously inspired, made it difficult for them to find a way in a Catholic culture that generally afforded two opportunities to women: becoming a nun, or becoming a wife and mother. Traditional convent life certainly held no appeal, as several women pointed out, because they considered themselves to be modern women and resented being restricted. Furthermore, their religiously motivated criticism of society seemed to call them for quite another vocation. Van Ginneken's plan held a much greater appeal. Lydwine van Kersbergen, one of the women, clearly expressed this clearly in her memoirs:

> [Prof. Van Ginneken's] ideas were big and totally caught me. [...] Yes, I already knew it at that time, I wanted to enclose the whole world, no tame Catholicism, but a heroic experience of the Gospel and a missionary zest, in which women would have a large part.[28]

The ultimate purpose of the association - explicitly voiced - was to convert the whole world. To emphasize this, one evening Van Ginneken and five leading women even divided up a map of the world. A particular part was allocated to each woman. As if it were a military operation, flags were stuck on to help them visualize the project and to illustrate the strategy. The enormous scale of the enterprise did not frighten the young women at all. On the contrary, as true soldiers of Christ they were determined to make their plan a success.[29]

Viewed from the outside, proud self-esteem and a powerful assertive performance appeared to be the distinctive characteristics of the movement. These were however counterbalanced by practices of joyous suffering and sacrifice within the group. The internal dynamics of the Women of Nazareth were characterized by a climate of militancy and suffering, in particular the administration of corporal punishment to oneself and to each other, both to accentuate the religious core of the association and to ensure discipline. The women embraced vicarious suffering as imitation of Christ's Passion, both aimed at their own salvation and at that of nonbe-

---

[27] Louise Veldhuis took her doctoral degree in 1931, Lydwine van Kersbergen in 1936, Liesbeth Allard in 1937 and Mia van der Kallen in 1938. E.g. Lucassen and Peeters, *Hora est*, 60-62.

[28] "[...] het waren grote ideeën [van Prof. Van Ginneken] en ik werd er totaal door gepakt. [...] Ja, ik wist het toen al, ik wilde de wereld omvatten, geen tam katholicisme, maar een heroïeke beleving van het evangelie en een missionair elan, waarin vrouwen een grote rol zouden hebben." Donders, *Lydwine van Kersbergen*, 14-15. Also: "Mia van der Kallen". Episode of KRO's radio program *Sporen in het achterland* (12 July 1984) with interviews.

[29] Donders, *Lydwine van Kersbergen*, 20; Id., *Geef mij 10.000 zielen*, 25.

lievers whom they hoped to save. With this active pursuit of voluntary suffering, the Women of Nazareth (and the Ladies of Bethany) echoed a practice that was especially known among French women in the second half of the nineteenth century, but that developed further during the interwar years while spreading to other countries.[30] Van Ginneken, who was very familiar with this culture through his contacts with Maritain (who, together with his wife Raïsa, was an adherent of this so-called mystic modernism[31]), was undoubtedly influenced by these examples. They served to balance the women's desires for self-determination and agency in the public sphere with their adherence to Catholic faith and church. The practice of physical and mental penances among the Women of Nazareth, which were hidden from the outside world, led to an atmosphere which was often strained. While this was challenging and gratifying for some members, it was damaging for others. Van Ginneken kept in close contact with the leading women to make sure these practices were maintained.

As said, part of the purpose of the corporal punishments was to balance religious devotion and public agency. The Women of Nazareth had a public agenda. In order to achieve their goal, they had to start things off on a modest scale. They began their work among non-Catholic adolescent girls, especially those employed in factories, because they believed that was where secularization began, at the core of rationality and technology. The women began to work in the factories themselves and organized clubs for working girls, both on their own properties and in rented houses in the cities. Like the Ladies of Bethany, they adopted a combined approach of entertainment and religious education. The women also assisted in running retreats for converts. Unlike the Ladies of Bethany, however, but true to their own goal, the Nazareth women also extended their work across the border. They nourished the ideal of the foundation of a Catholic Women's University on Java (Dutch Indies), from where the conversion of the Asian colonies was to start. This academic ideal indicates that for the learned Women of Nazareth, a women's university held an extra appeal.

However, this ideal received a setback when Johannes Aengenent, the new bishop of Haarlem (the diocese where the Nazareth association was based), ordered a change of direction in 1928. He bypassed Van Ginneken, who was constantly fighting his own battles with the clergy, and forced the women to take on the leadership of a new Catholic girls' movement. In return, they received considerable financial recompense from the parishes in the diocese, certain privileges and the bishop's unqualified support. It was this so-called Grail movement, that the Women of Nazareth planned, organized and led themselves which became the largest and most successful girls' movement in the Netherlands. At first, this change of plan discouraged the women, but gradually they incorporated the girls' movement into their own long-term goals. They made an effort to transfer their ideal to the girls and regarded the Grail as just another step on the road to a worldwide conversion.[32]

---

[30] Lösel, "Prayer, Pain, and Priestly Privilege". Also: Burton, *Holy Tears, Holy Blood*. An example from the USA gives Kane, "'She offered herself up'".
[31] Schloesser, *Catholicism in the Jazz Age*, 41-209.
[32] PANJ 345: Letters of Mia van der Kallen to Van Ginneken (1928).

THE PROUD CATHOLIC GIRL

The Grail became an eye-catching and expressive movement that was regularly commented upon in the press and other types of publication. Most of these comments were positive, at least when critics were taking into account the religious motives of the Grail members. With regard to their public display, however, a negative critical reflex surfaced. Among those critics were writers who belonged to the movement of the Young Catholics. One of them, Ernest Michel, labelled the Grail "hysterical", a movement for which "no real man can hold any respect". He criticized its public image and called its Catholicism "mere show". By contrast, Michel perceived the male Young Catholics as a true and "faith convinced" movement which avoided such outward appearances and strove instead to deepen religion.[33]

Why did this male writer, who was a radical religious critic of mainstream Catholic culture, judge so negatively and in such blatant gendered terms a movement of women and girls that itself was aiming at a more profound Catholicism? It could not have been his general dislike of a movement that wore uniforms, carried flags or marched in the streets, since Michel, like some other Young Catholics, became an adherent of Dutch national socialism during the 1930s. More likely, his confusion was caused by the about-turn in gender roles that the Grail movement displayed. Contrary to its restorative *religious* aim, this girls' movement adopted a variety of means and methods from modernity - and even appropriated those that at the time were associated with men. Sports, public manifestations, performances in stadiums, colourful uniforms, flags and their own private club houses, the use of photography, film and modern design, insights from psychology and pedagogy - everything was put to use to turn the Grail into an appealing movement that experimented successfully with a new kind of Catholic womanhood, one that allowed female agency in the public sphere and participation in modernity.[34]

Never before had Catholic girls marched through the streets, reciting religious verses that incited other girls to stand up and join their ranks: "Come on and blow the trumpets / Next to the powerful trace of men, woman wants / To put the fragile print of her foot / On the faith of all people, in all times and ages."[35] Despite words like "fragile" the Grail girls marched like "an large army of young women" or "female Percivals", as they called themselves, referring to the Grail saga where the knight Parsifal sets out to find the Holy Grail. The difference was that this time *girls* were starring in the hitherto male-focused story of the knight. Most girls merely enjoyed

---

[33] Michel, *Neo-Communisten*, quoted by Oostveen, "Ernest Michel. De wilde kreten van een heftig katholiek", in: *De Tijd* (31 December 1982); Michel, *Europeesche jeugd*, quoted in *Het Vaderland* (3 May 1933) 4.

[34] Andeweg, van Boven and Meijer have pointed at the persistence of similar criticism whenever women entered the public sphere, be it with expressions of a cultural, literary or religious nature. They perceive the Young Catholics as an essentially misogynist movement. "Een campobsessie met katholicisme", 61.

[35] "Komt op dan, vooruit nu en blaast de trompetten / De vrouw wil naast het machtige mannenspoor / Ook van haar vrouwenvoet de tere indruk zetten / Op het mensen lot aller eeuwen en tijden door" in: *Graalrangen* (n.p, n.y) [no pages].

the colourful settings and the activities that the movement provided. The Women of Nazareth, however, perceived the girls as proud and passionate apostles of Catholicism. For that reason they inculcated the same militant mentality in the girls of the Grail as they instilled within themselves.

A defining element of what could be described as 'Grail culture' was the emphasis on physicality. Although a pronounced sports culture had developed in mainstream Catholic culture, with football clubs appearing in even the smallest villages and a distinct Catholic competition, sport press and club culture, this was predominantly a male realm from which women were excluded or at most merely tolerated as spectators. Only gymnastics was generally perceived as an acceptable physical exercise for women, since it kept them healthy and fit enough to bear and raise children. Such modest physical activities were welcomed, provided, on the bishop's explicit orders, that only specific exercises, described in detail, were carried out and there were no public displays of women's gymnastic skill.[36] In general, although there certainly were exceptions, the 'muscular Catholic' was a man.[37] However, the ideal of a strong, fresh and proud Catholic (young) woman developed within the Grail movement.

Sport departments were established in all Grail divisions, partly because bishop Aengenent ordered all girls' gymnastic associations to join the Grail. But gymnastics was only one of the physical activities possible there: in general a typical Grail girl was an all-round athlete who rode her bike, was a rower and a canoeist, played tennis and hockey and could hike for hours and hours. There were competitions for each sport and each year a large Grail delegation participated in the famous Four Day Marches in Nijmegen.

Unlike in other sport clubs for women, that is, the gymnastics clubs, Grail girls did compete with each other and the results of their matches were published and commented upon in the Grail's magazine *The Silver Trumpet* (*De Zilveren Trompet*). The magazine also published articles on training, a phenomenon that until then was only known to appear in male sports culture: "Lithe and powerful and supple and strong our bodies will only then become, if we keep practicing all the time."[38]

Within the symbolic universe of the Grail movement, a true and proud Grail girl could stand everything and endure anything. This did not diminish her womanhood - on the contrary, in this way she was training herself to become a true female soldier of Christ. Within this conception, there were distinct echoes of the vicarious suffering that the leading Women of Nazareth practiced among themselves. The girls were immersed in a sacrificial spirituality that combined female suffering and male strength. This was certainly the foundation of the famous open-air plays in which thousands of costumed Grail girls showed off their gymnastic skills and mental endurance while performing a religious play and reciting verses. For these plays, such as "The Royal Easter play" and "The Blessing of Pentecost", the girls trained for months in a row and joyously overcame all hardship, knowing it was for

---

[36] Derks and Budel, *Sportief en katholiek*, 79-87.

[37] Derks, "Modesty and Excellence"; Id., "Fiere sportlijven en kenauturnsters"; Derks and Budel, *Sportief en katholiek*.

[38] "Lenig en krachtig en soepel en sterk zal ons lichaam alleen worden, wanneer wij voortdurend oefenen": "De technische organisatie van de sport in de Graal"; "Fierheid", 3.

a higher cause. The plays were written and directed by leading Women of Nazareth, and performed in sports stadiums like the Olympic Stadium in Amsterdam, as well as in London, Dublin and Berlin. Numerous clerical and secular authorities were among the spectators. Normally these stadiums were the temples of secular sports, but on these occasions they became the stage for proud Catholic girls.[39]

CLASHING WITH CLERICAL HIERARCHY

The Grail culture can be seen as an example of an ambiguous female Catholicism that displayed some distinctly masculine traits. Although the performances of the Grail drew reactions from the press and the authorities which were partly appreciative, they were also commented on in negative terms. Such public display was not thought appropriate for women and girls. Coupled with the relatively autonomous and wilful attitude of the Women of Nazareth, these displays also resulted in a series of conflicts with the clergy, with other youth movements and with school boards. The Grail was an all-consuming movement, led by self-aware women - a fact that did not please everyone. The Haarlem clergy, especially, became strong opponents because the parishes were obliged to contribute towards the costs of the Grail but were denied influence.

The Women of Nazareth established certain routines in the Grail houses that could be perceived as the prerogative of the clergy. For instance, the Grail houses had their own chapel, but no priest ever came there. In Grail clubs, girls had to confess aloud and were given penances by a Grail leader. No parish priest had any say in the organization of the clubs, as was the case with Catholic youth care in all other dioceses. What made matters worse, the Women of Nazareth, in general far better educated than most parish priests, easily out-manoeuvred them. On top of that, they did little to hide their pride in what they were doing and gloried in their freedom of action which was facilitated by the bishop's patronage.[40]

Such an overt display of authoritative female Catholicism had to lead to conflict since, despite the existence of a relatively influential women's organization such as the Women of Nazareth and their Grail movement, hegemonic power relations remained restricted to men. It can seriously be doubted whether their influence would ever have been as widespread without episcopal patronage. The Women of Nazareth thus became entangled in enduring conflict with the clergy. The outspokenness and authoritative attitude of the women, as well as the expansion of the Grail which spread to various European countries, to the United States and to Australia during the 1930s, became a problem for the Dutch clergy and for the Vatican. Confrontation was heightened when the movement manifested itself from 1933 onwards in

---

[39] For the experiences of participants see the interviews in Van Emmerik, *Gevaarlijk modern*, 61-67; interview of Derks with Donders and with Groothuizen; van Oostrum, "K(l)eurig, kwiek en katholiek".

[40] Bank, the biographer of bishop Aengenent, stated that the bishop was very taken with the Women of Nazareth and refused to express any criticism of the Grail: Bank, *Joannes Dominicus Joseph Aengenent*, 40-41; also see Voets, *Bewaar het toevertrouwde pand*, 236.

Nazi Germany, where it opened several Grail houses and where it participated in mass rallies. In addition, an unfortunate trip to perform in fascist Italy raised eyebrows. All this, as well as the unfamiliar symbols and rituals that the Grail had adopted (which some designated as 'pagan', but which Van Ginneken considered to be "of a religious core"), elicited restrictions from the Vatican.[41]

In 1935 the movement was incorporated into the hierarchical Catholic Action network, lost its privileges and had to submit to local clergy. The death of their patron, Bishop Aengenent, and the strict policy of his successor Huibers reinforced this position. Van Ginneken persisted in his rhetoric, but could not do anything to prevent it from happening. The Grail became a more traditional movement that stressed the stereotypical roles of girls and women, and the values of family life. The outbreak of the Second World War undermined its activities even further. After the war and the death of Van Ginneken, the Women of Nazareth evolved into an international religious movement for lay women without any claims to world conversion.

SOME CONCLUDING REMARKS

In this article, I have presented an account of the association of Catholic lay women, the Women of Nazareth, as well as an account of the Grail Movement, the girls' movement that they led. Both organizations aimed for conversion on a global scale, although the leaders were more explicit in their goal than the girls were. The women have been depicted against their social, personal and spiritual backgrounds, and an explanation given of their motivation and the activities that they carried out in order to realize their ideals. They represented the first generation of highly educated Catholic women, born and raised in a society that was not yet used to women wanting to step outside of the accepted ideals of motherhood and convent life. These women developed religiously worded ideals and ambitions which were, however, ambiguous and quite militant.

The gender perspective demonstrates that so-called 'different Catholics' could also be women. This may appear obvious, but it has not been acknowledged before. Dominant historiography has much preferred and appreciated the writing and discourse of the young Catholic men. Taking the experiences of women into account leads to a specification of 'different Catholics'. The women described in this article expressed their criticism of the predominating religious attitudes and practices in a radical, conservative and, in contrast to the men, in an embodied way. First, they made their body and soul, that is, their entire being, the subject of a religious battle and a conservative testimony, by cultivating militancy and personal suffering. More than that, they tried to spread the religious ideal to others, by organizing movements, houses and clubs for the purpose of religious conversion.

Despite the fact that both leaders and followers were of the female sex, the movement cannot be described as a feminine one. In addition, it did not contribute to any feminization of religion, but rather raises questions about the very concept. Although

[41] For an extensive explanation of this Vatican clash, known as "the question of the Sybils", see Derks, *Heilig moeten*, 300-319.

they articulated an almost exclusively female sphere, a social sphere of women only, they nevertheless had a distinctly masculine orientation. The women, inspired by their spiritual leader, cultivated an attitude of pride and defiance, presenting themselves as fearless crusaders and soldiers, and the true representatives of the original Catholicism. They identified with both an eclectic selection of women from Catholic tradition and with strong men. They frequently appeared in the public domain and did not hesitate to take over competences that were in fact restricted to the male clergy. This inevitably led to severe clashes both with the clergy and with other powerful men, since, however self-willed the women may have been, it was almost impossible for them to articulate a view of church and society and act upon it, without the help or at least consent of men in positions of authority. This in turn reinforces the argument against there having been an all-encompassing feminization of religion, since power within the Catholic Church was, and remained, exclusively in the hands of men.

The point of this article, therefore, is that gender is a very useful category of historical analysis, as Joan Scott has pointed out so well in her famous article which became the foundation of gender history.[42] Gender surpasses the idea that neutral human beings were historical subjects, and it enables us to differentiate between women and men. Although Scott did not apply this gender concept to the history of *religion*, a lot has changed since she published it in 1986.[43] However, the critical quality of the concept vanishes whenever the difference between female and feminine evaporates. Female refers to women; feminine refers to prototypical (traditional, stereotypical) qualities attributed to women.

In the concepts of feminization and masculinization, in which female and feminine are equated, this differentiation is lost and gone. In other words, the fruitfulness of an enlightening concept becomes overgrown and stereotypes are reproduced once again, this time in historiography itself. The ambiguities between female and feminine are pushed aside, as the concept 'feminization of religion' reiterates the opposition between male and female, and re-installs the polarities of this hierarchical binary dualism.

As a consequence, I argue that the masculinization and feminization of religion are not valid concepts and offer no adequate means for analysing religious history. Although challenging, this debate is in timely need of historical specification. The concept of feminization and its counterpart, masculinization, might illuminate some processes at certain times, as Bonnie Smith has pointed out in her study of French bourgeois ladies in the second half of the nineteenth century.[44] On the other hand,

[42] Scott, "Gender: A Useful Category".

[43] One of forerunners in historical religion and gender analysis is of course Bynum, e.g. *Fragmentation and Redemption*. During the same periode, Scott's plea for applying gender as a category of analysis was incorporated in Dutch religious history: see Derks and van Heijst, "Katholieke vrouwencultuur" and has been elaborated on ever since. Also see Derks, "Res Novae"; Van Heijst and Derks, *Terra incognita*; Derks and Eijt, "Wie kookte het laatste avondmaal?" and the publications mentioned on the website of *Echo*, a Dutch association on historical research on religion and gender (founded in 1995): www.stichting-echo.nl.

[44] Smith, *Ladies*; i.e. Lösel, "Prayer, Pain, and Priestly Privilege". Also see studies on the development of a "woman's sphere" in American religion, e.g. Hackett, *Religion and American Culture*.

the concepts might also eliminate our sensitivity towards historical differentiations that are so crucial in our understanding of the past. Therefore, I argue against concepts based on generalization and advocate differentiation in the assessment of feminization and masculinization alongside differentiation between social classes, between countries and regions, within age groups, concerning ecclesiastical status, and of course across historical periods. If anything, we need concepts that help us to understand the ambiguities of gender relations and the complex symbolic meanings of womanhood and manhood within religion.

By adopting the religious practice of male Catholic youth, Heliand girls broke with the feminine religiosity associated with late nineteenth century and early twentieth-century Catholicism. Heliand-Bund Bundestag, *Untermarchtal (Germany), 1936.*
[Speyer, Landesarchive: Heliand-Bund papers]

A FEMINIZED CHURCH?

GERMAN CATHOLIC WOMEN, PIETY, AND DOMESTICITY, 1918-1938

MICHAEL E. O'SULLIVAN

In the middle of an interview with an elderly member of a rural Kolping Association, I asked about the role of women in the Catholic Church during the 1930s. He smiled broadly and called to his wife in the kitchen: "The women are always more fervent, aren't they?"[1] His comment typified both popular and scholarly attitudes about the religiosity of women in modern German Catholicism. As one well-respected scholar argues, the 'feminization of religion' has become a "frequently cited topos".[2] While several essays engage the 'feminization' of German Catholicism during the nineteenth century, more empirical analysis of the theory is necessary for the first half of the twentieth century in order to shed light on the persistence of feminine domesticity and piety as a cultural trope.

American scholar Barbara Welter first argued that Christianity became feminized during the nineteenth century in the United States. Several academics, writing in the 1990s, found her conclusions applicable to the Catholic minority in Germany. Irmtraud Götz von Olenhusen suggests that nineteenth-century gender norms helped mothers and wives form a majority among practicing Catholics. As the bourgeois ideal of female domesticity became dominant, religious piety and instruction for children became a responsibility for women in the private sphere. Post-enlightenment men with active professional lives had less time or desire to participate in religious life.[3] Norbert Busch and others have also argued that this feminization represented a conscious strategy by the Church to increase religious participation. Bishops and priests emphasized 'emotional' elements of Catholic piety, such as the cults of the Virgin Mary and the Sacred Heart, which they believed would attract female congre-

---

[1] Interview with M.O. in Bad Münstereifel on 17 March 2004.
[2] Götz von Olenhusen, "Die Feminisierung von Religion und Kirche", 9.
[3] Ibid., 8-21; Welter, "The Feminization of American Religion: 1800-1860".

gants and prevent their participation in the women's movement.[4] Michael Gross also illustrates how Protestant liberals rhetorically gendered Catholicism feminine in order to attain greater hegemony for their own values in the political sphere.[5]

Few scholars of German Catholicism, however, concur with Welter's notion that the feminization of Christianity provided women opportunities for emancipation. Von Olenhusen suggests that the existence of a Church-controlled Catholic milieu made the German context different from the United States. This so-called milieu contained a network of lay associations for men and women with varying degrees of autonomy from clerical oversight. For example, the People's Association for Catholic Germany (*Volksverein für das katholische Deutschland*) functioned freely as a political organ for the Centre Party, while the Catholic Workers' Clubs endured careful supervision by representatives of the institutional Church. Von Olenhusen suggests that the clergy maintained strict control over female associations and used them to inhibit women's engagement with movements for emancipation.[6]

Relinde Meiwes' study about nineteenth-century nuns is one of the only monographs to support this element of the Welter thesis. Meiwes demonstrates that over two-thirds of those taking religious vows during the nineteenth century were women religious. Their access to new professional opportunities in charities, health care, and education as well as the relatively egalitarian structure of convents provided emancipatory opportunities.[7] David Blackbourn also analyses how nineteenth-century females seeing apparitions utilized Catholic piety for a limited amount of power. Women claiming to have seen the Virgin Mary 'inverted' the usual power relationship with men and priests in the village.[8]

Bernard Schneider raises significant questions about the extent to which the German Catholic Church actually underwent feminization. He emphasizes the masculine elements of nineteenth-century religious life, exemplified by the preservation of a patriarchal hierarchy led by male clergy. Furthermore, the associations and political organizations that most frequently represented the Church in the public sphere possessed overwhelmingly male members. Schneider reasons that if the public face and leadership structure of the Church remained masculine, it is unfeasible to generalize about Catholicism as a feminized religion.[9] The vast literature about the Catholic milieu during the nineteenth and twentieth centuries supports this critique by analysing many of its two hundred associations and their 5.7 million members as well as the powerful Centre Party. These studies argue that male associations and youth groups, such as the People's Association for Catholic Germany and the Kolping Associations, used modern organizational methods to delay contemporary secular impulses and uphold insular communities shaped by Catholic values until after 1945. Most milieu studies illustrate the continuing importance of activities by men in the public sphere,

---

[4] Busch, "Die Feminisierung der Frömmigkeit".

[5] Gross, *The War against Catholicism*.

[6] Götz von Olenhusen, "Die Feminisierung von Religion und Kirche", 17-19.

[7] Meiwes, *'Arbeiterinnen des Hernn'*.

[8] Blackbourn, *Marpingen: Apparitions of the Virgin Mary in Nineteenth-Century Germany*, 7-15, 30-31, 140-141, 261-263.

[9] Schneider, "Feminisierung der Religion".

despite the statistical trend toward a feminine Communion rail.[10] Schneider suggests that future research might examine how specific elements of Catholicism became feminized, rather than a universally apply of the theory. In sum, specific forms of piety, ritual, and domestic prayer became more feminine, while the public side of Church life retained masculine hegemony.

Schneider's ideas about the nineteenth century merit empirical analysis in the context of the twentieth century. It is important to understand the extent to which the partially feminized Roman Catholic community persevered and changed with the tumultuous events of the post-World War I era. Three case studies from Germany's somewhat distinctive confessional associations during the Weimar years add complexity to the historiography of feminized Catholicism in interwar Germany. First, the Mothers' Associations, which merged in the late 1920s to become the second largest national umbrella organization for Catholic women, advocated an ideal form of feminine domesticity and piety. They encouraged mothers to care for religious practice and moral behavior in the home. An overview of their activities during the Weimar Republic and the Third Reich reveals the areas of Church life where women remained prominent, gained power, and rejected increased professional opportunities. Second, the Marian Congregations (*Jungfraukongregationen*) represented the mainstream organization for young Catholic women. This group's traditional emphasis on ultramontane forms of piety illuminates the tensions involved with the younger generation's acceptance of the Virgin Mother as their model for domesticity and religiosity. Finally, the Catholic Youth Movement exemplified masculine forms of Catholicism as well as the ways in which girls from the educated middle class diverged from Church ideals about women's religious practice and domesticity. While Catholic boys used ideals of the youth movement to redefine how men dominated the public sphere of Church life, the girls who founded the *Heliand-Bund*, an organization for Catholic girls attending *Gymnasium*, transcended the rigid Catholic adherence to feminine domesticity with similar ideas.

Gender roles within German Catholicism reflected both clearly defined expectations and ambiguities in practice during the eras of Weimar democracy and Nazi dictatorship. Although domestic piety and religious morality remained areas of feminine hegemony, young women developed a public religious identity and reconciled professional opportunities with Catholic values. Furthermore, boys within the male youth movement used martial masculinity to lead public expressions of faith, but women and girls also joined the street demonstrations and sought opportunities for religious expression outside the confines of Church and home. The partially feminized German Catholic community possessed a female private sphere and a masculine public sphere, but the youth movement altered the lens through which girls viewed the domestic ideals of the late nineteenth century. Despite their restricted opportunities within the Catholic community, these young women leveraged religious organizations into empowerment in both religious and professional spheres.

---

[10] Kösters, *Katholische Verbände*; AKKZG, "Katholiken zwischen Tradition und Moderne"; Horstmann and Liedhegener, *Konfession, Moderne und Milieu*; Schank, '*Kölsch-Katholisch*'; Heilbronner, *Catholicism, Political Culture, and the Countryside*; Blaschke and Kuhlemann, *Religion im Kaiserreich*.

CATHOLIC MOTHERS

The historiography of Catholic women's organizations during the Weimar Republic indicates that they retained a dedication to patriarchal ideals and became even less flexible regarding gender norms as the Nazis rose to power, despite increased political participation after World War I. Most of this research has focused on the largest national women's organization, the *Katholische Deutsche Frauenbund* (KDF), because of its linkages to the Centre Party. Other confessional clubs and professional organizations within the Catholic subculture, such as groups for female teachers and social workers, also stressed chastity outside of marriage and opposition to abortion.[11] The Mothers' Associations also became increasingly significant during this era. These previously parish-based associations formed a national organization under the auspices of Catholic Action in the late 1920s. Analysis of this association demonstrates how clergy and female laity advocated a traditional ideal of domesticity, piety, and feminine morality, but it also illustrates how an increased emphasis on lay leadership provided women with more avenues to power.

Mainstream Catholicism maintained a patriarchal approach toward women after World War I. According to the secondary literature on German politics, the vast majority of female Catholic voters willingly chose the ideals of domesticity promoted by the clergy and sparked a revived interest in essentialist understandings of femininity in Weimar society. In the early years of the Weimar Republic, the Centre Party actually tolerated some progressive ideas, particularly from younger women who resisted clerical authority and advocated pacifism and flexible rules on birth control. After the rise of future chancellor Heinrich Brüning in 1929, the Centre Party converged with the conservative position of the clergy on maternal values and most women supported this policy shift at the ballot box.[12] In her book on women's voting, Julia Sneeringer argues that the Catholic Centre Party was so successful with female voters that conservative parties imitated their platform. Women constituted 60 percent of the Catholic Centre Party's electorate during the late 1920s. The party flourished with this majority because it stressed religious and maternal themes rather than rhetoric for emancipation.[13] The KDF also articulated self-confidence in their ability to uphold and defend Christian values, viewing women as the religious community's strongest asset. After the war, they argued that the family was the strongest 'defence' against the growing 'moral decay' in Germany and that the woman bore a special role in this effort as the "protector of popular morality".[14]

The clergy who led the *Müttervereine* fit into this larger context of normative gender values. For example, the association's journal expressed concern during World War I that the increased responsibilities of women outside the home eroded family piety and domestic discipline, and it fretted that total war compromised moral

---

[11] Sack, *Zwischen religiöser Bindung und moderner Gesellschaft*; Baumann, "Religion und Emanzipation".

[12] Sack, *Zwischen religiöser Bindung und moderner Gesellschaft*, 401.

[13] Sneeringer, *Winning Women's Votes*. See also Kaufmann, *Katholisches Milieu*, 77.

[14] BAT Abt. B III 14, 5, Bd. 1: Frauen- und Müttervereine, 1918-1942, "Katholischer Frauenbund Deutschlands, Zentralstelle (Köln)", 12 December 1919.

purity. Searching for stability in an uncertain time, they promoted a return to 'traditional' gender roles.[15] The association encouraged women to take the Virgin Mary as their model, serving as the 'queen' of the household, whose primary job was to bear children and take care of the home.[16]

During the second half of the 1920s, the Church recognized the importance of the Mothers' Associations and restructured them along the principles of Catholic Action, an initiative started by the Vatican in Italy.[17] Prelate Hermann Klens centralized the parish-based and loosely affiliated Mothers' Associations into a national organization in 1928. This group promoted active religious life among women, but also encouraged their role as missionaries to the rest of the Catholic community.[18] Previously neglected Mothers' Associations held one meeting and one communal mass a month. Under the reforms of Klens, these organizations now turned women into lay leaders charged with meeting the spiritual and maternal needs of others. They conducted seminars on how to counsel other congregants about family life and religious practice and hosted retreats for exhausted mothers. Female leaders also assembled members for 'group nights' to discuss contemporary issues.[19]

While some scholars view Catholic Action in Germany as a benign program that offered the laity more leadership positions,[20] several other historians criticize it as a repressive force that destroyed dynamic lay movements in order to strengthen the institutional power of the clergy. Both Dirk Müller and Joachim Köhler blame the hierarchy's suspicion of lay autonomy for the rapid decline of the People's Association for Catholic Germany and the Workers' Clubs during the implementation of Catholic Action policies. According to these researchers, Catholic Action made Catholicism apolitical and created the necessary context for the Concordat with National Socialism in 1933.[21] From the perspective of women's history, Doris Kaufmann argues that Catholic Action attempted to return Catholic communities to natural gender hierarchies by strictly separating male and female lay activists under the strict supervision of clergy.[22] The principles of Catholic Action undoubtedly restricted the agency of both men and women, especially in politically influential groups. The Mothers' Associations, however, already included strict supervision by local priests. Therefore, these women received more opportunities for leadership and had little autonomy to lose in the first place. While Church leaders perpetuated patriarchal themes that confined women, mothers also used Catholic Action to increase their power within the boundaries of religious life.

15 "Selbstvergessene Liebe"; "Ich habe keine Zeit"; "Wie ich mit meinen Kindern spiele"; "Unsere Jugend: Der kleine Kriegsheld"; "Unsere Jugend: Fritz will nicht beten/ Prinzetschen".
16 "Zur Einkehr".
17 Catholic Action in Germany differed from the program in France. In Germany, it avoided secular activities. For French women, see Whitney, "Gender, Class, and Generation", 487.
18 Klens, *Anwalt der Frauen*, 49, 88-89.
19 "Ein herzliches 'Grüß Gott' zum neuen Jahr"; "Aus unsere Verbandsfamilie - Aus unserem Gruppenabenden"; "Aus unserer Verbandsfamilie - Mutter erhole sich".
20 Klein, *Der Volksverein*, 218-240.
21 Müller, *Arbeiter, Katholizismus, Staat*; Köhler, "Ausbruch aus dem katholischen Milieu?".
22 Kaufmann, *Katholisches Milieu*, 8.

The most effective tool for communicating with this massive organization of over 2,000 associations and 900,000 women was its monthly journal, *Die Mutter*, which enjoyed over 920,000 subscribers by 1938.[23] Female editors, under the guidance of the clergy, articulated the primary aim of the association: to espouse Catholic feminine values against the challenge posed by the so-called 'new woman'. In a speech about Catholic values in cities, lay leader Minna Schumacher-Köhl asked: "Is it our fault that the image of the pious, chaste, simple, and authentic motherly woman is being displaced by the haughty, smug and worldly woman, the shallow sportswoman and the thoughtless fashion puppets?"[24] The associations championed maternal values of Catholicism in opposition to new images from 1920s popular culture and promoted a dichotomous perception of women as both deviously sexual and pillars of purity.

By reasserting maternal and family roles, lay leaders and the clergy charged women with saving Christian family life and protecting the ethical climate of the Catholic community. Encouraging increased moral authority in relation to their husbands, several articles called on Catholic women to "rescue the Christian family".[25] A fable in the journal depicts a boy crossing a clear stream of water after a May pilgrimage and throwing dirt in the water. His mother scolds: "If one clouds or dirties pure water, then one dirties the Virgin Mother."[26] In the minds of women, boys and men suffered most from sinful temptation and mothers guarded the moral order.[27] This rhetoric frequently sparked political action. For example, in 1932 the National Women's Caucus of the Centre Party led the religious backlash against 1927 reforms of prostitution laws by formally asking the Reich Minister of the Interior to criminalize prostitution.[28] Although constrained by Catholic affirmation of patriarchy, women utilized their religious mobilization to influence German society and spread their values to men, whom they sometimes portrayed as morally unreliable.

Catholic mothers also continued their roles as religious authorities within the home. The journal instructed mothers:

> Help your child pray. Go with him in the morning to Holy Mass. Say the morning and evening prayers with him, and then say the rosary together at dusk. Speak with the child often about the honor and happiness of Sundays and try to fill his heart with awe before the holy sacrament. The child encounters heaven through his mother's hands.[29]

Another article exhibited the gendered roles in the religious education of a child. When describing the preparation for First Communion, the journal stressed that the mother had to lead morning and evening prayers and oversee regular Mass atten-

[23] "Aus unsere Verbandsfamilie - Erste Gemeinschaftstagung von Leiterinnen der Frauen- und Müttervereine in Rhöndorf"; Klens, *Anwalt der Frauen*, 134.
[24] M. Schmacher-Köhl, "Christusträgerinnen in der Großstadt".
[25] "Rettet die Familie".
[26] "Unsere Jugend: Maigang".
[27] "David Gathen: Dein Junge im Beruf!".
[28] Roos, "Backlash against Prostitutes' Rights", 76.
[29] "Aus Kinderland: An der Mutter Hand".

dance. After the First Communion, mothers ensured the enduring faith of their children by making them participate regularly.[30]

Evidence suggests that women acted on this rhetoric. Many members of the Catholic Youth Movement acknowledged the religious influence of their mothers. In his memoir, male youth leader and future author Gisbert Kranz remembers his mother as caretaker of religion in the household. She taught him morning and evening prayers and made certain the family celebrated religious holidays, emphasizing religious values during Advent, teaching charity during St Martin celebrations, making Marian altars in May, and praying to the Sacred Heart in June. Kranz asserts: "The faith that my mother developed in me during my earliest years survived all that threatened to destroy it in later years."[31]

In congruence with the appeals of the Mothers' Association, women acted as the standard-bearers of religious practice. They attended Mass at a greater rate than men. While visitation reports complained about the participation of men, they never grumbled about women. The reports from the diocese of Trier included a gendered breakdown of Easter statistics indicating that men rarely attended Mass and received communion with less frequency than women.[32] At the pilgrimage site in Neviges, women constituted the majority of the participants. Women's organizations, such as the *Müttervereine,* arranged many Sunday events and most of the workday pilgrims were female as well.[33]

Some evidence indicates cracks in the façade of Catholic feminine unity in support of Catholic values - individual women sometimes chafed under these expectations. Isolated examples exist where Catholic women opposed Church teaching on birth control. For example, from two to five percent of participants in a rare 1931 Church survey opposed Church teachings on sexuality and family planning.[34] Although these numbers are small, any open defiance of Church teaching by devout mothers was exceptional and indicative of fissures beneath the surface of otherwise loyal congregations. In an era of dire economic need and improved access to birth control,[35] it is possible that tension existed between priests and women. However, clergy edited the journals published by lay women and oversaw the leadership of women's organizations. This patriarchal oversight limited the amount of public dissent over the probably contentious issue of family planning.

During the Third Reich, women eagerly rose to the challenges that Nazis posed to Catholicism. Mistrustful of institutional Christianity, the National Socialist state removed Catholic influence from the public sphere by dissolving most of its male associations, removing confessional influence from schools, cancelling outdoor events, and censoring the press. National Socialist leadership generally tolerated a greater degree of religious autonomy within the walls of churches and in the home. On the one hand, they preferred peace with the vocal Catholic minority after the antagonistic

---

[30] "Weißer Sonntag".

[31] Kranz, *Eine katholische Jugend im Dritten Reich*, 31-40.

[32] BAT Abt. 40, Nr. 362: "Dekanat Ottweiler" and "Dekanat Schweich".

[33] KaN 500: Pilgerstatistik, 1913-1929; KaN 28: Wallfahrtschronik, 1919-1940.

[34] Liedhegener, "Gottessuche, Kirchenkritik und Glaubenstreue", 348-351.

[35] Roos, "Weimar's Crisis through the Lens of Gender", 86.

and public Church Struggles of 1934 to 1937. Furthermore, NSDAP (National Socialist German Workers' Party) leaders seemed to attack men retaining aspects of Catholic identity more virulently than women who perpetuated devotion despite their totalitarian designs on the private as well as the public sphere.[36] In fact, they tolerated the publication of *Mutter und Frau* far longer than other Catholic journals because its contents converged with Nazi pro-natal policies for Aryan women. In this context, women became even more integral to the survival of Catholic traditions. Although emphasis on female domesticity persisted, women took advantage of their importance to the private sphere during the Nazi dictatorship to exercise even more power within the Church than they had during the 1920s. With a reduced role in schools and no youth groups, the clergy asked a loyal generation of Catholic mothers to preserve the spirituality of the Catholic population. In return, women became indispensable to the persistence of Catholicism and autonomous instructors of religious morality.

Priests aimed to make the family a micro-parish. On the eve of World War II, Hermann Klens declared that the "decisive task" of the Church was to "enable the woman and mother to organize the family as a small Church. ... She must be the focal point of all religious efforts."[37] Parish women instituted training sessions to prepare fellow mothers for this new task, previously undertaken by teachers and youth leaders. Parishes initiated special courses led by women on teaching Catechism and the Bible, while Mothers' Associations formed "conversation circles" for women overseeing First Communion or marriage preparation. Women performed tasks in the home that were once accomplished in school.[38] They now monitored attendance at workday masses as well. Before Nazi restrictions on the role of the Church in schools, religion instructors, Catholic schoolteachers, and clergy took children to morning Mass two or three times a week before the start of classes.[39]

Although some women undoubtedly disliked the burden of these new religious responsibilities, many embraced them to assist the Church and increase their own authority. One report commented: "Many women show much courage and loyalty in their religious and moral sense, up to the point of heroism. ... And it is not only a small core of loyalists that we can count on."[40] Some examples indicate that the steadfastness of women to Catholicism even sparked conflict at home. Men or children regularly critiqued pastoral letters for their politics or dry delivery, but women defended the clergy.[41] These examples suggest that Catholic mothers viewed a threat to the clergy as a challenge to their own power within the home. It is possible that they responded to the clergy's call for a more active role, not merely out of passive obedience, but from concern for a religious sphere that formed the basis of their moral authority.

---

[36] O'Sullivan, "An Eroding Milieu?".

[37] AEK, CR I 22.20, 2: Müttervereine, 1933-1941, Hermann Klens to Kardinal Schulte: Fragen der Frauenseelsorge, 1939.

[38] AEK, CR I 14.2, 10: Essen Alstadt-Mitte-Dekanatsbericht über 1939.

[39] "Unsere Kinder in der Werktagsmesse".

[40] AEK, CR I 22.20, 2: Hermann Klens to Schulte: Fragen der Seelsorge, 1939.

[41] HstAD, RW 35-9: Geheime Staatspolizei-Staatspolizei Aachen, Katholische Kirche 1941-1944, Betrifft: Hirtenbriefe über die religiöse Lage in Deutschland, 25 March 1942.

As many historians have noted, few women of this era challenged clerical associational control or Church positions about maternity, birth control, and popular culture. Ursula Baumann argues that the period after 1918 represented a "shift toward a more reactionary position" by Christian women that matched the emphasis on domesticity and patriarchy by the clergy.[42] Other work on German and Western European women suggests that economic and political volatility prevented the development of gender equality in many social and cultural spheres during the interwar years.[43]

The analysis of the Catholic Mothers' Associations supports this portrayal of the 1920s. However, these Christian mothers became active outside the home despite their affirmation of domestic femininity, and used maternal themes to create opportunities for greater equality. Through their mobilization in the Mothers' Associations, they contributed to the political platforms of the Centre Party and increased their moral authority within the Church. As the Nazis restricted male associations, Catholicism became even more feminized. This process empowered Catholic women within their own cultural context by granting them authority in public matters of piety, spirituality, and morality.[44]

CATHOLIC YOUTH

Many scholars credit the Catholic Youth Movement, which integrated the emphasis on nature, music, and critiques of bourgeois society by non-confessional youth into the practice of Catholicism, with revitalizing the Church for a brief time in the late Weimar Republic.[45] This movement's ideas spread from a few elite organizations, such as *Quickborn* and *Bund Neudeutschland*, to influence how young Catholics of all social classes understood their roles within religious communities. Young men in numerous German associations for Catholics expressed masculine forms of religious identity more forcefully in the public sphere. However, Catholic girls also used the ideas of the youth movement to acquire acceptance for their professional activities and public forms of feminine piety.

The cultural 'feminization' of Christianity starting in the nineteenth century caused some men to avoid religious rituals in the Weimar era. After World War I, the feminine image of the Church caused it great difficulty because of the competing masculine identities for young men that emerged. On the one hand, a new cult of masculinity arose after the camaraderie of the trench experience. George Mosse demonstrates that during the 1920s, films, memoirs, and monuments glorified the male war experience, creating a "new religion" where war volunteers represented the "saints and martyrs".[46] On the other hand, members of the labor, women's, and

---

[42] Baumann, "Religion, Emancipation, and Politics", 301-302.
[43] Roos, "Weimar's Crisis Through the Lens of Gender", 86; Bridenthal, Grossmann and Kaplan, *When Biology Became Destiny*; Hagemann, *Frauenalltag und Männerpolitik*; Grayzel, *Women's Identities at War*.
[44] For the theoretical stimulus of this interpretation, see Taylor Allen, *Feminism*.
[45] Ruff, *The Wayward Flock*, 20-27, 40-41.
[46] Mosse, *Fallen Soldiers*.

peace movements viewed the war as a transition that would improve partnership in marriage.[47] As a result of decades of 'feminization' in the eyes of non-Catholics and the strict hierarchy and moral codes of the Church, Catholicism struggled to define a youthful male image in accordance with these new forms of masculinity. For example, one author from *Die Wacht* complained that he often heard from men: "The rosary is only for old and fragile women."[48]

Men left Church-affiliated associations in droves. Membership in the People's Association for Catholic Germany declined from 805,000 in 1914 to 308,000 in 1932 because the group retreated from its traditional emphasis on social justice and adhered more strictly to clerical doctrine. Furthermore, 800,000 men left Catholic workers' clubs during the Weimar era in favor of socialism or communism because the Church privileged religious life over economic needs.[49] Catholicism, moreover, lost many male believers in the early 1920s because of its failure to appeal to the competing visions of masculinity after the Great War.[50]

During the second half of the Weimar period, however, the Catholic Youth Movement introduced a new image for young Catholic men.[51] First, it emphasized hiking, nature, and athletics. A member of the *Sturmschar*, a section of the *Katholischen Jungmännerverband* inspired by the Youth Movement, wrote: "We steel ourselves and train our bodies. We live simply and honestly in close connection with nature."[52] Besides emphasizing physical activity and nature, the Catholic Youth Movement promoted strict morality. Youth members guarded their moral purity by abstaining from alcohol and sexual relationships. In fact, youth leaders encouraged a revival of 'chivalry'.[53] The calls for physical fitness and "a new chivalry" reawakened central themes of mainstream nineteenth-century masculinity in an era when bourgeois rhetoric encouraged men to remain physically healthy in order to maintain moral strength.[54]

Toward the end of the 1920s, 'martial' or militarized masculinity became more hegemonic among the generation that had just missed fighting in the war.[55] Reacting to this more aggressive male image, Catholic organizations also portrayed their men as militant fighters. In his recent article, Raymond C. Sun demonstrates how struggling workers' associations courted men with militant rhetoric.[56] While these appeals failed in the realm of adult workers, they achieved success with young men. In the second half of the decade, the Catholic Youth Movement couched its rhetoric in the language of war memory.[57] For example, an article describing a meeting of

---

[47] Hagemann, "Introduction".

[48] "Zur Einkehr: Der Rosenkranz, das Gebet der Männer".

[49] Sun, "Catholic-Marxist Competition"; Köhler, "Ausbruch aus dem katholischen Milieu?", 130.

[50] For men departing the Church because of its feminine image, see Schank, *'Kölsch-Katholisch'*, 133-134.

[51] Kaufmann, *Katholisches Milieu*, 97-113.

[52] Winandi, *In seiner Spur bleiben für eine bessere Welt!*, 49.

[53] "Nochmals Jungmann und Mädchen".

[54] Sun, "'Hammer Blows'", 255.

[55] Hagemann, "Introduction", 12-15.

[56] Sun, "'Hammer Blows'".

[57] Kaufmann, *Katholisches Milieu*, 97-113.

Sturmschar leadership called upon young men to defend the Catholic faith by "fighting for heaven" and "bringing the sword" to Godlessness.[58] During a national meeting in Trier, *Sturmschar* leadership read a "Vow to Fight for Germany". It called all pious young men to "arm themselves for a fight" with "discipline and order, devotion and brotherly love". Unlike the masculine appeals to Catholic workers analysed by Sun, the new masculinity of the Catholic Youth Movement inspired religious revival. Mass demonstrations of Catholic youth became typical. Observing the national meeting in Trier, one reporter wrote, "Whoever saw the *Katholischer Jungmännerverband* at its meeting in Essen five years ago and first saw it again in Trier, would not recognize it. … What have changed are the masses of youth."[59] The dynamism of young Catholic men contrasted sharply with the decline of adult males affiliated with Church institutions and the Centre Party.

The emphasis on new forms of male piety created enthusiasm beyond the boundaries of the Catholic Youth Movement. Some adult men practiced Catholicism while simultaneously abandoning the Centre Party and its affiliated organizations, such as the People's Association. The enthusiasm of young men generated stronger male participation in pilgrimages. In the late 1920s and 1930s, the Marian shrine of Neviges boasted strong involvement from men and boys. One newspaper reported on the worship of working-class men: "What struck the Cologne participants were the large throngs of men; men of all ages. At the main mass, at the steps of the main altar, and at the prayers, one saw almost only men."[60] The attraction of Neviges resulted in part from the introduction in 1932 of "*Sturmandachten*", a Mass where believers 'stormed' the heart of the Virgin Mary and took part in emotional prayer and fierce devotion.[61] These rituals included assertive hymns of Catholic identity favored by the Catholic Youth Movement as well as organized chants and structured communal prayer. Although men became less prominent in political Catholicism, masculine worship increased in realms of piety usually gendered as feminine.

The revival of male youth receded as the Nazi campaign against public Catholicism intensified from 1935-1945. The NSDAP removed clerical oversight from schools, dissolved youth groups, restricted adult associations, and prohibited Catholic newspapers and journals. As the regime took a harder line about Church policy, however, the Church became more conciliatory. The hardship and uncertainty that fuelled the religious reawakening receded as Germans increasingly supported National Socialist rule and economic conditions appeared to improve. The core of the Catholic Youth Movement remained resistant to National Socialism and continued underground meetings. However, the Church and the majority of the youth movement, supportive of many aspects of Nazism, accepted the dissolutions of youth groups and associations in relative peace after 1935 in exchange for religious freedom within the privacy of church and home.[62] During the 1930s, young Catholic men, once contributors to

---

[58] "Wir wollen! Wacht-Rufe".

[59] Clemens, *Ruf von Trier*, 192.

[60] KaN 28: *Kath. Kirchenzeitung der Pfarre St. Ursula, Köln*, July 11, 1926; "Pilgerfahrt der Zwölfhundert: Machtvolle Kundgebung der hl. Familie in Neviges", July 12, 1932; "Bußprozession in Wuppertal: Eine Anregung", 1932.

[61] Haun, *Die Wallfahrt nach Neviges*.

[62] Schellenberger, *Katholische Jugend und Drittes Reich*.

religious life, lapsed into growing spiritual indifference. The Church lost young men as a result of the dissolution of their organizations. While mothers persevered in their private religious roles, the nature of the Nazi dictatorship made public male piety more difficult.

Through both coercion and consent in the Hitler Youth (HJ), the Nazis constructed a hegemonic model of youthful masculinity that excluded Catholicism. Like the Catholic Youth of the 1920s, the HJ encouraged boys to be aggressive, physical, active, and loyal to their *Volksgemeinschaft*. They tied these ideals to membership in the Hitler Youth and National Socialist ideology and pressured children to reject confessional organization. Participation of young men in mandatory state programs during the Third Reich demonstrated the ways that the feminine image of Catholicism inhibited male devotion. Programs such as the Land Year, the Labor Service, and the Land Service forced young people to live away from home and parish under the direction of anti-Catholic youth leaders, who confiscated religious publications and encouraged the children to abandon their parents' doctrines.[63]

The clergy tried unsuccessfully to convince young people to maintain their faith despite National Socialist pressure. Despite pleas from the clergy for letters that they requested in pre-departure preparation,[64] only 10 percent of the Catholic Land Year, Labor Service, and Land Service participants wrote back to their parishes by 1939.[65] According to a study of religious practice in 1937, mass attendance also fell far below the usual rate of participation for these boys in their home parishes.[66] The primary cause of this male indifference was pressure from youth leaders and peers. For example, one Land Year participant wrote: "Yesterday night, six to seven of the strongest boys came and cut my hair like a priest. The group leaders laugh at me because I pray at the table."[67] The Nazis made institutional Catholicism less appealing to boys by perpetuating past stereotypes of the Catholic Church as feminine. Although a small devoted core of enthusiasts for the Catholic Youth Movement retained a prominent religious identity, most boys assimilated into the National Socialist state.

An examination of the male youth illustrates the fluidity of feminized Christianity. The cultural association of Catholicism with femininity aided Hitler Youth attempts to marginalize the Catholic Youth Movement. Both fear of persecution and enthusiasm for Nazism meant that only the most committed members remained loyal to their parish groups throughout the Third Reich. At the same time, the Catholic Youth Movement was a new attempt by young men to dominate the public life of the Catholic community. By seizing the most prominent position in public pilgrimages and demonstrations, they pushed the more numerous women further into the private sphere. Similar to men's organizations, such as the Kolping Associations and the St

---

[63] USHMM, RG-15.007M: Records for the *Reichssicherheitshauptamt*, Reel 46, "Katholisches Elternhaus und Landjahr".

[64] USHMM, RG-15.007M: Chaplain Hartel to Land Year children.

[65] "Referat Kallers über die Wandernde Kirche, 22 August 1940".

[66] AEK, Gen. I 4.31: Wandernde Kirche, 1934-1941: Bericht über die Tagung des Katholischen Seelsorgedienstes für die Wandernde Kirche am 14./ 15. Dezember 1937.

[67] AEK, Gen. I 26.53: Landjahr der Schulentlassenen, 1934-1940: Joseph Jochum to his parents, Oedenkoven, 13 May 1935.

Sebastian Shooting Clubs, they developed a code of masculine behavior that resonated with men and refuted the stereotype of the 'feminized Church.'

The Catholic Youth Movement also altered the relationship of girls to the Catholic gender values of the early twentieth century. In her examination of the KDF, female members of the Centre Party, and the Catholic association for female teachers, Birgit Sack argues that a generational conflict developed between young and adult women of the Catholic milieu over issues such as sexuality, birth control, abortion, and professional life in the late 1920s.[68] In the relationship between the Mothers' Associations, Marian Congregations, and the *Heliand-Bund*, no open generational conflict existed. Rather, subtle differences emerged where Catholic girls sought more maneuverability within the confines of Catholic patriarchy.

The Marian Congregations (*Jungfraukongregationen*), founded in the late nineteenth century, organized the activities of female parish youth around worship of the Virgin Mary. Mary was the "soul of their community" and girls regularly heard speeches from male clergy about "female chastity and Marian ideals".[69] This focus on Marian piety and sexual purity perpetuated the ultramontane gender values of the nineteenth century. Von Olenhusen views such organizations as part of the Catholic milieu's attempt to thwart the values of the women's movement and restrict emancipation.[70]

The leadership, piety, and morality of the congregations during the 1920s illustrate their traditionally rigid approach. In existence at the parish level for decades, the congregations organized on a national level in the late 1920s under the leadership of Prelate Klens. While long-serving regional prelates and local priests maintained strict oversight of the Marian Congregations, older lay women led weekly activities. For example, the Prefect of a group in Essen-Steele, a member since 1878, celebrated her 25th anniversary in a leadership role in 1928.[71] Such older leaders demanded adherence to the ideal of feminine domestic piety. In published responses to letters of inquiry from her 170,000 subscribers, Aenne Unterberg, editor of the organization's journal, reminded girls of their duty to guard the piety of men. In 1932, she asked one congregation member to convince her brother not to convert to Protestantism, and she warned another girl to bring her fiancé back to Catholicism before marrying him.[72] Finally, journal leaders expected strict chastity from their members before marriage. Typical speeches for individual groups included "Emergency and Danger for the Girl's Soul in Modern Times" and "Catholic Female Youth and their Stance toward Marriage and Family in Opposition to Modern Morality". These appeals mirrored the conservative turn of the Centre Party during the late 1920s. For example, associations for female schoolteachers also demanded chastity from their members so that they would set a good example for their students.[73] Clergy feared that the

---

[68] Sack, *Zwischen relgiöser Bindung und moderner Gesellschaft*, 154-165, 250-273.

[69] "Verbandsfamilie"; "Verbandsfamilie - St. Urbanus in Buer".

[70] Götz von Olenhusen, "Die Feminisierung von Religion", 17-19.

[71] "Verbandsfamilie"; "Verbandsfamilie - Diözesanverband Köln"; "Verbandsfamilie - Jungfraukongregation in St. Bonifaz in Duisburg".

[72] "Kranzbriefe"; Ibid., 84; KFD 675: Führer durch die Zeitschriften.

[73] "Verbandsfamilie-Breslau"; Sack, *Zwischen religiöser Bindung und moderner Gesellschaft*, 152-154.

growing number of girls in the professions and the increased appeal of consumer culture would damage the sexual values of young women.

Much like the Mothers' Associations, Marian Congregations asked women to care for the morality of men as well as themselves. When discussing the dangers of the workplace, Aenne Unterberg wrote: "The danger is present that after hard, empty labor, the burning desire for pleasure in the evening will lead ... girls to boys who make the slightest mention of love." However, she also believed that women in the workplace were responsible for guarding male purity as well as their own: "Girls have a sacred duty in the factory: they must convert men who no longer understand the chastity and honor of a woman because of their environment."[74] In another example from 1928, a young man wrote to *Der Kranz* complaining about a female speaker who demanded more chivalry from men. He said that the more pressing need was for girls who could teach young men "authentic Christian manliness". The female journal editors agreed with the young man, calling it the "duty" of young women to help boys find their "buried chivalry".[75] Finally, when the German bishops complained about the state of alcohol abuse, the girls' congregations undertook a week of abstinence. They expected the girls to win over their men for this "week of sacrifice", asking them to make the home so "comfortable" that the men would not seek pleasure in the "tavern".[76] As in the Mothers' Associations, public morality was a feminine area of responsibility.

It is not clear whether Catholic girls accepted the rhetoric on sexuality from Church leadership. Tension emerged between older and younger generations about sexuality, especially during the Third Reich. Catholic prelates expressed concern about the loosening of sexual mores among younger women. Hermann Klens argued that "sexual themes" offered the gravest concern for religious work among females.[77] One report complained that teenagers displayed little regard for honor, and that too many young women attended "questionable" bars, cabarets, theatres, and movies in a "spirit of immorality".[78]

Frequently, the encouragement of sexual experimentation by elements of Nazi youth leadership exasperated Catholic women and clergy alike. Dagmar Herzog argues that several Nazi youth leaders advocated pre-marital sex. The Labor Service organized co-ed social events to find partners for young people while they were away from home. Catholic leadership clashed with the regime throughout the 1930s and 1940s about the Nazis' inconsistent stances on sexuality. While NSDAP leaders made public pronouncements in support of marriage and maternal roles for women, radical elements within the party simultaneously promoted more open sexual attitudes.[79] Michael H. Kater's recent book about the Hitler Youth confirms Herzog's findings. According to his research, 900 young women from the League of German Girls (BDM) departed the Nuremburg Party Rally of 1936 pregnant and over half of them did not

---

[74] "Wie wir das Leben sehen!".
[75] "Fragen wir uns einmal...".
[76] "Was geht uns die Alkoholfrage an?".
[77] AEK CR I 22.20, 2: Hermann Klens to Kardinal Schulte: Fragen der Frauenseelsorge, 1939.
[78] AEK CR I 22.20, 2: "Die religiöse und sittliche Lage der Frauenwelt", 1938.
[79] Herzog, *Sex after Fascism*, 61-62.

know the identity of the father.[80] Mothers shuddered at the thought of their youth under the tutelage of authority figures encouraging pre-marital sex. For example, the lay leader of the *Mädchenschutzverein* in Aachen held several lectures for mothers and girls condemning the sexual practices of the Land Year and Labor Service.[81] Women perpetuated their moral values in opposition to those of Nazi men, while their daughters discovered an opportunity to escape their parents' dogmas on sexuality in youth programs. It would seem that at least some members of the Marian Congregations utilized the Nazi youth programs to escape the inflexible teachings on sexuality by their Catholic associations.

Typically, members of the Girls' Congregations attempted more subtle challenges to the ideal of feminine domesticity. The national journal, *Der Kranz*, maintained a more open attitude toward female employment than *Die Mutter*. On one hand, journal editors strongly encouraged female domesticity. They argued that a woman's God-given role was in the home and encouraged women who had to work to seek domestic labor which would train them for their future roles as wives and mothers. On the other hand, they recognized the economic reality of 11 million working women during the Weimar Republic. They requested group members to write in about their work experiences and published several of these letters. Through their commentary and selection of letters, journal editors constructed a narrative of struggle and perseverance in the workplace.

Editors and readers depicted female professionalism as an albatross whether one worked in an office, the factory, or as a sales clerk. Work was 'struggle' because it contradicted a woman's 'natural' role as mother and wife. Several letters complained about exposure to flexible sexual morality in the workplace and the toll that paid work took on their labor in the home. Young Catholic women were to overcome this 'burden' through faith in the aid of the Virgin Mary and 'proper femininity'. Besides praying for intercession, they needed their feminine virtues to make the workplace morally pure. Adopting the rhetoric of "spiritual motherhood" (*geistige Müttterlichkeit*), congregation leaders asked young women to utilize their feminine values in order to improve the quality of the public sphere. *Der Kranz* advised young women: "In the cool social and professional setting, where there is little personal contact, bring love: affectionate, understanding, cooperative, and maternal love!"

In their published letters about professional employment, some girls departed slightly from the editors' overarching narrative. A few took the notion of "spiritual motherhood" to the point that they viewed the workplace rather than the home as their "God-given role". There were several examples of religious young women finding fulfilment through professional labor. One young textile worker wrote: "Textile work means more to me than just making enough money to live; it is also a life duty. ... Through this work, I earn my bread, but I also serve God and other people ... the results of my work will without doubt find their way to people and be useful." A bank teller and an office assistant both found meaning in their labor through their feelings of power and accomplishment when they gained the trust of their superiors as well as increased responsibility. In sum, some young Catholic women viewed the workplace

---

[80] Kater, *Hitler Youth*, 108.

[81] HStAD, RW 35-9: Betrifft: Katholischer Mädchenschutzverein, 16 November 1942.

as fulfilling and natural for them as the home, despite their leaders' wish that they understand it as an unnatural condition.[82]

The members of the Marian Congregations also joined the sphere of public piety dominated by the young men in the demonstrative culture of the late 1920s and early 1930s. Similar to young men, young women emphasized public displays of Catholic loyalty by wearing the Congregation's symbol in public and by carrying their banners in street processions. They also marched in demonstrations of Catholic identity that had become trademarks of the 'martial masculinity'. One article declared, "Enter the … struggle for public life without fear and with clear goals. You want to demonstrate in public the will of the German Catholic Youth. Where things are great and worthwhile for the youth, girls and women have not failed! We are also participants!"[83] *Der Kranz* tempered this approach somewhat in 1932:

> We sisters are happy about our Catholic young men! If they shout and march through the streets carrying torches, then we must silently stand aside with the wish that there will always be worldly carriers of Christ's message. … The way they write '*Sturm*' on their banners and march through the streets is something that we cannot and should not do. That is the nature of boys! … And we must live within our nature as girls and women! It is quieter, contemplative and deeper.[84]

While some girls participated in the street culture of the late Weimar era, the leaders of the Congregations viewed such public piety as a violation of the domestic ideal supported by Church leadership.

Educated daughters of middle-class Catholic families founded the Heliand-Bund, an elite organization that offered more resistance to the ideals of domestic piety while remaining within the framework of Church teaching about women. The origins and structure of this group offered it more freedom from the institutional Church. Inspired by the fusion of the German Youth Movement with Catholic youth activities in *Bund Neudeutschland*, Catholic girls studying in the *Gymnasium* founded the *Heliand-Bund* in the mid-1920s. Women in their teens and early twenties assumed leadership as the group grew to 10,000 members by the end of World War II. They required a spiritual leader to receive official Church recognition, a role filled by the Jesuit Georg Kifinger. Father Kifinger rode a motorcycle and went by "Kif", leaving most of the organization's decisions to its young leaders.[85] The youthfulness of their leadership and the autonomy granted to them by their spiritual advisor made this the most independent Catholic girls' organization in Germany.

Independent male youth organizations, such as *Quickborn* and *Bund Neudeutschland*, stood at the forefront of the Catholic Youth Movement, but the young women who founded Heliand raised significant concerns from the Catholic commu-

---

[82] "Verbandfamilie-Einmütige Zusammenarbeit"; "Dr. Ernst Breit: Vor dem Maialtar"; "Wie wir das Leben sehen!", 50-51, 144-161, 172-189.

[83] "Junge Front".

[84] Heinemann, "Aufbruch katholischer Jugend!".

[85] Doerry, *Mädchen- und Frauenbildung*, 10-12.

nity. The very idea of an association with girls in roles usually deemed masculine caused dissonance with Catholic sensibilities. In the chronicle of a local branch of Heliand in southern Germany, a young leader asked: "A girl's youth movement? Is this even possible?"[86] Families and parish communities struggled with the idea of their daughters camping, meeting, praying, and organizing charity work without the direct supervision of adults. The group arranged "parent evenings" in order to assuage the fears of potential new members.[87] A group leader from Neuhausen reported that her 'strict' father articulated reservations about an association that caused her to wait for a streetcar to take her home at 10:30 on weekday evenings.[88] Although boys formed similar groups, the Heliand girls required more initiative and independence to participate in the same activities as *Quickborn* and *Bund Neudeutschland* boys.

Despite this freedom from institutional oversight, *Heliand* emphasized many of the same themes in the areas of Marian piety and morality as other confessional women's organizations of the Weimar Republic and the Third Reich. The Virgin Mary remained important, if not central, to the *Heliand-Bund*. The 1932 version of their "guiding principles" (*Leitsätze*) asserted: "Mary, the Virgin Mother, is the model of authentic femininity and maternal service." These principles also demanded strict abstinence from sex or contact with boys. A Heliand speech from 1931 proclaimed: "A woman's life must be an evolution toward motherhood. Therefore sexuality should never disturb this pure womanly honour."[89] "Young Man and Girl" was frequently the title of conversation evenings in branch meetings and they emphasized the imperative of feminine purity in midst of challenges from modern industrialization and consumer society. The girls were also trained to become role models of morality for the rest of society. One lecturer suggested: "In the business of public life, the woman is influential through her presence and example. Her pure nature as a woman has a universal meaning. The woman is a benchmark for the culture of a people, where one can measure moral values."[90] The founders of the *Heliand-Bund* remained devoted to the ideals of Marian piety and their role as moral guardians.

Although strict on issues of morality, the *Heliand-Bund* experimented with forms of piety not typical of 'feminized' Catholicism. The Virgin Mary was important to the Heliand Bund, but they placed worship of Jesus at the forefront of their prayer. In an attempt to tone down what they viewed as superstitious attachments to Mary, Heliand emphasized the importance of Jesus above all other religious figures.[91] The three most common forms of worship in the *Heliand-Bund* differed radically from the passive practice of mainstream associations for female youth. Spiritual life centred on communal Mass, Christ discussion circles (*Christuskreise*), and the spiritual exercises of the Jesuits. In each of these expressions of faith, the organization encouraged intellectual study of the Bible and active participation by girls. This crossover into

---

[86] LaS, T-84. Archiv des Heliand-Bundes: 083, Liebfrauengau, 1926-1968, "Aus der ersten Chronik, von 28.8.1926."

[87] Doerry, *Mädchen- und Frauenbildung*, 10, 15; *Rundbrief des Heliandbundes Sommer 1932*.

[88] LaS, T-84. 083: Liebfrauengau, 1926-1968, "Anfänge des Heliand-Bundes."

[89] LaS, T-84. 338: Referate/Aufsätze vor 1945, "Mütterlichkeit."

[90] Schaeffler-Laub, *Der Heliandbund in seinen Gründungsjahren*, 20, 42, 83, 85-86.

[91] LaS, T-84. 339: 1a, Vorträge, Aufsätze, Predigten, "HH Domvikar Ziegelbauer, "Christozentrische Frömmigkeit."

the 'masculine' piety of male youth formed part of a wider embrace of the Liturgical Movement in the 1920s and 1930s. The Liturgical Movement offered alternative rituals where the laity played a more active role in 'communal masses' and where participants recited prayers in German rather than Latin. Within the framework of these masses in the *Heliand-Bund*, members served as altar girls long before the reforms of the Second Vatican Council in the 1960s.[92] By adopting the religious practice of male Catholic youth, Heliand girls broke with the feminine religiosity associated with late nineteenth-century and early twentieth-century Catholicism.

The devotion to the Liturgical Movement, as well as the principles of the Catholic Youth Movement, provided these middle-class girls with occasions to express their religious identities publicly. They sought opportunities at the National Catholic Congress of 1931 to openly display their devotion. The group's journal declared: "Yes, finally we are allowed to demonstrate for the Catholic public. We observe that we girls can also march in step with a disciplined row, singing hiking songs."[93] They sent hundreds of girls to the national demonstrations of Catholic Youth throughout the 1930s.[94] Some members of the *Heliand-Bund*, however, attempted to feminize this public piety. For example, Alice Schnee described the public behavior of a local celebration: "The Heliand youth chant through the streets! Honestly the marching in step and sharp turns are not completely successful. We are not men. We are girls – soon to be women. We want to serve the Fatherland with helpful love and a soldierly attitude does not belong." In a speech, the fifteen-year-old Bertl Schudrowitz explained: "And we, the young Church have important tasks. ... But not with fire and sword, but rather with the love of our God and master Jesus Christ."[95] While girls used the Liturgical Movement to gain access to the previously restricted world of public piety, they also tried to define this entry into the public sphere as feminine. They distinguished between their public marches and the martial masculinity of male youth.

The non-religious activities of Heliand also provided subtle subversions of the Catholic ideal of feminine domesticity. The organization encouraged sports for girls. "Body Culture" was a frequently discussed theme among the local branches and hiking became a staple of the association. They also encouraged gymnastics, folk dancing, and other non-competitive forms of exercise. In providing opportunities for sport, Heliand demanded adherence to gender norms. In an essay about girls' sports, one leader from Offenbach wrote: "We must leave the competitive sports to the boys. They are born to fight; it is natural law. We are only allowed to partake in sports in so far as it helps us maintain the health of our bodies and revive our spirit."[96] Despite this separation of spheres within sports participation, Heliand girls viewed their secular activities as emancipatory. Isa Paulus recalled that hiking, folk dancing, travelling, and "sleeping on straw" in barns without supervision were "outrageous" endeavors

---

[92] Doerry, *Mädchen- und Frauenbildung*, 31; Schaeffler-Laub, *Der Heliandbund in seinen Gründungsjahren*, 34, 90.

[93] *Rundbrief des Heliandbundes*, Christkönigsfest 1932, 11-12.

[94] LaS, T-84. 313: Liebfrauengau, 1945-1952, "Aus der Heliand Geschichte Landshuts", no date.

[95] Doerry, *Mädchen- und Frauenbildung*, 35; Schaeffler-Laub, *Der Heliandbund in seinen Gründungsjahren*, 29.

[96] LaS, T-84. 057: Rundbriefe Bundesamt, 1927-1968, "Rundbrief 1931- Gedanken über den Frauensport."

for girls from well-regarded families. Participation in Heliand allowed them to "break out of the sheltered family circle".[97] Such examples indicate that despite the powerful Catholic rhetoric about feminine domesticity, religious girls used associational life as a release from household expectations.

Perhaps the most important element of the *Heliand-Bund* was its approach to the future careers of young members. Like other groups, the association emphasized maternal responsibilities and values for women.[98] Nonetheless, it aimed to prepare girls for professional careers. When founding a new branch of Heliand, one young woman wrote: "Girls should make themselves free and later do more than stand at the oven; rather they must be active in the professions, teaching, and education. This is a result of the emergency of our times."[99] This statement adhered in part to Catholic teaching about working women. It implied that women only should pursue careers because it was necessary during difficult economic periods. However, the association provided members with leadership roles, charitable opportunities, lectures, and discussion groups to enrich their education and prepare them for a life in the workforce. Heliand assumed educated girls would work in careers not usually reserved for women. For example, Maria Bauer wrote:

> We must undertake self-education to strive for advancement. We must prepare ourselves to use our especially feminine traits to solve the difficult problems of the modern world. Our groups should produce practical and efficient girls for a public life. Recently someone asked me, 'Are there more girls like Dr. ... from Heliand? Such a marvelous woman and mother is rare.'

Maria's words indicate Heliand's dedication to high academic achievement and professional advancement in the context of 'spiritual motherhood.'[100] They encouraged women to use their specifically feminine traits as positive contributions to a society struggling with economic depression and political turmoil. This faith in 'spiritual motherhood' did not prevent girls from practicing professions usually reserved for men; several Heliand girls became doctors and lawyers as well as teachers, social workers, and nuns.

Like the Mothers' Associations and the Marian Congregations, *Heliand-Bund* members utilized opportunities from confessional associations to seize a greater role within the public sphere. While remaining within the framework of Catholic teachings about feminine domesticity, the youthful leaders of the Heliand-Bund undertook some of the most progressive steps toward prominent roles for women in rituals. Furthermore, they attempted a reconciliation of Christianity and careers for women. While they did not openly confront or dissent against Catholic patriarchy, they used the opportunities available to them within the Catholic Youth Movement to subtly challenge the ideals of feminine piety and domestic motherhood. Heliand added aspects of femininity to the otherwise masculine public sphere of the German Catholic community.

---

[97] Schaeffler-Laub, *Der Heliandbund in seinen Gründungsjahren*, 21.
[98] Doerry, *Mädchen- und Frauenbildung*, 18.
[99] LaS, T-84. 083: Liebfrauen-Gau, 1926-1968, "Aus der ersten Chronik, von 28.8.1926."
[100] LaS, T-84. 057: Rundbriefe Bundesamt, 1927-1968, "Rundbrief 1931: Maria Bauer, Johannisgruppe

CONCLUSION

The interwar period was a time of both continuity and change for gender norms in German Catholicism. The Mothers' Associations encouraged values other historians have associated with the feminization of Christianity during the nineteenth century. They advocated faith in the Virgin Mary, motherhood, domesticity, emotional piety, maternal religious instruction of children, and feminine oversight of the family's morality. The reorganization of these associations under the guidelines of Catholic Action in the late 1920s, however, increased the public visibility of its members. Despite the intent of the clergy to limit the autonomy of the laity, women of the Mothers' Associations benefited more from this reform movement than most other associations. After decades of using these associations to inhibit female entrance into the public sphere, this reform offered restricted opportunities for female agency. Mothers gained prominent positions within Church life and moral authority as the clergy encouraged their roles as disciplinarians in the home. With Catholic associational life severely damaged during the late Nazi years, mothers became even more important to the survival of Catholic traditions. While fighting for feminine domesticity, these women gained increased power in the family and greater access to politics and parish leadership roles.

The Catholic Youth Movement altered gender roles for both boys and girls. The male youth found new ways for men to dominate the public sphere of religious life. As women's associations became more prominent, the new cult of martial masculinity became a centrepiece of public demonstrations of Catholic identity and even pilgrimages that had been previously dominated by women. The militarization of Catholic processions undermines any universal use of the feminization of religion thesis and illustrates how male associations exercised hegemony over public rituals, even if men were less prevalent than women at the communion rail and in the confessional.

Young women remained enthralled by the ideal of feminine domesticity but nevertheless utilized the youth movement to gain greater access to public ritual and the public sphere. The Marian Congregations, a mainstream organization of hundreds of thousands, remained under the careful scrutiny of parish priests and older women. It stressed emotional piety, maternal values, and spiritual motherhood in the workplace. At the same time some of its members sought to reconcile fulfilment at work with religious practice, and they marched in public demonstrations. The *Heliand-Bund* was much more progressive in its challenge to feminine domesticity. They remained within the framework of Catholic teaching but sought greater professional and religious flexibility in the Church's approach to women. While a clear minority, Heliand represented an active attempt by young middle-class Catholic women to maneuver beyond the rigid ultramontane boundaries of the nineteenth century.

Analysis of these primarily female associations illustrates the difficulty with any general application of the feminization of religion thesis in context of interwar German Catholicism. Women represented the majority of participants, but the Catholic community encompassed a diverse mix of men and women from city and countryside. Moral teaching, First Communion preparation, Marian worship, and family prayers continued as spheres for urban and rural mothers. Men remained the public carriers of Catholic identity and they maintained central roles in street rituals despite the disintegration of the People's Association and the Centre Party. Male youth provide one example of how men used values associated with the masculine areas of influence, such as work, sports, or military, to retain places of prominence in the patriarchal order of the Catholic community. Young Catholic women provide another example in their attempts, always tentative and subtle, to challenge this gender order. While remaining within the boundaries of Catholic rhetoric about gender, young women ambiguously sought active roles in public ritual; alternative expressions of faith; and long-term careers beyond Catholic motherhood and feminine domesticity. Partially feminized Christianity was limited and adapted to the everyday needs of each generation.

BIBLIOGRAPHY

Abbreviations

AEK: Historisches Archiv des Erzbistums Köln
AFJ: Archives of the Flemish Jesuits (Archief der Vlaamse Jezuïeten)
AG: Archives of Grail Movement
AKKZG: Arbeitskreis für kirchliche Zeitgeschichte
BAT: Bistumsarchiv Trier
BB: Bondsblad voor Bonden van het Heilig Hart
BME: Archives of the Belgian Southern Province of the Company of Jesus (Archives de la Province Belge Méridionale de la Compagnie de Jésus)
Bode: Bode van het Heilig Hart van Jesus
BZKT: Breslauer Zeitschrift für katholische Theologie
EKZ: Evangelische Kirchen-Zeitung
HPB: Historisch-politische Blätter
HstAD: Hauptstaatsarchiv Düsseldorf
IKZ: Internationale Kirchliche Zeitschrift
KaN: Klosterarchiv Neviges
KFD: Archives of the Katholische Frauengemeinschaft Deutschlands
LaS: Landesarchiv Speyer
MM: Maandelijksche Mededeelingen voor Bonden van het Heilig Hart
PANJ: Provinciaal Archief Nederlandse Jezuïeten (Provincial Archives of the Dutch Jesuits)
PAOD: Archief van de Nederlandse Provincie van de Orde der Dominicanen (Provincial Archives of the Dutch Province of the Order of the Dominicans)
SB: Sonntagsblatt für katholische Christen
SKB: Süddeutsches Kirchenblatt
USHMM: United States Holocaust Memorial Museum
YMCAA: YMCA Archives

Archives

Berg en Dal (NL), Archives Sint Willebrord
Private Collection

Birmingham (UK), University of Birmingham Library
YMCA Archives: A27, A47, A49

Bruges (BE), Episcopal Archives Bruges
File minor seminary 1859-1869

Cologne (DE), Historisches Archiv des Erzbistums Köln (AEK)
CR I 22.20, 2; 14.2, 10
Gen. I 4.31; I 26.53

Derby (UK), Derby Local Studies Library
Manuscripts, BA796.33

Düsseldorf (DE), Archives of the Katholische Frauengemeinschaft Deutschlands (KFD)
675

Düsseldorf (DE), Hauptstaatsarchiv (HstAD)
RW 35-9

Ghent (BE), Episcopal Archives Ghent
Fund minor seminary Sint-Niklaas.

Louvain (BE), KADOC KU Leuven
Archives of the Flemish Jesuits (Archief der Vlaamse Jezuïeten) (AFJ):
Archives of the Leagues of the Sacred Heart (Bonden van het Heilig Hart)
COA 1.6; 1.10; 4.6; 4.7; 6.4; I.1; I.2; I.3; I.7; I.8; I.9; III.2; III.4; III.5; IV.3; V.4; V.10; IX.1
Image Collection
Archives of the Belgian Southern Province of the Company of Jesus (Archives de la Province Belge Meridionale de la Compagnie de Jésus) (BME):
Apostolat de la Prière
II.4

Neviges (DE), Klosterarchiv (KaN)
28, 500

Nijmegen (NL), Katholiek Documentatiecentrum (KDC)
Archives of Grail Movement (AG)
1, 40
Archives Henri Bruning
520
Provinciaal Archief Nederlandse Jezuïeten
(Provincial Archives of the Dutch Jesuits) (PANJ)
345, 913

Roeselare (BE), Archives of Roeselare minor seminary
Fund Zouave corps and Library of the Zouave students

Sint Agatha (NL), Erfgoedcentrum Nederlands Kloosterleven, Archief van de Nederlandse Provincie van de Orde der Dominicanen (Provincial Archives of the Dutch Province of the Order of the Dominicans) (PAOD)
779, 785, 2574, 2775, 5865, 5867, 5869, 6181, 6393, 8097b, 8529

Sint-Niklaas (BE), Archives minor seminary Sint-Niklaas
Logbook of the Literary Society, 1848-1888

Speyer (DE), Landesarchiv Speyer (LaS)
T-84. 057, T-84. 083, T-84. 313, T-84. 338, T-84. 339

Trier (DE), Bistumsarchiv (BAT)
Abt. B III 14, 5, Bd. 1
Abt. 40, Nr. 362

Washington (USA), United States Holocaust Memorial Museum (USHMM)
RG-15.007M

Interview made by Marieke Smulders
Herman van Run, 10 July 2006.

Interviews made by Marjet Derks
Rachel Donders, 19 January 1996.
Dammaris Groothuizen, March 1992.

Interview made by Michael E. O'Sullivan
M.O. in Bad Münstereifel, 17 March 2004.

"Mia van der Kallen". Episode of KRO's radio program Sporen in het achterland *(12 July 1984) with interviews.*

Literature

"Aartsbisdom Herenthout". *Bondsblad voor Bonden van het Heilig Hart*, December (1938), 4.

A.B. "Een monnik-schilder. Pater Raymond van Bergen o.p.". *Opgang* (1924), 892-893.

Abel, Wilhelm. *Massenarmut und Hungerkrisen im vorindustriellen Deutschland*. Göttingen, 1986.

Abrams, Lynn. *The Making of the Modern Woman*. London, 2002.

Accati, Luisa "Explicit Meanings: Catholicism, Matriarchy and the Distinctive Problems of Italian Feminism". *Gender and History*, 7 (1995) 2, 241-259.

Adams, Julia; Clemens, Elisabeth S. and Schola Orloff, Ann. "Introduction: Social Theory, Modernity and the Three Waves of Historical Sociology" in: Id., eds. *Remaking Modernity: Politics, History, and Sociology*. Durham-London, 2005, 1-72.

Airiau, Paul. "Le prêtre catholique: masculine, neutre, autre? Des débuts du XIXe siècle au milieu du XXe siècle" in: Régis Revenin, ed. *Hommes et masculinités de 1789 à nos jours. Contributions à l'histoire du genre et de la sexualité en France*. Paris, 2007, 192-207.

AKKZG, Münster. "Katholiken zwischen Tradition und Moderne. Das katholische Milieu als Forschungsaufgabe". *Westfälische Forschungen*, 43 (1993), 588-590.

Albert, Marcel. "Ordensleben in der ersten Hälfte des 19. Jahrhunderts" in: Erwin Gatz, ed. *Klöster und Ordensgemeinschaften*. Geschichte des kirchlichen Lebens in den deutschsprachigen Ländern seit dem Ende des 18. Jahrhunderts VII. Freiburg, 2006, 149-204.

Alderson, David. *Mansex Fine: Religion, Manliness and Imperialism in Nineteenth-Century British Culture*. Manchester, 1998.

"Algemeen Secretariaat van de Bonden van de Vrienden van het Heilig Hart" in: *ODIS databank*: <www.odis.be>, Record 14564.

Allen, L. Dean. *Rise Up, O Men of God: The "Men and Religion Forward Movement" and the "Promise Keepers"*. Macon, Ga., 2002.

Allitt, Patrick. *Catholic Converts: British and American Intellectuals Turn to Rome*. Ithaca-London, 1997.

Amalvi, Christian. "La construction des héros nationaux à l'école et au foyer familial, de 1800 à 1914" in: Odile Faliu and Marc Tourret. *Héros d'Achille à Zidane*. Paris, 2007.

Amalvi, Christian. "Le Mythe de Rome dans la littérature catholique destinée aux écoles et aux foyers chrétiens de 1830 à 1930" in: H. Multon et al. *L'Idée de Rome: pouvoirs, représentations, conflits*. Chambéry, 2006.

Anderson, Margaret Lavinia. "Piety and Politics: Recent Work on German Catholicism". *Journal of Modern History*, 63 (1991) 4, 681-716.

Andeweg, Agnes; Van Boven, Erika and Meijer, Maaike. "Een campobsessie met katholicisme". *Spiegel der Letteren*, 41 (1991) 1, 57-67.

Appleby, R. Scott. [Review Alden V. Brown. The Grail Movement]. *Church History*, 62 (1993) 2, 300-302.

Armstrong, Karin. *The Battle for God*. New York, 2000.

Art, Jan. "Documents concernant la situation de l'Eglise catholique en Belgique en vue du concile de Vatican I (1869-1870)". *Bulletin de l'Institut historique belge de Rome*, 48-49 (1978-1979), 452-508.

Art, Jan. "Kerkgeschiedenis na Drewermann: naar een psychohistory van de r.k. clerus?" in: D.J. Wolffram, ed. *Om het christelijk karakter der natie. Confessionelen en de modernisering van de maatschappij*. Amsterdam, 1994, 179-191.

Art, Jan. "Mannen als bruiden van de bruidegom? Enkele verklaringspogingen" in: Marjet Derks; José Eijt and Marit Monteiro, eds. *Sterven voor de wereld. Een religieus ideaal in meervoud*. Hilversum, 1997, 35-48.

Art, Jan and Buerman, Thomas. "Anticléricalisme et genre au XIXe siècle. Le prêtre catholique, principal défi à l'image hégémonique de l'homme". *Sextant*, 27 (2009), 323-337.

Art, Jan and Buerman, Thomas. "Is de katholieke man wel een echte vent? Suggesties voor onderzoek naar mannelijkheid, katholicisme en antiklerikalisme". *Historica*, 30 (2007) 2, 27-29.

Arts, L., S.J. "Mannelijk Christendom". *Bode van het Heilig Hart*, (1936), 32-35.

Arts, L., S.J. "Mannelijke vroomheid". *Bode van het Heilig Hart*, (1936), 421-424.

Asad, Talal. "The Construction of Religion as an Anthropological Category" in: Id. *Genealogies of Religion: Discipline and Reasons of Power in Christianity and Islam*. Baltimore, 1999, 27-55.

"Aus Kinderland: An der Mutter Hand". *Die Mutter*, March 1929.

"Aus unsere Verbandsfamilie-Aus unserem Gruppenabenden". *Die Mutter*, September 1929.

"Aus unsere Verbandsfamilie-Erste Gemeinschaftstagung von Leiterinnen der Frauen- und Müttervereine in Rhöndorf". *Die Mutter*, May 1930.

"Aus unsere Verbandsfamilie-Mutter erhole sich". *Die Mutter*, January 1932.

Bagchi, David. "Poets, Peasants, and Pamphlets: Who Wrote and Who Read Reformation Flugschriften?" in: Kate Cooper and Jeremy Gregory, eds. *Elite and Popular Religion*. Papers Read at the 2004 Summer Meeting and the 2005 Winter Meeting of the Ecclesiastical History Society. Bury St. Edmunds, 2006, 189-196.

Baldwin, Peter. *The Narcissism of Minor Differences: How America and Europe Are Alike*. Oxford, 2009.

Bank, Franciscus. *Joannes Dominicus Joseph Aengenent*. Amsterdam, 1996.

Barendse, B.A.M. *Thomas van Aquino: een geloof op zoek naar inzicht*. Baarn, 1968.

Bartholmä, Johann G. *Die barmherzigen Schwestern in München im Bezug auf Krankenpflege*. Augsburg, 1838.

Baumann, Ursula. "Religion, Emancipation, and Politics in the Confessional Women's Movement in Germany, 1900-1933" in: Billie Melman, ed. *Borderlines: Genders and Identities in War and Peace, 1870-1930*. New York-London, 1998, 285-306.

Baumann, Ursula. "Religion und Emanzipation: Konfessionelle Frauenbewegung in Deutschland 1900-1933" in: Irmtraud Götz von Olenhusen, ed. *Frauen unter dem Patriarchat der Kirchen. Katholikinnen und Protestantinnen im 19. und 20. Jahrhundert*. Stuttgart-Berlin, 1995, 89-119.

Bayly, Christopher A. *Die Geburt des modernen Welt. Eine Globalgeschichte 1780-1914*. Frankfurt-New York, 2006.

Becker, Annette. *War and Faith. The Religious Imagination in France 1914-1930*. Oxford, 1998.

Bederman, Gail. "'The Women Have Had Charge of the Church Work Long Enough': The Men and Religion Forward Movement of 1911-1912 and the Masculinization of Middle-class Protestantism". *American Quarterly*, 14 (1989) 3, 432-165.

Bell's Life in London, 1836, 1846, 1851.

Berlis, Angela. "Der Bund Alt-Katholischer Frauen und sein Engagement für Frauenrechte" in: Gisela Muschiol, ed. *Katholikinnen und Moderne. Katholische Frauenbewegung zwischen Tradition und Emanzipation*. Münster, 2003, 199-220.

Berlis, Angela. "Einde aan een kaste buiten de maatschappij. Rond de opheffing van de celibaatsverplichting in de Oud-Katholieke Kerk van Nederland" in: Marit Monteiro and Gian Ackermans, eds. *Mannen Gods. Klerikale identiteit in verandering.* Metamorfosen 7. Hilversum, 2007, 53-71.

Berlis, Angela. *Frauen im Prozeß der Kirchwerdung. Eine historisch-theologische Studie zur Anfangsphase des deutschen Altkatholizismus (1850-1890).* Frankfurt, 1998.

Berlis, Angela. "Johann Friedrich von Schultes Stellung zu Zölibat und Priesterehe" in: Rüdiger Althaus, Klaus Lüdicke and Matthias Pulte, eds. *Kirchenrecht und Theologie im Leben der Kirche, Festschrift für Heinrich J.F. Reinhardt zur Vollendung seines 65. Lebensjahres.* Münsterischer Kommentar zum Codex Iuris Canonici, Beiheft 50. Essen, 2007, 51-71.

Berlis, Angela. "Maria in alt-katholischer Sicht". *IKZ*, 99 (2009), 33-66.

Berlis, Angela. "Seelensorge verträgt keine Teilung. Ignaz von Döllinger (1799-1890) und die Frage des Zölibats". *Annali di studi religiosi*, 6 (2005), 249-281.

Berlis, Angela. *Vergelijking als weg tot historische kennis.* Publicatieserie Stichting Oud-Katholiek Seminarie 40. Amersfoort-Sliedrecht, 2007.

Beschlüsse der ersten Synode der Altkatholiken des deutschen Reiches, gehalten zu Bonn am 27., 28. und 29. Mai 1874. Amtliche Ausgabe, 3rd edition. Bonn, 1875.

Bethouart, Bruno and Lottin, Alain, eds. *La dévotion mariale de l'an mil à nos jours.* Arras, 2005.

Bienvenue, Louise and Hudon, Christine. "Entre franche camaraderie et amours socratiques. L'espace trouble et ténu des amitiés masculines dans les collèges classiques (1870-1960)". *Revue d'histoire de l'Amérique française*, 57 (2004) 4, 481-507.

Bienvenue, Louise and Hudon, Christine. "'Pour devenir homme, tu transgresseras...' Quelques enjeux de la socialization masculine dans les collèges classiques québécois (1880-1939)". *The Canadian Historical Review*, 86 (2005) 3, 485-511.

"Bij onze Waalsche broeders". *Maandelijksche Mededeelingen voor Bonden van het Heilig Hart*, June (1937), 2-3.

Bircher, Patrick. "Religious Communities and the Catholic Poverty Discourse in the First Half of the Nineteenth Century: Aspects of the Relationship between Charitable Service and Denomination-Specific Identity as Reflected in the Church Press" in: Urs Altermatt and Franziska Metzger, eds. *Religious Institutes and Catholic Culture in Nineteenth Century Europe.* KADOC Studies on Religion, Culture and Society. Leuven (forthcoming).

Bischof, Franz Xaver. *Theologie und Geschichte. Ignaz von Döllinger (1799-1890) in der zweiten Hälfte seines Lebens.* Stuttgart, 1997.

Bischoff, Claudia. *Frauen in der Krankenpflege. Zur Entwicklung von Frauenrolle und Frauenberufstätigkeit im 19. Jahrhundert.* Frankfurt, 1997.

Blackbourn, David. *Marpingen: Apparitions of the Virgin Mary in Bismarckian Germany.* Oxford, 1993.

Blackbourn, David. "The Catholic Church in Europe since the French Revolution". *Comparative Studies in Society and History*, 33 (1991), 778-790.

Blaschke, Olaf. "Das 19. Jahrhundert: Ein Zweites Konfessionelles Zeitalter". *Geschichte und Gesellschaft*, 26 (2000), 25-62.

Blaschke, Olaf. "Der Dämon des Konfessionalismus. Einführende Überlegungen" in: Olaf Blaschke, ed. *Konfessionen im Konflikt. Deutschland zwischen 1800 und 1970: ein zweites konfessionelles Zeitalter.* Göttingen, 2002, 13-69.

Blaschke, Olaf. "Fältmarskalk Jesus Kristus: religiös remaskunlinisering i Tyskland" in: Yvonne Maria Werner, ed. *Kristen manlighet. Ideal och verklighet 1830-1940.* Lund, 2008, 22-60.

Blaschke, Olaf, ed. *Konfessionen im Konflikt. Deutschland zwischen 1800 und 1970: ein zweites konfessionelles Zeitalter.* Göttingen, 2002.

Blaschke, Olaf. "The Unrecognized Piety of Men. Strategies and Success of the Re-masculinization Campaign around 1900" in: Yvonne Maria Werner, ed. *Christian Masculinity. Men and Religion in Northern Europe in the 19th and 20th Century.* Leuven, 2011, 21-45.

Blaschke, Olaf and Kuhlemann, Frank-Michael, eds. *Religion im Kaiserreich: Milieus-Mentalitäten-Krisen.* Gütersloh, 1996.

Bloemen geplukt op het graf van mijnheer August De Rijnck, gewezen pauselijk zouaaf. Roeselare, 1871.

Blum, Peter. *Staatliche Armenfürsorge im Herzogtum Nassau 1806-1866.* Wiesbaden, 1987.

Bock, Gisela. *Frauen in der europäischen Geschichte. Vom Mittelalter bis zur Gegenwart.* Munich, 2000.

Bondsblad voor Bonden van het Heilig Hart. 1930.

Bonomi, Patricia U. *Under the Cope of Heaven: Religion, Society, and Politics in Colonial America.* New York-Oxford, 2003[2].

Bonvan, B. *Lacordaire-Jandel. Suivi de l'édition originale et annotée du Mémoire Jandel. La restauration de l'Ordre dominicain en France après la Révolution écartelée entre deux visions du monde.* Paris, 1989.

Borutta, Manuel. "Antikatholizismus, Männlichkeit und Moderne. Die diskursive Feminisierung des Katholizismus in Deutschland und Italien (1850-1900)". *AIM-Gender Tagung*, s.l., s.d. <http://www.ruendal.de/aim/pdfs/Borutta.pdf>

Borutta, Manuel. "Genealogie der Säkularisierungstheorie: Zur Historisierung einer großen Erzählung der Moderne". *Geschichte und Gesellschaft*, 36 (2010), 347-376.

Bos, David. "A Good Enough Parson: Early Nineteenth-Century Dutch Discourse on Requirements for the Pastoral Ministry in the Reformed Church" in: Th. Clemens and W. Janse, eds. *The Pastor Bonus. Papers Read at the British-Dutch Colloquium at Utrecht, 18-21 September 2002* (*Dutch Review of Church History*, 83 (2004)), 333-370.

Boss, S. J. *Empress and Handmaid: On Nature and Gender in the Cult of the Virgin Mary.* London, 2000.

Boutry, P. *Prêtres et paroisses au pays du curé d'Ars.* Paris, 1986.

Bowler, Peter J. "Christianity and the Sciences" in: Hugh McLeod, ed. *World Christianities c. 1914-c. 2000.* Cambridge History of Christianity 9. Cambridge, 2006, 569-581.

Boyarin, Daniel. *Unheroic Conduct: The Rise of Heterosexuality and the Invention of the Jewish Man.* Berkeley, 1997.

Bradstock, Andrew et al., eds. *Masculinity and Spirituality in Victorian Culture.* Basingstoke, 2000.

Brasher, Brenda E. *Godly Women: Fundamentalism and Female Power.* New Brunswick-New Jersey-London, 1998.

Braude, Ann. "Women's History *is* American Religious History" in: Thomas A. Tweed, ed. *Retelling US Religious History.* Berkeley, 1997, 87-107.

Braunschweig, Sabine. "Introduction" in: Sabine Braunschweig, ed. *Pflege – Räume, Macht und Alltag. Beiträge zur Geschichte der Pflege.* Zurich, 2006, 9-25.

Breitenbach, Sonja. *Frauen gestalten soziale Arbeit. Soziale Arbeit zwischen geistiger Mütterlichkeit und Profession.* Münster, 1999.

Brelivet, A. *La formation chrétienne dans les grands colleges catholiques (Bretagne 1920-1940).* Paris, 2001.

Brentano, Clemens. *Die Barmherzigen Schwestern in Bezug auf Armen- und Krankenpflege. Nebst einem Bericht über das Bürgerhospital in Coblenz und erläuternden Beilagen.* Koblenz, 1831 (Mainz, 1852).

Bresciani, Antonia. *Olderico, o lo zuavo pontificio.* S.l., 1861.

Breslauer Zeitschrift für katholische Theologie, 1832-1833.

Bridenthal, Renate; Grossmann, Atina and Kaplan, Marion, eds. *When Biology Became Destiny: Women in Weimar and Nazi Germany.* New York, 1984.

British Sport and Sportsmen, Past and Present. London, 1908. 2 vols.

Brown, Alden V. *The Grail Movement and American Catholicism, 1940-1975.* Notre Dame, 1989.

Brown, Callum G. *Religion and Society in Twentieth Century Britain.* London, 2007.

Brown, Callum G. "Secularization, the Growth of Militancy and the Spiritual Revolution: Religious Change and Gender Power in Britain, 1901-2001". *Historical Research*, 80 (2007) 209, 393-418.

Brown, Callum G. *The Death of Christian Britain: Understanding Secularization 1800-2000.* London, 2001.

Brown, Callum G. and Snape, Michael, eds. *Secularisation in the Christian World: Essays in Honour of Hugh McLeod.* Farnham-Burlington, 2010.

Bruce, Steve. *God is Dead: Secularization in the West.* Oxford, 2002.

Bruce, Steve. *Religion in the Modern World: From Cathedrals to Cults.* Oxford, 1996.

Bruley, Y. "La romanité catholique au XIXe siècle: un itinéraire romain dans la littérature française". *Histoire, économie & société*, 21 (2002) 1, 60-61.

Bruning, Henri. *Onze priester.* Revisie en richting. Amsterdam, 1933.

Buerman, Thomas. *Katholieke mannelijkheden in België in de 19de en 20ste eeuw.* Diss. Doct. UGent. Gent, 2010.

Burleigh, Michael. *Earthly Powers: The Clash of Religion and Politics in Europe from the French Revolution to the Great War.* New York, 2005.

Burton, Richard. *Holy Tears, Holy Blood: Women, Catholicism and the Culture of Suffering in France, 1840-1970.* London, 2004.

Busch, Norbert. "Die Feminisierung der Frömmigkeit" in: Irmtraud Götz von Olenhusen, ed. *Wunderbare Erscheinungen, Frauen und katholische Frömmigkeit im 19. und 20. Jahrhundert.* Paderborn, 1995, 203-219.

Busch, Norbert. "Fromme Westfalen. Zur Sozial- und Mentalitätsgeschichte des Herz-Jesu-Kultes zwischen Kulturkampf und Erstem Weltkrieg". *Westfälische Zeitschrift*, 144 (1994), 329-350.

Busch, Norbert. *Katholische Frömmigkeit und Moderne. Die Sozial- und Mentalitätsgeschichte des Herz-Jesu-Kultes in Deutschland zwischen Kulturkampf und Erstem Weltkrieg*. Gütersloh, 1997.

Buß, Franz Josef. *Der Orden der barmherzigen Schwestern. Uebersicht seiner Entstehung, Verbreitung, Gliederung, Leitung, Nothwendigkeit und Zweckmäßigkeit in der Gegenwart*. Schaffhausen, 1847.

Bynum, Caroline W. *Fragmentation and Redemption: Essays on Gender and the Human Body in Medieval Religion*. New York, 1992.

Bynum, Caroline W. *Jesus as Mother: Studies in the Spirituality of the High Middle Ages*. Berkeley-Los Angeles, 1982.

Carroll, John. *Guilt: The Grey Eminence behind Character, History and Culture*. London, 1985.

Carroll, Michael P. *American Catholics in the Protestant Imagination: Rethinking the Academic Study of Religion*. Baltimore, 2007.

Carroll, Michael P. *Catholic Cults and Devotions: A Psychological Inquiry*. Kingston, 1989.

Carroll, Michael P. *Madonnas that Maim. Popular Catholicism in Italy since the Fifteenth Century*. Baltimore, 1992.

Carroll, Michael P. "Previous Explanations of the Mary Cult" in: Michael P. Carroll. *The Cult of the Virgin Mary*. Princeton, 1986, 22-48.

Carroll, Michael P. *The Cult of the Virgin Mary: Psychological Origins*. Princeton, 1986.

Carroll, Michael P. *Veiled Threats: The Logic of Popular Catholicism in Italy*. Baltimore, 1996.

Cathrein, Victor, S.J. *Die Frauenfrage*. S.l.,1901. (transl. *Het vrouwenvraagstuk*. Leiden, 1907),

Cautereels, Peter Jozef. *De pauselijke zouaven: hunne heldenfeiten in 1867*. Mechelen, 1868.

Chadwick, Owen. *A History of the Popes 1830-1914*. Oxford, 1998.

Charmot, F. "Le prêtre et la très sainte Mère de Dieu". *Le recrutement sacerdotal*, 1933, 120-133.

Châtellier, Louis. *La religion des pauvres. Les sources du christianisme moderne XVIe-XIXe siècles*. Paris, 1993.

Châtellier, Louis. *L'Europe des dévots*. Paris, 1987.

Chélini-Pont, Blandine. "French Catholics, Secularization, and Politics" in: Alec G. Hargreaves, John Kelsay and Sumner B. Twiss, eds. *Politics and Religion in France and the United States*. Lanham, 2007, 79-94.

Cholvy, Gérard and Hilaire, Yves-Marie. *Histoire religieuse de la France contemporaine*. Vol. 1-2. Toulouse, 1985-1986.

Chotard, Jean-René. *Séminaristes... une espèce disparue? Histoire et structure d'un petit séminaire. Guérande (1822-1966)*. Québec, 1977.

Christie, Nancy. *Households of Faith: Familiy, Gender and Community in Canada 1760-1969*. London, 2002.

Clark, Christopher. "The New Catholicism and the European Culture Wars" in: Christopher Clark and Wolfram Kaiser, eds. *Culture Wars: Secular-Catholic Conflict in Nineteenth-Century Europe*. Cambridge, 2003, 47-76.

Clemens, Jakob, ed. *Ruf von Trier: Bericht über die VI. Reichtagung des Katholischen Jungmännerverbandes Deutschlands 1931 zu Trier*. Düsseldorf, 1931.

Collins Tony and Vamplew, Wray. *Mud, Sweat and Beers: A Cultural History of Sport and Alcohol*. Oxford, 2002.

Connell, Robert William. *Masculinities*. Cambridge: Polity Press, 1995.

Connell, Robert William and James, W. Messerschmidt. "Hegemonic Masculinity: Rethinking the Concept". *Gender & Society*, 19 (2005) 6, 829-859.

Cookson, Peter W. and Hodges Persell, Caroline. *Preparing for Power: America's Elite Boarding Schools*. New York, 1985.

Coppa, Frank. "Italy: The Church and the *Risorgimento*" in: Sheridan Gilley and Brian Stanley, eds. *The Cambridge History of Christianity: World Christianities c. 1815-1914*. Cambridge, 2006, 233-249.

Corrado Pope, B. "Immaculate and Powerful: The Marian Revival in the Nineteenth Century" in: C.W. Atkinson et al., eds. *Immaculate and Powerful: The Female in Sacred Image and Social Reality*. Boston, 1985, 173-200.

Cott, Nancy F. *The Bonds of Womanhood: Women's Sphere in New England 1780-1835*. New Haven, Conn.-London, 1977.

Cox, Jeffrey. "Master Narratives of Long-Term Religious Change" in: Hugh McCleod and Werner Ustorf. *The Decline of Christendom in Western Europe, 1750-2000*. Cambridge, 2003, 201-217.

Cox, Jeffrey. "Secularization and Other Master Narratives of Religion in Modern Europe". *Kirchliche Zeitgeschichte*, 14 (2001) 1, 24-35.

Crottogini, Jakob. *Werden und Krise des Priesterberufes*. Einsiedeln, 1995.

Curtis, Sarah Ann. *Educating the Faithful: Religion, Schooling, and Society in Nineteenth-Century France*. DeKalb, 2000.

Daems, Servaas Domien. *Voor twee vaders: tafereelen uit het leven der pauselijke zouaven.* Brussels, 1868. (transl. *The Double Sacrifice: A Tale of Castelfidardo.* London, 1871.)

Dalarun, Jacques. *'Dieu changea de sexe, pour ainsi dire'. La religion faite femme, XIe-XVe s.* Paris, 2008.

Danzinger, Danny. *Eton Voices.* London, 1988.

Dauzet, Dominique-Marie. *La mystique bien tempérée. Ecriture féminine de l'expérience spirituelle XIXe-XXe siècle.* Paris, 2006.

"David Gathen: Dein Junge im Beruf!". *Die Mutter*, April 1929.

Dawson, Christopher. *Christianity and European Culture. Selections from the Work of Christopher Dawson, edited by Gerald J. Russello.* Washington DC, 1998.

De Becdelièvre, L.A. *Souvenirs de l'armée pontificale.* Paris-Lyon, 1867.

DeBerg, Betty A. *Ungodly Women: Gender and the First Wave of American Fundamentalism.* Minneapolis, 1990.

"De Bonden en de aanstaande verkiezingen". *Maandelijksche Mededeelingen voor Bonden van het Heilig Hart*, March 1936, 3-4.

De Corte, J.-B. *Lijkrede, Uitgesproken in Onze Lieve Vrouw-Kerk te Brugge, door J.-B. De Corte, Missionaris en geestelyken schoolopziener des Bisdoms, Ter gelegenheid van den plegtigen Lykdienst aldaer op 6 November 1860 gevierd voor de gesneuvelden van het Pauselyk Leger.* Ghent-Bruges, 1860.

"De eerste Bondsmis". *Bondsblad voor Bonden van het Heilig Hart*, November 1936, 2.

De Fiores, S. "Marie (sainte vierge), le 19e siècle" in: *Dictionnaire de spiritualité*, vol. X. Paris, 1980, 467-473.

"De godsvrucht tot het Heilig Hart. Vastenbrief van 1899 van Z.D.H. Mgr Doutreloux". *Bode van het Heilig Hart van Jesus*, 1899, 45.

Deil, M. van. "Raymond van Bergen" in: *Glas in lood in Nederland 1817-1968.* The Hague, 1989, 207.

De Keizer, Madelon. "Inleiding" in: Madelon de Keizer and Sophie Tates, eds. *Moderniteit. Modernisme en massacultuur in Nederland 1914-1940.* Zutphen, 2004.

De Kok, J.A., O.F.M. *Acht eeuwen Minderbroeders in Nederland. Een oriëntatie.* Hilversum, 2008.

De Kruif, José and Meijer Drees, Marijke, eds. *Het lange leven van het pamflet. Boekhistorische, iconografische, literaire en politieke aspecten.* Hilversum, 2006.

Dellepoort, J.J. *De priesterroepingen in Nederland. Proeve van een statistisch-sociografische analyse.* 's-Gravenhage, 1955.

Delves, Anthony. "Popular Recreation and Social Conflict in Derby 1800-1850" in: Eileen and Stephen Yeo, eds. *Popular Culture and Class Conflict 1590-1914.* Brighton, 1981, 89-127.

De Maeyer, Jan. "The Concept of Religious Modernization" in: Jan De Maeyer et al., eds. *Religion, Children's Literature and Modernity in Western Europe 1750-2000.* Leuven, 2005, 43-49.

De Maeyer, Jan; Leplae, Sofie and Schmiedl, Joachim. "Introduction" in: Jan De Maeyer, Sofie Leplae and Joachim Schmiedl, eds. *Religious Institutes in Western Europe in the Nineteenth and Twentieth Centuries. Historiography, Research and Legal Position.* Leuven, 2004, 7-26.

De Maeyer, Jan; Leplae, Sofie and Schmiedl, Joachim, eds. *Religious Institutes in Western Europe in the Nineteenth and Twentieth Centuries. Historiography, Research and Legal Position.* KADOC Studies on Religion, Culture and Society 2. Leuven, 2004.

Derby Mercury, 26 February 1845.

Derks, Marjet. "Fiere sportlijven en kenauturnsters. Katholieke percepties van moderne sportbeoefening, 1910-1940" in: Dirk-Jan Wolffram, ed. *Om het christelijk karakter der natie. Confessionelen en de modernisering van de maatschappij.* Amsterdam, 1994, 59-88.

Derks, Marjet. *Heilig moeten. Radicaal-katholiek en retro-modern in de jaren twintig en dertig.* Hilversum, 2007.

Derks, Marjet. "Modesty and Excellence: Gender and Sports Culture in Dutch Catholic Schooling". *Gender & History*, 20 (2008) 1, 8-26.

Derks, Marjet. "Religion, Suffering and Female Heroism: Transformations in the Meaning of Sacrifice in a Catholic Conversion Movement" in: Joachim Duyndam et al., eds. *The New Fascination of Sacrifice.* Leiden, 2012 (forthcoming).

Derks, Marjet and Budel, Marc. *Sportief en katholiek. Geschiedenis van de katholieke sportbeweging in Nederland in de twintigste eeuw.* 's-Hertogenbosch-Nijmegen, 1990.

Derks, Marjet and Eijt, José. "Wie kookte het laatste avondmaal? Over de zichtbaarheid van vrouwen in religiegeschiedenis" in: Theo Hoogbergen and Maurice Ackermans, eds. *Kloosters en religies leven. Historie met toekomst.* 's-Hertogenbosch, 2002, 195-203.

Derks, Marjet and Van Heijst, Annelies. "Katholieke vrouwencultuur. Een theoretische terreinverkenning" in: Marjet Derks and Catharina Halkes. *"Roomse dochters". Katholieke vrouwen en hun beweging*. Baarn, 1992, 325-346.

Derks, Marjet et al. "Res Novae. Evoluties in de historische beeldvorming over katholieke vrouwen". *Ex Tempore*, 11 (1992) 2, 121-134.

Derks, Marjet; Nissen, Peter and de Raat, Judith, eds. *Het licht gezien. Bekeringen tot het katholicisme in de twintigste eeuw*. Hilversum, 2000.

Der Spiegel, 6 July 2006.

Der vierte Altkatholiken-Congress in Freiburg im Breisgau im Jahre 1874. Stenographischer Bericht. Officielle Ausgabe. Bonn, 1874.

Desan, Suzanne. *Reclaiming the Sacred: Lay Religion and Popular Politics in Revolutionary France*. Ithaca, New York, 1990.

De Saussure, T. "Questions psychanalytiques sur la prévalence masculine dans la religion chrétienne". *Etudes théologiques et religieuses*, 70 (1995) 3, 405-417.

De Ségur, A. *Les Martyrs de Castelfidardo*. Paris, 1862.

De Smet, J. "Ronseling van minderjarigen voor de pauselijke zouaven 1864". *Biekorf*, 59 (1958), 358-362.

Despland, M. "A Case of Christians Shifting their Moral Allegiance: France 1790-1914". *Journal of the American Academy of Religion*, 52 (1984) 4, 671-690.

"De technische organizatie van de sport in de Graal". *De zilveren trompet*, 1 (1931), 122-123.

Dethlefs, Silvia. "Frauengeschichte - Geschlechtergeschichte: ein Versuch anhand der Überlieferung des Magdalenen-Hospitals im 19. Jahrhundert" in: Franz-Josef Jakobi et al., eds. *Strukturwandel der Armenfürsorge und der Stiftungswirklichkeit in Münster im Laufe der Jahrhunderte*. Münster, 2002, 145-257.

De Turck de Kersbeek, Théodore. *Letter To His Father, 20 of March 1862* in: Edouard Terwecoren. *Auguste Misson, zouave pontifical*. Brussels, 1862, 60-66.

Deutsche Reichs-Zeitung, 7 (1878).

De Vries, Jacqueline. "Rediscovering Christianity After the Postmodern Turn". *History Compass*, 4 (2006) 4, 698-714.

Die Mutter, 1919, 1929, 1930, 1932.

di Giorgio, Michaela. "La bonne catholique" in: Georges Duby and Michelle Perrot, eds. *Histoire des femmes en Occident*. Vol. 4. Paris, 1991, 169-194.

di Giorgio, Michaela. "Das katholische Modell" in: Geneviève Fraisse and Michelle Perrot, eds. *19. Jahrhundert*. Frankfurt, 1994 and (paperback) 1997 (*Geschichte der Frauen*, 4), 187-220.

Dinges, Martin. "Einleitung: Geschlechtergeschichte - mit Männern!" in: Id., ed. *Hausväter, Priester, Kastraten: zur Konstruktion von Männlichkeit in Spätmittelalter und früher Neuzeit*. Göttingen, 1998, 7-28.

Dinges, Martin. "'Hegemoniale Männlichkeit' – Ein Konzept auf dem Prüfstand" in: Martin Dinges, ed. *Männer – Macht – Körper. Hegemoniale Männlichkeiten vom Mittelalter bis heute*. Frankfurt, 2005, 7-33.

Dittes, James E. "Psychological Characteristics of Religious Professionals" in: M.P. Strommen, ed. *Research on Religious Development. A Comprehensive Handbook*. New York, 1971, 355-390.

Dobbelaere, Karel. "Assessing Secularization Theory" in: Id. *Secularization: An Analysis at Three Levels*. Brussels, 2002, 229-254.

Doerry, Sigrid. *Mädchen- und Frauenbildung im Heliand-Bund, 1926-1950*. Mutterstadt: Kreis Katholische Frauen im Heliand Bund, 1997.

Dols, C. *De geesel der eeuw. Katholieke drankbestrijding in Nederland, 1852-1945*. Zaltbommel, 2007.

Donders, Rachel. *Geef mij 10.000 zielen. Levensschets van Debborah Bouwman*. 's-Hertogenbosch, 1940.

Donders, Rachel. *History of the International Grail 1921-1971*. Grailville, 1983.

Donders, Rachel. *Lydwine van Kersbergen 1905-1990. Een vrouw van de twintigste eeuw*. Voorburg, 2000.

Douglas, Ann. *The Feminization of American Culture*. New York, 1977.

Dowe, Christopher. *Auch Bildungsbürger. Katholische Studierende und Akademiker im Kaiserreich. Kritische Studien zur Geschichtswissenschaft 171*. Göttingen, 2006.

Downes Miles, Henry. *Pugilistica: The History of British Boxing*. Edinburgh, 1906, 3 vols.

"Dr. Ernst Breit: Vor dem Maialtar". *Der Kranz*, 22 (1928), 113-114.

Drewermann, Eugen. *Kleriker. Psychogramm eines Ideals*. Olten, 1990.

Droste zu Vischering, Clemens August. *Ueber die Genossenschaften der barmherzigen Schwestern, insbesondere über die Errichtung Einer derselben und deren Leistungen in Münster*. Münster, 1833.

Dubuisson, Daniel. *The Western Construction of Religion. Myths, Knowledge, and Ideology*. Baltimore, 2003.

Dufau, T., S.J. *Beautés de l'âme contemplées dans le cœur de Jésus et suivies de guide pratique des Zélateurs et Zélatrices de l'Apostolat de la Prière et des associés de l'archiconfrérie*. Leuven, 1869.

Duffy, Eamon. *Saints and Sinners: A History of the Popes*. Cambridge (U.S.), 1997.

Duperray. "La Dévotion à Marie et les Vocations". *Le recrutement sacerdotal*, 1937, 204-222.

Dusausoit, Xavier. *Les collèges jésuites et la société belge du XIXème s. (1831-1914)*. Unpublished doctoral thesis, Université Catholique de Louvain. Louvain-la-Neuve, 2005.

Dussel, Enrique. "World Religions and Secularization from a Postcolonial and Anti-Eurocentric Perspective" in: Derek R. Peterson and Darren R. Walhof, eds. *The Invention of Religion: Rethinking Belief in Politics and History*. London-New Brunswick NJ, 2002, 179-189.

Eckkart, Wolfgang U. and Jütte, Robert. *Medizingeschichte. Eine Einführung*. Cologne, 2007.

Eder, Manfred. *Helfen macht nicht ärmer. Von der kirchlichen Armenfürsorge zur modernen Caritas in Bayern*. Altötting, 1997.

"Een wensch van Z.H. Leo XIII". *Bode van het Heilig Hart*, 1899, 234-235.

"Ein herzliches 'Grüß Gott' zum neuen Jahr". *Die Mutter*, January 1929.

Eksteins, Modris. *Rites of Spring: The Great War and the Birth of the Modern Age*. London, 1989.

Elgershuizen, J., C.Ss.R. *Een kroniek van vijfenzeventig jaar Nebo*. Nijmegen, 2003.

Engelhardt, Carol Marie. "Victorian Masculinity and the Virgin Mary" in: Andrew Bradstock et al., eds. *Masculinity and Spirituality in Victorian Culture*. Basingstoke, 2000, 44-57.

Engelhardt Herringer, Carol. *Victorians and the Virgin Mary: Religion and Gender in England, 1830-1885*. Manchester-New York, 2008.

Fairfax-Blakeborough, John. *Northern Turf History*. Vol. 3: *York and Doncaster Races*. London, s.d.

Felski, Rita. *The Gender of Modernity*. Cambridge-London, 1995.

"Fierheid". *De zilveren trompet*, 1 (1931) 11, 3.

Fitzgerald, Timothy. *The Ideology of Religious Studies*. New York, 2000.

Flüchter, Antje. *Der Zölibat zwischen Devianz und Norm. Kirchenpolitik und Gemeindealltag in den Herzogtümern Jülich und Berg im 16. und 17. Jahrhundert*. Cologne-Weimar-Vienna, 2006.

Ford, Caroline. *Divided Houses. Religion and Gender in Modern France*. Ithaca-London, 2005.

Ford, Caroline. "Religion and Popular Culture in Modern Europe". *Journal of Modern History*, 65 (March 1993), 152-175.

Fouilloux, Étienne. "Femmes et catholicisme dans la France contemporaine. Aperçu historiographique". *Clio*, 2 (1995). <http://clio.revues.org/index498.html>

Fouilloux, Étienne. "Le catholicisme" in: *Histoire du christianisme des origines à nos jours*. Vol. XII: Jean-Marie Mayeur, ed. *Guerres mondiales et totalitarismes (1914-1958)*. Poitiers, 1990, 116-239.

Fouilloux, Étienne. "Le due vie della pieta cattolica nel XX secolo" in: Guiseppe Alberigo and Andrea Ricardi, eds. *Chiesa e papato nel mondo contemporaneo*. Rome, 1990, 287-353.

"Fragen wir uns einmal...". *Der Kranz*, 22 (1928), 98-99.

Franke, A. *Nicht nach Canossa! Eine Erzählung aus den jüngsten Tagen*. Regensburg, 1872.

Franke, A. *Priesterthum oder Hochzeit? Beitrag zum Verständnisse einiger Tagesfragen*. Würzburg, 1873.

Freedman, Estelle. *No Turning Back: The History of Feminism and the Future of Women*. New York, 2002.

Frei, Carl. *Clara oder "Erfahrungen einer gemischten Ehe"*. Würzburg, 1876.

Frevert, Ute. *'Mann und Weib, und Weib und Mann'. Geschlechter-Differenzen in der Moderne*. Munich, 1995.

Fuchs, Rachel G. *Gender and Poverty in Nineteenth-Century Europe*. Cambridge, 2005.

Fuller, Margareth, *Woman in the Nineteenth Century*. S.l., 1845.

Gabriëls, Leen. *De Bonden van het H. Hart in het Bisdom Gent 1920-1945*. Aartrijke, 1991.

Gadbois, Geneviève. "'Vous êtes presque la seule consolation de l'Eglise'. La foi des femmes face à la déchristianisation de 1789 à 1880" in: Jean Delumeau, ed. *La religion de ma mère. Le rôle des femmes dans la transmission de la foi*. Paris, 1992, 301-326.

Galarneau, Claude. *Les collèges classiques au Canada français*. Montréal, 1978.

Ganiage, Jean. "Mentana (combat de), 3 novembre 1867" in: Jean Tulard, ed. *Dictionnaire du Second Empire*. Paris, 1995, 810.

Ganiage, Jean. "Rome (Question de)" in: Jean Tulard, ed. *Dictionnaire du Second Empire*. Paris, 1995, 1128.

Die Gartenlaube. Illustriertes Familienblatt, 1869-1870, 1872-1874.

Gatz, Erwin. *Kirche und Krankenpflege im 19. Jahrhundert. Katholische Bewegung und karitativer Aufbruch in den preußischen Provinzen Rheinland und Westfalen*. Munich, 1971.

Gatz, Erwin. "Kirchliche Mitarbeit in der öffentlichen Armenpflege. Die Neuanfänge einer eigenständigen kirchlichen Armenpflege" in: Erwin Gatz, ed. *Caritas und soziale Dienste*. Munich, 1982, 57-70.

Gause, Ute. *Kirchengeschichte und Genderforschung. Eine Einführung aus protestantischer Perspektive*. Tübingen, 2006.

Gay, Peter. *Schnitzler's Century: The Making of Middle-Class Culture 1815-1914*. New York-London, 2002.

Gentile, Emilio. "New Idols: Catholicism in the Face of Fascist Totalitarianism". *Journal of Modern Italian Studies*, 11 (2006) 2, 143-170.

Gevers, Lieve. "De 'belle époque' van de kerk in België. 1830-1940" in: Peter Nissen, ed. *Geloven in de lage landen. Scharniermomenten in de geschiedenis van het christendom*. Leuven, 2004, 170-182.

Gibson, Ralph. *A Social History of French Catholicism, 1789-1914*. London-New York, 1989.

Gibson, Ralph. "Le Catholicisme et les femmes en France au XIXe siècle". *Revue de l'Histoire de l'Église en France*, 79 (1993), 63-94.

Gill, Sean. "How Muscular Was Muscular Christianity? Thomas Hughes and the Cult of Christian Manliness Reconsidered" in: Robert N. Swanson, ed. *Gender and the Christian Religion*. Woodbridge, 1998, 421-430.

Glöe, Elke. "Frauenarmut in Münster im 19. Jahrhundert" in: Franz-Josef Jakobi et al., eds. *Strukturwandel der Armenfürsorge und der Stiftungswirklichkeit in Münster im Laufe der Jahrhunderte*. Münster, 2002, 261-293.

Goddeeris, John. *De Pauselijke Zouaven: met opgave van de vrijwilligers uit West Vlaanderen*. Handzame, 1978.

Godin, André. *Psychologie de la vocation. Un bilan*. Paris, 1975.

Godin, André. "Psychologie de la vocation" in: *Dictionnaire de spiritualité*. Vol. 16. Paris, 1994, 1158-1167.

Gods zegen over het Retraitenhuis van Lier. Plechtige Feestvergadering voorgezeten door Z.E. Kardinaal Mercier. Lier, 1909.

Goetz, Leopold. *Der Ultramontanismus als Weltanschauung auf Grund des Syllabus quellenmäßig dargestellt*. Bonn, 1905.

Gola, Sabine. *Un demi-siècle de relations culturelles entre l'Italie et la Belgique 1830-1880*. Vol. 1. Brussels, 1999.

Golan, Romy. *Modernity and Nostalgia: Art and Politics in France between the Wars*. New Haven-London, 1995.

Gorski, Philip S. "Historizing the Secularization Debate: Church, State, and Society in Late Medieval and Early Modern Europe, ca. 300 to 700". *American Sociological Review*, 65 (2000), 138-167.

Götz von Olenhusen, Irmtraud. "Die Feminisierung von Religion und Kirche im 19. und 20. Jahrhundert: Forschungsstand und Forschungsperspektiven (Einleitung)" in: Imtraud Götz von Olenhusen, ed. *Frauen unter dem Patriarchat der Kirchen. Katholikinnen und Protestantinnen im 19. und 20. Jahrhundert*. Stuttgart-Berlin, 1995, 9-21.

Graalrangen, s.l., s.d.

Graf, Friedrich W. "Le politique dans la sphère intime. Protestantisme et culture en Allemagne au XIXe siècle". *Annales HSS*, 57 (2002) 3, 773-787.

Grayzel, Susan R. *Women's Identities at War: Gender, Motherhood, and Politics in Britain and France during the First World War*. Chapel Hill, 1999.

Gross, Michael B. *The War Against Catholicism: Liberalism and the Anti-Catholic Imagination in Nineteenth-Century Germany*. Ann Arbor, 2004.

Guenel, Jean. *La dernière guerre du pape: les zouaves pontificaux au secours du Saint-Siège, 1860-1870*. Rennes, 1998.

Habermas, Rebekka. *Frauen und Männer des Bürgertums. Eine Familiengeschichte (1750-1850)*. Göttingen, 2000.

Hackett, David G., ed. *Religion and American Culture: A Reader*. New York, 2003².

Hagemann, Karen. *Frauenalltag und Männerpolitik: Alltagsleben und gesellschaftliches Handeln von Arbeiterfrauen in der Weimarer Republik*. Bonn, 1990.

Hagemann, Karen. "Introduction" in: Karen Hagemann and Stephanie Schüler-Springorum, eds. *Home/Front: The Military, War, and Gender in Twentieth Century Germany*. New York-Oxford, 2002, 14.

Hähner-Rombach, Sylvelyn, ed. *Quellen zur Geschichte der Krankenpflege*. Frankfurt, 2008.

Hall, Donald E., ed. *Muscular Christianity: Embodying the Victorian Age*. Cambridge Studies in Nineteenth-Century Literature and Culture. Cambridge, 1994 [2006].

Hardy, J., S.J. *Het werk der Bonden van het Heilig Hart*. Lier, 1912.

Hardy, J., S.J. *Practische wenken voor het stichten en in bloei houden der Bonden van het H. Hart*. Lier, 1911.

Harris, Ruth. "Les miraculées de Lourdes" in: Nicole Edelman et al., eds. *Les femmes dans les sciences de l'homme (XIXe-XXe siècles). Inspiratrices, collaboratrices ou créatrices?* Paris, 2005, 287-300.

Harris, Ruth. *Lourdes: Body and Spirit in the Secular Age*. New York, 1999.

Harrison, Carol E. "Zouave Stories: Gender, Catholic Spirituality, and French Responses to the Roman Question". *The Journal of Modern History*, 79 (2007), 274-305.

Harvey, Adrian. *The Beginnings of a Commercial Sporting Culture in Britain, 1793-1850*. Aldershot, 2004.

Hastings, Adrian. *The Construction of Nationhood: Ethnicity, Religion and Nationalism*. Cambridge, 1997.

Hastings, Derek K. "Fears of a Feminized Church: Catholicism, Clerical Celibacy, and the Crisis of Masculinity in Wilhelmine Germany". *European History Quarterly*, 38 (2008) 1, 34-65.

Haun, Gerhard. *Die Wallfahrt nach Neviges*. Wuppertal, 1981.

Haupt, Heinz-Gerhard and Langewiesche, Dieter, eds. *Nation und Religion in Europa. Mehrkonfessionelle Gesellschaften im 19. und 20. Jahrhundert*. Frankfurt-New York, 2004.

Haynes, Carolyn. "Women and Protestantism in Nineteenth-Century America" in: Peter W. Williams, ed. *Perspectives on American Religion and Culture*. Malden Mass.-Oxford UK, 1999, 300-318.

Healy, Róisín. "Anti-Jesuitism in Imperial Germany: The Jesuit as Androgyne" in: Helmut Walser Smith, ed. *Protestants, Catholics and Jews in Germany, 1800-1914*. Oxford-New York, 2001, 153-181.

Healy, Róisín. *The Jesuit Specter in Imperial Germany*. London, 2003.

Heerma van Voss, Lex; Pasture, Patrick and De Maeyer, Jan, eds. *Between Cross and Class: Comparative Histories of Christian Labour in Europe 1840-2000*. Bern-Oxford, 2006.

Heilbronner, Oded. *Catholicism, Political Culture, and the Countryside: A Social History of the Nazi Party in the Countryside*. Ann Arbor, 1998.

Heimann, Mary. *Catholic Devotion in Victorian England*. New York, 1995.

Heinemann, A. "Aufbruch katholischer Jugend!". *Der Kranz*, 26 (1932), 191-196.

Hellemans, Staf. "Die Transformation der Religion und der Grosskirchen in der zweiten Moderne aus der Sicht des religiösen Modernisierungsparadigmas". *Schweizerische Zeitschrift für Religions- und Kulturgeschichte*, 99 (2005), 11-35.

Hellemans, Staf. *Het tijdperk van de wereldreligies. Religie in agrarische civilizaties en in moderne samenlevingen*. Zoetermeer, 2007.

Hellemans, Staf. "How Modern is Religion in Modernity?" in: Judith Frishman, Willemien Otten and Gerard Rouwhorst, eds. *Religious Identity and the Problem of Historical Foundation: The Foundational Character of Authorative Sources in the History of Christianity and Judaism*. Leiden, 2004, 76-94.

Hellemans, Staf. *Strijd om de moderniteit. Sociale bewegingen en verzuiling in Europa sinds 1800*. Leuven, 1990.

Henkelmann, Andreas. *Caritasgeschichte zwischen katholischem Milieu und Wohlfahrtsstaat. Das Seraphische Liebeswerk (1889-1971)*. Paderborn, 2008.

Henvaux, L., S.J. "Le Problème de la Piété Eucharistique chez les hommes". *Hostia*, 10 (1936), 150-155.

Herf, Jeffrey. *Reactionary Modernism: Technology, Culture and Politics in Weimar and the Third Reich*. Cambridge, 1984.

Hermans, Hyacinth. "Em. Pastoor Orie". *De Waalbode*, 1939.

Herringer, Carol E. *Victorians and the Virgin Mary. Religion and Gender in England 1830-85*. Manchester, 2008.

Herzog, Dagmar. *Sex after Fascism: Memory and Morality in Twentieth-Century Germany*. Princeton, 2005.

"Het Pilatushoekske!". *Bondsblad voor Bonden van het Heilig Hart*, December 1936, 2.

Het Vaderland, 1933.

"Het zevende eeuwfeest der Dominicaner-orde". *De Maasbode*, 1916.

Heward, Christine. *Making a Man of Him: Parents and their Son's Education at an English Public School 1929-50*. London, 1988.

Heynen, Hilde. "Modernity and Domesticity: Tensions and Contradictions" in: Hilde Heynen and Gulsum Baydar, eds. *Negotiating Domesticity. Spatial Productions of Gender in Modern Architecture*. London, 2005, 1-28.

Heywood, Sophie. "Les 'petits garçons modèles'. La masculinité catholique à travers l'œuvre de la comtesse de Ségur" in: Régis Revenin, ed. *Hommes et masculinités de 1789 à nos jours. Contributions à l'histoire du genre et de la sexualité en France*. Paris, 2007, 208-219.

Historisch-politische Blätter, 1848.

Hödl, Klaus. "Performative Beiträge zum Diskurs über den effeminierten Juden" in: Annette Runte and Eva Werth, eds. *Feminisierung der Kultur? Féminisation de la civilization? Krisen der Männlichkeit und weibliche Avantgarden – Crises de la masculinité et avant-gardes féminines.* Saarbrücker Beiträge zur Vergleichenden Literatur- und Kulturwissenschaft 33. Würzburg, 2007, 137-155.

Hölscher, Lucian. *Datenatlas zur religiösen Geographie im protestantischen Deutschland; Von der Mitte des 19. Jahrhunderts bis zum Zweiten Weltkrieg.* Berlin, 2001, 4 vols.

Honegger, Claudia. *Die Ordnung der Geschlechter. Die Wissenschaften vom Menschen und das Weib, 1750-1850.* Frankfurt, 1991.

Horaist, Bruno. *La Dévotion au pape et les catholiques français sous le pontificat de Pie IX (1846-1878) d'après les archives de la Bibliothèque apostolique vaticaine.* Rome, 1995.

Horstmann, Johannes and Liedhegener, Antonius, eds. *Konfession, Moderne und Milieu: Konzeptionelle Positionen und Kontroversen zur Geschichte von Katholizismus und Kirche im 19. und 20. Jahrhundert.* Schwerte, 2001.

Hosp, Eduard. *Kirche Österreichs im Vormärz 1815-50.* Vienna, 1971.

Howat, Gerald. *Village Cricket.* Newton Abbot, 1980.

Hudson, Paul. *The History of Derby Shrovetide Football.* Derby, 2005.

Hufton, Olwen. "The Reconstruction of the Church, 1796-1801" in: Gwynne Lewis and Colin Lucas, eds. *Beyond the Terror: Essays in French Regional and Social History, 1794-1815.* Cambridge-New York, 1983, 21-52.

Hughes, Thomas. "How To Be Bodily Strong in a Town". *St Peter's, Derby, Parish Magazine,* (1861), 2.

Hughes, Thomas. *Tom Brown's School Days.* Oxford, 1989. [1st pub. 1857].

Huppertz, Hubert. "Auf dem Weg zu neuen Döllingerbiographien". *Internationale Kirchliche Zeitschrift,* 89 (1999), 45-62.

Huppertz, Hubert. "Ignaz von Döllinger (1799-1890): Opfer einer fixen Idee oder Zeuge der Wahrheit?" *Internationale Kirchliche Zeitschrift,* 89 (1999), 65-95.

Hürten, Heinz. "Zukunftperspektiven kirchlicher Zeitgeschichtsforschung" in: Ulrich von Hehl and Konrad Repgen, eds. *Der deutschen katholizismus in der Zeitgeschichtlichen Forschung.* Mainz, 1988, 97-116.

Huyssen, Andreas. *After the Great Divide: Modernism, Mass Culture, Postmodernism.* Bloomington, 1986.

"Ich habe keine Zeit". *Die Mutter*, January 1916.

Irigaray, Luce. *Je, tu, nous: Towards a Culture of Difference.* New York, 2007. (transl. *Je, tu, nous.* Paris, 1990).

Itzkowitz, David C. *Peculiar Privilege: A Social History of English Foxhunting 1753-1885.* Brighton, 1977.

Jacobs, P.M.J. *Beeldend Nederland.* Tilburg, 1993.

Jarry, E. "Zouaves, Papal" in: Catholic University of America, ed. *New Catholic Encyclopedia.* Vol. 14. New York, 1967, 1136.

Jonas, Raymond. "Anxiety, Identity, and the Displacement of Violence during the Année Terrible: The Sacred Heart and the Diocese of Nantes, 1870-1871". *French Historical Studies*, 21 (1998) 1, 55-75.

Jonas, Raymond. *France and the Cult of the Sacred Heart. An Epic Tale for Modern Times.* Berkeley, 2000.

Joosten, L.M.H. *Katholieken en fascisme in Nederland 1920-1940.* Hilversum-Antwerpen, 1964.

"Junge Front". *Der Kranz*, 26 (1932), 245.

Juster, Susan. "The Spirit and the Flesh. Gender, Language, and Sexuality in American Protestantism" in: Harry S. Stout and D.G. Hart, eds. *New Directions in American Religious History.* New York-Oxford, 1997, 334-361.

Kaiser, Wolfram. "'Clericalism – That Is Your Enemy!' European Anticlericalism and the Culture Wars" in: Christopher Clark and Wolfram Kaiser, eds. *Culture Wars: Secular-Catholic Conflict in Nineteenth-Century Europe.* Cambridge, 2003, 11-46.

Kall, Alfred. *Katholische Frauenbewegung in Deutschland. Eine Untersuchung zur Gründung katholischer Frauenvereine im 19. Jahrhundert.* Paderborn, 1983.

Kalven, Janet. *Women Breaking Boundaries: A Grail Journey, 1940-1995.* New York, 1999.

Kalyvas, Statys N. *The Rise of Christian Democracy in Europe.* Ithaca-London, 1996.

Kane, Paula. "'She offered herself up': The Victim Soul and Victim Spirituality in Catholicism". *Church History*, 71 (2002) 80, 80-119.

Kater, Michael H. *Hitler Youth.* Cambridge, 2004.

Katholik, 1836, 1840, 1841, 1845, 1847, 1849.

Katholische Blätter. Organ des Schweizerischen Vereins freisinniger Katholiken, 1875-1877.

Katholische Kirchen-Zeitung, 1830.

Katholische Sonntagsblätter zur Belehrung, 1845.

Kaufmann, Doris. *Katholisches Milieu in Münster 1928-1933*. Düsseldorf, 1984.

Kaufmann, Franz-Xaver. *Kirche begreifen. Analysen und Thesen zur gesellschaftlichen Verfassung des Christentums*. Freiburg, 1979.

Kessel, Maria. "The 'Whole' Man: The Longing for a Masculine World in Nineteenth Century Germany". *Gender & History*, 15 (2003), 1-31.

Kieft, Ewoud. *Het plagiaat. De polemiek tussen Menno ter Braak en Anton van Duinkerken*. Nijmegen, 2006.

Kieft, Ewoud. *Tot oorlog bekeerd. Religieuze radicalisering in West-Europa, 1870-1918*. Utrecht, 2011.

King, Ursula. "Religion and Gender: Embedded Patterns, Interwoven Frameworks" in: Teresa A. Meade and Merry Wiesner-Hankes, eds. *A Companion to Gender History*. Oxford-Melbourne, 2004, 70-85.

Kirchliches Handbuch. Vol. 2: 1908/09. Freiburg, 1909.

Kirkley, Evelyn A. "Is it Manly to Be Christian? The Debate in Victorian and Modern America" in: Stephen D. Boyd et al., eds. *Redeeming Men: Religion and Masculinities*. Louisville, 1996, 80-88.

Klein, Gotthard. *Der Volksverein für das katholische Deutschland, 1890-1933: Geschichte, Bedeutung, Untergang*. Paderborn, 1996.

Klens, Hermann. *Anwalt der Frauen: Leben und Werk*. Düsseldorf, 1978.

Köhler, Joachim. "Ausbruch aus dem katholischen Milieu? Katholikinnen und Katholiken in Württemberg 1918 bis 1933" in: Rainer Lächele and Jörg Thierfelder, eds. *Württembergs Protestantismus in der Weimarer Republik*. Stuttgart, 2003, 122-138.

Köppen, Ruth. *Die Armut ist weiblich*. Berlin, 1985.

Köser, Silke. *Denn die Diakonisse darf kein Alltagsmensch sein. Kollektive Identitäten Kaiserswerther Diakonissen 1836-1914*. Leipzig, 2006.

Kösters, Christoph. *Katholische Verbände und moderne Gesellschaft: Organizationsgeschichte und Vereinskultur im Bistum Münster, 1918-1945*. Paderborn, 1996.

Kracht, Hans-Joachim. *Leidenschaft für die Menschen*. Vol. 1: *Margaretha Rosa Flesch – Leben und Wirken*. Trier, 2005.

Kranz, Gisbert. *Eine katholische Jugend im Dritten Reich: Erinnerungen, 1921-1947*. Freiburg, 1990.

"Kranzbriefe". *Der Kranz*, 26 (1932), 55-56.

Kriege, Anneliese. *Geschichte der Evangelischen Kirchen-Zeitung unter der Redaktion Ernst Wilhelm Hengstenbergs (vom 1. Juli 1827 bis zum 1. Juni 1869). Ein Beitrag zur Kirchengeschichte des 19. Jahrhunderts*. Unpublished Theol. Diss. Bonn, 1958.

Kroon, Henk. *Pubers voor God. Het leven op een kleinseminarie in de jaren vijftig*. Nijmegen, 2001.

Kselman, Thomas. *Miracles and Prophecies in Nineteenth Century France*. New Brunswick, 1983.

Kynaston, David. *Bobby Abel, Professional Batsman*. London, 1982.

Lamberts Bendroth, Margaret. "Fundamentalism and Femininity: Points of Encounter between Religious Conservatives and Women, 1919-1935". *Church History*, 61 (1992) 2, 221-233.

Lamberts Bendroth, Margaret. *Fundamentalism and Gender, 1875 to the Present*. Yale, 1993.

Lamberts Bendroth, Margaret. *Growing Up Protestant: Parents, Children, and Mainline Churches*. New Brunswick, 2002.

Lamberts, Emiel, ed. *Een kantelend tijdperk. De wending van de Kerk naar het volk in Noord-West-Europa/ Une époque en mutation. Le catholicisme social dans le Nord-Ouest de l'Europe/ Ein Zeitalter im Umbruch. Die Wende der Kirche zum Volk im nordwestlichen Europa (1890-1910)*. KADOC-Studies. Leuven, 1992.

Landwehr, Achim. *Geschichte des Sagbaren. Einführung in die Historische Diskursanalyse*. Tübingen, 2004.

Langlois, Claude. *L'autobiographie de 1895. Lecture du manuscrit A de Thérèse de Lisieux*. Paris, 2009.

Langlois, Claude. *Le catholicisme au féminin. Les congrégations françaises supérieure générale au XIXe siècle*. Paris, 1984.

Langlois, Claude. *Le désir de sacerdoce de Thérèse de Lisieux*. Paris, 2002.

Langlois, Claude. "Le temps des séminaires. La formation cléricale au XIXe et XXe siècles" in: *Problèmes d'histoire de l'éducation. Actes des séminaires organisés par l'Ecole française de Rome, 1980*. Rome, 1980, 229-254.

Langlois, Claude. "'Toujours plus pratiquantes'. La permanence du dimorphisme sexuel dans le catholicisme français contemporain". *Clio*, 2 (1995). <http://clio.revues.org/index533.html>

"La piété italienne". *Revue de Bruxelles*, 5 (1841), 115-143.

Launay, Marcel. "Essor ou déclin des petits séminaires?" in: Id. *Les séminaires français aux XIXe et XXe siècles*. Paris, 2003.

Launay, Marcel. *Le bon prêtre: le clergé rural au XIXe siècle*. Paris, 1986.

Leconte, L. "Les Belges au Service de Rome (1860-1870). Aux Tirailleurs franco-belges et aux Zouaves pontificaux". *Carnet de la Fourragère*, 2 (1927-1929), 179.

Lehmann, Hartmut, ed. *Säkularisierung, Dechristianisierung, Rechristianisierung im neuzeitlichen Europa: Bilanz und Perspektiven der Forschung*. Göttingen, 1997.

Leinweber, Winfried. *Der Streit um den Zölibat im 19. Jahrhundert*. Münsterische Beiträge zur Theologie 44. Münster, 1978.

"Leve Paus Pius XI". *Bondsblad voor Bonden van het Heilig Hart*, February 1939, 1.

Lewis, Jane. *Women and Social Action in Victorian and Edwardian England*. Brighton, 1991.

Lewis, Jane. *Women's Welfare, Women's Rights*. London, 1983.

Liedhegener, Antonius. "Gottessuche, Kirchenkritik und Glaubenstreue unter Münsters Katholiken in den Krisenjahren der Weimarer Republik. Untersuchungen zur katholischen Deutungskultur anhand einer frühen pastoraltheologischen Meinungsumfrage". *Westfälische Forschungen*, 47 (1997), 323-372.

Lindman, Janet Moore. "Acting the Manly Christian: White Evangelical Masculinity in Revolutionary Virginia". *William and Mary Quarterly*, 3 (2000) 57, 393-416.

Lindman, Janet Moore. "The Body Baptist: Embodied Spirituality, Ritualization and Church Discipline in Eighteenth Century America" in: Janet Moore Lindman and Michele Lise Tarter, eds. *A Centre of Wonders: The Body in Early America*. Ithaca, 2001, 177-190.

Loeff, J.A. et al. *Het Katholieke Nederland 1813-1913. Blijde herinneringen aan het eerste eeuwfeest onzer nationale onafhankelijkheid*. Nijmegen, 1913.

Loewenberg, Peter. "The Psychohistorical Origins of the Nazi Youth Cohort" in: Id. *Decoding the Past: The Psychohistorical Approach*. London, 1985, 240-284.

Longman, Chia. "De marginalisering van 'religie' binnen genderstudies: een pleidooi voor een intersectionele benadering via de sociale wetenschappen". *Tijdschrift voor sociologie*, 24 (2003) 2-3, 261-276.

Lorette, J. "Historiographie des zouaves pontificaux belges 1860-1980" in: *Actes du colloque d'histoire militaire belge (1830-1980), Bruxelles, 26-28 mars 1980*. Brussels, 1981, 151-163.

Lösel, Steffen. "Prayer, Pain, and Priestly Privilege: Claude Langlois's New Perspective on Thérèse of Lisieux". *Journal of Religion*, 88 (2008) 3, 273-306.

Lowerson, John. *Sport and the English Middle Classes 1870-1914*. Manchester, 1993.

Lucassen, Hetty and Peeters, Thea. *Hora est. Gepromoveerde vrouwen aan de KUN, 1923-1940*. Nijmegen, 1988.

Lupson, Peter. *Thank God for Football*. London, 2006.

Lüttgen, Magdalena. *Die Elisabethvereine. Frauen im Dienst am Nächsten seit dem Jahre 1840 insbesondere in Rheinland und Westfalen*. Siegburg, 2003.

Luykx, Paul. "'Andere katholieken': een nieuwe visie". *Bijdragen en Mededelingen betreffende de Geschiedenis der Nederlanden/ Low Countries Historical Review*, 124 (2009) 3, 75-81.

Luykx, Paul. *Andere katholieken. Opstellen over Nederlandse katholieken in de twintigste eeuw*. Nijmegen, 2000.

Luykx, Paul. '*Daar is nog poëzie, nog kleur, nog warmte'. Katholieke bekeerlingen en moderniteit in Nederland, 1880-1960*. Hilversum, 2007.

Maandelijksche Mededeelingen voor Bonden van het Heilig Hart, 1930-.

Maguire, Joe. "Images of Manliness and Competing Ways of Living in Victorian and Edwardian Britain". *British Journal of Sports History*, 3 (1986), 278-279.

Maitre, Jacques. *Mystique et féminité*. Paris, 1997.

Maltha, Andreas, O.P. in: *Theologisch Woordenboek*. Vol. 2. Roermond, 1956, 1661-1675.

"Mannen- en Vrouwenbonden". *Maandelijksche Mededeelingen voor Bonden van het Heilig Hart*, December 1936, 2.

Mansi, J.D. *Sacrorum conciliorum nova et amplissima collectio*. Vol. 21. Florence, 1756.

Marks, Lynne. "'A Fragment of Heaven on Earth'? Religion, Gender and Family in Turn-of-the-Century Canadian Church Periodicals". *Journal of Family History*, 26 (2001) 2, 251-271.

Martin, David. "Integration and Fragmentation: Patterns of Religion in Europe" in: Krzysztof Michalski, ed. *Religion in the New Europe*. Budapest-New York, 2006, 65-84.

Marx, J. "De cultus van het Heilig Hart: een materialistische en politieke devotie" in: Anne Morelli, ed. *Devotie en godsdienstbeoefening in de verzamelingen van de Koninklijke Bibliotheek*. Dossier van de Koninklijke Bibliotheek Albert I, 26. Brussels, 2005, 97-112.

Mausbach, Joseph. *Die Stellung der Frau im Menschheitslebens. Eine Anwendung katholische Grundsätze auf die Frauenfrage*. Mönchengladbach, 1906. (transl. *Het standpunt der vrouw in de maatschappij: eene toepassing der katholieke leer op het vrouwenvraagstuk*. Leiden, 1908.)

McCutcheon, Russell T. *Manufacturing Religion: The Discourse on Sui Generis Religion and the Politics of Nostalgia*. New York, 1997.

McDannell, Colleen. *The Christian Home in Victorian America 1840-1900*. Bloomington, 1986.

McDevitt, Patrick F. "Muscular Catholicism: Nationalism, Masculinity and Gaelic Team Sports, 1884-1916". *Gender & History*, 9 (1997) 2, 262-284.

McLeod, Hugh. "New Perspectives on the Religious History of Western and Northern Europe 1815-1960". *Kyrkhistorisk Arsskrift*, 100 (2000) 1, 135-145.

McLeod, Hugh. *Piety and Poverty: Working Class Religion in Berlin, London and New York 1870-1914*. New York, 1996.

McLeod, Hugh. *Religion and the People of Western Europe*. Oxford-New York, 1997.

McLeod, Hugh. *Secularization in Western Europe, 1848-1914*. Basingstoke, 2000.

McLeod, Hugh. "The Religious Crisis of the 1960s". *Journal of Modern European History*, 3 (2005) 2, 205-230.

McLeod, Hugh. "Thews and Sinews: Nonconformity and Sport" in: David Bebbington and Timothy Larsen, eds. *Modern Christianity and Cultural Aspirations*. London, 2003, 29-30.

McLeod, Hugh. "Weibliche Frömmigkeit-männlicher Unglaube? Religion und Kirchen im bürgerlichen 19. Jahrhundert" in: Ute Frevert, ed. *Bürgerinnen und Bürger. Geschlechtsverhältnisse im 19. Jahrhundert*. Göttingen, 1988, 123-156.

McMillan, James. "'Priest Hits Girl': on the Front Line in the 'War of the Two Frances'" in: Christopher Clark and Wolfram Kaiser, eds. *Culture Wars. Secular-Catholic Conflict in Nineteenth-Century Europe*. Cambridge, 2003, 77-101.

McSweeney, Bill. "Catholic Piety in the Nineteenth Century". *Social Compass*, 34 (1987) 2-3, 203-210.

Meerman, Dick and Van Oostrum, Hilde. "'Een groote vrouw waar vindt men haar!' Katholieke vrouwen in de jaren dertig: de Graal" in: Grietje Dresen and Annelies van Heijst, eds. *Een sterke vrouw...? Over het zoeken van vrouwen naar religieuze identificatiefiguren*. Amersfoort, 1984, 93-113.

Meesen, G., S.J. *La belle histoire des Ligues du Sacré-Cœur*. S.l., s.a.

Meeus, J., S.J. "De Bonden van het Heilig Hart in het Aartsbisdom". *Bode van het Heilig Hart*, 1939, 264.

Meeus, J., S.J. "Mannen- en Vrouwenbonden". *Maandelijksche Mededeelingen voor Bonden van het Heilig Hart*, June 1936, 2-3.

Meeus, J., S.J. "Mannen- en Vrouwenbonden. II. Eenige Toepassingen". *Maandelijksche Mededeelingen voor Bonden van het Heilig Hart*, July 1936, 2-3.

Meeus, J., S.J. "Mannen- en Vrouwenbonden. III. Kommuniemis". *Maandelijksche Mededeelingen voor Bonden van het Heilig Hart*, August 1936, 2-3.

Meeus, J., S.J. "Mannen- en Vrouwenbonden. IV. Apostolaat". *Maandelijksche Mededeelingen voor Bonden van het Heilig Hart*, September 1936, 1-3.

Meeus, J., S.J. *Mannen- en Vrouwenbonden van het Heilig Hart*. Mechelen, 1936.

Meiwes, Relinde. *'Arbeiterinnen des Herrn'. Katholische Frauenkongregationen im 19. Jahrhundert*. Frankfurt-New York, 2000.

Meijer, G.A. *Studiën over de Dominicanen-Orde*. Zwolle, 1910.

Menozzi, Daniele. *Sacro Cuore. Un culto tra devozione interiore e restaurazione cristiana della società*. Rome, 2001.

Menozzi, Daniele. "Un rêve de chrétienté à la fin du XIXe siècle: le règne social du Christ dans les congrès eucharistiques internationaux" in: Laurence Van Ypersele and Anne-Dolorès Marcelis, eds. *Rêves de Chrétienté. Réalités du monde. Imaginaires catholiques. Actes du colloque, Louvain-la-Neuve, 4-6 novembre 1999*. Paris-Louvain-la-Neuve, 2001, 141-158.

Mergel, Thomas. "Die subtile Macht der Liebe. Geschlecht, Erziehung und Frömmigkeit in Katholischen Rheinischen Bürgerfamilien 1830-1910" in: Irmtraud Götz von Olenhusen, ed. *Frauen unter dem Patriarchat der Kirche, Katholikinnen und Protestantinnen im 19. und 20. Jahrhundert*. Stuttgart, 1995, 22-47.

Metcalfe, Alan. *Leisure and Recreation in a Victorian Mining Community*. London, 2006.

Metz, Karl Heinz. *Die Geschichte der sozialen Sicherheit*. Stuttgart, 2008.

Mews, Stuart. "Clergymen, Gentlemen and Men: World War I and the Requirements, Recruitment, and Training of the Anglican Ministery" in: Theo Clemens and W. Janse, eds. *The Pastor Bonus. Papers read at the British-Dutch Colloquium at Utrecht, 18-21 September 2002 (Dutch Review of Church History, 83 (2004))*, 435-447.

Michel, Ernest. *Europeesche jeugd*. Malden, 1933.

Michel, Ernest. *Neo-Communisten*. S.l., [1932].

Michelet, Jules. *Du prêtre, de la femme, de la famille*. Paris, 1845. (transl. *Priests, women and families*. London, 1845; *Der katholische Priester in seiner Stellung zum Weibe und zur Familie*. Leipzig, 1845; *Over den priester, de vrouw en het huisgezin*. Amsterdam, 1845.)

Miegge, Giovanni. *La Vergine Maria: saggio di storia del dogma*. Torre Pellice, 1950. (Transl. *The Virgin Mary: The Roman Catholic Marian Doctrine*. Textbook Publishers, 2003.)

Miller, Lori. "The (Re)Gendering of High Anglicanism" in: Andrew Bradstock et al., eds. *Masculinity and Spirituality in Victorian Culture*. Basingstoke, 2000, 27-43.

Mirbt, Carl and Aland, Kurt. *Quellen zur Geschichte des Papsttums und des Römischen Katholizismus*. Tübingen, 1967.

Monteiro, Marit. "Catholic Intellectual Elites in the Netherlands: Fruitful and Vulnerable Alliances during the Interbellum" in: Urs Altermatt, Franziska Metzger and Jan De Maeyer, eds. *Religious Institutes and Catholic Culture 19th and 20th Century Europe. Relins-Europe International Workshop*. KADOC Studies on Religion, Culture and Society. Leuven (forthcoming).

Monteiro, Marit. *Gods Predikers. Dominicanen in Nederland (1795-2000)*. Hilversum, 2008.

Monteiro, Marit. "Mannen Gods: historische perspectieven op clericale identiteit en clericale cultuur" in: Marit Monteiro and Gian Ackermans, eds. *Mannen Gods. Clericale identiteit in verandering*. Hilversum, 2007, 9-32.

Morbach, Annika. *Der katholische Diskurs über die Barmherzigen Schwestern in der ersten Hälfte des 19. Jahrhunderts*. Unpublished Diplomthesis at the Theological Faculty of Trier. Trier, 2008.

Morcillo, Aurora. *True Catholic Womanhood: Gender Ideology in Franco's Spain*. DeKalb-Nothern Illinois, 2000.

Mosse, George L. *Fallen Soldiers: Reshaping the Memory of the World Wars*. New York-Oxford, 1990.

Mosse, George L. *The Image of Man: The Creation of Modern Masculinity*. New York-Oxford, 1998.

Müller, Dirk H. *Arbeiter, Katholizismus, Staat: Der Volksverein für das katholische Deutschland und die katholischen Arbeiterorganizationen in der Weimarer Republik*. Bonn, 1996.

Munting, Roger. "Social Opposition to Gambling in Britain: An Historical Overview". *International Journal of the History of Sport*, 10 (1993).

Mutter und Frau, 1932, 1937.

Nathanel, 1849.

Neue Theologische Zeitschrift, 1832.

Neuner, Peter. *Döllinger als Theologe der Ökumene*. Paderborn-Munich, 1979.

Nippold, Friedrich, ed. *Die Einführung der erzwungenen Ehelosigkeit bei den christlichen Geistlichen und ihre Folgen: ein Beitrag zur Kirchengeschichte von Johann Anton Theiner und Augustin Theiner*. Barmen, 1891-1898, 3 vols.

"Nochmals Jungmann und Mädchen". *Die Wacht*, 20 (1924-1925), 68-70.

Nye, Robert A. "Western Masculinities in War and Peace". *The American Historical Review*, 112 (2007) 2.

Obelkevich, James. *Religion and Rural Society: South Lindsey 1825-1875*. Oxford, 1976.

Oeyen, Christian. *Die Entstehung der Bonner Unions-Konferenzen im Jahr 1874*. Unpublished Habilitationsschrift, Christkatholische Fakultät, University of Bern. Konstanz, 1971.

Offen, Karen. *European Feminisms, 1700-1950: A Political History*. Stanford, 2000.

O'Malley, Patrick R. *Catholicism, Sexual Deviance, and Victorian Gothic Culture*. Cambridge, 2006.

Onslow, G.M. "Physical Recreation: Its Use and Abuse". *Official Report of the Church Congress*, 1892, 301-317.

"Onze Zondagmis". *Bondsblad voor Bonden van het Heilig Hart*, June 1939, 4-5.

Oostveen, Ton. "Ernest Michel. De wilde kreten van een heftig katholiek". *De Tijd*, 1982.

Oraison, Marc. *Le célibat. Aspect négatif, réalités positives*. Paris, 1966.

Orsi, Robert A. "Abundant History: Marian Apparitions as Alternative Modernity" in: Randall J. Stephens, ed. *Recent Themes in American Religious History: Historians in Conversation*. Columbia, 2009, 127-139.

Orsi, Robert A. *The Madonna of 115th Street: Faith and Community in Italian Harlem, 1880-1950*. New Haven/London, 2002.

Osbaldeston, George. *Squire Osbaldeston: His Autobiography*. London, 1926.

O'Sullivan, Michael E. "An Eroding Milieu? Catholic Youth, Church Authority, and Popular Behavior in Northwest Germany during the Third Reich, 1933-1938". *Catholic Historical Review*, 90 (2004) 2, 236-259.

Palau, G., S.J. *De Katholiek van de Daad*. Alken, 1929.

Parker, Charles. *Faith on the Margins: Catholics and Catholicism in the Dutch Golden Age*. Cambridge MA, 2008.

Pasture, Patrick. "De-Christianization and the Changing Spiritual Landscape in Europe and North America since 1950. Comparative, Transatlantic and Global Perspectives" in: Nancy Christie, Michael Gauvreau and Stephan Heathorn, eds. *Dechristianization as History: The Sixties and Beyond*. Toronto, in press.

Pasture, Patrick. "Religion in Contemporary Europe: Contrasting Perceptions and Dynamics". *Archiv für Sozialgeschichte*, 49 (2009), 319-350.

"Pater/schilder Raymundus van Bergen (95) overleden". *Zwolsche Courant*, 24-11-1978.

Pearce, Joseph. *Literary Converts: Spiritual Inspiration in an Age of Unbelief*. London, 1999.

Perry, Jos. *Jongens op kostschool. Het dagelijks leven op katholieke jongensinternaten*. Utrecht, 1991.

Perry, Nicholas and Echeverria, Loreto. *Under the Heal of Mary*. London, 1988.

Pesch, Rudolf. *Die kirchlich-politische Presse der Katholiken in der Rheinprovinz vor 1848*. Mainz, 1967.

Peterson, Derek R. and Walhof, Darren R., eds. "Rethinking Religion" in: Derek R. Peterson and Darren R. Walhof, eds. *The Invention of Religion: Rethinking Belief in Politics and History*. London-New Brunswick NJ, 2002, 1-18.

Peterson, Derek R. and Walhof, Darren R., eds. *The Invention of Religion: Rethinking Belief in Politics and History*. London-New Brunswick NJ, 2002.

Petit, Bernard. "Zouaves" in: Jean Tulard, ed. *Dictionnaire du Second Empire*. Paris, 1995, 1345-1346.

Pijfers, Herman. *Het Katholieken Boek*. Zwolle, 2006.

Pijfers, Herman and Roes, Jan. *Memoriale. Een eeuw katholiek leven in Nederland*. Zwolle, 1997.

Pirotte, Jean. *Images des vivants et des morts: la vision du monde propagée par l'imagerie de dévotion dans le Namurois 1840-1965*. Louvain-la-Neuve, 1987.

Pirotte, Jean. "L'empreinte des gens d'Eglise sur les images de dévotion. Les images diffusées dans le Namurois de 1840 à 1965". *Annales de Bretagne*, 98 (1991) 2, 134-136.

Pirotte, Jean. "Le paradis de papier de l'imagerie dévote. Quelle société céleste pour quels chrétiens? (1840-1965)" in: Emma Fattorini, ed. *Santi, culti, simboli nell'età della secolarizzazione (1815-1915)*. Rome, 1997, 67-104.

Planert, Ute. *Antifeminismus im Kaiserreich. Diskurs, soziale Formation und politische Mentalität*. Kritische Studien zur Geschichtswissenschaft 124. Göttingen, 1998.

Prestjan, Anna. "The Man in the Clergyman: Swedish Priest Obituaries" in: Yvonne Maria Werner, ed. *Christian Masculinity: Men and Religion in Northern Europe in the 19th and 20th Century*. KADOC Studies on Religion, Culture and Society 8. Leuven, 2011, 115-125.

Pruvost, Alexandre. *Notice sur la vie et la mort du comte Alfred de Limminghe*. Brussels, 1861.

Putney, Clifford. *Muscular Christianity: Manhood and Sports in Protestant America, 1880-1920*. Cambridge, 2001.

Pyka, Marcus. "Geschichtswissenschaft und Identität. Zur Relevanz eines umstrittenen Themas". *Historische Zeitschrift*, 280 (2005), 381-392.

Quaghebeur, Patricia. "De Eucharistische Kruistocht (1920-1963)" in: Patricia Quaghebeur and Rita Ghesquière, eds. *Averbode: een uitgever apart 1877-2002*. Averbode-Leuven, 2002, 92-173.

Rae, Simon. *W.G. Grace: A Life*. London, 1998.

Ratzinger, Georg. *Geschichte der kirchlichen Armenpflege*. Freiburg, 2001 (reprint of the Freiburg edition 1884).

"Referat Kallers über die Wandernde Kirche, 22 August 1940" in: Ludwig Volk, ed. *Akten Deutscher Bischöfe über die Lage der Kirche 1933-1946*. Vol. 5. Mainz, 1983, 138.

Reid, Douglas A. "Beasts and Brutes: Popular Blood Sports c.1780-1860" in: Richard Holt, ed. *Sport and the Working Class in Modern Britain*. Manchester, 1990, 12-28.

Reinkens, Joseph Hubert. *Die Barmherzigen Schwestern vom heil. Carl Borromäus zu Nancy, geschichtlich dargestellt nach den bisher nur statt handschriftlicher Mittheilung gedruckten Berichten und officiellen Rundschreiben der geistlichen Oberen der Congregation*. Bonn, 1847.

Report of the First Conference of the Young Men's Christian Associations of Great Britain and Ireland, held in Leeds September 1858. Leeds, 1858.

"Rettet die Familie". *Die Mutter*, February 1930.

Reul, C. et al., ed. *Het vierde Rolduc, 1946-1971. Geschiedenis van een klein-seminarie*. Kerkrade, 1983.

Rey, Karl Guido. *Das Mutterbild des Priesters*. Zurich, 1969.

Rich, Paul John. *Chains of Empire: English Public Schools, Masonic Cabalism, Historical Causality and Imperial Clubdom*. London, 1991.

Rich, Paul John. *Elixer of Empire: The English Public Schools, Ritualism, Freemasonry and Imperialism*. London, 1989.

Richardson, Mary E. *The Life of a Great Sportsman (John Maunsell Richardson)*. London, 1919.

Righart, Hans. *De katholieke zuil in Europa. Het ontstaan van verzuiling onder katholieken in Oostenrijk, Zwitserland, België en Nederland*. Meppel-Amsterdam-Boom, 1986.

Rion, P. "Une illustration du patriotisme du Cardinal Van Roey: sa position relative au culte du Sacre-Coeur et la Basilique de Koekelberg durant les années 1940-1944". *Centre de recherches et d'études historiques de la Seconde Guerre mondiale. Bulletin*, 11 (1981), 27-33.

Rogier, L.J. and de Rooij, N. *In vrijheid herboren. Katholiek Nederland 1853-1953*. The Hague, 1953.

Roos, Julia. "Backlash against Prostitutes' Rights: Origins and Dynamics of Nazi Prostitution Policies". *Journal of the History of Sexuality*, 11 (2002), 67-94.

Roos, Julia. "Weimar's Crisis through the Lens of Gender: The Case of Prostitution". *Bulletin of the German Historical Institute*, 23 (2003), 85-92.

Rosen, David. "The Volcano and the Cathedral: Muscular Christianity and the Origins of Primal Manliness" in: Donald E. Hall, ed. *Muscular Christianity: Embodying the Victorian Age*. Cambridge Studies in Nineteenth-Century Literature and Culture. Cambridge, 1994 [2006], 17-44.

Roussel, Jean-Francois. "Roman Catholic Religious Discourse About Manhood in Quebec: From 1900 to the Quiet Revolution (1960-1980)". *The Journal of Men's Studies*, 11 (2003) 2, 145-155.

Ruff, Mark Edward. "The Postmodern Challenge to the Secularization Thesis". *Schweizerische Zeitschrift für Religions- und Kulturgeschichte*, 99 (2005), 385-401.

Ruff, Mark Edward. *The Wayward Flock: Catholic Youth in Postwar Germany, 1945-1965*. Chapel Hill-London, 2005.

Rulla, Luigi M. *Structure psychologique et vocation. Motivations d'entrée et de sortie*. Rome, 1978.

Rundbrief des Heliandbundes, Christkönigsfest 1932.

Rutten, Martin. *Lettres d'un Zouave Pontifical (de 1863 à 1870)*. Paris, 1949.

Rutz, Andreas. *Bildung-Konfession-Geschlecht. Religiöse Frauengemeinschaften und die katholische Mädchenbildung im Rheinland (16.-18. Jahrhundert)*. Mainz, 2006.

Sachße, Christoph. *Mütterlichkeit als Beruf. Sozialarbeit, Sozialreform und Frauenbewegung 1871-1929*. Frankfurt, 1986.

Sachße, Christoph and Tennstedt, Florian. *Geschichte der Armenfürsorge in Deutschland*. Vol. 1: *Vom Spätmittelalter bis zum 1. Weltkrieg*. Stuttgart, 1998.

Sack, Birgit. *Zwischen religiöser Bindung und moderner Gesellschaft: katholische Frauenbewegung und politische Kultur in der Weimarer Republik (1918/19-1933)*. Münster, 1998.

Sailer, Johann Michael, ed. *Sebastian Winkelhofers vermischte Predigten*. Vol. 2. Munich, 1834.

Salemink, Theo and Borgman, Erik. "Katholieken en de eerste feministische golf" in: Bert van Dijk, Liesbeth Huijts and Trees Versteegen, eds. *Katholieke vrouwen en het feminisme. Een onderzoek door de Acht Mei Beweging*. Amersfoort-Leuven, 1990, 14-35.

Sánchez-Eppler, Karen. *Dependent States: The Child's Part in Nineteenth-Century American Culture*. Chicago, 2005.

Sanders, Mathijs. "Dominicus in de *Jazz Age*. Cas Terburg en de Nederlandse katholieke jongeren rond 1925". *Zacht Lawijd*, 5 (2006) 4, 43-60.

Sanders, Mathijs. *Het spiegelend venster. Katholieken in de Nederlandse literatuur, 1870-1940*. Nijmegen, 2002.

Sanders, Mathijs. "Maritain in the Netherlands: Pieter van der Meer de Walcheren and the Cult of Youth" in: Rajesh Heynickx and Jan De Maeyer, eds. *The Maritain Factor: Taking Religion into Interwar Modernism*. KADOC Studies on Religion, Culture and Society 7. Leuven, 2010, 84-99.

Sanfilippo, Matteo "Du Québec à Rome et de Rome au Québec: voyageurs canadiens-français en Italie et voyageurs italiens au Canada français entre la deuxième moitié du XIXe siècle et le début du XXe" in: Jean-Pierre Wallot et al., eds. *Constructions identitaires et pratiques sociales*. Ottawa, 279-302.

Sassen, Jan, O.P. *Het klooster: cultuur historische beschouwingen*. Roermond, 1922.

Sauer, Joseph. *Die Elisabetherinnen in Breslau*. Breslau, 1837.

Savart, Claude. *Les catholiques en France au XIXe siècle. Le témoignage du livre religieux*. Paris, 1985.

Schaeffler-Laub, Maria. *Der Heliandbund in seinen Gründungsjahren, 1924-1932: Ein Beitrag zur Geschichte katholischer Mädchen und Frauen*. Aus dem Archiv des Heliandbundes Nr. 6. Munich: Kreis Katholischer Frauen im Heliandbund, 2001.

Schaffer, Wolfgang. "Staatliche Neuordnung der Armenpflege seit Aufklärung und Säkularization" in: Erwin Gatz, ed. *Caritas und soziale Dienste*. Geschichte des kirchlichen Lebens in den deutschsprachigen Ländern seit dem Ende des 18. Jahrhunderts, 5. Freiburg i.Br., 1997, 39-56.

Schank, Christoph. *'Kölsch-Katholisch'. Das katholische Milieu in Köln, 1871-1933*. Cologne-Weimar-Vienna, 2004.

Schaper, Hans-Peter. *Krankenwartung und Krankenpflege. Tendenzen der Verberuflichung in der ersten Hälfte des 19. Jahrhundert*. Opladen, 1987.

Scheidgen, Hermann-Josef. *Der deutsche Katholizismus in der Revolution von 1848/49. Episkopat - Klerus - Laien - Vereine*. Cologne, 2008.

Schellenberger, Barbara. *Katholische Jugend und Drittes Reich: Eine Geschichte des katholischen Jungmännerverbandes 1933-1939 unter besonderer Berücksichtigung der Rheinprovinz*. Mainz, 1975.

Scheutz, Martin. "Demand and Charitable Supply: Poverty and Poor Relief in Austria in the 18th and 19th Centuries" in: Ole Peter Grell et al., eds. *Health Care and Poor Relief in 18th and 19th Century Southern Europe*. Aldershot, 2005, 52-95.

Schloesser, Stephen. *Catholicism in the Jazz Age: Mystic Modernism in Post-War Paris 1919-1933*. Vol. 2. Toronto, 2005.

Schmacher-Köhl, Minna. "Christusträgerinnen in der Großstadt". *Mutter und Frau*, October 1932.

Schmale, Wolfgang. *Geschichte der Männlichkeit in Europa (1450 - 2000)*. Vienna, 2003.

Schmid, Pia. "Weib oder Mensch, Wesen oder Wissen? Bürgerliche Theorien zur weiblichen Bildung um 1800" in: Elke Kleinau and Claudia Opitz, eds. *Geschichte der Mädchen und Frauenbildung*. Vol. 1. Frankfurt, 1996, 327-345.

Schnabel-Schüle, Helga. "Vierzig Jahre Konfessionalisierungsforschung – eine Standortbestimmung" in: Olaf Blaschke, ed. *Konfessionen im Konflikt. Das zweite konfessionelle Zeitalter zwischen 1800 und 1970*. Göttingen, 2002, 71-93.

Schneider, Bernhard. "Feminisierung der Religion im 19. Jahrhundert. Perspektiven einer These im Kontext des deutschen Katholizismus". *Trierer theologische Zeitschrift*, 111 (2002), 123-147.

Schneider, Bernhard. *Katholiken auf die Barrikaden? Europäische Revolutionen und deutsche katholische Presse 1815-1848*. Paderborn u.a., 1998.

Schneider, Bernhard, ed. *Konfessionelle Armutsdiskurse und Armenfürsorgepraktiken im langen 19. Jahrhundert*. Frankfurt, 2010.

Schneider, Bernhard. "'Poverty Need No Longer Despair...'. Observations on the Dignity of the Poor in Late-enlightenment Catholic Prayer Books." Presentation at the conference "The Dignity of the Poor: Concepts, Practises, Representations", German Historical Institute, London, 7-9 Dec. 2006 (forthcoming).

Schnell, Rüdiger. "Text und Geschlecht. Eine Einleitung" in: Rüdiger Schnell. *Text und Geschlecht. Mann und Frau in Eheschriften der Frühen Neuzeit*. Frankfurt, 1997, 9-46.

Schoon, Dick J. *Van bisschoppelijke Cleresie tot Oud-Katholieke Kerk. Bijdrage tot de geschiedenis van het katholicisme in Nederland in de 19e eeuw*. Nijmegen, 2004.

Schulz, Gerhard. "Armut und Armenpolitik in Deutschland im frühen 19. Jahrhundert". *Historisches Jahrbuch*, 115 (1995), 388-410.

Schulze Wessel, Martin. *Nationalisierung der Religion und Sakralisierung der Nation im östlichen Europa*. Stuttgart, 2006.

Schweikardt, Christoph. *Die Entwicklung der Krankenpflege zur staatlich anerkannten Tätigkeit im 19. und frühen 20. Jahrhundert*. Munich, 2008, 42-45.

Scott, Joan W. "Gender: A Useful Category of Historical Analysis". *American Historical Review*, 91 (1986) 5, 1053-1075.

Scott, Joan W. "On Gender, Language and Working-Class History" in: Id. *Gender and the Politics of History*. New York, 1999², 53-67.

Seeley, Paul. "O Sainte Mère: Liberalism and the Socialization of Catholic Men in Nineteenth-Century France". *Journal of Modern History*, 70 (1998) 4, 862-892.

"Selbstvergessene Liebe". *Die Mutter*, January 1916.

Sensbach, Jon F. "Before the Bible Belt: Indians, Africans, and the New Synthesis of Eighteenth-Century Southern Religious History" in: Beth Barton Schweiger and Donald G. Mathews, eds. *Religion in the American South: Protestants and Others in History and Culture*. Chapel Hill-London, 2004, 5-29.

Shoemaker, Robert. *Gender in English Society, 1650-1850: The emergence of separate spheres?* London, 1998.

Showalter, Elaine. *Sexual Anarchy: Gender and Culture at the Fin de Siècle*. New York, 1990.

Siemann, Wolfram. *Vom Staatenbund zum Nationalstaat. Deutschland 1806-1871*. Munich, 1995.

Sintzel, Michael. *Geschichte der Entstehung, Verbreitung und Wirksamkeit des Ordens der barmherzigen Schwestern*. Regensburg, 1847.

Sion, 1832, 1836, 1837, 1842, 1843.

Sipe, A.W. Richard. *Celibacy in Crisis: A Secret World Revisited*. New York, 2003.

Smith, Anthony D. *Chosen Peoples: Sacred Sources of National Identity*. Oxford, 2003.

Smith, Bonnie. *Ladies of the Leisure Class: The Bourgeoises of Northern France*. Princeton, 1981.

Smith, Jonathan Z. "Religion, Religions, Religious" in: Mark C. Taylor, ed. *Critical Terms for Religious Studies*. Chicago, 1989, 269-284.

Snape, Michael. *Clergy under Fire*. Woodbridge, 2007.

Sneeringer, Julia. *Winning Women's Votes: Propaganda and Politics in Weimar Germany*. Chapel Hill-London, 2002.

Sonntagsblatt für katholische Christen, 1842, 1850.

Starink, Jan et al. *Hoe wij slaagden: een reconstructie van het leven op het Sint Canisius College te Nijmegen tussen 1900 en 1950*. Hilversum, 1982.

Starkey, Pat. "Women Religious and Religious Women: Faith and Practice in Women's Lives" in: Deborah Simonton, ed. *The Routledge History of Women in Europe since 1700*. London-New York, 2006, 177-215.

Steinhoff, Anthony J. "Ein zweites konfessionelles Zeitalter?". *Geschichte und Gesellschaft*, 30 (2004), 549-570.

Stevens, F.E. "Een goudmijn voor genealogisten en geschiedschrijvers. De dienstverbintenissen bij de pauselijke troepen 1860-1870". *Belgisch Tijdschrift voor Militaire Geschiedenis*, 20 (1973), 53-78.

Stobbe, Heinz-Günther. "Konflikte um Identität. Eine Studie zur Bedeutung von Macht in interkonfessionellen Beziehungen und im ökumenischen Prozeß" in: Peter Lengsfeld, ed. *Ökumenische Theologie*. Stuttgart, 1980, 190-237.

Stockums, W. *Priesterschap en ascese. Godsdienstig-ascetische gedachten voor theologanten en priesters*. Amsterdam, 1939.

Stray, Christopher. "From Monopoly to Marginality: Classics in English Education" in Ivor F. Goodson, ed. *Social Histories of the Secondary Curriculum*. London, 1985, 19-52.

Strobbe, Johan. *200 jaar dichters, denkers en durvers. Het Klein Seminarie van Roeselare. Biografie van een college*. Tielt, 2007.

Struyker Boudier, C. *Vijftig jaar Nebo. De Nebo vijftig jaar*. Nijmegen, 1978.

Süddeutsches Kirchenblatt, 1845.

Süddeutsche Zeitung für Kirche und Staat, 1845.

Suleiman, Susan R. *Authoritarian Fictions: The Ideological Novel as a Literary Genre*. New York, 1983.

Sun, Raymond C. "Catholic-Marxist Competition in the Working-Class Parishes of Cologne during the Weimar Republic". *Catholic Historical Review*, 83 (1997) 1, 20-44.

Sun, Raymond C. "'Hammer Blows': Work, the Workplace, and the Culture of Masculinity among Catholic Workers in the Weimar Republic". *Central European History*, 37 (2004), 245-271.

Suszczynski, Josaphat Sylvester. *Denkschrift des Propstes von Mogilno*. Königsberg, 1876.

Sutherland, Douglas. *The Yellow Earl*. London, 1965.

Tacke, Andreas, ed. *"…Wir wollen der Liebe Raum geben". Konkubinate geistlicher und weltlicher Fürsten um 1500*. Göttingen, 2006.

Taylor Allen, Ann. *Feminism and Motherhood in Germany, 1800-1914*. New Brunswick, 1991. (Transl. *Feminismus und Mütterlichkeit in Deutschland 1800-1914*. Weinheim, 2000.)

Taylor Allen, Ann. *Feminism and Motherhood in Western Europe, 1890-1970: The Maternal Dilemma*. London, 2005.

Terburg, Cas. *Het innerlijk leven*. Utrecht, 1925.

"Terug naar de Zondagmis!". *Maandelijksche Mededeelingen voor Bonden van het Heilig Hart*, May 1937, 2.

"Terug naar de Zondagsmis. De tijden zijn rijp!". *Maandelijksche Mededeelingen voor Bonden van het Heilig Hart*, October 1938, 3.

Terwecoren, Edouard. *Auguste Misson, zouave pontifical*. Brussels, 1862.

Terwecoren, Edouard. *Ludovic De Taillart, zouave pontifical*. Brussels, 1862.

"The football slaughter". *The Young Man*, April (1889), 73-75.

The Official Report of the Church Congress, 1869, 1892.

Thomas Aquinas. *Summa Theologiae*. Latin text, ed. and transl. Edmund Hill. London, 1964.

Tihon, André. "Les mouvements des laïcs aux XIXe et XXe siècles. Rapport general" in: *Miscellanea historiae ecclesiasticae. VII: Congrès de Bucarest août 1980*. Brussels, 1985, 143-177.

Tihon, André. "Les religieuses en Belgique du XVIIIe au XXe siècle. Approche statistique". *Revue belge d'histoire contemporaine*, 7 (1976) 1-2, 1-54.

Tozer, Malcolm. *Physical Education at Thring's Uppingham*. Uppingham, 1976.

Tromp, W. et al. *Meer dan het geweest is: 100 jaar met Canisius College, Mater Dei, Canisius Mavo, Pius XII Mavo, Poels-Roncalli, De Kronenburg, Michaël Mavo en hun voorgangers*. Nijmegen, 2000.

Troughton, Geoffrey M. "Jesus and the Ideal of the Manly Man in New Zealand after World War One". *Journal of Religious History*, 30 (2006) 1, 45-60.

Tschannen, Olivier. *Les théories de la sécularisation*. Geneva, 1992.

"Uit het leven". *Bondsblad voor Bonden van het Heilig Hart*, October 1936, 2.

"Uit het Walenland". *Bondsblad voor Bonden van het Heilig Hart*, May 1937, 4.

"Unsere Jugend: Der kleine Kriegsheld". *Die Mutter*, January 1916.

"Unsere Jugend: Fritz will nicht beten/ Prinzetschen". *Die Mutter*, March 1916.

"Unsere Jugend: Maigang". *Die Mutter*, April 1930.

"Unsere Kinder in der Werktagsmesse". *Mutter und Frau*, September 1937.

"Van Bode tot Boodschap". *Jezuïeten*, 1 (1991), 2.

Van Boven, Erika. "De viriele generatie van 1918". *Tijdschrift voor Nederlandse Taal- en Letterkunde*, 117 (2001) 2, 109-132.

Vance, Norman. *The Sinews of the Spirit: The Ideal of Christian Manliness in Victorian Literature and Religious Thought*. Cambridge, 1994.

Van Coillie, Jan and Ghesquière, Rita. *Uit de schaduw. Een beknopte geschiedenis van de West-Vlaamse en de Westfaalse jeugd- en kinderliteratuur*. Bruges, 1996.

Van den Haterd, Lex. *Om hart en vurigheid. Over schrijvers en kunstenaars van tijdschrift en uitgeverij De gemeenschap 1925-1941*. Haarlem, 2004.

Van der Meer de Walcheren, Pieter. *Menschen en God*. Vol. 1: *1911-1929*. Utrecht, [1940].

Vandermeersch, Patrick and Westerink, Herman. *Godsdienst-psychologie in cultuurhistorisch perspectief*. Amsterdam, 2007.

Van der Plas, Michel. *Uit het rijke Roomsche Leven. Een documentaire over de jaren 1925-1935*. Utrecht, 1963 [Baarn, 1992].

Van der Veer, Peter and Lehman, Hartmut, eds. *Nation and Religion: Perspectives on Europe and Asia*. Princeton, 1999.

Van der Veken, Floris, S.J. "De mannen en de godsvrucht tot het H. Hart". *Pastor Bonus*, 1936, April, 49-53.

Van der Veken, Floris, S.J. *Handleiding van de Bonden van het H. Hart*. Mechelen, 1942.

Van de Sande, Ton. "Decadente monniken en nonnen: aard en functie van een antipapistisch motief (ca. 1500-1853)" in: Marit Monteiro, Gerard Rooijakkers and Joost Rosendaal, eds. *De dynamiek van religie en cultuur. Geschiedenis van het Nederlands katholicisme*. Kampen, 1993, 239-260.

Van de Velde, Fernand. *Priester Poppe op Sint Coleta 1916-1918*. Roeselare, 1985.

Van Duinkerken, Anton. "De onherkenbare priester". *De Gemeenschap. Maandschrift*, 7 (1931) 9, 382-386.

Van Emmerik, Ine, eds. *Gevaarlijk modern. Levende geschiedenis van vrouwen in de Graalbeweging*. S.l., 2001.

Van Ginneken, Jacques. "Die Konversionsbewegung in Holland". *Stimmen der Zeit*, 106 (1923-1924) 1-2, 1-19.

Van Haver, Jozef. *Voor U, Beminde Gelovigen. Het Rijke Roomse Leven in Vlaanderen, 1920-1950*. Tielt, 1995.

Van Heijst, Annelies and Derks, Marjet, eds. *Terra incognita. Historisch onderzoek naar katholicisme en vrouwelijkheid*. Kampen, 1994.

Van Hulsem, J.B. *Het pauselijk zoeavenleven na de slag van Castelfidardo*. Roeselare, 1863.

Van Kersbergen, Kees and Manow, Philip, eds. *Religion, Class Coalitions and Welfare State Regimes*. Cambridge, 2009.

Van Lieshout, Huub. *Onze onevenwichtige jongeren*. Tilburg, 1933.

Van Molle, Leen. "De nieuwe vrouwenbeweging in Vlaanderen, een andere lezing". *Belgisch tijdschrift voor nieuwste geschiedenis*, 34 (2004) 3, 359-397.

Van Oostrum, Hilde. "K(l)eurig, kwiek en katholiek. Het verhaal van de Graal". *Vrij Nederland bijlage*, 28 August 1982.

Van Osselaer, Tine. "'A lot of women have good reason to complain about their husbands': Ideals of Catholic masculinity in the household". *Sextant*, 24 (2009), 339-357.

Van Osselaer, Tine. "Christening Masculinity? Catholic Action and Men in Interwar Belgium". *Gender & History*, 11 (2009) 2, 380-401.

Van Osselaer, Tine. "'Heroes of the Heart': Ideal Men in the Sacred Heart Devotion". *Journal of Men, Masculinities and Spirituality*, 3 (2009) 1, 22-40.

Van Osselaer, Tine. *The Pious Sex: Catholic Constructions of Masculinity and Femininity in Belgium (1800-1940)*. Diss. Doct. KU Leuven. Leuven, 2009.

Van Osselaer, Tine. "'Une oeuvre essentiellement virile'. De 'masculinisering' van de Heilig Hart-devotie in België?". *Tijdschrift voor Genderstudies*, 11 (2008) 3, 33-45.

Van Osselaer, Tine and Buerman, Thomas. "Feminization Thesis: A Survey of International Historiography and a Probing of Belgian Grounds". *Revue d'histoire ecclésiastique*, 103 (2008), 497-544.

Van Osselaer, Tine and Maurits, Alexander. "Heroic Men and Christian Ideals" in: Yvonne Maria Werner, ed. *Christian Manliness - A Paradox of Modernity*. Leuven, 2011, 63-94.

Van Osselaer Tine and Pasture, Patrick et al., eds. *Households of Faith: Domesticity and Religion*. KADOC Studies on Religion, Culture and Society. Leuven (Forthcoming).

Van Sante, Raymund. *Gezag*. Roermond, [1932].

Van Schaik, Ton. *Katholieken in de twintigste eeuw*. Amsterdam, 1999.

Van Wely, Joseph. *Waar Sint Dominicus nog toe roept: gedachtenisrede*. Zwolle, 1921.

Van Zuthem, John. *'Heelen en halven': orthodox-protestantse voormannen en het 'politiek' antipapisme in de periode 1872-1925*. Hilversum, 2001.

Veith, Johann Emanuel. *Charitas [!]. Neun Kanzelvorträge…*. Vienna, 1851.

Veith, Johann Emmanuel. "Woran liegt es, daß bei Frauen mehr wahre Frömmigkeit sich findet, als bei Männern?". *Nathanael*, 1 (1845), 738-742.

"Veldslag van Mentana". *De Eeklonaar*, 17 November 1867 in: Albert Maes. *De Zomergemse zoeaven*. Zomergem: Komitee Pausviering, 1983, 33-35.

"Verbandsfamilie". *Der Kranz*, 22 (1928), 25-27.

"Verbandsfamilie - Breslau". *Der Kranz*, 22 (1928), 51.

"Verbandsfamilie - Diözesanverband Köln". *Der Kranz*, 22 (1928), 50-51.

"Verbandsfamilie - Einmütige Zusammenarbeit". *Der Kranz*, 22 (1928), 81.

"Verbandsfamilie - Jungfraukongregation in St. Bonifaz in Duisburg". *Der Kranz*, 22 (1928), 106-109.

"Verbandsfamilie - St. Urbanus in Buer". *Der Kranz*, 22 (1928), 50-52.

Verhandlungen der dritten General-Versammlung des katholischen Vereines Deutschlands. Regensburg, 1849.

Verheylezoon, Louis S.J. *Handboek van het Apostolaat des Gebeds*. Alken, 1930.

Verheylezoon, Louis S.J. *Het Apostolaat des Gebeds en de parochie*. S.l., 1928.

Verhoeven, Timothy. "Neither Male or Female: Androgyny, Nativism and International Anti-Catholicism". *Australasian Journal of American Studies*, (2005) 24, 5-19.

Viaene, Vincent. *Belgium and the Holy See from Gregory XVI to Pius IX (1831-1859)*. Brussels, 2001.

Viaene, Vincent. "The Roman Question: Catholic Mobilization and Papal Diplomacy during the Pontificate of Pius IX (1846-1878)" in: Emiel Lamberts, ed. *The Black International. L'internationale noire 1870-1878: The Holy See and Militant Catholicism in Europe. Le Saint-Siège et le catholicisme militant en Europe*. Leuven, 2002, 135-178.

Vicaire, M.H., O.P. "Dominique (saint)" in: *Dictionnaire de Spiritualité ascétique et mystique: doctrine et histoire*. Vol. 3. Paris, 1957, 1519-1532.

Vickery, Amanda. "Historiographical Review. Golden Age to Separate Spheres? A Review of Categories and Chronology of English Women's History". *The Historical Journal*, 36 (1993), 383-414.

Vigneron, Paul. *Histoire des crises du clergé français contemporain*. Paris, 1976.

Vijverberg, M. "In memoriam Fons van Bergen". *Bulletin*, 14 (1979) 2, 7-8.

Voets, Bernard. *Bewaar het toevertrouwde pand. Het verhaal van het bisdom Haarlem*. Hilversum, 1981.

Von Hehl, Ulrich and Kronenberg, Friedrich, eds. *Zeitzeichen. 150 Jahre Deutsche Katholikentage 1848-1998*. Paderborn, 1999.

Von Schaching, Otto. *Ein gefangener Bischof*. Würzburg, 1874.

Von Schulte, Johann Friedrich. *Der Altkatholizismus. Geschichte seiner Entwicklung, inneren Gestaltung und rechtlichen Stellung in Deutschland. Aus den Akten und anderen authentischen Quellen dargestellt*. Aalen, 1965 [Giessen, 1887].

Von Schulte, Johann Friedrich. *Der Cölibatszwang und dessen Aufhebung*. Bonn, 1876.

"Voorbeeldig Bondslid". *Bondsblad voor Bonden van het Heilig Hart*, December 1937, 2.

"Vrouwenbonden". *Maandelijksche Mededeelingen voor Bonden van het Heilig Hart*, January 1935, 1.

"Waarom ik Bondslid ben: 10 doorslaande redenen". *Maandelijksche Mededeelingen voor Bonden van het Heilig Hart*, July 1938, 3.

Wagner, Marion. *Die himmlische Frau. Marienbild und Frauenbild in dogmatischen Handbüchern des 19. und 20. Jahrhunderts*. Regensburg, 1999.

Wagner, Peter. "Fest-Stellungen. Beobachtungen zur sozialwissenschaftlichen Diskussion über Identität" in: Aleida Assmann and Heidrun Friese, eds. *Identitäten. Erinnerung, Geschichte, Identität*, 3. Frankfurt, 1999, 44-72.

Wakeford, John. *The Cloistered Elite: A Sociological Analysis of the English Public Boarding School*. London, 1969.

Walford, Geoffrey. *Life in Public Schools*. London, 1986.

Walter, Ilsemarie. "Krankenpflege in Österreich 1784-1938" in: Sabine Braunschweig, ed. *Pflege - Räume, Macht und Alltag. Beiträge zur Geschichte der Pflege*. Zurich, 2006, 29-38.

Walter, Ilsemarie. *Pflege als Beruf oder aus Nächstenliebe? Die Wärterinnen und Wärter in Österreichs Krankenhäusern im langen 19. Jahrhundert*. Frankfurt, 2004.

Walz, Angelus, O.P. *Compendium Historiae Ordinis Praedicatorum*. Rome, 1930.

Walz, Angelus, O.P. *Wahrheitskünder. Die Dominikaner in Geschichte und Gegenwart 1206-1960*. Essen, 1960.

Warne, Randi R. "Making the Gender-Critical Turn" in: Tim Jensen and Michael Rothstein, eds. *Secular Theories on Religion: Current Perspectives*. Copenhagen, 2000, 249-260.

Warner, Marina. *Alone of all her Sex*. London, 1976.

"Was geht uns die Alkoholfrage an?". *Der Kranz*, 22 (1928), 72-73.

Weiß, Otto. "Veith, Johann Emanuel" in: *Biographisch-Bibliographisches Kirchenlexikon*. Vol. 12, 1194-1204.

"Weißer Sonntag". *Die Mutter*, April 1930.

Welter, Barbara. "The Cult of True Womanhood: 1820-1860". *American Quarterly*, 18 (1966), 51-74.

Welter, Barbara. "The Feminization of American Religion: 1800-1860" in: Mary Hartman and Lois Banner, eds. *Clio's Consciousness Raised*. New York, 1974, 137-157.

Wendt, Wolf Rainer. *Geschichte der sozialen Arbeit*. Vol. 1: *Die Gesellschaft vor der sozialen Frage*. Stuttgart, 2008.

Werner, Yvonne Maria, ed. *Christian Masculinity: Men and Religion in Northern Europe in the 19th and 20th Century*. Leuven, 2011.

Werner, Yvonne Maria. "Feminin manlighet? Katholska missionärer I Norden" in: Yvonne Maria Werner, ed. *Kristen manlighet. Ideal och verklighet 1830-1940*. Lund, 2008, 139-160.

Werner, Yvonne Maria, ed. *Kristen manlighet. Ideal och verklighet 1830-1940*. Lund, 2008.

Werner, Yvonne Maria. "Manliness and Catholic Mission in the Nordic Countries". *Journal of Men, Masculinities and Spirituality*, 1 (2007) 1, 3-18.

Werner, Yvonne Maria. "Studying Christian Manliness: An Introduction" in: Yvonne Maria Werner, ed. *Christian Masculinity: Men and Religion in Northern Europe in the 19th and 20th Century*. Leuven, 2011, 7-17.

Wetterer, Angelika. "Konstruktion von Geschlecht. Reproduktionsweisen der Zweigeschlechtlichkeit" in: Ruth Becker and Beate Kortendiek. *Handbuch Frauen- und Geschlechterforschung. Theorie, Methoden, Empirie*. Wiesbaden, 2004, 122-131.

Weyns, N.J. "Daems, Servaas" in: *Nationaal Biografisch Woordenboek*. Vol. 8. Brussels, 1979, 214-222.

Wheeler, Michael. *The Old Enemies: Catholic and Protestant in Nineteenth-Century English Culture*. Cambridge, 2006.

Whitney, Susan B. "Gender, Class, and Generation in Interwar French Catholicism: The Case of the Jeunesse Ouvrière Chrétienne Féminine". *Journal of Family History*, 26 (2001), 480-507.

Wickham, E.R. *Church and People in an Industrial City*. London, 1957.

"Wie ich mit meinen Kindern spiele". *Die Mutter*, January 1916.

"Wie wir das Leben sehen!". *Der Kranz*, 26 (1932), 50-51, 144-161, 172-189.

Williams, Jack. "Churches, Sport and Identities in the North of England" in: Jeff Hill and Jack Williams, eds. *Sport and Identity in the North of England*. Keele, 1996, 114-117.

Winandi, Klaus, ed. *In seiner Spur bleiben für eine bessere Welt! Eine unverwechselbare Spur, ein kostbares Zeichen sind wieder neu zu entdecken: Aufzeichnungen aus einem ungewöhnlichen Freundkreis, 1919-1999*. Aachen, 1999.

Winner, David. *Those Feet*. London, 2006.

"Wir wollen! Wacht-Rufe". *Die Wacht*, 20 (1924-1925), 98.

Wiseman, Nicholas Patrick. *Fabiola: Or, The Church of the Catacombs*. S.l., 1860.

Witte, Els. "The Battle for Monastries, Cemetries and Schools: Belgium" in: Christopher Clark and Wolfram Kaiser, eds. *Culture Wars: Secular-Catholic Conflict in Nineteenth-Century Europe*. Cambridge, 2003, 117-118.

Wijfjes, Huub. *Het Stanislas. School- en jeugdcultuur op een katholiek college te Delft, 1948-1998*. Delft, 1998.

Wolfs, P., O.P. *Van oude en nieuwe schooljaren*. Nijmegen, 1986.

Woodcock, Henry. "Betting and Gambling". *Primitive Methodist Quarterly Review*, 33 (1891), 97-113.
<www.sfb600.uni-trier.de>
<www.stichting-echo.nl.>

Zalar, Jeffrey T. "The Process of Confessional Inculturation: Catholic Reading in the 'Long Nineteenth Century'" in: Helmut Walser Smith, ed. *Protestants, Catholics and Jews in Germany, 1800-1914*. Oxford-New York-Berg, 2001, 121-152.
"Zedenverwildering". *Maandelijksche Mededeelingen voor Bonden van het Heilig Hart*, July 1935, 1-2.
"Zevende Eeuwfeest der Dominicaner-orde". *De Gelderlander*, 1916.
Zock, Hetty. "The Predominance of the Feminine Sexual Mode in Religion: Erikson's Contribution to the Sex and Gender Debate in the Psychology of Religion". *International Journal for the Psychology of Religion*, 7 (1997) 3, 187-198.
"Zur Einkehr". *Die Wacht*, 20 (1924-1925), 43-44.
"Zur Einkehr: Der Rosenkranz, das Gebet der Männer". *Die Wacht*, 20 (1924-1925), 163-164.

CONTRIBUTORS

Jan Art retired as Professor of History at the University of Ghent in 2010. He has taught and published widely on 19th- and 20th-century cultural and religious history, the application of social scientific methodology in history, and psychohistory.

Angela Berlis is Professor for the History of Old Catholicism and General Church History, Theological Faculty, University of Berne (CH). She works on the history of 18th-20th-century Old Catholicism, Anti-Ultramontanism, women and gender history from a historical-theological perspective, and ecumenical subjects.

Thomas Buerman defended his PhD in History on Catholic manliness in Belgium in the 19th and 20th centuries at the University of Ghent in May 2010. He is currently a staff member of the International Relations Office of the University of Ghent.

Marjet Derks is lecturer and Postdoctoral Research Fellow at the Radboud University in Nijmegen. In 1995 she founded the independent Stichting Echo to stimulate critical historical research into religion, men and women religious and the significance of religion for daily life. Her current research focuses on intellectual Catholic women and their transnational networks.

Hugh McLeod is Emeritus Professor of Church History at the University of Birmingham since 2010 and a specialist on the social history of religion in Western Europe and the United States in the 19th and 20th centuries. His next project will be a book on *Religion and the Rise of Sport in Modern England*.

Marit Monteiro is Professor of the History of Dutch Catholicism at the Radboud University in Nijmegen. She focuses on the significance of, and connections between religion, culture and identity in an international comparative perspective. She has published extensively on clerical cultures and in particular on the history of the Dominicans in the Netherlands.

Michael E. O'Sullivan is Assistant Professor of History at Marist College in Poughkeepsie, NY. Building on his dissertation, his current research project is 'Lived Catholicism in Germany: Gender, Reform, and Religious Miracles, 1918–1965'. He is a list editor for H-Catholic.

Patrick Pasture is Professor of History and Director of the Centre for European Studies at the University of Leuven. He is currently working on a transatlantic history of Christendom in Western Europe and North America since 1650 and on different issues related to the religious globalization of Europe.

Bernhard Schneider is Professor of Medieval and Modern Church History at the University of Trier, where he directs a major research project on 'Poor relief and Catholic identity: Poverty and the poor in Catholic Germany during the early nineteenth century'. He has published extensively on the history of Catholic piety and poor relief.

Marieke Smulders prepares a PhD on Catholic elite education and training in the Netherlands 1920-1970 at the Radboud University in Nijmegen.

Tine Van Osselaer is a Postdoctoral Fellow of the Fund for Scientific Research Flanders and works on a study on Marian apparitions in Belgium during the interwar period. She has published on the 'feminization' and 'masculinization' of religion, domesticity and religion, and on Christian heroes.

COLOPHON

This book has been realized in the framework of the research project of the FWO (Research Foundation Flanders) *In search of the good Catholic m/f. Feminization and masculinity in Belgian Catholicism (c 1750-1950)* with additional funding from KADOC-KU Leuven and the Arts faculties of the universities of Ghent and Leuven. We wish to thank all who contributed to this publication: the funding agencies, the authors as well as the publishing staff at KADOC and UPL, in particular Luc Vints .

FINAL EDITING
Luc Vints

COPY EDITING
Lieve Claes
Joke Depuydt

LAY-OUT
Alexis Vermeylen

KADOC-KU Leuven
Documentation and Research Centre for Religion, Culture and Society
Vlamingenstraat 39
B - 3000 Leuven
www.kadoc.kuleuven.be

Leuven University Press
Minderbroedersstraat 4
B - 3000 Leuven
www.lup.be